D1368425

the
LEADERSHIP
MACHINE

Architecture to develop leaders for any future

10th anniversary edition

Michael M. Lombardo
Robert W. Eichinger

The Leadership Machine
Architecture to develop leaders for any future

www.kornferry.com

ISBN 978-1-933578-41-5 • Print
ISBN 978-1-933578-42-2 • eBook

Item number 82147

The Leadership Machine
Architecture to develop leaders for any future

Printings:

1st Printing February 2001
2nd Printing January 2002 Second Edition
3rd Printing January 2003 Third Edition
4th Printing October 2004 Third Edition
5th Printing June 2006 Third Edition
6th Printing July 2007 Third Edition
7th Printing September 2008 Third Edition
8th Printing December 2011 Anniversary Edition
9th Printing April 2012 Anniversary Edition
10th Printing February 2014 Anniversary Edition
11th Printing February 2015 Anniversary Edition
12th Printing February 2017 Anniversary Edition
13th Printing September 2017 Anniversary Edition
14th Printing December 2018 Anniversary Edition

Table of Contents

Preface

This is a book about the development of effective leaders and managers—for organizations and for individuals. The need for great talent and leaders has only increased as the world gets more complex and tougher.

We make a case, hopefully a strong one, that the best way to do this is with fundamental rules of talent development and best developmental practices that don't change much over time. In the time since we first published this book, research and practice has shown that the fundamentals still stand and the basics still work. What we said before holds true today.

We have also made new observations in the twilight of our careers. We cannot underestimate the importance of self-awareness. The most successful executives are aware of their strengths and weaknesses. Armed with that information, they don't try to fix every weakness. They find workarounds.

For those of you who are wondering, our research and recommendations apply universally. Regardless of global region, industry, gender, or ethnic background, study after study shows the same elements leading to success or failure.

Your time is valuable and scarce. If you don't have time to read the whole book, at least not all at once, the following is a guide.

We still recommend that everyone reads Chapter 1 because it lays out the basic argument for the rest of *The Leadership Machine*.

For readers primarily interested in how people learn, grow, and change, pay special attention to Chapters 2–6 and 8.

For bosses, we hope the book gives you insight on how to get the best from all of your people and, in exchange, do the best for them in enhancing their job performance and careers. Acquiring, developing, and deploying talent is still job one. It hasn't gotten any easier. And, it can't happen without you. You should especially note Chapters 15 and 16.

For top management, we hope you will take the book to heart and be passionate about establishing your own version of the best practices found in the book. Many independent research studies have shown that commitment at the top for talent management is the number one requirement. Nothing much happens without it. It can't happen without you either. You should especially note Chapters 17, 18, and 19.

For HR, you are the group that must stand up and make this happen. Someone has to run the talent machine. The best practices are well known and usually presented and discussed at every HR conference. Well known doesn't mean they are well done. Top management has to own it and HR has to run it. You should read the whole book, no exceptions. The various systems HR runs will be of particular interest to you. These are covered in Chapters 11–20.

For the CEO, we hope you make leadership development part of your legacy. As our colleague Jim Collins has said, "You have to get the right people on the bus—the talent bus." We would add you have to have the right driver who knows the destination. That's you. It, for sure, doesn't happen without you. You also need to read the whole book in order to lead the effort. Pay special attention to Chapter 17.

For the individual, we hope you gain an understanding of the bigger picture of career management and take the biggest slice of the pie you are capable of. Who cares the most about you? Who has the most to gain? Who has the most to lose? Who can make things happen? Surprise! It's you. Nothing happens without you. Others can be very helpful, but if you are not the active agent for your development, others can't do it for you. If you are primarily interested in managing your own career, focus on Chapters 7–10. If your goal is a senior management position, focus on Chapters 2–6 and 17–19 to learn how The Leadership Machine works and how it applies to you.

We are indebted to all those who helped us with the creation of this book. Larry Clark, David DeVries, Pat Pinto, Linda Hodge, Adrienne Johns, Dan Moss, Roland Nelson, Jim Peters, Evelyn Rogers, Kathy Spinelli, David Ulrich, Les Woller, George Hallenbeck, Vicki Swisher, Erica Lutrick, Julie Scott, Michael Harper, and Karen Dorece, all of whom provided valuable feedback and contributions. We would like to express our gratitude to Evelyn Orr who did an outstanding job on this 10th anniversary edition. Products did its usual fine job in supporting and producing this effort. We especially thank Lesley Kurke, Doug Lodermeier Sr. and Paul Montei for their fine work. A large thank you goes to Bonnie Parks for her excellent editing and proofing of this work. And of special note is the Center for Creative Leadership, where much of the content of this book began.

Finally, a special thanks to the tens of thousands of people who have read previous editions of this book. And the thousands of companies around the world that are implementing its recommendations. We have heard many wonderful stories from users who say that the book helped their organizations do a better job implementing and running the talent machine.

Robert W. Eichinger and Michael M. Lombardo

V

About the authors

Michael M. Lombardo

Mike Lombardo has over 30 years experience in executive and management research and in executive coaching. He is one of the founders of Lominger Limited, Inc., publishers of the Leadership Architect® Suite of management, executive, and organizational development tools. With Bob Eichinger, Mike has authored 40 products for the suite, including *FYI® For Your Improvement,* the *Career Architect® Development Planner,* Choices Architect® learning agility suite, and VOICES® 360° feedback assessment. During his 15 years at the Center for Creative Leadership,  Mike was a co-author of *The Lessons of Experience,* which detailed which learnings from experience can teach the competencies needed to be successful. He also co-authored the research on executive derailment revealing how personal flaws and overdone strengths caused otherwise effective executives to get into career trouble, Benchmarks®, a 360° feedback instrument, and the Looking Glass® simulation. Mike has won five national awards for research on managerial and executive development.

Robert W. Eichinger

Bob Eichinger has been working with managers and executives on leadership development for over 50 years. He is one of the founders and the former CEO of Lominger Limited, Inc. and co-creator of the Leadership Architect® Suite of management, executive, and organizational development tools. During his career, he has served as Vice Chairman of the Korn/Ferry Institute, worked inside companies such as PepsiCo and Pillsbury, and as a consultant in Fortune 500 companies in the United States, Europe, Japan, Canada, and Australia. Dr. Eichinger lectures extensively on the topic of executive and management development  and has served on the Board of the Human Resource Planning Society. He has worked as a coach with more than 1,000 managers and executives. Some of his books include *100 Things You Need to Know: Best People Practices for Managers & HR,* written with Mike Lombardo and Dave Ulrich, and *FYI® for Strategic Effectiveness*, written with Kim Ruyle and Dave Ulrich.

Chapter 1

The change vaccine: Developing leaders for any future

No one knows what specific challenges we will face in 2020, but we have a strong idea of what the leaders who can meet those challenges will look like and how they will get to be that way.

Only monks and hermits hiding in caves have not read about or, more likely, not experienced the rapid, chaotic change the world has undergone and is undergoing. The fastest conveyance for our great-grandparents was the same as for Hannibal two millennia before. Most kids today have never seen a 33 1/3 record, much less a 78. But unlike many adults, kids can change settings on their mobile devices and are comfortable with computers and many adults can't and aren't. An eight-year-old said to his dad the other day on the golf course, "How can I hand you a wood? These are all titanium clubs."

The past 100 years have produced more change than what occurred in all the eons before. Although change is a constant, the rate, pace, and extent of change that we face is a break from the past. The nature of change is indeed changing.

The premise of this book is that the best way to deal with accelerating change is with fundamentals that don't change much, if at all.

To develop the men and women who can lead us going forward, we need to rely on what stays fairly constant. Life is always lived forward, and each leader has to make the next jump to deal with whatever change occurs in his or her career or lifetime. The issue is what predictably happens when change occurs and what are the most effective strategies to cope with it. And the nature of that issue hasn't changed.

Much is known about how to develop people who can contribute superior performance and leadership to organizations. There is a set of research-based practices that can be used to develop people aggressively and support them with a system that works—what we call "The Leadership Machine."

Performance can be improved, leaders can be better equipped, and all of us can learn to deal with changing demands better. In this book, we will detail practices to help accomplish all these goals.

Note: To make reading smoother, we are going to relegate footnotes and all secondary support for our arguments to the Notes section at the end of the book. Each chapter has a Notes section for the critical and the curious.

The leadership supply problem

During the last decade, one-third of the CEOs in the Fortune 500 lasted less than three years. Top executive failure rates are variously estimated as high as 75 percent and rarely lower than one-third. A McKinsey study found that the pipeline for future executives is broken as well. Responding to the statement "We develop people well," only 3 percent said yes.

The demand for those who can deal with change and ambiguity and fragmentation is increasing, but the supply of people who can do those things is pretty much what it has always been. (And according to McKinsey, that supply will shrink over the next 15 years.) In AT&T's assessments of high-potential managers, only 12 percent could cope effectively with the ambiguity and fragmentation of rapidly changing conditions. So the need for leaders is greater than ever, but there is a problem on the supply side.

As an illustration, few changes are as difficult to pull off as a successful merger. A 1997 study found 71 percent were negative 12 months after the deal. A.T. Kearney's study found that 58 percent of mergers fail to reach the goals they set out to achieve, and an additional 14 percent added no value to the company. Cost reduction and short-term revenue growth strategies actually destroyed value, both in stock prices and profits. In contrast, focusing on a clear growth vision and rapid integration increased shareholder return by 25 percent. One of the study's major conclusions: handle leadership as the central issue before closing the deal.

According to all major studies of mergers we have seen, failures have much more to do with lacking the soft skills—leadership and change management. Rarely do failures result because hard business skills are lacking.

The penalty for less-than-able leadership is huge, as is the payoff when leadership is present. The difference between so-so performers and high performers is vast. As early as 1991, research indicated that a high-performing executive was 15 percent better than an average one, or worth $25 million after taxes for a Fortune 500 company. Dan Goleman reported that top performers exceeded revenue targets by 15 to 20 percent. In another large study, top performers had 19 to 48 percent higher output than average performers. For sales jobs, it can be far greater than this, and many claim that top performers routinely outperform the lowest performers by 100 percent. Depending on the job, the performance differences reported can be staggering. Among computer programmers, superb performers were 1,272 percent better than average performers; superior account managers produced 600 percent more revenue than average account managers.

The bottom line? Companies scoring in the top quintile of talent management practices outperform their industry's mean return to shareholders by 22 percentage points.

1

Our argument assumes not only that such stellar performers can be developed, but also that the people to whom these fundamental principles would be applied have not changed greatly from the managers and executives of 20 years ago. With all the talk about Generation Xers growing up in the "postmodern era," are they really the same as the last demographic surge—the Baby Boomers?

According to the 1997 National Study of the Changing Workforce, Gen Xers are better educated, more racially diverse, work longer hours, and find their jobs more demanding than young workers (Boomers) of 20 years earlier. They are just as loyal as older workers and are not job-hoppers. They are hardly a bunch of slackers.

Additionally, exactly the same things that workers in general respond to now are the same things that motivated workers 20 years ago:

- Work quality – job autonomy, challenges to learn on the job, and the meaning that people find in their work.
- A supportive workplace – family friendly, supportive supervisors, relationships with coworkers.

These indicators are not only the same, Gen Xers report higher job quality and job support than did Boomers 20 years earlier. The study concludes that job and workplace characteristics are far more important predictors of productivity than pay and benefits.

The findings from 20 years ago were the same—pay was 12th, benefits 16th. At the top of the list were accomplishing something worthwhile, autonomy, and chances to learn new things.

Gen Xers respond to the same forces that their mothers and fathers did and still do.

What doesn't change much: The four fundamentals of management and leadership development

In the world of management and leadership development, four fundamentals (constants) have changed little, if at all, over time. They also are not likely to change much going forward. The fundamentals are:

1. The competencies/skills that matter for leading in new and different situations.
2. How these skills are learned and developed.
3. Who is equipped to learn these skills.
4. What it takes to make skill development work.

Bold statements, but true. In this case, knowledge of history informs the future. The history of the development of managers and leaders who could make whatever next jumps they faced in the past tells us what we face going forward.

1. The competencies/skills that matter (have and always will matter) for leading in new and different situations

We are going to use the words "skill" and "competency" interchangeably, although we recognize they have somewhat different meanings. A competency is a measurable characteristic of a person that is related to success at work. It may be a behavioral skill, a technical skill, an attribute (such as intelligence), or an attitude (such as optimism). As all competencies are measurable, they are often called skills, even though this is not entirely accurate.

What if 85 percent of the common skills that lead to effective management and leadership were known? *They are.*

| 5

What if there was a way to quickly determine the remaining 15 percent? *There is.*

1 Throughout the history of layered and organized work, there have always been start-ups, turnarounds, shutdowns, acquisitions, divestitures, expansions, new technologies, contractions, conflict, and consolidations. Each of these situations—although across a wide range of time, content, settings, and contexts—requires about the same set of skills. Hannibal taking the elephants over the Alps was a start-up requiring the same skills (and maybe more) as any modern start-up. Elephants had never crossed mountains before, just as more recently, books had never been electronic before.

Thousands of studies have attacked the question of common versus unique competencies from every angle—looking at executives, managers, supervisors, scientists, flight crews, reporters, government officials, military officers, sales, marketing, etc., across industries, countries, and economic models. Each of these types of jobs may have unique aspects, but they are mostly unique technical job knowledge in nature. The behavioral and attitudinal skills it takes to do a job are known, have been known for quite some time, and are mostly consistent across situations. *We have seen no evidence anywhere, anytime that more rapid change has somehow required the creation of any new skills or competencies to deal with that change.* CEOs of e-companies may deal with more change more rapidly than Hannibal or George Washington did, but the essence of dealing with change is the same—tolerance for ambiguity, incremental experiments, and quick learning.

All research-based skill models come from the same source—the study of human behavior. All are easily translatable into each other. They are virtually identical in underlying meaning, just not in wording or categorization. In the Hay-McBer competency studies across 286 situations, entrepreneurs, technical, professional, sales, human service, and managerial jobs were studied in industry, government, military, health care, education, and religious institutions. The same set of 21 competencies was used to describe superior performance. The unique competencies (which might be technical or something related to the values of the organization) ranged from 2 to 20 percent of the jobs. Development Dimensions International's (DDI) taxonomy of competencies—in development for over 30 years—uses the same 70 competencies worldwide to describe all jobs.

Both science, as in the Hay-McBer or DDI studies, and practice indicate that competencies are roughly 85 percent the same across different job situations. In one internal company study, models were collected from roughly 100 organizations. The competencies listed were 85 percent the same across models, and even the remaining 15 percent were sometimes there and sometimes not. Everyone had essentially the same skills, but some models included more than others did.

So the same type of job (executive, marketing manager) in one company is much more similar to like jobs in other companies than to a different job position within the same firm. The same findings hold for salespeople, human services, manufacturing, military officers, etc.

What differs is not what the skills are, but how much they matter in a particular job, a level, a function, or an organization at this time. A common skill may or may not matter, and the examples may be slightly different, but the skill or competency is the same everywhere. Strategic thinking is "strategic thinking," perseverance means "never giving up" everywhere, and listening means "listening."

There are a number of research-based lists of competencies from respected institutions like the Center for Creative Leadership, Saville Holdsworth Limited (SHL), Development Dimensions International, Hay-McBer, and PDI-Ninth House, and respected instruments from researchers like Bernard Bass and Clark Wilson, as well as the list we will use in this book, the Leadership Architect® competencies.

We strongly contend that there is little difference in any of these models. Some are oriented higher and some lower, they are all worded differently, and they use somewhat different indicators (such as planning). But, and this is our core point, they end up measuring the same underlying competencies.

If many respected worldwide firms have looked at the research from a number of different angles and derived roughly the same library of personal, managerial, and leadership competencies, what does that say?

If all rigorous, study-based organization success profiles that are customized and tailored specifically to that firm can be mapped into any of those research models, what more do you need to know?

Since 85 percent of the common competencies are known, and most commercial models that measure those competencies are fundamentally the same, this leads us to a strongly held recommendation: don't reinvent the wheel.

Pick a research-based model, any model. Select the one with the words that fit your culture best and the firm you like to work with and be done with it.

Said another way, making up your own model is a waste of time and shareholders' money. You are paying to rediscover and rename the periodic table of the elements—in this case the elements of management and leadership. If you are determined to tailor, buy a license and start with one of the research-based models. Why would anyone want to conduct a study to discover that you too have a competency called "Listening" or "Planning"?

Yet one study said that 60 percent of companies giving 360° feedback to their employees were developing custom models. The reasons given for this aren't very sound:

- *We are unique.* What you do may be; what competencies it takes to do it are not.

- *We have to get buy-in via participation in creating the model.* This argument has always struck us as weak leadership from HR and line management. No one gets buy-in on the periodic table of the elements or the FASB rules. Buy-in, in fact, ruins some well-developed models. People tinker with the wording, try to shorten the model for ease of use, and reduce even good models to mush. Two years later, the firm is looking for another magic bullet. We've seen it countless times. Getting buy-in would be much easier if the process were more efficient.

- *The model must be valid.* Studying your firm through interviewing, or whatever method, has little to do with validity beyond your organization. Unless you are number one or a strong number two in your market, why would you want to study yourself for the keys to success? (In fairness, responsible consulting firms do compare internal models with their work in other companies, but why bother? If your competencies can be easily compared or benchmarked with those of other successful companies, what exactly are you paying for?)

What actually seems to happen is that the "not invented here" syndrome is alive and well. Firms spend massive amounts of money to rediscover listening skills just so they can have wording that feels right to them. They could get exactly the same thing with an 85 percent solution—starting with a research-based model, then tailoring and wording it to fit their culture. Less time. Fewer resources. More professional.

There is further illogic to such approaches. If we are dealing with rapid change, why would we want to study current incumbents who are having trouble with change? Will the standards change? Then we would want a broader model that includes all known competencies related to the history of dealing with change.

What do we do with the model once we have it? Can we just select people who have the skills we need? Fifty years of research would answer a strong "No" to that question. We'll deal with this topic in Chapter 2.

1

If we can't just select perfect people, does the model have strong ties to developing these missing competencies? If the model were truly unique, it could not have strong ties to development plans that work. Each organization would have to be studied separately. But, in all cases we've ever seen, the models are then mapped to existing developmental materials. You'd think that would tip off organizations to the fact that there was nothing unique to begin with. We have mapped more than 200 built-from-scratch models into the Leadership Architect® competencies and it's very, very rare to find anything unusual.

Creating their own model also allows organizations to follow another poor practice: measurement has to be brief. The same survey we mentioned above found that most firms are after 10 or fewer core competencies. The rationale is that we're very busy people. We have to focus. The organization can't handle more than 10. Behavior is as complex as it is—you can't describe people with 10 categories any more than you can describe the universe that way. If success could be fully or usefully described with less than 10 competencies, Plato would have known about it.

We will deal in depth with this issue in Part I of this book where we discuss competencies and how to make them more useful. To pique your interest, we'll also hint at what else we have to say in this section:

- The wrong competencies are often used to measure people.
- Even with the right competencies, it doesn't usually matter because hardly anyone is developed to perform well at them past hire.
- Simplistic views of talent and how people develop often lead to the failure of countless able people.
- Competency models can also lead to a vain search for people who rarely exist.

2. How skills are developed

What if it were known which types of developmental experiences lead to the development of the skills in the library of competencies? *It is known (enough to make a difference).*

The world would be an easier place if organizations could just measure and select for the skills they need, making development unnecessary. Indeed, many organizations act as if that were the case. They select a person for a certain job and if he or she is successful, they throw the person into a tougher job without much thought about what skills, if any, the person needs or if the person has them. This, in turn, leads to many failures.

There are, undoubtedly, some competencies that should be selected for, including intelligence, character, technical skill, and basic interpersonal orientation. But beyond these, there is no choice but to develop people, and much is known about how and where competencies develop.

In Part II, we'll discuss the critical experiences that can teach— how job challenges, other people, and even failures help people hone and grow skills that they weren't born with and can't be selected for. No one, regardless of how talented, waltzes into an organization at age 25 knowing how to be strategic or how to turn around a failed unit. Many, many things must be learned as we go.

3. Who is best equipped to learn these skills

What if it were fairly predictable who has the best chance of building the key skills necessary for any future situation? *It is.*

Also in Part II, we will discuss how some people learn far better from experience than others, and we will detail what those people look like. Although you can select for "learners," there aren't many to go around. Fortunately, learning agility can be developed as well.

Another hint to keep you reading: the best learners probably aren't who you think they are.

4. What it takes to make development work

What if there were a set of best practices and a system that would lead to the most effective use of resources to produce current and future managers and leaders? *There are and there is (with slight adjustments for specific situations).*

At this point you might be asking yourself, "If the developmental situation is so bad, why did we somehow manage to post record earnings the last eight quarters?" Our straightforward answer is that you have enough individuals with enough skills to get the job done currently. People compensate for weaknesses by developing proficiencies according to personal tastes, or because they have had a developmental boss, or they attended a course at the right moment in time.

Many people will rise to the occasion, but this almost-random process isn't a good way to keep an organization vibrant. A Secretariat will come along and run you into the dust, just as more than one-third of the Fortune 500 firms from 1970 don't exist as independent entities anymore. Right now you may be running neck and neck, but to beat the next Secretariat, you will need to raise the developmental bar. Leadership performance across time doesn't just happen.

You might also be asking yourself, "If all of this is known, why is it that our organization doesn't do most of these practices?" To this question, we have three answers: time lag, false prophets, and courage.

Reasons why organizations avoid development practices

1. Time lag

The cure for scurvy was known 150 years before it was implemented in the British navy. Similarly, what caused common ulcers was discovered long before it became common knowledge. (It's actually *Helicobacter pylori* bacteria—not prolonged stress.) The major research on management and leadership development, however, is still a young, evolving set of findings, and the systems around it haven't been mature enough to necessarily work in a practical manner. While it's nice to say this is known, it's another thing to convince everyone, and far more difficult to make it happen when companies also have to fight competitors, meet payroll, and have time left over to sleep.

2. False prophets

Organizations also have to contend with false (but possibly with fine intentions) prophets. There is no shortage of books, speeches, and consulting practices pushing theories and systems of management and leadership. Among the customers for this message and material are all of the current and aspiring managers and leaders around the world. Many times, they are easily swayed with the new, the simple, the catchy, and the loud. It's hard sometimes to separate the wheat from the chaff and the bread from the cheese.

A corollary to this is that many managers and leaders think they are experts on people because they have been around people all their lives. This has led to a lot of homegrown models which, unfortunately, don't get the job done and can lead to quick adoption of another model, and another, and another.

3. Courage

As the research findings and the systems that support them become better known and accepted, the issue becomes the courage to act on what we know to be true. That's when the trouble really starts: Who gets the job? Do we take a chance or use a safe fill? Are the jobs that develop people the same as our most critical jobs? Can we develop people faster? What do you mean you're sending Sally on a foreign assignment? I need her here. Should I tell Sally she is a high potential?

People hoard talent, make irrational arguments about whom to promote, won't make tough calls on stagnant performers, and do all the things we do to protect ourselves. It's called human nature.

What it takes to deal with natural reluctance is, first, knowledge of what works and, second, the establishment of systems and practices that mirror the patterns of real people. As we will argue, real people can only be developed through systems that mirror how human beings grow. And that hasn't changed either.

We'll deal with all of these questions and many others in the final three sections of the book. In Part III, we'll cover personal development. Because the findings are so bleak on how well organizations develop people, we'll explain how to develop yourself so you're not done-in by the poor practices of your organization. In Part IV, we'll cover the five basic systems organizations need to have in place to make development work. They are:

1. Setting success targets so you know who and what you're measuring.
2. Preventing the derailment of your people.
3. Constructing feedback.
4. Coaching processes that work.
5. And, most essential, how to think about and design work as both a learning and a performance challenge.

The five basic systems help master the present by developing a more competent workforce.

To drive against future demands, one more system is needed. In Part V, we'll explain what drives The Leadership Machine—how to use succession planning to develop people to meet future demands and how to make the calls on who gets the jobs. Ensuring the future through development also requires individual leadership and courage. Someone has to change the systems that prevent us from responding to the change swirling around us.

Just because change swirls doesn't mean that people are developed to effectively deal with it. As we'll see in Chapter 2, few people handle change well, and just as few are being developed to deal with it going forward.

Part I

The skills
that matter

Chapter 2

Leadership competencies: What effective leadership looks like

If we don't define leadership competencies well, nothing much else matters.

Competencies are the universal common denominator. They drive much of work and performance. As we'll detail, workers have plenty of some of the skills needed for success, very little of others, and there are even some skills that we don't try to develop until it's too late. The competencies that are critical can be developed if we are purposeful about work challenges early enough rather than simply seeing work as tasks and goals to be done today.

Since competencies drive the majority of job success, knowing what the key skills are and measuring them reasonably well makes all your systems work better—recruiting, deployment, development, performance, succession. Without this common denominator, you may as well rely on reading bumps on people's heads because you haven't defined what effective leadership looks like.

If you know what your critical competencies are and you develop your people to be better at them, you have a competitive edge that is very hard to duplicate. Although your competitors can buy some talent, no one can buy away the thousands to millions of hours invested in growth. You will have bench strength to replace those lured away. Most important, you'll have more and different skills—skills that make your organization better, more agile, and more productive.

The leadership competencies important to performance and/or potential

There are many methods of finding the key competencies that drive success: obtain or create a good competency model; observe people in different jobs or levels; get a panel of experts (incumbents, bosses, or consultants) to decide on the importance of various competencies for jobs and levels; create behavioral definitions; measure fairly, etc. Another method is to do critical-incident interviews with people who do their jobs well and create a model of what they do that average performers either don't do or don't do as well.

In our opinion, going out and creating your own set of leadership competencies from scratch would be like trying to rediscover all of the chemical elements in your garage. The work has already been done. Core leadership competencies have already been identified, so do not waste precious time and resources conducting a study to figure out what leadership competencies exist. The Leadership Architect® competencies document the leadership competencies that have been discovered through research. It is a research-based, scientifically validated tool used by organizations to profile and assess leadership behaviors. The development of the Leadership Architect® Competency Library was based on the early work at the Center for Creative Leadership, Hay-McBer, Sears, Exxon, AT&T, and other organizations that seriously studied success at work.

The competencies in the Leadership Architect® Competency Library fall into 6 Factors and 21 Clusters. These factors and clusters are statistically derived from factor analysis and ongoing normative studies. Within the 6 Factors and 21 Clusters there are 67 Competencies which are the positive skills and behaviors required for success. The Library also includes 7 Global Focus Areas that outline critical skills when working outside of one's home country. Organizations can work with the Library at the factor, cluster, competency, or aspect (not shown) level. However, some applications are more appropriate at certain levels than others.

Figure 2.1 Leadership Architect® library structure

GLOBAL FOCUS AREAS
- Global Business Knowledge
- Cross-Cultural Resourcefulness
- Cross-Cultural Agility
- Assignment Hardiness
- Organizational Positioning Skills
- Cross-Cultural Sensitivity
- Humility

**FACTOR I:
Strategic Skills**

Cluster A. Understanding the Business
- Business Acumen
- Functional/Technical Skills
- Technical Learning

Cluster B. Making Complex Decisions
- Decision Quality
- Intellectual Horsepower
- Learning on the Fly
- Problem Solving

Cluster C. Creating the New and Different
- *Dealing with Ambiguity*
- Creativity
- Innovation Management
- Perspective
- Strategic Agility

**FACTOR II:
Operating Skills**

Cluster D. Keeping on Point
- *Timely Decision Making*
- Priority Setting

Cluster E. Getting Organized
- Organizing
- Planning
- Time Management

Cluster F. Getting Work Done Through Others
- Delegation
- Developing Direct Reports and Others
- Directing Others
- Informing
- Managing and Measuring Work

Cluster G. Managing Work Processes
- Process Management
- *Managing Through Systems*
- Total Work Systems

**FACTOR III:
Courage**

Cluster H. Dealing with Trouble
- Command Skills
- Conflict Management
- Confronting Direct Reports
- Managerial Courage
- Standing Alone

Cluster I. Making Tough People Calls
- Hiring and Staffing
- Sizing Up People

**FACTOR IV:
Energy and Drive**

Cluster J. Focusing on the Bottom Line
- Action Oriented
- Perseverance
- *Drive for Results*

**FACTOR V:
Organizational Positioning Skills**

Cluster K. Being Organizationally Savvy
- Organizational Agility
- Political Savvy

Cluster L. Communicating Effectively
- Presentation Skills
- Written Communications

Cluster M. Managing Up
- Career Ambition
- Comfort Around Higher Management

**FACTOR VI:
Personal and Interpersonal Skills**

Cluster N. Relating Skills
- Approachability
- Interpersonal Savvy

Cluster O. Caring About Others
- Caring About Direct Reports
- Compassion

Cluster P. Managing Diverse Relationships
- Boss Relationships
- Customer Focus
- *Managing Diversity*
- Fairness to Direct Reports
- Peer Relationships
- Understanding Others

Cluster Q. Inspiring Others
- Motivating Others
- Negotiating
- *Building Effective Teams*
- *Managing Vision and Purpose*

Cluster R. Acting with Honor and Character
- Ethics and Values
- Integrity and Trust

Cluster S. Being Open and Receptive
- Composure
- Humor
- Listening
- Patience
- Personal Disclosure

Cluster T. Demonstrating Personal Flexibility
- *Dealing with Paradox*
- Personal Learning
- Self-Development
- Self-Knowledge

Cluster U. Balancing Work/Life
- *Work/Life Balance*

2

Why are there so many competencies? Because work and the people who do it are quite complex. This is a complete library of competencies meant to apply to an entire career—from entry to retirement—as well as across types of work responsibilities and all of the types of activities in which organizations engage.

Quite understandably, organizations want to reduce the number of competencies dealt with for any specific application. Commonly, 67 are too many to measure, and so organizations use various methods to get the list down to a manageable size. In this chapter, we recommend how to do this. A first step is to understand the skills that are in high supply and which are rare in the general population. This can help you understand which ones are price-of-admission and which are going to give you a competitive edge.

Leadership Architect® norms

Since 1996, we have collected data on individual contributors, managers, and executives—a total sample of more than 9,000 people from over 140 companies. Almost 50,000 bosses, peers, direct reports, and customers rated these individual contributors, managers, and executives. On 2,000 of these women and men, we also have independent ratings of performance; for about 1,000 we have data on promotion; for 500 we have ratings of potential. Our database consists of multi-rater feedback on the 67 Competencies and the 19 Career Stallers and Stoppers (see Chapter 4 for more information on stallers) from the Leadership Architect® Competency Library. The competencies and stallers and stoppers can be measured reliably and have numerous relationships with organizational outcome measures—including profit, retention, both current and long-term performance, promotion, potential, and stock and bonus differentials. Typically, a person completes his or her self-ratings on a five-point scale and receives feedback from an average of nine others (boss, peers, direct reports, and/or customers). Ratings are ordinarily done electronically.

After collecting and analyzing data over the years, we see the same patterns emerge. In fact, the norms are extremely stable. Rank orders of skill in the current normative study are highly correlated with the rank orders from normative studies conducted in 2006 ($r = 0.97$) and 2003 ($r = 0.94$).

What most people are good at

2

When people start out their careers, they tend to be good at a certain set of skills. As people get promoted into new and bigger jobs, the requirements for success change but what changes for most people is very little. A lot of individual contributor skills start high and stay high. Table 2.1 illustrates this point and comes from our database described earlier. (Here we have ordered the ratings—for example, of the 67 competencies, Integrity and Trust is the highest-rated skill for individual contributors, the second highest skill for managers, and the third highest for executives.)

There are a couple of ways to look at this: (1) it will be very easy to hire people who already have these common skills, and (2) it will be necessary to build the skills that people do not naturally develop through the course of their careers.

Table 2.1 Top 10 skills across levels

Top 10 skills	Overall	Individual contributors	Managers	Executives
Integrity and trust	1	1	2	3
Ethics and values	2	2	1	1
Intellectual horsepower	3	4	3	2
Functional/ technical skills	4	3	4	5
Action oriented	5	8	5	4
Customer focus	6	5	6	10
Perseverance	7	11	7	8
Approachability	8	7	8	15
Managing diversity	9	6	9	13
Drive for results	10	13	10	7

An important finding from our research is the tremendous similarity of leadership skills around the globe. To study this, we looked at the data across six regions: North America including Canada, the United States, and Mexico; Europe including Eastern Europe and Russia; New Zealand and Australia; Asia including the Middle East; South America including Central America; and Africa. When we look at leaders across six regions of the world, the top 10 skills can be captured in just 15 competencies. Not only are top skills common across position levels, the top skills are common among leaders around the world (Table 2.2).

2

Table 2.2 Top 10 skills across regions

Competency	North America	Europe	New Zealand/ Australia	Asia	South America	Africa
Ethics and values	1	4	2	2	1	2
Integrity and trust	2	2	1	1	3	1
Intellectual horsepower	3	3	4	4	2	6
Functional/technical skills	4	1	3	6	5	4
Customer focus	5	6	10	7	13	11
Managing diversity	6	13	8	22	14	16
Action oriented	7	5	7	3	7	3
Perseverance	8	7	9	10	6	5
Approachability	9	8	5	9	18	9
Drive for results	10	9	14	8	8	7
Comfort around higher management	11	17	12	11	9	8
Standing alone	12	10	6	13	11	12
Technical learning	13	11	17	18	4	14
Boss relationships	15	18	11	5	16	10
Learning on the fly	18	19	23	12	10	32

Note: The top 10 rank orders by region are highlighted.

What most people struggle with

We've shown that what starts high stays high. The corollary is also true. What starts low stays there for the most part. In Table 2.3, we look at the 10 competencies that come up most often in our studies as critical but are lower skills.

Table 2.3 Bottom 10 skills across levels

Bottom 10 skills	Overall	Individual contributors	Managers	Executives
Developing direct reports and others	67	63	66	66
Dealing with paradox	66	66	67	62
Conflict management	65	64	64	59
Personal disclosure	64	50	60	67
Personal learning	63	49	62	64
Managing vision and purpose	62	61	65	52
Confronting direct reports	61	62	61	61
Motivating others	60	65	59	58
Innovation management	59	55	58	57
Creativity	58	42	63	55

The bottom 10 leadership competencies by region are displayed in Table 2.4. Again, there is similarity across regions. A total of 19 competencies are needed to capture the 10 weakest skill areas. People, regardless of region, were relatively weak in these areas. You may notice that many of the skills that made the bottom 10 list are personal and interpersonal skills (noted with an asterisk).

Table 2.4 Bottom 10 skills across regions

Competency	North America	Europe	New Zealand/ Australia	Asia	South America	Africa
Humor*	21	12	13	58	36	19
Caring about direct reports*	26	33	31	44	58	26
Hiring and staffing	40	49	46	63	49	48
Work/life balance	51	57	48	53	66	65
Patience*	52	41	56	52	64	35
Political savvy	53	54	41	50	44	61
Creativity	54	66	61	66	56	60
Innovation management	56	60	58	65	47	59
Total work systems	57	46	55	59	61	37
Managing through systems	58	53	51	49	62	45
Understanding others*	59	58	59	64	65	58
Motivating others*	60	56	62	56	60	62
Managing vision and purpose	61	63	64	60	53	63
Confronting direct reports*	62	67	57	54	63	50
Conflict management*	63	65	63	61	59	66
Personal disclosure*	64	61	60	67	67	57
Personal learning*	65	59	67	36	51	56
Developing direct reports and others*	66	62	65	62	55	67
Dealing with paradox*	67	64	66	57	54	64

Note: the bottom 10 rank orders by region are highlighted.
* Many of the skills in the bottom 10 are personal and interpersonal skills.

What we can conclude from the norms:

- Individual skills start high and stay high.
- Skills that are absolutely essential to change management such as Conflict Management, Motivating Others, Innovation Management, and *Managing* Vision and Purpose start low and stay there even though requirements change.
- Skill in Self-Development lags in the middle, even as level goes up. Personal Learning, a competency that measures picking up on the need to change, is always among the lowest.
- Skills essential to day-to-day business such as Planning, Directing Others, and Managing and Measuring Work languish.
- Perhaps most telling, the ultimate test: Developing Direct Reports and Others is 67th out of 67 competencies overall. No wonder the leadership shelves aren't stocked with a lot of skilled people. Many organizations haven't learned how to run the development store yet.
- Very little changes until people reach executive levels. Then Political Savvy, Business Acumen, Perspective, Strategic Agility, and Command Skills (leading during tough times) increase in skill level. What goes down? Day-to-day managing, creativity, and many interpersonal skills.

The conclusion is inescapable. Individual skills are rewarded and little gets developed effectively. The only good news is that at least executives appear to be selected based on some of the skills most required for their roles. But those things are mostly cognitive skills, not people-orchestration skills. In most cases, it looks like strengths stay strengths, and downsides accumulate over time.

Now that we see which leadership competencies are in high supply and low supply, the next step is to identify which competencies to include in your leadership competency model.

Finding the magic formula: Building a core competency model

Many organizations are seeking the list of 10 or fewer core competencies that drive success. Here we are not referring to business strategies or organizational values that are sometimes called core competencies. The search for core competencies to drive business strategy has to do with operational excellence. Core values, or beliefs, have to do with the social contract people are asked to enter into as members of the organization.

By core competencies, we mean the leadership skills and behaviors that drive success in the organization for individuals. Once determined, organizations want these 10 or fewer competencies to be applied to everyone in the organization regardless of job, business unit, location, or level. These 10 core competencies are then applied throughout the HR system for things like selection, deployment, and development.

Is there such a list of core competencies? *There is an 85 percent solution.*

Is it 10 or fewer? *Can't be. There are several sets of core competencies needed to cover an entire enterprise.*

Why more than 10? Because the process of getting to a usable list of core competencies is quite complex and not as obvious as it appears to be. Our view of core competencies focuses on competitive-edge competencies that can be used to differentiate superior from average jobholders. To do this, a competency model has to take five types of competencies into account.

Observation | **The 85 percent solution**

A reliable common theme that I hear in almost every company is "We're different." It's a very difficult conversation because I know, after 50 years and 250 companies, that companies are mostly the same. The "we're different" theme is a point of pride and branding and a reason for being. That is, if we were the same as every other company, that wouldn't be very exciting. I know from science that companies are more the same than different. Meaning that the principles of talent management and leadership development best practices are basically the same. On the other hand, companies are somewhat different, and I would put a number of 10 to 15 percent different. Those differences are and can be important, but they are mostly differences in style and culture and method of operation. They are probably not different in terms of leadership and managerial skills necessary to be successful. It's more values and style than skills and competencies.

Five types of competencies

1. Price-of-admission competencies – important across all levels and many people are good at them.

2. Competitive-edge competencies – equally important but few people are good at them.

3. Competitive-edge competencies that are level-driven – unique differences among levels.

4. Competitive-edge competencies that are common to superior performers.

5. Competitive-edge competencies that are job-driven – unique differences between jobs.

1. Price-of-admission competencies – important across all levels and many people are good at them.

The usual core competency list is a mixed bag of skills that almost everyone already has (like action orientation), some a few have (like communication skills), and some very few have (like managing innovation). Rarely do all the competencies apply to all levels and all jobs, even in a loose sense. The usual list is much, much too short to serve for more than a public-relations purpose and is often stacked with things most people are already good at—like being trustworthy and results oriented.

The core competency list we will present is different from this. Our list contains only competencies that most people are fairly good at and that are usually important in any job. We call these competencies price-of-admission skills.

2

Our first recommendation is that you should select for the competencies most people are good at that are essential across levels. Why fool around? If people who are good at them are in reasonable supply, why do anything else?

This, of course, requires information on which competencies are critical across the board—all levels and all jobs. There are 12 competencies in our studies on which many people receive relatively high ratings (in the top third of all competencies rated). All are significant with performance and/or promotion or potential across levels. This list is not exhaustive and cannot be totally correct. Samples will differ, but this is a reasonable starting point, especially if your organization lacks data on critical skills.

The good news: price-of-admission competencies predict performance across levels and the skill level is generally high:

Strategic Skills

- Decision quality
- Functional/technical skills
- Intellectual horsepower
- Learning on the fly
- Problem solving

| 31

Operating skills

- Organizing

Courage

- Standing alone

Energy and drive

- Action oriented
- Perseverance
- *Drive* for results

Organizational positioning skills

- Comfort around higher management

Personal and interpersonal skills

- Customer focus

The point here is that if something is readily available and you need it, select for it. Up to the 85 percent level—85 percent of these should play in most jobs—should be selected for. They might not appear on a core competency profile, however, because with a few exceptions we'll note later, they won't differentiate much if they are high to begin with. Consider them price-of-admission or knockout factors.

An analogy may help make this point better. If we pick basketball players based on height, we will, indeed, have a better chance of success. A team with 5' 10" average height wouldn't win a game beyond middle school. Once we do this, height still matters to win games but no longer tells us who among the players will be the best at making baskets. Similarly, if we use Intellectual Horsepower as a screen for a top-management team, once selected, Intellectual Horsepower can no longer differentiate excellent from average executives because everyone has it.

2. Competitive-edge competencies – equally important but few people are good at them.

The first set of competitive-edge competencies would make a difference in the success of the organization, but most people aren't good at them. We like to call these the Big 8. These are the key competencies to drive change, form new strategies, and inspire people to achieve. These are the competencies that can make your organization unique. These competencies would drive a competitive-edge difference if a critical mass of your top executives and aspiring executives had them.

In the list of competencies below, all are generally related to performance, promotion, and/or potential across jobs and levels. They are not in high supply and must ordinarily be developed. We present these as probabilities, not truth. The question for any organization is what competencies are critical across levels (or for managers and executives) and not in high supply? Hire for them if you can, but mostly develop these.

What people are consistently not very good at, that is often related to performance:

Strategic skills
- *Dealing with* ambiguity
- Creativity
- Innovation management
- Strategic agility

Operating skills
- Planning

Personal and interpersonal skills
- Motivating others
- *Building effective* teams
- *Managing* vision and purpose

So far we are up to 20 core competencies, a daunting number, but we would argue that organizations should focus their efforts

|

on the time bombs above and, then, not all at once. But not just those. There are two more groupings of competitive-edge competencies to consider as you build your model.

3. Competitive-edge competencies that are level-driven – unique differences among levels.

The second set of competitive-edge competencies is unique to levels. They partly drive performance once someone is in the job at any specific level. As we'll see, they form a mixed bag—some are in high supply and some are in very low supply. Select for these if possible, but mostly develop these.

The types of competencies in Table 2.5 form more of your competitive edge. When jobs—and especially levels—change, so do the competencies required. The competencies that get someone into a job may be important to performance, but they probably won't spell the difference between average and superior performance since many of the current incumbents already have these competencies.

Once in a job, the critical competencies may be a different list altogether, a combination of the eight low-supply competencies above as well as demands unique to a person's level in the organization. Each level has certain unique features—from performing as an individual contributor, to managing the people and the processes, to forming and inspiring others toward an organizational direction. While everyone may do all of these things at times, the amount of time spent, the emphasis on a competency, and oftentimes the formal responsibility will change dramatically across levels.

Table 2.5 What's most different across levels?

Individual contributors	Managers	Executives
Emphasis on:	Emphasis on:	Emphasis on:
• Interpersonal skills • Assessing people	• Day-to-day tactical operations skills • Developing direct reports and others • Conflict skills • Creating something new	• Strategy • Negotiation • Business acumen • Command skills

Based on research samples of 2,000 individual contributors, managers, and executives.

You should develop these in advance if possible and then select against them; however, many of these competencies are hard to see in advance. For example, most of the low competencies for managers require having others to direct when the stakes are high.

Our recommendation is that you select for all the level-based competencies in which most people are rated high, measure and reinforce the middles, and aggressively develop the lows (see Table 2.7). As we'll demonstrate later, people do not have to walk into a job cold. Small versions of these challenges can be provided early and often in a career.

4. Competitive-edge competencies common to superior performers.

If you know the few competencies that distinguish superior from average performers, this knowledge can drive much of selection and development. Then you can boost the average performance of your workforce. Superior performers (top 15 percent) are significantly better than low performers on two-thirds of our competencies, so in our most recent study, we decided to pare down our findings to just those competencies that differentiated superior from average performers. In essence, what's the difference between the good (performing fine in current job) and the great (top 15 percent) performers?

The answer is, not much. As others have found, superior performers are really good at a few competencies and are average on many. We looked manager-by-manager and executive-by-executive to see how many of these competencies someone had to score significantly higher on (rated in the top quarter) in order to be considered a superior performer (in the top 15 percent). Managers need to be really good at five competencies. Executives need to be really good at eight. But it matters which ones.

When we looked across superior-performing managers and executives (top 15 percent of performers), they were better at 17 of our 67 competencies than were average performers. Also, they had no issue whatsoever with one of the 19 career stallers. These 18 areas varied by level with 8 being common. We present these as an example of what superior performance might look like in an organization. Think of these competencies as boosters toward excellence. They have to be on top of or in addition to a solid base to begin with. Also, superior performers tend to have good self-awareness, which they use to neutralize weaknesses and keep themselves out of career trouble.

Table 2.6 Competitive-edge competencies common to superior performers

Managers	Executives
Strategic skills: ■ Decision quality ■ Functional/technical skills ■ Learning on the fly ■ Business acumen ■ *Dealing with* ambiguity ■ Strategic agility ■ Technical learning **Operating skills:** ■ Process management **Courage:** ■ Command skills ■ Conflict management ■ Standing alone **Energy and drive:** ■ Action oriented ■ *Drive for* results **Organizational positioning skills:** ■ Comfort around higher management **Personal and interpersonal skills:** ■ Listening ■ Personal learning ■ Composure	**Strategic skills:** ■ Decision quality ■ Functional/technical skills ■ Learning on the fly ■ Problem solving ■ Innovation management **Operating skills:** ■ Process management ■ *Timely* decision making ■ Planning **Courage:** ■ Sizing up people **Energy and drive:** ■ Perseverance ■ *Drive for* results **Organizational positioning skills:** ■ Comfort around higher management ■ Written communications **Personal and interpersonal skills:** ■ Listening ■ Personal learning ■ Boss relationships ■ Self-development
Career stallers: ■ (Not having) overdependence on a single skill	**Career stallers:** ■ (Not having) defensiveness

Out of the 18 areas at the manager level and the 18 areas at the executive level, there are eight competencies in common:

- Comfort around higher management
- Decision quality
- Functional/technical skills
- Learning on the fly
- *Drive for* results
- Listening
- Personal learning
- Process management

Interestingly, the first five of these have already appeared in our price-of-admission list. What this means is that average performers are good to quite good at many of these competencies, but superior performers are noticeably great (top 15 percent) at many of them.

These boosters, or differentiators, are even more powerful in pairs. Someone who is good at either *Drive for* Results or Listening scored below the 50th percentile in overall performance in our studies. Someone good at both scored at the 90th percentile.

The point of this list is that superior performers excel (the top 15 percent) at only a few things, and these may give an organization some indication of what those few things may be. With the exception of Personal Learning (which is the subtle skill of picking up on cues and changing one's behavior quickly), all could be selected for.

Still, directing others on a short-term project is not exactly the same challenge as directing full-time employees. Organizations need to develop whatever proficiency can be developed, but many competencies are only really learned when the heat is on and the pressure is high.

There are ways to develop these competencies on the job as a part of normal work. Thinking about real work differently will most likely develop these skills, and most challenging work tasks can develop three to five of these competencies at once.

That's just the way it is. Jobs, organizations, and people are quite complex. Demands change. Different skills are required. Ten competencies won't do the job for you.

2

Later in this chapter, we'll put all the competencies together in a model for you. But first, most of you have no doubt wondered "How did we get into this condition?" Development is indeed marginal in most organizations—people are often quite unqualified to do the jobs they are asked to do.

Why this happens to be and what to do about it forms the basis for this book. What happens and doesn't happen across careers is what a good competency model can partially fix for you. We say *partially* because there is another piece to the puzzle. You also need to have the systems in place to select, measure, and develop your people.

The best way to make our argument is to go back in time and show you what happens to the best and the brightest in most organizations.

Most of us were hired for our individual contributor skills and asked to perform in a technical area—we are an accountant or a salesperson or an HR person. We get ahead by performing our jobs well and showing some other skills that spell performance at entry level. These tend to be skills like Peer Relationships, Technical Learning, Approachability, and Interpersonal Savvy. If we build technical skill and show that we are not all knees and elbows, we can horse-trade with peers, form some solid work relationships, and build foundational career skills. One, we have a marketable skill. Two, we can network in a way that helps get things done.

39

If we are good enough, we are promoted to supervisor or manager. Now from a logical standpoint, this is the greatest transition of all—from doing the work to seeing that it is done by others, from being motivated to motivating others, from being developed to developing others, from managing our work to managing the work of a unit, from working to delegating.

2

Although not supervisors or managers yet, individual contributors do a lot of management-style projects, so many companies have them receive feedback on what are commonly thought of as managerial skills—Motivating Others, Delegation, Developing Direct Reports and Others, *Building Effective* Teams, Planning, and the like. To make this transition, these are core skills that would help accomplish the tasks mentioned above.

But none of these managerial competencies change significantly across levels.

The picture doesn't change much for the other huge transition— manager to executive. Here, people go from managing processes and people to managing systems, forming strategy and policy, and engaging in high-stakes negotiations. The proverbial buck stops here, and the pressure can be immense. But competency proficiency hardly budges.

5. Competitive-edge competencies that are job-driven – unique differences between jobs.

These specific job- or function- or organization-based competencies comprise 2 to 20 percent of the job according to the Hay-McBer studies we cited in Chapter 1 and are borne out by hundreds of core competency profiling sessions we have conducted.

While the competency profiles are all more the same than different, their differences matter. A business unit that is in a start-up phase will have a different profile than one that's in a turnaround stage. Marketing will have a different profile than manufacturing, and so on.

An 85 percent model of leadership effectiveness

Our approach focuses on the competitive-edge competencies. What good do these competitive-edge competencies do? They drive change strategically and operationally, fueled by people who grow themselves and grow others. In sum, they revolve around organizational renewal or change. What better competitive edge could there be than having competencies your competitors don't?

To make our case and to demonstrate our point, we will use the 67 competencies we developed and have conducted research on since 1992—the Leadership Architect® Competency Library. One caution: you should not view these suggestions as any more than that. We are introducing a way of thinking more than recommending that you follow the competency recipes.

The first line of solution is to have a leadership target—a clear set of competencies that drive performance and relate to potential within and across levels. In Table 2.7, we present a starter model of leadership effectiveness across time. In Appendix A, we lay out a rationale for why we selected what we did. Here, we will outline the core of the argument:

- Select for competencies that are in high supply. For each level, we list the competencies most likely to be related to performance and people are rated well on.
- Develop competencies that are likely weaknesses on the job.
- Measure and reinforce all competencies that are critical to performance once a person gets into a particular job.
- Develop competencies in low supply a level before they are needed, to the extent possible.
- Develop individual contributors and managers, but select executives.

Table 2.7 The 85 percent solution

	Individual contributors	Managers	Executives
Select for:	■ Action oriented ■ Decision quality ■ Functional/ technical skills ■ Intellectual horsepower ■ Learning on the fly ■ Perseverance ■ Problem solving ■ Process management ■ *Drive for* results ■ Standing alone ■ Technical learning	■ Action oriented ■ Comfort around higher management ■ Customer focus ■ Functional/ technical skills ■ Integrity and trust ■ Intellectual horsepower ■ Organizing ■ Perseverance ■ Problem solving ■ *Drive for* results ■ Standing alone	**High supply:** ■ Business acumen ■ Comfort around higher management ■ Command skills ■ Customer focus ■ Decision quality ■ Functional/ technical skills ■ Intellectual horsepower ■ Learning on the fly ■ Organizing ■ Problem solving ■ *Drive for* results **Moderate supply:** ■ *Dealing with* ambiguity ■ Negotiating ■ Perspective ■ Political savvy ■ Priority setting ■ Process management ■ Strategic agility **Low supply:** ■ Creativity ■ Innovation management ■ Motivating others ■ *Managing* vision and purpose

Table 2.7 The 85 percent solution–continued

	Individual contributors	Managers	Executives
Most likely weaknesses:	■ Motivating others ■ Personal learning ■ Strategic agility ■ *Managing* vision and purpose	■ *Dealing with* ambiguity ■ Command skills ■ Conflict management ■ Confronting direct reports ■ Creativity ■ Developing direct reports and others ■ Directing others ■ Hiring and staffing ■ Informing ■ Innovation management ■ Managing and measuring work ■ Motivating others ■ Perspective ■ Political savvy ■ Self-knowledge ■ *Building effective* teams ■ Managing vision and purpose	

2

| 43

Table 2.7 The 85 percent solution–continued

	Individual contributors	Managers	Executives
Measure and reinforce:	■ Creativity ■ Informing ■ Interpersonal savvy ■ Listening ■ Organizing ■ Peer relationships ■ Planning ■ Total work systems	■ Command skills ■ *Timely* decision making ■ Decision quality ■ Managing and measuring work ■ Presentation skills ■ Priority setting ■ Process management ■ Self-development ■ Time management	
Develop early (for high potentials):	■ Command skills ■ Conflict management ■ Creativity ■ Managing and measuring work ■ Motivating others ■ Perspective ■ Planning	■ *Dealing with* ambiguity ■ Creativity ■ Innovation management ■ Motivating others ■ Negotiating ■ Perspective ■ Political savvy ■ Strategic agility ■ *Managing* vision and purpose	

We constructed the 85 Percent Solution table to be viewed in two ways—by level and across a career. Each level can be viewed independently. From our studies, these are a reasonable starter set of competencies to select for, likely weaknesses, skills that need development a level early, and skills that need reinforcement because they matter for performance both now and across time.

When we get to the executive level, we split the competencies by probability—the ones that are in high, moderate, or low supply.

This also makes our point visually: develop individual contributors and managers; select executives. There is no other way to do it. People with all these skills don't exist in any number. You have to begin to develop executive skills long before they get there. By then, it's much too late to talk about developing creativity or strategic skills.

In the 85 Percent Solution table, across a career, we list competencies in high supply only once. Select for them, and then view them as price-of-admission skills for the next level. They are necessary but not sufficient for future performance. The most likely weaknesses are just that—the competencies most often related to performance that are in the lowest supply. The measure and reinforce list consists of skills in moderate supply critical to current performance. The develop early list is for high potentials only. If a person is eligible for promotion to the next level, it is essential that development on these competencies begins immediately. The develop early list ordinarily includes competencies that are weak at all levels.

Of special emphasis should be the measure and reinforce list. Lyle Spencer's research shows that improving average competencies (with feedback, training, and development) has two to three times the payoff than selecting better people. The reason for this is that people are starting with at least adequate levels of competence and improving in very specific job- and organizational-relevant behaviors (writing better computer code, finishing a project faster). It's easier to improve if you have some proficiency to begin with, and in many ways, this is the developmental best bet.

Even though the 85 Percent Solution is a research-based list, we view it as a starter set for organizations with no data on effectiveness. It cannot be totally accurate. It will vary with the strategy, the functional emphases, and how the business is doing. We present it primarily as a way of thinking—select for what is in high supply, work on common weaknesses on current job, measure and reinforce all competencies important for current performance, and develop critical competencies a level early.

Story

2

A superior performer's leadership competencies

The right leader can influence the vision, direction, and success of an organization. But to see transformation in just two years takes remarkable leadership skills.

Take the story of the San Francisco giants. Until 2008, Barry Bonds had been the golden goose—a player who could be relied upon to win game after game. But despite the star's performance, the giants were unable to win a world series.

When the giants let bonds go after the 2007 season, the focus was on transition to a new era. Enter william Neukom, the giants' new managing general partner and CEO. How did the giants win the world series three years after losing bonds and two seasons after Neukom joined?

Some might say luck. But over the course of his career, Neukom had honed an exceptional combination of leadership skills that he employed to shape the culture, the team, and the talent of the giants organization.

- *Listening – rather than shaking things up, neukom focused on understanding what people needed to be able to do their jobs well.*

- *Sizing up people – a keen eye for talent helped neukom identify homegrown players who were the antithesis to the high-priced, star-studded lineup of other teams.*

- *Decision quality – Neukom erred on the side of inclusion for any key discussions or decisions made by the organization. The result was open dialogue, better understanding across departments, and better decisions.*

> ■ *Managing vision and purpose – Neukom's "giants' way" laid out a philosophy, a direction, and a strategic vision that would provide the guiding principles that shaped the culture of the organization. Instead of a collection of individual goals, the giants organization had a set of shared goals.*
>
> *The result? A back-to-basics organization that valued collaborating, working hard, and sharing the credit for successes. Neukom's vision of collaboration and inclusiveness extends all the way to the banners above the streets of san francisco: "together we're giant."*

Building a case for development

Our core competency argument supposes that people will actually be developed to perform these competencies well, and as we have shown, this is rarely the case. Beginning with Chapter 5, we will elaborate on what has to happen for development to occur. For now, we will mention the core of the argument and illustrate with five killers—competencies that are generally important across levels and at which very few people are highly skilled:

- ■ *Dealing with* ambiguity
- ■ Creativity
- ■ Planning
- ■ Strategic agility
- ■ *Managing* vision and purpose

You may be wondering why these five showed up as killers, especially when Strategic Agility and *Managing* Vision and Purpose are not competencies most would associate with the lower levels of organizations. We believe the reason is that change skills have come to the fore. As Gary Hamel and C. K. Prahalad have argued in their strategy work, most of what spells success needs to be found outside the organization one is in, and it must be hunted and used by as many people as possible. What they call the "democratization of strategy" is what people proficient in these five competencies can do. They look outside the box, don't try to fit all knowledge into neat categories, and spend the head time necessary to come up with plans and visions to implement something new or different.

For these five killers, what if some of the following began happening within six months on the job as an individual contributor:

- Manage a group of people who are towering experts but he/she is not.
- Take on a task he/she dislikes or hates to do.
- Is part of a study group to see how the media organizes to deal with the chaos of events.
- Teach/coach someone how to do something he/she is an expert in.
- Lead an ad hoc group on a work project.
- Plan for and start up something small (secretarial pool, athletic program, suggestion system, program, etc.).
- Study the history of a similar situation and draw parallels for a current business issue or problem, and present the findings to others for comment.
- Make peace with an enemy or someone he/she has disappointed with a product or service or someone he/she has had some trouble with or didn't get along with very well.
- Study some aspect of his/her job or a new technical area he/she hasn't studied before but needs in order to be more effective.

See the beginnings of Planning, *Dealing with* Ambiguity, Creativity, *Managing* Vision and Purpose, and Strategic Agility?

Going further, what if the person is promoted to management?

- Do a one-year stint at corporate in business planning.
- Serve on a start-up team.
- Serve on four business strategy projects, where the recommendations, if accepted, would be implemented by some of the project members.
- Manage a group of people in a rapidly expanding or growing operation.
- Work a few shifts in the telemarketing or customer service department, handling complaints and inquiries from customers.
- Work in a unit where frequent experiments are necessary to improve quality.
- Work on a project that involves travel and study of an international issue, acquisition, or joint venture, and report back to management.
- Go to the Aspen Institute to study the great philosophers.

You don't have to rely on guesswork to orchestrate activities that can create competency growth. Each competency, as we'll see later, has a set of fingerprints—challenging tasks, job demands, and learning opportunities that have a rhyme to them.

Conclusion

Competencies are the universal common denominator. They drive work and performance. Some should be selected for and some nurtured. The competencies that are critical can be developed if we are purposeful about work challenges rather than simply seeing work as tasks and goals.

But don't reinvent the wheel, and don't fall prey to the short, simple, 10-or-fewer argument. Use whichever research-based model you like. The Leadership Machine will run with any of them.

Chapter 3

Leadership types: The effectiveness patterns of real people

Do most of the people in your organization have good scores on all of your core competencies? No. Is that good or bad? Maybe neither. Maybe it's just the way people are.

There are hundreds of studies of the characteristics of leaders. Via one method or another, there are a number of, let's say, excellent and not-so-excellent managers chosen. Data are collected on each about leadership style, strengths, and weaknesses. Finally, a statistical profile is computed explaining which variables of style or skill differentiate the more able from the less able. This produces a list of the competencies of effective managers.

Impressive. Ten or 20 characteristics of successful managers. But wait a minute. If we look back over the competencies, hardly anyone may have them all. Bad research? Not at all. It is certainly true that better managers as a group, in fact, excel at these skills. It is just as true that few managers will have them all.

Success is more complex than any model can portray. There are multiple ways to be successful and effective. In real life, not many managers and leaders look like the success profile. A study of 200 consensus geniuses reached the same conclusion: few geniuses had all the characteristics of genius. Because Einstein worked in spurts, he appeared to be lazy to some people, for example.

So what's going on? And what does this mean for organizations?

Common questions from line leaders about so-called core competencies are, "Do we really want all of our managers and leaders to look the same? Do we want to clone managers and leaders? Won't this single list of competencies produce a single type of leader?"

Well it hasn't yet. And luckily, it never will, because line managers are right. They sense that having all leaders look the same wouldn't lead to success. This is because people have different gifts and all contribute to the success of the organization.

There have been few studies that classify people into groups and determine what variables differentiate them from each other. Some of these are mentioned in the Notes section at the end of the book. For our purposes, before we tackle the issue of how to develop people to meet the enduring challenges of work, we thought it useful to ask what types of people show up at work each day. After all, this is what we have to work with.

Using a statistical technique called cluster analysis, we analyzed our sample three ways. We split it in two, ran clusters and compared them for similarity; then we ran the entire sample to see if the patterns held. While the matches were not exact in most cases, they were close enough to say that there may be at least seven patterns that characterize real people. We say *may* because, as far as we can tell, this is the first time this particular sort of analysis has been done with an extensive competency model. So, at the least, these seven patterns are a beginning. To help you understand these patterns, we repeat the factor structure that our competencies group into. See Figure 3.1 for what the competencies important to success look like.

Figure 3.1 Leadership Architect® library structure

GLOBAL FOCUS AREAS
- Global Business Knowledge
- Cross-Cultural Resourcefulness
- Cross-Cultural Agility
- Assignment Hardiness
- Organizational Positioning Skills
- Cross-Cultural Sensitivity
- Humility

FACTOR VI:
Personal and Interpersonal Skills

Cluster N. Relating Skills
- Approachability
- Interpersonal Savvy

Cluster O. Caring About Others
- Caring About Direct Reports
- Compassion

Cluster P. Managing Diverse Relationships
- Boss Relationships
- Customer Focus
- *Managing Diversity*
- Fairness to Direct Reports
- Peer Relationships
- Understanding Others

Cluster Q. Inspiring Others
- Motivating Others
- Negotiating
- *Building Effective Teams*
- *Managing Vision and Purpose*

Cluster R. Acting with Honor and Character
- Ethics and Values
- Integrity and Trust

Cluster S. Being Open and Receptive
- Composure
- Humor
- Listening
- Patience
- Personal Disclosure

Cluster T. Demonstrating Personal Flexibility
- *Dealing with Paradox*
- Personal Learning
- Self-Development
- Self-Knowledge

Cluster U. Balancing Work/Life
- Work/Life Balance

FACTOR III:
Courage

Cluster H. Dealing with Trouble
- Command Skills
- Conflict Management
- Confronting Direct Reports
- Managerial Courage
- Standing Alone

Cluster I. Making Tough People Calls
- Hiring and Staffing
- Sizing Up People

FACTOR IV:
Energy and Drive

Cluster J. Focusing on the Bottom Line
- Action Oriented
- Perseverance
- *Drive for Results*

FACTOR V:
Organizational Positioning Skills

Cluster K. Being Organizationally Savvy
- Organizational Agility
- Political Savvy

Cluster L. Communicating Effectively
- Presentation Skills
- Written Communications

Cluster M. Managing Up
- Career Ambition
- Comfort Around Higher Management

FACTOR I:
Strategic Skills

Cluster A. Understanding the Business
- Business Acumen
- Functional/Technical Skills
- Technical Learning

Cluster B. Making Complex Decisions
- Decision Quality
- Intellectual Horsepower
- Learning on the Fly
- Problem Solving

Cluster C. Creating the New and Different
- *Dealing with Ambiguity*
- Creativity
- Innovation Management
- Perspective
- Strategic Agility

FACTOR II:
Operating Skills

Cluster D. Keeping on Point
- *Timely Decision Making*
- Priority Setting

Cluster E. Getting Organized
- Organizing
- Planning
- Time Management

Cluster F. Getting Work Done Through Others
- Delegation
- Developing Direct Reports and Others
- Directing Others
- Informing
- Managing and Measuring Work

Cluster G. Managing Work Processes
- Process Management
- *Managing Through Systems*
- Total Work Systems

| 53

The effectiveness patterns of real people

(We distinguish high performance from average and average performance from low using a one-half standard deviation difference, which is a common rule of thumb when comparing groups.)

Before we begin, an obvious question is, who are in these groups? Were there more individual contributors, more managers, or more executives? The answer for all seven clusters is that all the levels are represented in relatively equal proportions. Put another way, any of the seven clusters are as likely to have an executive in it, as it is to have an individual contributor or a manager.

1. The stars

First, the good news. There is a group of people who scored high on almost all the factors. Maybe 15 percent of people averaged high on all the factors except personal balance (and were moderate there). So at best, 15 percent fit the success pattern.

2. The near stars

Perhaps 10 percent of the sample looks like the Star group in many respects. They are quite high in the strategic skills which are most valued in organizations, along with their other highs— energy and drive for results. Adequate in most other areas, they do have some difficulties with conflict. Perhaps this is a group of people who do fine under most circumstances but struggle when they have to deal with ambiguity or push through changes against resistance. Because day-to-day operational skills are also highly valued, their average scores may also not be good enough to propel them forward.

These first two groups look much like the analysis we presented in Chapter 2. Both are high where it matters most—strategic skills and drive, with high or moderate interpersonal skills. However, interpersonal skills are much lower relative to the other factors. In rank-order terms, the interpersonal factor comes in fifth out of sixth for both groups.

3. The solid performers (Seasoned citizens, high professionals)

About one-fifth (20 percent) of the sample really knows how to get the job done. They drive hard for results, take initiative, and push things through. They are at least average on everything else.

4. Nice people (Good time managers, relationship managers)

About one-fifth (20 percent) of the sample scores high on personal and interpersonal skills and fairly moderate on everything else, except for one factor—they are not the people to help in times of turmoil or conflict. They don't confront well, show much courage, size up people accurately (or won't admit it), or take charge in a crisis. It's a fair assumption that their genuine concern for others is their greatest strength and their greatest weakness.

5. The poor managers (Technocrats?)

About one-fifth (20 percent) of the sample looks to be very poor managers. While adequate at some of the factors such as the fact they also drive for results, have some strategic skills, and are interested in self-development, they also score very low on most operating skills, matters of courage, and dealing with change. They appear, at best, to be technically adept caretakers who shouldn't manage. Unfortunately, 85 percent of them do.

6. The galley masters

Maybe 10 percent fit the stereotypic media view of poor performers—sky-high drive coupled with subterranean interpersonal and conflict-management skills. They would be the boss you hope you never have. They probably resist every change but are adequately organized and planful to appear to be doing many of the right things. On the other hand, they'll never win any awards from their coworkers, and are probably viewed as marginal in many organizations due to their crippling lack of any sort of conflict-resolution or inspirational skills.

7. The not-so-goods

Now the truly bad news. About 10 percent of people didn't do well at anything. They were either the lowest or close to lowest on all six factors. There was no level pattern here. The lowest performers were equally likely to be individual contributors, managers, and executives.

While at PepsiCo, Andy Pearson built a fearsome reputation as one of *Fortune's* first *Toughest Bosses* by setting high standards and eliminating the lowest 10 percent of performers each year. You may recall the Roman legions did the same thing. This is where we get the word *decimate*. Pearson, of course, didn't kill the bottom 10 percent as the Romans did, but he was adamant that these people were not suited to perform in large organizations and would be better off elsewhere. Looks like he was right.

We can't emphasize enough that as of this writing, these patterns are meant only to be suggestive. There simply isn't enough research to say these are the only patterns we may find. Other analyses with different samples may well find more nuance than we can at this point. Nonetheless, these patterns come from a national database with all major types of organizations represented. They are a reasonable start.

We conclude from this first analysis that there are multiple ways to manage and lead, and all but one of the clusters has at least one significant upside. What any organization most likely needs (and will get nonetheless) is a portfolio of these types. Sometimes you need a relationship manager or a driver or a technocrat. While too many of one type might lead to imbalance and failure, our contention is that all types have value. There are simply not enough superstars to go around, even after the elaborate culling processes that go on in organizations, and organizations would be well served to work with whom they have (other than cluster seven).

The problem is not that each cluster—except cluster one—has obvious flaws. (And if we looked deeply enough, individuals in that cluster would have a few flat sides as well.) The problem, as we have pointed out repeatedly, is that no one is developing much. We see the same result again here as these seven patterns have nothing to do with level. It's fair to conjecture that nice people stay nice people and drivers stay drivers. It's hardly likely they started out any other way.

Further, the fact that level doesn't matter means that, proportionally, there are just as many poor performers, poor managers, and conflict avoiders at executive levels as there are among 25-year-olds.

The challenge

We can better select what the right competencies for a job are; we can be more realistic about the people who walk in the door every day; and, hopefully, we can avoid inadvertently derailing them. But before we do this, we need to consider the nature of development and what the people look like who develop most. Only then can we begin to put this knowledge to work in organizational systems.

Chapter 4

Derailment: the failure on the other side of success

Success isn't just a matter of piling up wins. Quite often it's the wins that derail careers.

Common sense and research findings fly out the door when many organizations assess and promote people. Myths and legends pave the path from early success to later derailment, and it is a broad path. With downsizing, delayering, globalization, and rapid change, the assignments are larger, the jumps across levels are larger, and as we saw in Chapter 2, most people aren't prepared to handle them.

Here, we do not refer to the never successful but, rather, to those who are respected in early and middle career, then run into trouble as executives (or flame out as high potentials who never get promoted past the middle ranks). As an example, five CEOs of five Fortune 100 companies were fired by their boards after less than two years of service. All five had stellar careers that led to their selection as CEO. But something happened. What? Overnight failures? Or failures that had been building for years or even decades before?

The other side of success works like this: None of us gets up in the morning to approach our day in a neutral, open fashion. We were born with and learn strong drives which we express through our personalities—the bundle of tactics, likes, and dislikes we use to satisfy what drives us. To achieve, to have power, to be loyal, to promote harmony, to worship aesthetics, to have fun—these are some of the core forces that lie underneath the surface of

59

our actions. Not surprisingly, people select occupations that will satisfy their drives if they can. Therefore, formal organizations are chock-full of individual achievers, those who want power, and those who are loyal and diligent.

Now the conspiracy begins, with us as oh-so-willing accomplices. Say you are hired to be a salesperson, and an eager one you are. You want to control your own destiny, like to talk and persuade, and are bored by strategy and paperwork and anything other than what contributes to your personal measure of success— closing the deal, making the sale, winning the sales contest.

What would you focus on? Results, customer transaction skills, and product knowledge would be a good start. What wouldn't you focus on? Maybe anything in a team (you're an individual achiever after all), anything involving other functions (boring, so what does this have to do with selling?), and anything remotely resembling administration. You're in the perfect job, you sell a lot of stuff, and your performance reviews are glowing. In fact, in your last two reviews, you only had one nit—you're not very cooperative with others unless they can help you make a sale. This little nit was glossed over; it took about 15 seconds in your performance appraisal and has long since slipped from consciousness. There are other nits as well, but no one has noticed them yet because they're not relevant to selling.

You roll along, building on your selling and individual contributor strengths, tackling problems with what works, and honing your closing skills. You're extremely good at it, and life is pretty comfortable. Steady pay increases. Increasing bonuses. A lot of recognition.

The conspiracy is now complete: In a world of do more with less, organizations are comfortable assigning you to do what you already know how to do, telling you how well you are doing it, and you don't mind a bit.

Until something changes.

The product lines you sell get spun off; or 60 percent of what you sell becomes a cold, hands-off, e-commerce transaction; or sales become a matter of cajoling and negotiating with huge key customers and joint venture partners.

Observation | Derailment

Over the course of my 50-year career, I have watched many leaders move from one job to the next. In the 50 years I've been practicing, the reasons why people derail have not changed much. This is not just my observation; meta-analysis of derailment studies over the last 50-year period shows that derailment has stayed basically the same. For the most part, it is an issue of poor interpersonal and relationship skills. What's frustrating as a practitioner is that we have known about these derailment characteristics for a very long time. There shouldn't be an HR professional or a line manager who is not aware of the findings or phenomena of derailment.

In the twilight of our careers, we're dealing today with derailment events in our current client assignments the same as we did 50 years ago when we began. The derailment characteristics are easy to assess, easy not to hire, and relatively easy to address once they occur inside a company. What's also frustrating is that we have followed a group of people over the course of our careers who have derailed repeatedly, company after company, for the same set of poor interpersonal skills. So far, the record is six (firings), several people are at five, and a large number are at four or less. Basically, they keep getting hired by new organizations and failing for the same reasons.

4

Where the trouble starts

In Exercise 4.1, there are eight common patterns of early success that were uncovered in research at the Center for Creative Leadership (CCL). We later adapted this into the following exercise for a course we designed for CCL. (We have further updated the exercise for presentation here.) Please take a minute to fill it out on yourself or someone who is struggling at the senior ranks.

Exercise 4.1 Eight common patterns of early success

Check no more than two strengths that you believe are primarily responsible for your (or their) success to date:

_____ 1. Bright, driver, ambitious, high standards, tough on laggards.

_____ 2. Independent, likes to do it alone.

_____ 3. Extremely loyal to organization, a team player.

_____ 4. Controlling, results oriented, single-minded, really nails down technical detail.

_____ 5. Personable, relies on relationships to get things done.

_____ 6. Creative, conceptually strong, ball of fire, finger in many pies.

_____ 7. Has a single notable characteristic such as tons of energy, raw talent, or a long-term mentor.

_____ 8. Contentious, likes to argue, takes strong stands, usually right.

©1990 Center for Creative Leadership. Adapted from Tools for Developing Successful Executives, designed by Michael M. Lombardo and Robert W. Eichinger. Used by permission.

The process of derailment

In Table 4.1, find the two strengths that you checked in Exercise 4.1 as primarily responsible for your (or their) success to date and read across the row. Does anything on the right look familiar? Are your (or their) strengths becoming weaknesses as well?

Table 4.1 The process of derailment

Early strengths	"Little" problems/ Untested areas	As time goes by	May slide into trouble due to
___ 1. Bright, driver	• Overly ambitious, bruises others • Needs no one else • Abrasive, lacks composure • Handles others' mistakes poorly • Doesn't know how to get the most out of other people, appreciate what they can do	• Friends come and go, but enemies accumulate and they are getting more powerful too; bringing out the best in others becomes required	• Arrogant • Insensitive • Betrayal of trust • Ethics and values • Overly ambitious • Lack of composure
___ 2. Independent	• Doesn't develop direct reports • Doesn't resolve conflict • Poor delegator	• Team building, staffing, developing others becomes a necessity • Conflicts can't be ignored forever	• Can't build a team • Can't rally people to his or her side (performance problems) • No network— political missteps

| 63

Table 4.1 The process of derailment–continued

Early strengths	"Little" problems/ untested areas	As time goes by	May slide into trouble due to
__ 3. Loyal, team player	• Selects in own image • Not challenging • Has never built a staff	• Team building, standing alone, staffing become essential across time	• Overmanaging • Can't be counted on when times are tough • Failure to staff effectively • Can't build a team
__ 4. Controlling, results oriented	• Has trouble in new jobs, situations • Gets irritated when things don't go right • Not strategic	• Giving up old ways of doing things in order to succeed in new situations	• Overmanaging • Non-strategic • Unable to adapt to differences • Lack of composure
__ 5. Personable	• Not strategic • Has problems with deep analysis • Not very flexible	• Jobs get more complex and cognitive • Relationships will only take one so far	• Non-strategic • Blocked personal learner
__ 6. Creative	• Lacks attention to detail • Disorganized, speedboats along • Hasn't really completed anything	• Depth, nitty-gritty required to do many jobs • Ramifications of failure to follow through get huge	• Poor administrator • Betrayal of trust
__ 7. Single notable characteristic	• Too many eggs in one basket • Staying with the same person too long	• Increasing complexity calls for broader skills and standing alone	• Standing alone • Key skill deficiencies • Over-dependence on a single skill or advocate

Table 4.1 The Process of Derailment–Continued

Early strengths	"Little" problems/ untested areas	As time goes by	May slide into trouble due to
__ 8. Contentious, usually right	• Doesn't know how to sell a position • Has to win • Trouble adapting • Hasn't learned how to lose gracefully	• The higher you go, the more powerful your peers and bosses get	• Unable to adapt to differences • Political missteps • Insensitive to others

©1990 Center for Creative Leadership. Adapted from Tools for Developing Successful Executives, designed by Michael M. Lombardo and Robert W. Eichinger. Used by permission.

None of the above is inevitable, but it is probable unless feedback and additional development occur. Even superb early performers get into later trouble when something changes, and it always does. Then the personal side of the conspiracy comes into play:

- *Strengths become weaknesses.* Under enough stress, people normally fall back on their strengths. This is the "if more is good, then a lot is even better" fallacy. We see the bright light of our success but never see what's in the darkness beyond. We ignore or are blind to our flaws. Our performance is great, and we're bulletproof. We get a bit overconfident.

- *Our experience is too narrow.* We have obvious untested areas—challenges we've never faced and haven't been prepared for. Even if we've been promoted, our experience is silo-based—we've done the same thing over and over.

- *We don't know how to learn anything new.* Not to be confused with reading and learning facts, we don't know how to come up with a new strategy, learn a new personal skill, or do something differently from what we've done in the past.

- *Transitions do us in.* The greatest learning or the greatest flameouts occur during transitions. A new job, a new boss, new job demands require skills we don't have and may not even be sure of what they are. So we lead with what we know how to do.

In short, we become victims of our past success. Our chance of changing quickly is fairly bleak—no actionable feedback, no broadened perspective, don't know how to learn anything new. Performance is all that matters, and our numbers don't look so good anymore.

Organizations do an excellent job of derailing people—it's one of the things they do best from a people point of view. Many set the conspiracy in motion by hiring for the current job and often taking a very superficial view of the dynamics of growth and careers. People get done-in psychologically with poor feedback and simplistic views of what success is. But they also get done-in structurally through poor developmental practices almost guaranteed to produce the very derailers that cause hand-wringing when they flame out.

How to derail your competitors for advancement

Sometimes it's more informative and more fun to argue cases in the reverse. Say you really dislike a few people. They are much too talented to fire in the short-term, so you have to rely on a 10-year strategy, one that will leave you looking like a saint because you were right about them all along.

Following are your two best practices lists. The first list is for organizational consumption. The second list contains your little secrets.

Best practices in development of our best young people

1. *We assign our best and highest-potential people to our best-performing units.* To be the best, one must learn from the best. At International Widget (IW), we carefully select excellent units, then make sure our promising, early-career people are exposed to their best practices.

2. *We promote almost entirely from within.* Functional and business excellence is the hallmark of our firm. We ensure smooth transitions and the continuity of the firm by promoting people on sheer merit in their specialty area.

3. *We promote broadness in our starting-career people through an intensive job rotation program.* We invest in our new people; indeed, their first two years are spent in a standard program (our fast-track Future Leaders program) designed to expose and teach every aspect of our business. Those selected spend three or more months in all of the functions and business units. This experience is augmented through the years with courses that provide updated information related to our changing business environment.

4. *We focus on real work.* Rather than divert people into interesting but tangential worklike projects, we develop core expertise first, then assign people to projects once they are ready to handle the demands.

5. *We don't punish people for mistakes.* Even the best of us stumble from time to time. Here at IW, we know this and guarantee that thoughtful mistakes will not be punished.

6. *We develop people fast.* Average job tenure is one to two years for fast-trackers. In this rapidly changing world, only those who move fast and think fast will succeed. IW offers career excitement for ambitious and aggressive learners.

7. *We ensure development through real-time performance feedback.* With our up-to-the-minute technology, we offer instant performance feedback on a number of key performance indicators so people always know how they are doing.

8. *We mentor the best with the best.* All high potentials are assigned to bosses and mentors who are also high potentials. Here at IW, we believe that the best learn best from the best.

9. *We develop the expertise of our people.* People here at IW can expect to spend their careers in their functional or business area. We develop experts here, not jacks-of-all-trades who know a little bit about everything.

10. *We reward performance with promotion.* We don't lateral people off into oblivion at IW. For our best people, performance in current job leads to promotion to greater responsibilities.

11. *We develop collegial spirit in our young people.* Our high potentials regularly meet with one another during special events and courses constructed just for them. Continuous improvement and networking help them develop further.

12. *We accentuate the positive.* We don't believe that beating on your best people is the way to help them grow. Feedback and growth at IW focuses on building on one's strengths, not on cataloging the inevitable weaknesses all of us have.

In real life, the practices above are well intentioned, and all of them have a grain of truth in them. For example, one good reason to assign people to the best units is to help high potentials get better pay and bonuses. Unfortunately, here is how these practices often play out.

Twelve surefire ways to derail your worst enemy

1. *We assign our best and highest-potential people to our best-performing units.* This will ensure a suitably narrow background where they never learn most of what is necessary to lead or cope with change. If the unit is high performing enough, little of what they do will make any real difference anyway, and they may even learn to grossly overestimate their impact.

2. *We promote almost entirely from within.* Promote them into their boss's job and then his boss's job and...this is the least powerful developmental move a person can ordinarily make. Regardless of whatever merits the job may have, developmentally, it's basically more of the same people and same work. It's also irrational. Why would the best salesperson make the best sales manager? Are the jobs really similar? If they are, then why is it that few great basketball players have been great coaches?

3. *We promote broadness in our new people through an intensive job rotation program.* Put them in a rotation program the first two or three years so they can get exposed to all parts of the business. This may get them to quit, as it does many young people. Rather than develop a core competence that they can rely on like a tree trunk later, they can be exposed to all the functions or businesses they'll never really work in and where no one will want them. They'll be given training assignments and make-work instead.

4. *We focus on real work.* Eschew any developmental project as a distraction to real work. Business projects, especially those that are multifunctional in nature, are the all-purpose developer of people. Make sure to staff all projects with high professionals who can already do the work.

5. *We don't punish people for mistakes.* Airlift them out of any failures and mistakes because "they are too valuable to lose." This will encourage learning nothing from mistakes and help a worker develop defense scripts of blame and denial. Successful managers are much more likely to report more failures and mistakes in their careers—it's a primary motivation for getting better.

6. *We develop people fast.* Have them declared fast-track and get them moved every two years or so. It's very important to move people so fast they never really finish a job. Their mistakes never catch up with them; deep problem solving never takes place. As Jack Gabarro showed in his research, there are inexorable learning phases in taking charge of a job. People go through them whether they think they have the time or not. Interrupt the sequence and they learn very little, even if they apparently succeeded.

7. *We ensure development through real-time performance feedback.* Give a lot of "what you did" feedback, but not "how you did it" feedback. Studies indicate that high-potential managers get less developmental feedback (and ask for less). If they move fast enough, they may never get any feedback.

8. *We mentor the best with the best.* Make sure they have a series of bosses who are high potentials and who change jobs quickly. If they move fast and their bosses move fast, this provides further insurance against anything developmental happening.

9. *We develop the expertise of our people.* Encourage same function and same business throughout their careers. This is critical in developing vertical movement, especially if they can go straight up the hierarchy in units that are doing at least reasonably well. If they succeed long enough, they'll run into the dreaded "T" promotion (they go straight up the line of the T, then hit the broad horizontal bar of the T). In a T promotion, they will suddenly be wrenched from their functional cocoons into a multifunctional nightmare where they'll be managing functions they know nothing about and can't really understand how to manage. This best practice works in strong parallel with number four above (We focus on real work).

10. *We reward performance with promotion.* Only consider promotions as legitimate job opportunities. The careers of successful people are zigzags, not straight lines. Avoid any job that would require them to perform under first-time and different conditions. They would be quite likely to learn some useful skills.

11. *We develop collegial spirit in our people.* Encourage networking with other high potentials. This is an excellent way to help them develop a limited view of successful people as confident, aggressive, and independent. Send them all to prestigious courses to cement the relationships.

12. *We accentuate the positive.* Give a lot of feedback focusing on strengths. Your final insurance policy, critical to developing the arrogance and hubris that people like to see so that they don't feel so guilty about derailing a talented person.

Tongue in cheek? Not at all. These are common practices, and they were just as common as when we started observing them years ago. With the widespread use of 360° feedback instruments, only numbers seven (We ensure development through real-time performance feedback) and twelve (We accentuate the positive) aren't as severe as they used to be, and they are hardly without controversy. A major survey questioned the value of 360s—too expensive, too unsettling—and one major consulting firm takes an "only give feedback on strengths" position. The argument goes that it's pointless to push people into areas they will never be any good at, and better to get all the strengths represented on a team so the person can focus on honing his or her gifts.

Sounds good, but there are some significant flaws in the argument. First, organizations that don't have good competency models and don't develop people also don't have teams with all the strengths. Second, all people use their strengths to attack their weaknesses—what else could they use? Third, this argument leaves out the developmental best bet—moving an average skill toward the strong side. Much research indicates that this approach pays off better than selection because the development is focused on specific work issues with someone already adequately skilled in the area.

The truth is that strengths reinforced and unmoderated by any sense of their dark sides could go into overdrive. The focus-on-strengths argument essentially advocates that what you drive fast, you should drive faster. Not much point in looking at the road signs, even the ones displayed on diamond shapes with black borders.

So don't worry. Your secrets are safe. Given enough time, you can still derail anybody in most organizations with the above list.

What is most likely to stall and stop careers

Paraphrasing Tolstoy, all happy families look alike but each unhappy family is miserable in its own way. So it is with the bright and dark sides of competence. The bright side looks remarkably similar everywhere—individual contributors, managers, and executives share common strengths as we saw in Chapter 2. But derailment is a different story.

In our most recent round of studies, we looked at over 1,500 people across a one-year period. We had performance, promotion, and/ or termination information for all.

For managers and executives, performance is fairly straightforward. Good judgment, strategic skills, creating something new, tactical skills, and personal drive dominate it. Promotion is another matter entirely. While it has a strong get-out-the-work component to it, relationships, networking, and learning agility largely determine who gets ahead.

4

Table 4.2 The five best predictors of promotion for managers and executives

Relationships	Learning	Motivation and energy
■ Boss relationships ■ Peer relationships ■ Customer focus	■ Learning on the fly	■ *Drive* for results

Getting fired is more the flip side of promotion than performance. People may excel at most of the competencies fairly important to performance, yet get dismissed. In termination, we found many competencies where being better at them did not get people promoted, but being worse at them got them fired. What happens is that people run out of people to work with, wreck relationships, and destroy trust, and this inevitably erodes their ability to perform. While few sheer relationship skills ordinarily relate to performance, they play heavily in who gets ahead, who gets left behind, and who gets shown the door.

Table 4.3 What gets managers and executives fired

What gets managers fired?	What gets executives fired?
Weak relationships/networks	Weak relationships/networks
Lower ratings in: ■ Approachability ■ *Managing* diversity ■ Integrity and trust ■ Patience ■ Political savvy	Lower ratings in: ■ Comfort around higher management ■ Listening ■ Peer relationships
Higher ratings in: ■ *Lack of* ethics and values ■ Insensitive to others	Higher ratings in: ■ Defensiveness ■ *Lack of* ethics and values ■ Political missteps
Not getting work out	Not getting work out
Lower ratings in: ■ Managing and measuring work ■ Organizing	Lower ratings in: ■ Customer focus ■ Functional/technical skills ■ *Drive for* results ■ Total work systems
Higher ratings in: ■ *Poor* administrator	Higher ratings in: ■ *Poor* administrator ■ Failure to staff effectively
	Not managing strategy: ■ Non-strategic

4

73

Excerpt

What to stop

Among the myriad wise things I have heard Peter Drucker say, the wisest was, "We spend a lot of time teaching leaders what to do. We don't spend enough time teaching leaders what to stop. Half the leaders I have met don't need to learn what to do. They need to learn what to stop."[†]

[†]From *What Got You Here Won't Get You There*. Marshall Goldsmith. (2007). New York, NY: Hyperion.

We began this chapter using the example of a salesperson who "gets away" with certain behavior until something changes. This pattern runs throughout our data. Getting promoted for an individual contributor is a matter of sheer energy and drive. Nothing else predicts. High performers with strong drive get ahead, regardless of relationship or learning skills. Across time, however, what you can get away with early catches up with you. For example, boss ratings of career stallers have nothing to do with promotion until a person becomes an executive. Then they are strongly related and, of course, it's too late to do anything about it. The person is simply fired.

It has become fashionable with recent scandals to trash executives, and our research could be read that way. Peer and direct report ratings of executives are sharply critical, almost scathing. Most of the relationships are negative. According to them, executives who cut corners, lack ethics, play favorites, and are insensitive to others perform better and get ahead.

We take a different view, seeing the problem as a massive systems failure. No feedback or feedback on strengths alone, myths about what matters, pitiful developmental efforts, fads, and the vain search for people who arrive with all the skills take their toll over time. Raters paint a favorable picture of individual contributors, a favorable picture of managers, then blast executives.

It is not believable that these men and women turned to the dark side once they hit the executive suite. They were grown or not grown that way long before, but no one was looking; they could get away with it, or it didn't really matter. The harsh view of executives painted by our raters is a reflection of failed systems.

It is also true that derailment is more dependent on organizational context. If an organization puts a premium on relationships, insensitivity to others might get people in trouble earlier. If it puts a premium on results, insensitivity may be related to performance and promotion. (Both are actual research findings.) Of course, it wouldn't be called insensitivity—it would be referred to as high standards and candor. So it goes with derailment.

Interpersonal skills seem to matter most at the extremes. People with relationship problems get into trouble in the executive suite. But people who excel at interpersonal skills get into the same trouble for different reasons.

Look at the two sets of competencies below. If you can't have everything, would you rather have people who are high in Set A and moderate in Set B, or would you rather have the opposite?

Set A	Set B
■ Approachability	■ Creativity
■ Caring about direct reports	■ *Timely* decision making
■ Compassion	■ Learning on the fly
■ Delegation	■ Managing and measuring work
■ Fairness to direct reports	■ Organizing
■ Interpersonal savvy	■ Planning
■ Listening	■ Process management
	■ *Drive for* results
	■ Strategic agility
	■ Time management

Most would say the latter, Set B over Set A, which was the case in our executive data. Plateaued or "left company" executives were higher in every Set A competency than they were in the Set B competencies. Executives rated as high potentials were higher in every Set B competency than they were the Set A competencies. And the differences were high versus moderate. High potentials excelled at Strategic Agility, for example, and were OK at Approachability. People whose affiliation skills exceed the more important business skills don't last as executives either.

Since high potentials don't exceed at everything, what is their hedge? They know themselves. They are unlikely to stumble into a disaster because they think they are great at something at which others say they are just OK or even poor.

What Table 4.4 – Knowing Yourself means is that high-potential executives are more critical of their skills and more critical of their flaws than are those who rate them. But they are also in closer agreement with their raters than are average or derailed executives. They know better how they are seen and set a higher standard for themselves. In our research, the higher the self-rating compared with the ratings of others, the more likely a person is to be fired. Those who were promoted rated themselves lower than any rater group. In fact, the only relationship of self-rating to performance is just this self-awareness component. Self-ratings don't relate to performance; they don't relate to promotion. On one side, they signal an oversized ego or an unaware one; on the other, they signal a self-critical learner.

Table 4.4 Knowing Yourself

Self-Rater	Left Company	Plateaued	Key Player	High Potential
Rates self higher or lower than others on competencies	Rates self higher	Rates self higher	Rates self higher	Rates self lower
Rates self higher or lower on flaws	Rates self lower	Rates self lower	Rates self lower	Rates self higher

So what should we look for to improve the effectiveness of our workforce and prevent derailment?

We'll have much more to say on this topic in Chapter 13. We will discuss programmatic interventions such as early warning systems and vaccinating against career derailment, as well as what to do when the worst has already happened and people need rescuing. We'll also return to the "Twelve Best Practices" and talk about what best practices would actually look like. In Chapter 16, we'll discuss the special problem of coaching those about to derail.

For now, we'll mention the first line of defense against talent waste management: measurement of derailment factors, feedback, knowing what actual talent looks like, and realism.

You get what you measure for (or don't expect what you don't inspect). One company lost a lot of money with bad expatriate selections. Their selection profile, like most, concentrated on results in similar kinds of assignments. Yet they had 86 failures in one year alone, so they instituted derailment factor feedback. Their notion was you had to neutralize the flaw before even being considered for an expatriate assignment. People were given feedback, coaching, and development plans. Those involved signed off that the flaw had been neutralized (e.g., they weren't warm and fuzzy, but they no longer made people feel stupid; they would never be confused with Douglas MacArthur, but they had some strategic skills). The result: the company saved more than $40 million the first year of the program in recruitment and relocation costs alone. No more people with stunning results histories who, within two months, cause an entire plant to quit—not strike, quit. No more arrogant types who can't adjust to other cultures. No more tacticians who can't spot business climate shifts.

We love to overdo. It's the human condition. If more is good, a lot is great. Without feedback, our strengths may well tip over and become darkly hued. The key to this is heightened self-awareness, and the best tool to achieve this is 360° feedback coupled with coaching, more 360°, and more coaching. Without it, strengths go into overdrive, and people lack awareness of the full picture of themselves they need for a successful career. Getting no developmental feedback or feedback on strengths alone are time bombs which explode in managerial and executive roles.

Look for learners. As we will demonstrate in Chapter 6, if there is a magic talent that guarantees success, it's recognizing—then learning to do—what you don't know how to do. Learning agility can be spotted early and nurtured. Look for those who show interest in developing the competencies most people are neither very good at nor very interested in and which few organizations reward. Look for those who respond to feedback by changing a bit. Look for those who are intrigued by the new and different, who like fresh challenges.

Let's quit kidding ourselves. As we saw in Chapter 3, the people described on the average profile rarely exist and undoubtedly never will. Another key to preventing derailment is to be realistic—someone high in Strategic Agility probably won't be high in Approachability. Jobs being what they are, a manager with high management skills and moderate interpersonal skills is better than other combinations and the best we're going to get in most cases. While we shouldn't ignore any key competency, our expectations have to be in line with human nature.

We'll close this chapter the way we started it: Success untempered breeds "instant" failure once the transitions required outstrip the old skills portfolio. Simplistic notions about how to develop people against simplistic models accelerate the process. Knowing yourself and lifelong learning are more than homilies—they are the foundations of success.

4

79

Part II

How skills
are developed

Chapter 5

Learning from experience: Experience is still the best teacher

People don't come to organizations ready to handle everything, no matter how talented they are. If self-knowledge is the foundation of success, then the right on-the-job experience is the building.

The case for growth through experience

Experience finishes what nature starts.

Our argument supposes that we can't always select whom we need to begin with, that we can't just find all the people who will either have or will develop the right skills. As we have tried to demonstrate in previous chapters, such people don't seem to readily exist, and even if they did, most organizations have no idea how to arrange for their growth. It seems to be true that while certain skills and attributes can and should be selected for, that what happens after hiring a person has as much or more impact on long-term worth as anything that has gone before.

Beginning many years ago, AT&T assessed thousands of men and women on hundreds of variables, from IQ to administrative skills to personal adjustment. The assessments were evaluated and people were assigned a grade on potential for advancement. The data were held in secret so that decision makers never saw the results. Only in this way could the AT&T researchers find out, many years later, who would make it and who would not.

They first looked at the actual progress people had made eight years later and compared it to the test results. There were some expected results: intelligent people who could deal with ambiguity did better. And there was one fairly large surprise: those who were assessed low for potential were often more successful if they had developmental jobs and developmental bosses. In fact, a greater percentage of those who were assessed low were promoted than those who were assessed high if their developmental opportunities were noticeably better.

Some years later, the Center for Creative Leadership (CCL) took up the issue of what it is about experience that can make it powerful. They asked what these experiences are, what characterizes them, why they are developmental, and what can be learned from them. The CCL researchers (which included one of the authors, the other author served as a research advisor) concluded that there is some consistent rhyme to experience:

5

- Certain types of experience appeared again and again in all organizations studied. (Many studies since then have supported these findings, including in other countries.)

- People in all organizations learned the same lessons from the same types of experiences. It did not matter whether they were drilling for oil, analyzing health claims, or designing computers. The types of experiences that teach specific competencies are universal.

- Some people learn much more from experience than others. Some learn more new perspectives and behaviors from life and work and some less. For example, successful executives had a strong and similar pattern of learning from key job assignments. The derailed executives, all of whom had been successful for many years before derailing and who had gone through many of the same key assignments as the successful executives, had virtually no pattern of learning from jobs. Their learning appeared to be virtually random.

- Learning to benefit from experience is developable. It is possible to help people learn how to learn. Efforts by CCL, Bob Sternberg and Rick Wagner's work on tacit knowledge (street smarts), and Dan Goleman's work in emotional intelligence have all shown that people can learn how to learn.

People don't come out of school knowing all of the following: how to shut down a business, get along with a difficult boss, solve an ambiguous problem, handle a drunk at work, or form complex strategy. At best, they come with an understanding of the technical aspects of what they are to do and with whatever wisdom they have gleaned from their previous work and life experiences. What comes after makes a huge difference.

Following is a thumbnail sketch of which experiences are most likely to make a difference and why they matter. Interested readers should see the Notes at the end of the book for further references.

5

The experience catalog

People learn most of the skills they need on the job.

There are four kinds of experiences reported by everyone who has been studied, including executives, managers, professionals, teachers, principals, coaches, men, women, and high school students.

1. Key jobs
2. Important other people
3. Hardships
4. Courses (and books, tapes, internet)

Depending on the study, skill development is reported as 75 to 90 percent learned on the job. The events that matter most occur there.

1. Key jobs

Most of the hard job skills that matter for performance (Strategic Agility, Planning) are learned on the job when people hit fresh challenges. The jobs most likely to teach are starting something from nothing or almost so, fixing something broken or torn, switching from line to staff, big changes in scope or scale, or various kinds of projects (see the following Developmental Jobs definitions for detail).

The jobs that are least likely to teach are straight-upward promotions, doing the same type of job again and again, and job switches aimed at exposure rather than tough challenges.

Essentially, development is the land of the first time and the difficult. Comfortable circumstances applying skills we already have not only do not lead to growth, they lead to stagnation and retirement in place. Lack of challenge also prompts talented people to look for another employer.

People who succeeded usually had survived and learned from all or almost all of the jobs listed below.

What are the most developmental jobs? (Listed alphabetically)

- **Chair of projects/task forces** – Leader of a group with an important and specific goal. One-time, short-term events usually lasting from a few weeks to a year. Much of the work in today's flatter, less hierarchical organizations can be classified as project work. Typical examples: implementing new ideas, product launches, systems development, acquisitions, joint ventures, one-time events like reorganizations.

- **Change manager** – Leader of a significant effort to change something or implement something of significance. Typical examples include: Total Work Systems like TQM, ISO, or Six Sigma; business restructurings; installing major systems and procedures for the first time; M&A integrations; responding to major competitor initiatives; extensive reorganizations; and long-term post-corporate scandal recovery.

- **Crisis manager** – Leader responsible for an unpredictable, unique crisis of significant proportion. Typical examples of crisis management would be: a product safety recall; product failure; unexpected death, termination, or scandal involving a CEO or senior corporate executive; trouble with a key customer or supplier; natural disasters; terrorist attacks; kidnapping or arrest of employees; violent crime against employees.

- **Cross-moves** – Move to a very different set of challenges. Typical examples would be: changing divisions or functions, field/headquarters shifts, country switch, or changing lines of business.

- **Fix-its/Turnarounds** – Cleaning up a mess where this is a last chance to fix it. Usually accompanied by serious people issues and morale problems. Typical examples: failed business/unit; disasters like mishandled labor negotiations, strikes, thefts, fraud, obsolete staff; restructuring; product liability events; system/process breakdowns.

- **Heavy strategic demands** – Requires new or significant strategic redirection; visible and watched by senior people. Typically part of a major job switch.

- **International assignments** – First time working in the country. Usually features new language, business rules, different cultural norms, and assigned for more than a year.

- **Line to staff switches** – Visible role in a staff function, often at headquarters. Typical examples: business/strategic planning role, heading a staff department, assistant to senior executive, head of a task force, Human Resources role.

- **Member of projects/Task forces** – Member of a group with an important and specific goal. One-time, short-term events usually lasting from a few weeks to a year. Much of the work in today's flatter, less hierarchical organizations can be classified as project work. Typical

5

examples: implementing new ideas, product launches, systems development, acquisitions, joint ventures, one-time events like reorganizations.

- **Scale (size shifts) assignments** – Jump in the size of a job in the same area for the person. Typically involves much more budget, volume of business, people, layers of the organization.

- **Scope (complexity) assignments** – Managing substantially more breadth. Typically involves new areas of business, increase in visibility, complexity. Typical scope jobs are: moving to a new organization, adding new products or functions or services, moving from staff to line, and numerous first-time jobs such as first-time manager, managing managers, executive, or team leader.

- **Significant people demands** – Involves a sizable increase in either the number of people managed or the complexity of the people-challenges faced. Typical examples are: going to a team-based management structure, changing to a quality format for work, and working with groups not worked with before.

- **Small entrepreneurial** – Founder or core team member of a company or brand. Typically, there is a personal financial stake in the business's success or failure. Typical examples include: being a small business owner, starting an incubator business or a new business line, launching a new brand or new product line.

- **Staff leadership (influencing without authority)** – Significant challenge where one has the responsibility but not the authority. Typical examples: planning project, installing new systems, troubleshooting systems problems, negotiating with outside parties, working in a staff group.

- **Staff to line shifts** – Moving to a job with an easily determined bottom line or results, managing bigger scope and/or scale, requires new skills/perspectives, unfamiliar aspects of the assignment.

- **Start-ups –** Starting something new for the organization. Typical examples are: building a team, creating new systems or facilities or products, heading something new, establishing a branch operation, and moving a successful program from one unit to another.

2. Important other people

As with jobs, the people who developed most had the widest variety of other people to observe and learn from. Role models play a critical role throughout life, and learning from others is a large category of learning in organizations. Those most remembered are usually bosses and those higher up.

Bosses matter because of what they model—how values play out in the workplace. The so-called soft skills come into focus here— how people walk their talk, deal with poor performers, make trade-offs between results and compassion, deal with diversity, or solve ethical dilemmas. They also matter because they are a substitute for direct experience—role models can teach through their actions. A novice can learn how a superb marketing manager thinks through marketing plans or observe how an experienced negotiator reaches agreements.

They were also quite likely to mention learning from bad bosses, not restricting their learning to the best. The people most likely to be remembered were remarkable for something, but that something wasn't necessarily good.

The best way to summarize the impact of notable people is that they challenge one's thinking, not that they were direct teachers.

Who is the most memorable at work?

- **Good bosses** – who model values and skills. They are rarely teachers, and most learning is by observing and questioning them.

- **Bad bosses** – who teach how not to be and, therefore, what to do instead. People are more likely to learn about compassion and integrity from the bad rather than the good. Why? Because they learned directly how horrible it felt to be subjected to someone who was a bad boss.

- **Both** – Bosses with big strengths and big weaknesses provided an object lesson for people about human foibles.

- **Mentors** – These men and women took younger people into their care and personally guided their careers. Mentors are rare for men and somewhat more common for women and people of color. Natural mentors have more impact than assigned mentors. Same-sex and ethnic background mentors are more effective. Much research indicates that women learn more from other people and from each other than men do.

3. Hardships

No one started out to have hardships, they just happened to people—missed promotions, demotions, getting fired, business blunders, career ruts, intractable or impossible direct reports, and the like. The key here was what people learned from the bad bounces of life.

One key difference between the successful and the less so is that the successful were more likely to report blunders they made and had to rally from. They were much more likely to embrace whatever happened to them, whether they created the situation or not. Rather than resorting to blame, successful people were much more likely to see what could be learned from the situation.

Hard times:

- Business mistakes
- Problems with direct reports
- Getting fired or demoted
- A missed promotion
- A lousy job
- A personal trauma
- Feeling discriminated against
- Breaking out of a career rut and changing jobs

4. Courses

Curiously, at first, we noticed that the content of coursework came in second when people talked about the value of coursework. (The Harvard Business School had a similar finding.) What we came to understand as we looked further was that timing was everything. It was less what the course was about and more what the person needed badly right then to perform on the job. A developmental course looked more like the other job events than one would think—it was first time, different, and difficult. The number one gleaning from courses was self-confidence— the belief that a person could grow, change, and improve when demanded.

Developmental courses: Basically, whatever the person needed at the moment.

Most likely to be mentioned next:

- Self-insight courses
- Problem-solving courses
- Strategy courses

The catalog of experiences people most remember is the same everywhere.

| 91

The nature of experience

Development only occurs when there is something at stake.

Certain challenges teach, but why do developmental experiences look alike? What unites them?

Exercise 5.1 The impact of experience

> Think back through your life, focusing on work and school experiences. Pick four experiences—that may have lasted for a few minutes or for years—that had the most lasting impact on you. Regardless of their length, they share a common truth—they made a lasting impact on you as a person, how you respond to the world and, in this case, how you approach work. You learned more from these experiences than any others.
>
> 1. _____
>
>   _____
>
>   _____
>
> 2. _____
>
>   _____
>
>   _____
>
> 3. _____
>
>   _____
>
>   _____
>
> 4. _____
>
>   _____
>
>   _____

5

Perhaps you thought of each of the four categories of experiences discussed above.

For a job, you remembered starting a new business or serving on a joint venture project in a new business area, or taking an international assignment, or working in a rapidly expanding business where all the systems became obsolete quickly.

For other people, you thought of a boss who was remarkable in some way. The odds are about 2 to 1 that you remember that person as a positive experience.

For a hardship, you remembered something that hit you like a truck—a missed promotion, a truly awful job, a blunder, or having to fire someone.

For a course, you recalled the course that opened a door in your mind permanently, just when you needed it most.

You remembered all these experiences for the same reasons.

You knew very little about it going in. You had little or no experience in the area. Development is the world of the first time and the different. The varied and the adverse create a need to learn, and most learning occurs while we are in transition.

You felt you had a significant chance of failure. One of the truths of the human psyche is people try hardest when there is between one-half and two-thirds chance of success. More, and it's too easy; less than one-half, and we start to cut our losses. Although there were some strengths you had to fall back on, you thought you might fail. You learned because you had to get through the situation. For the job and the boss, your skills weren't quite up to the challenge; for the hardship, you didn't know if or how you could bounce back. The temptation to blame and deny was tremendous. For the course, it was just-in-time training for your job. Something in the course, whether it was personal self-awareness or a job skill, was pivotal in your performance. Having something at stake facilitates the learning.

You had to make a difference. You had to take charge and lead. You didn't have time to check off with everyone nor collect all of the data you needed.

You felt a tremendous amount of pressure. When the stakes are highest—such as impending deadlines, people looking over your shoulder, travel, or overwhelming workload—is when we are also most motivated to learn.

There are many other challenges that create learning, but these are the common denominators people recall from any key event or experience. Development is a demand pull. *The experience demands that we learn to do something new or different, or we fear we will fail.*

Development is full of paradoxical conditions: adverse, difficult, first time, varied, full of new people, bosses, good and poor legacies, strong emotions, lack of significant skills, closely watched, and lonely. It is usually not that pleasant at the time, but it is exciting—much more so than straight-line promotions or succeeding at jobs we already basically know how to do. Development is discomfort because comfort is the enemy of growth. Staying in our comfort zone or building our nest encourages repetition. Going against the grain—being forced or venturing outside the cozy boxes of our lives—demands that we learn.

5

Observation | Going against the grain

One of the things we've learned about getting better at learning agility is the so-called GAG assignment (going against your natural grain). If you're not paying attention, human beings are habituated and tend to repeat patterns of behaviors and preferences—operate inside the box, in the comfort zone, and are nest-builders. The best practice for developing learning agility is to go outside your comfort zone, do things you've never done before, things you have feared doing, things you are not looking forward to.

This best practice is backed up by brain research. There is the notion of "use it or lose it." Many studies have shown the health advantage of being mentally active into old age. And we've also found that it's possible to dig new neural networks by doing new things that you've never done before. The effectiveness of your brain is benefited by as many neural networks as you can create.

Since I ran into this finding many decades ago, I've gone out of my way in my life to make sure I don't get habituated. A small example of that is to change your mouse hand. Wear your watch on your other wrist. Take different routes to work. Force yourself to eat at restaurants out of your comfort zone. Go to international festivals other than your own ethnic background. And buy different makes of cars. All examples of getting out of your comfort zone. The learning strategy of the GAG assignment has support in brain research.

5

Developmental heat

Now think of your current job as it exists for you today. Look at Exercise 5.2. Compared with other jobs you have had, how would you rate each of the following on a five-point scale?

|

Exercise 5.2 Developmental heat

Developmental heat: Rate each of the following on a five-point scale.

1 = Little challenge when compared to other jobs
2 = Some challenge
3 = Like other jobs
4 = More challenging than other jobs
5 = Much more challenging than other jobs

1. _____ Success or failure are both possible and would be obvious to myself and others. I think I could fail or not perform well at this job.

2. _____ Requires take-charge, aggressive, individual leadership.

3. _____ Involves working with new people, a lot of people, or people with different skills.

4. _____ High personal pressure (deadlines, high stakes, large shift in scope or scale, travel, long hours, work is viewed as critical).

5. _____ Requires influencing people, activities, and factors over which I have no control (supervisors besides boss, lateral relations, partners, peers, outside parties, political situations, customers).

6. _____ Involves high variety of tasks; doing something very different from what I've done in the past (line/staff switch, promotion to headquarters, changing functions or lines of business/ technology).

7. _____ Is closely watched and monitored by people whose opinions count.

8. _____ Requires building a team or something from scratch, or fixing/turning around an operation in trouble (downsizing, restructuring, new product line, new business, establishing a new operation, poor-performing unit, major staffing issues, inheriting a failing unit).

9. _____ Involves a tremendous intellectual/strategic/problem-solving challenge with little or no history for guidance.

10. _____ Involves interacting with a significant boss (whether supportive or not, the boss's view is critical to success in this job).

11. _____ Am missing something important (lack of management support, limited resources, not aligned with strategy or core of the business, poor legacy, missing key skills or technical knowledge, lack of credentials/credibility).

Adapted from Eighty-Eight Assignments for Development in Place: Enhancing the Developmental Challenge of Existing Jobs by Michael M. Lombardo and Robert W. Eichinger. © 1989 Center for Creative Leadership. Used by permission.

We developed this Developmental Heat checklist from CCL's studies of developmental assignments. The research team deduced the core elements (reasons why an experience was developmental) of more than two thousand experiences recounted in detail by executives and middle managers.

We used this as an exercise in a course for some years. Thousands of people have filled it out, and many organizations use it to rate the developmental potential of jobs and other experiences.

Developmental heat interpretive guidelines

If you scored above 45 (out of 55 possible), this is a very developmental job for you. You are probably in a start-up, a fix-it, or an international assignment. There is very little about this job you have ever done before. Unfortunately, the job may also be too large a jump for you or anyone else.

If you scored 35–45, this is where most developmental jobs fall. One-half or more of the challenges are present in a big way.

If you scored 21–34, you may have been in this job for three years or more, it may be a straight-line promotion, or you changed companies (but not basic responsibilities) some time ago. Your performance might not be as good as it once was; you may be getting bored.

If you scored 20 or less, you are comfortable coasting and retired on the job or you are plotting ways to change your situation or quit. Your resume may be on the street. You've been in the job too long, it's old hat, it's no longer challenging, and you probably dread going to work in the morning.

Later we'll show how organizations can use this same line of thinking in developing people and in designing jobs.

How do some people get to be so good?

All overnight successes start with a thousand repetitions.

What in life have you truly mastered? Perhaps you are an excellent pianist, golfer, accountant, gardener, stockbroker, or gin rummy player.

How did that happen? Most would say it was because of the talent you were born with and nurtured, and there is truth to that. But just because you started playing with numbers or taking apart broken appliances at age four doesn't magically grow into mastery.

Studies from sports psychology and from the University of Chicago inform us about the nature of talent. Given at least reasonable aptitude to begin with, talent has more to do with small steps from the ground up than anything else. Whether musicians or tennis players or mathematicians or swimmers, people who go on to excel in an area learn small skills that they practice through endless repetition until they can execute them perfectly.

They also have a plan for what they do. They don't just repeat; rather, they take the basic motions or mental operations they have learned and practice them in new situations. As Jack Nicklaus once said, "I have learned how to practice differently. If I play a round in which I don't hit a three iron, I may go practice that first rather than what I did poorly that day." After Tiger Woods won the Masters in his first full year on the PGA tour, he revamped his swing for the longer haul. He had won six tournaments in roughly a year, yet was willing to make major changes and practice those until he reached another level of excellence.

It is the same for those who go on to succeed in management and leadership. As mentioned earlier, we found that they first focused very narrowly on their technical field, working to excel at it regardless of the conditions they faced. They built their management skills the same way; for example, learning how to deal with balky people, then learning how to integrate balky people into a team, then learning how to manage balky people from a distance. Or they learned the difference between managing people and managing processes and managing systems as they went. Each had to be learned fully before the next could be learned fully.

What makes mastery possible is control over the conditions of growth. It is a fair assumption that there are many more excellent golfers and accountants than there are managers and leaders. The former group has a much greater chance of practicing and seeing the maximum variety of conditions before the stakes get too high. Only in management settings do we sometimes ask Little League pitchers to hurl in the World Series. We do that because of many mistaken views about the core experiences (and core competencies that can result from them) which account for excellence.

True development

Traditional career paths are many times narrow dead ends. It's experience paths that matter.

As we have argued previously, traditional career paths generally produce narrow and limited specialists. Experience paths leading to general management and leadership are, in reality, a zigzag of challenges that have little to do with job titles. They are, by their nature, predictable only in the sense that we know the enduring challenges or experiences that create the conditions for growth. This year's dead-end assignment may be tomorrow's golden goose if the answers to the questions below are yes.

- Am I missing significant skills?
- Will my performance in this role make an obvious difference in the performance of the unit?
- Do I get the chance to be a big fish in a small pond?
- Will the role expose me to different types or new groups of people?

- Do important people care what happens in this role?
- Is there something particularly adverse or contentious about this role?
- Is there a lot of variety in what I will have to do?

The list could go on, but the core of development is always the same—variety, adversity, jobs, people, courses, and hard times for which you're not quite ready. We'll show how to integrate this into more realistic experience paths later in the book.

For experience to matter...

- *People need to master something first.* Healthy branches spring from sturdy trunks. Interfering with the process of mastery makes people feel like impostors later.

- *People need to experience an optimum variety of job challenges.* It's starting things and fixing things and forming strategies at an early point that eventually lead to skills growth. Just like for fledgling tennis pros, development is about the small wins that become big wins later.

- *Development involves heat, emotions, and stakes.* We endorse the Mark Twain approach: "People say if a cat wants to sit on a hot stove lid, let her. She'll learn. Now that is true, but she'll never sit on a cold one again either." Development is much more than throwing people into nasty situations and seeing who swims. The goal is to learn to perform, not simply to survive.

- *Skills come back around in more sophisticated forms.* Skills are built hierarchically—you really do need to learn *A* before *B*. Interfering with this leads to derailment.

- *What the person does has to make an obvious, measurable difference.* People don't learn much from situations they are caught in, that they didn't create, and where they couldn't influence the outcome. To learn to manage and lead, you have to manage and lead—the success or failure of something has to depend unambiguously on what you do.

Experience paths are the forces that set development in motion, yet only the most enlightened organizations pay much attention to them. Job assignments are done with safe fills and guaranteed returns—people who can already do the job or who have the right pedigree. We'll deal with correcting this situation in Part V.

Even for the enlightened, little may come of it. As T. S. Eliot said, "We have had the experience, but we have missed the meaning."

How to benefit from experience is the next topic we will take up as we deal with the question of why some people benefit from hot stove lids and some people miss the meaning of them.

5

101

Chapter 6

Learning agility: The silver bullet

Everyone wants to know the secret of success, and there is one. It's called continuously learning to do what you don't know how to do.

If a company hires smart people and recruits experienced people from only the top organizations, success is assured, right?

Apparently not. Most organizations we've worked with or even heard about seem to be lacking bench strength for key management and leadership roles. If success were essentially a matter of IQ and grades in school, we would have that talent and bench problem solved. If success were highly related to amount (length of time) of experience, similarly, talent and bench would not be an issue.

So IQ, grades, and time spent in job and career alone don't do it. Long-term success in the face of faster-paced challenges actually rests on three legs:

- Basic intelligence, which most organizations assure through their hiring practices.
- Variety of experience, as we saw in the last chapter.
- Continuously learning to do something new or different.

It's the last two that cause our troubles. Few people have the requisite experiences needed for managing and leading in the world of change, and fewer still have any idea how to learn from those experiences. Not surprisingly, many organizations don't know how to help them either.

Three strong assertions about learning agility

Since so much press is given to learning, we'll begin this chapter by making three strong assertions.

1. Learning to learn (or learning from experience or learning agility) and IQ have little to do with each other

Large organizations hire for IQ, even if they are not doing it intentionally or testing IQ directly. They do it by hiring college graduates and those with advanced degrees. This assures the minimum amount of IQ needed for most management and leadership roles. The average IQ of a person (mostly managers and executives) coming through the Center for Creative Leadership's assessment center is 121, well into the top 10 percent of smarts.

IQ is quite valuable. It leads to analytical skill and acquiring new technical knowledge. It doesn't, however, lead to acquiring new behaviors. New behaviors are the currency of high learners— who now go by many synonyms. They are variously called street smart, savvy, emotionally intelligent, adaptable, learning agile or, simply, learners from experience. Whatever they are called, research from Yale University by Bob Sternberg states that scores on a measure of learning from experience were unrelated to IQ scores.

This means that when a company hires engineers with a high grade point average from premier technical universities like MIT or MBAs from the top schools, how well they will learn new behaviors is unknown. All organizations more or less know this and have taken stabs at dealing with the problem through interviews (usually unstructured) or references, but neither of these are reliable sources. A few use assessments like structured interviewing, which can reveal something about learning acumen,

6

but all too many resort to the weight of the opinion of untrained interviewers.

2. Bet on learners

In our research, learning and drive for results are the strongest predictors of promotion. Again, in Sternberg's research, the best predictor of position level attained was a measure of learning from experience; second best was IQ. So if IQ is a must to get in the game, learning agility is essential to excel at the game for the long haul.

There are different approaches to measuring those who are most adaptable—assessment centers, instruments, structured interviews, different kinds of intelligence measures. But whichever way one turns, learners win.

One company had the usual 50 percent failure rate in five years for executives brought in from the outside. Organ transplant rejection by the culture. They used the typical approach of headhunter-qualified candidates, intensive interviewing, and multiple raters. Their approach was thorough but the results were about like everyone else's, so they added one wrinkle. They had a headhunter who was experienced in learning interviews pass judgment on the final candidates. Their success rate soared to over 90 percent. Similar results have been reported for those using learning instruments to select people for expatriate assignments.

In both cases, in addition to the usual credentials, they were checking for the ability to adapt.

3. Trying to select only learners is a losing long-term strategy

Since many companies do not yet do this, selection may work for a while. But, long-term, most organizations will be fighting over a narrow slice of pie. The pie consists of high-achieving academic students (guaranteed sufficient IQ) who are also high learners. This cannot be more than 5 percent of graduates if the research to date is more or less accurate. Companies essentially hire from the top 10 percent of IQs, and it is random whether they are high learners or not. If we accept those in the top one-half of a learning measure, we're down to 5 percent (high on IQ and high on learning agility).

So chasing the few people who naturally exist out there as high-IQ/high-learner types is only a strategy for those with good assessment, major money, and a very attractive business proposition. For the rest of us, we'll make two suggestions, both of which are good news for the budget-conscious:

1. *A lot of high learners already work for you.* One benefit of the random-selection process for learners is that you already have some of these people around. You just have to find out who they are.

2. *To some extent, learning to learn is a developable skill.* Rather than repeat the research summary from the previous chapter, we'll just reinforce that there is plenty of evidence people can learn how to learn better.

What do learners look like?

Probably somewhat like you would expect. If asked what type of person would learn to do something new or different, most of us would respond, "the curious and the risk-takers." That much is true, but being curious and taking risks have only to do with finding the opportunity, not making sense of the experience.

In a nutshell, people who learn best are, indeed, curious and risk-takers. This sets the stage for learning. What brings it into focus are some more unusual skills:

- *They are willing to feel and look stupid.* This is the only way to learn to perform well in new situations—admit you don't know what to do and hit it with everything you've got.

- *They are keen observers of themselves, others, and situations.* You know that little person we all have who sits on our shoulder and gives advice to us all the time, the hall monitor in our mind? Learners have one also, but this monitor is fairly objective and dispassionate: What's going on here? How are people reacting? Why? What's working? What isn't? Is there anything I can take away that is repeatable? Learners are sense-makers, and a great way to make sense of events is to pepper them with process questions.

- *More is indeed better.* Learners have more ways to handle situations because they have more conscious learning tactics. They will try anything. They'll keep a journal, write down a plan, engage in a visioning exercise. In one study, effective supervisors had five times more methods to handle difficult employees than did the average supervisors. That's learning in action.

- *They are comparers.* Learners will search the past for parallels, look at history, ask others, read a biography. They know there is nothing really new—that history repeats itself, if only in broad themes. Whenever Harry Truman faced a "first-time" crisis in the White House, he consulted what he called his "council of presidents." He would go to the presidential archives, find as many roughly parallel situations as he could, and see how previous presidents thought them through.

- *They make sense through rules of thumb.* Many learners keep lists, mental or otherwise, of things that might be true most of the time. These are guiding principles and trends they use to view situations. Colin Powell is a famous example of someone who keeps such a list.

- *They are likely to have a plan and measures of success and failure.* While the plan is not likely to be written, they know what they are going to try and why. They evaluate what they did, decide on what worked, and understand why it worked. Then they try again and again. The more tries, the more chances to learn to get it right.

Eventually, as Sternberg's research indicates, they pile up at the top of organizations. They had more diverse experiences, spent far more time making sense of them and, as a result, developed more skills and performed better. In the Center for Creative Leadership (CCL) studies, the findings were similar.

We define learning agility as *the willingness and ability to learn from experience, and subsequently apply that learning to perform successfully under new or first-time conditions*. Learners are willing to go against the grain of what they know how to do and prefer to do. Why? To get better and to learn new skills and ways of behaving.

Story

Learning agility

Audrey ran the toy business at a major retailer:

"I went through a retail boot camp there; I learned a lot, but I was ready for my next challenge. I played flute in band—what's the point of this instrument when no one can hear it. I want to play the drums! Drive a lot of change, new business, and contribute to the bottom line.

"I came to my new job because they wanted someone to start up their licensing business. I told them I would do it, but that they needed to leave me alone and let me do it."

Audrey pulled from her past experience—she knew that relationships and connections would be key.

"I pursued a guerilla business strategy. It was a breakthrough in this business. All about relationships. I just have to do whatever it takes to form those relationships.

"We needed a credible strategic partner. So what do I do? I called a guy who had a friend who knew someone who worked for the company I wanted to partner with—I stalked her at a conference and built a relationship with her, and we're going to start working together. I approached her and said, 'I think I can help you make money.' Now, we're on the brink of testing something.

6

"The goal for the first year was $50 million. We did $100 million and we'll do more this year."

Licensing was new to this retailer and new to Audrey, but in this unfamiliar challenge, she had ideas about how to approach it. She was resourceful and pulled from her past lessons in "retail boot camp." Her strong drive, versatility, and her demand for independence all contributed to the first-year revenue coming in at 200 percent to goal. As a learning-agile person, Audrey knew what to do when she didn't know what to do.

Learning agility research

During the past 10 years, we have collected data on thousands of employees using the Choices Architect® online survey, a validated assessment of learning agility. Here is what we know:

- *Learning agility predicts success.* Our research has consistently found that learning agility predicts job performance following a promotion. In the last two years, we have analyzed data from two large global companies, one in the pharmaceutical industry and the other in consumer products. We found a significant correlation ($p < .001$) between learning agility and potential ($r = 0.42$) as well as learning agility and performance ($r = 0.37$).

- *When it comes to learning agility, most people fall somewhere in the middle.* Overall, learning agility has been found to have a normal distribution in the employee population. When learning agility assessments are administered to a general group of employees, the scores show a normal distribution.

- *Doesn't matter if you are male or female.* In general, learning agility scores are unrelated to gender. Women scored slightly higher than males on the People Agility subscale. Women appear to be more attuned to others, learn more from others, and have more versatile interpersonal skills on average than do men. Overall, there were no statistically significant differences between male and female mean scores on *overall* learning agility.

6

- *Doesn't matter how old you are.* Learning agility generally is unrelated to age. There is some evidence that younger individuals tend to score slightly higher than older ones on the Change Agility subscale. However, *overall* learning agility mean scores were not statistically different across age groups.

- *Ethnic background doesn't matter.* There also is no evidence suggesting ethnicity-related differences on learning agility.

- *Doesn't matter where in the world you are.* Data obtained from different regions of the world—North America, South America, Europe, Asia, Australia/New Zealand—show consistent results.

- *People score relatively higher on Results Agility and Mental Agility than on People Agility and Change Agility.* This scoring pattern is consistent across the five international regions we looked at.

- *People tend to lack awareness of their learning agility.* When we placed employees into three groups—high, middle, and low—and then compared their self-ratings with others' ratings, we saw that people in the *low* learning agility group *overrate* themselves. People in the *high* learning agility group tend to *underrate* themselves. This is consistent with the findings on other multi-rater assessments.

- *Learning agility is very related to being labeled high potential.* One Fortune 500 special materials company identified approximately 100 "high potentials" through a series of talent review sessions. Of the 100, 70 percent had very high learning agility scores and the other 30 percent had higher-than-average learning agility scores. The Choices Architect® online survey learning agility scores had good overlap with an independent assessment of potential.

Learners in more detail

People high in learning agility do four things particularly well:

1. **Mental agility** – They are excellent critical thinkers who are comfortable with complexity and ambiguity, examine problems

carefully, and make fresh connections. These individuals can clearly explain their logic and thinking to others.

2. **People agility/self-awareness –** They know themselves and can readily deal with a wide variety of people and tough situations. They are cool and resilient under the pressures of change.

3. **Change agility –** They are curious, like to experiment, and can effectively deal with the discomfort of change. These individuals have a passion for ideas and are highly interested in continuous improvement.

4. **Results agility –** They deliver results in first-time situations by inspiring teams and have significant presence. They exhibit the sort of presence that builds confidence in themselves and others.

The downsides of learners

Learners have their downsides as well. People interested in shaking things up and challenging the status quo tend to be somewhat perfectionistic and independent with a low need to be liked. As a group, they are not especially people-oriented, and their "can-do" attitudes can tip into overuse at times. In sum, it's hard for them to stop an initiative, they tinker too much, and they can run into trouble with others because they are so unsettling. They can be stress carriers and noise generators.

People high in learning agility are sometimes driven to learn as a value in itself. They can appear to be interested in people, ideas, etc., in order to learn. For example, they may not build a team because it is a "good thing to do." If they build a team, it is because they think a team is absolutely necessary to carry out an experiment or push a change through. In other circumstances, they might be indifferent or even scoff at the value of teams. If they help others solve problems, it is probably as much for the mental discipline of learning about problem solving as it is in helping others. If they believe in diversity, it's because they know they can learn more from difference than sameness. Their characteristic behaviors are largely instrumental to their continued growth.

Tinkerers can get into a lot of trouble in organizations, which necessarily run largely off systems designed to ensure sameness and handle exceptions. Since high learners can be like fingernails on a blackboard at times, they stay out of trouble mainly through self-knowledge. They know who they are and are especially likely to know their limits and learn from their mistakes. They apparently don't suffer from an excess of self-confidence. This may help them get away with being different—pushing change, enduring the heat, and being somewhat uncompromising, yet balancing this with no glaring weaknesses and showing their concern for others through helpfulness and listening.

Their profiles typically look like this:

- High performers but not the highest – They are learning to be better, so at a point in time they are always a work in process.

- High self-confidence – Allows them to jump into the unknown.

- Rate themselves lower than others rate them – They set a higher bar.

- High self-knowledge – Their saving grace. They know what they are good at and what they aren't. They are aware enough of others to push change without creating a deadly backlash.

- Somewhat uncompromising and resilient – They are all about improvement and change, whether personal, in work systems, or in skill levels. One can't get better by shying away from conflict.

- No notable flaws – In Chapter 4, we spoke of the common flaws of people. In a pilot study we conducted, none of the high learners had any rated flaws by any single rater. Out of 26 possible trouble statements, no one gave a single "maybe" or "yes" rating. This is not to say that learners are nearly perfect, only that they do not usually evidence major career-derailing flaws, like lack of a strategic sense or arrogance. As mentioned earlier, they can push change too hard and be somewhat perfectionistic. They need development just like everyone else.

6

In studying successful and derailed executives, we heard many case studies of learners and those who failed to do so. We discussed this previously in Chapter 4. A typical scenario was promotion to a general management role. Those who derailed were likely to be victims of their past success. They went to the boss for guidance, studied functions new to them through reading or asking others the answers, and relied on whatever skill set they currently had. Successful executives more often took another route. They were likely to use direct experience to learn.

Following are some of their tactics:

- Volunteer for a project with functions unfamiliar to them.

- Ask experts how they thought about a business problem they were dealing with. For example, an attorney says, "I think about this problem in this manner. You're a marketer; what do you see? What are the five buckets you put concepts in? What numbers do you look at?"

- Offer up their strengths to help others. For example, a marketing manager offered to show manufacturing managers how his perspective could be beneficial in production. He asked the same of them.

- Analyze past successes to see what works best. Many would question veterans in areas unfamiliar to them to see what patterns of success existed. Another common tack was the debrief after any successful effort to uncover the principles that drove it. One executive called this the search for "repeatables."

- Do a self-analysis to see where they came up short. One executive decided his negotiation skills were too primitive for the role. He assigned himself small negotiations, accompanied high professionals to negotiations, took copious notes, tried to guess what they were thinking, debriefed them afterward, had high professionals buddy with him and critique him in larger negotiations.

- Develop others to do what they don't know how to do. Many worked closely with talented direct reports to make them better. "Even if you know little about an area, you can figure out the logic of it and ask good questions," one said.

Why don't we have more high learners?

First of all, assessing learning agility can be tricky. How do you select candidates who have the right amount of learning agility for the job? How can you help people develop learning agility? It is critical to have validated tools such as the Choices Architect® online survey, viaEDGE™ self-assessment, or Learning From Experience™ interviews to measure learning agility.

Second, we could do a lot more to help people learn how to learn. There is a false assumption that given the right rich experiences, good people will learn. When we studied developmental events and learning at CCL, we reached some conclusions outlined in Chapter 5. We found that:

- Developmental events are the same everywhere. How often they occur varies with the particular business a firm is in.

- People learn the same lessons (competencies) from the same events. Managers and executives learn the same lessons from a start-up, regardless of what company they work for or how often start-ups occur within that company. This also means, as we have argued throughout, that competencies (other than technical skills) are universal. The same ones matter everywhere. How much they matter depends on the point in time for the business.

There is one notable exception to the second bullet. This finding held for high-performing executives and managers only. Low performers were hardly incompetent. Most were performing competently but they were not candidates for further promotion. So even among the best of the best—the few in any organization who rose to near the top—there was a massive difference in learning.

While there was little difference in the developmental events reported by high and low performers, the high performers drew 16 major predictable skill lessons from the jobs we outlined in Chapter 5; low performers drew three. For example, a start-up is the most logical and powerful source for learning how to develop others through team building. High performers consistently learned this skill from that source, while low performers did not. Curiously, low performers tended to report this learning as having occurred before they ever had a start-up assignment.

Low-performing executives seem to have much more difficulty learning from experience. They tend to form preconceived and general notions of, for example, how to develop others. The average age at which this was reported was before they had their first management job, so it had to be a hypothesis rather than a learning for them. High performers reported this learning when one would expect—when they hit their first big promotion and they had to develop others or sink, since they couldn't do it all alone. No low-performing executive reported this learning from such a job.

The point here is that learning new behaviors, skills, and attitudes is tough. We can't expect managers, even those who advance to executive levels before stagnating, to waltz into a new job, deduce where they are deficient, and efficiently learn those skills.

So why is it that many people with high IQs, wildly successful, with superb track records don't learn new behaviors?

They head down the path of habit. As we have discussed previously, it's more comfortable to stay with what we know, immersing ourselves in the technical detail of a new area while assuming that our other (management and personal) skills will carry the day.

They confuse being a manager with being a technical expert. The assumption all too often is that one's role is to become an expert, to master the content of an assignment, and be a technical expert for all seasons. While this might be a comfortable belief,

6

it isn't possible to realize and isn't the way to effectiveness. Being able to work with and conceptually understand different businesses and functions is what is critical. All management jobs are tests, but the test is whether one can manage something new without having to master it first. Being a quick study, asking good questions, grasping the concepts, and working with others to get the job done are the more effective tactics.

The deeper reasons why we don't have more high learners

Learning tactics are fairly simple to describe and would seem simple to do. But they aren't. Very few people are eager to do what we have described here.

The essential reason is that after a career built on technical proficiency, even mastery of an area, a person is asked to give up control and certainty. Once we face that we don't know how to do something, or that we'll never master it, we open up some elemental fears—of being viewed as a nincompoop, of being wrong while everyone watches.

This is part of the conspiracy (see Chapter 4) to keep us doing what we already know how to do. It's scary to go into new skill areas, while it's comfortable to lead with the familiar. As we are rarely required to expose ourselves as numbskulls, fresh challenges are quite threatening. If we don't know how to form a strategy or have never dealt with an e-commerce technical expert, it's not obvious what to do. Under stress, most people fall back on their skill sets and bags of tricks.

Our familiar selves are basically an expression of our drive and the bundle of personality tactics we use to satisfy it. In Chapter 3, we showed the major clusters of real people that we see at work. Their skill sets and lack thereof don't develop randomly. Partly, they are limited by job experiences they have had but, even more so, they are an expression of what they prefer and don't prefer to do.

Decades of personality and interest research has proven the argument above. In Holland's vocational types (contained in the widely used Strong Interest Inventory®), there are six strong interest patterns that lead people toward certain occupations. Realistic types may prefer outdoor work; investigative types prefer research jobs; and social types may feel more comfortable in teaching or social welfare occupations. The profile of a business manager looks much like that of a professional gambler—cool, calculating, rational.

Going against our natural grain is not easy and not preferred. Unless some powerful demands are thrust upon us, we don't change much.

The first step in developing learning skills is a thorough assessment of who we are—skill sets, personality and interest profile, experiences we have had and not had. The goal is to learn what is relatively easy and tough for us to do.

Observation | The land of the uncomfortable

6

Let's take an example from a research intervention conducted when one of us was at the Center for Creative Leadership. We followed 55 high-potential managers for a year to see how they grappled with learning to learn. One was Ed, a plant manager for a utility. Smart, funny, perfectionistic, Ed was "the kind of guy who squares the papers on his desk every day." As was fairly common for people like Ed, he was controlling, didn't develop people, liked to have his fingers in everything, and was viewed as talented but too tactical by his organization.

In detailing his developmental experiences, Ed listed a series of tasks and assignments where he was in charge. None of his experiences included learning from other people. What Ed's data revealed was a lifelong pattern of building up skills around his preferences, putting himself in situations where he could control the outcomes, and getting away with it by being smart, likable, and funny.

|

The challenge for Ed in going against the grain of his preferences and experiences wasn't something he looked forward to. "Let's see," he said, "you want me to try some experiences I've spent my life avoiding and attack them with fresh learning tactics since the ones I'm using serve only to control situations. I can't wait."

Yep, Ed. That's the nature of learning something new. It's the land of the uncomfortable.

Ed and about half the others had the motivation to give it a try. For Ed, the reasons were personal and professional. He didn't feel as close to his children as they reached the teenage years and strained against his authority. At work, his direct reports often felt the same way, and his tactical orientation threatened to plateau his career. It took Ed three months or so to come to these conclusions, and only then did he attack his needs with any conviction.

Ed volunteered for every strategy and acquisition task he could find. He instituted meetings with his direct reports where they scoped out projects—he gave them the benefit of his thinking, set guidelines and deadlines, then he got out of the way. In a clever move, he asked his children to plan the family vacation in the same manner, and co-taught Sunday school with his son. Ed was also having extreme difficulty with one of his direct reports who was not particularly competent, and he began to keep a journal detailing his efforts to deal with the person.

The results were quite good. As Ed said, "I hated it all at first, but then I started to see some benefits. Things actually did go better at home and at work. I think my stock is going up. Do I like doing these things? No, but now I merely dislike them, not hate them. It's important not to confuse what you like to do with what's necessary to do."

6

The principles that underlie what Ed did are the core principles of learning to learn:

- Self-awareness of our patterns and portfolio of skills.
- Motivation to do something differently because our current modes are no longer acceptable to us (both family and work).
- Direct experiences and developmental tasks that force the issue.
- New learning tactics (all Ed's other tactics were around controlling events and people).

Ed tried some methods of learning he had rarely tried before—methods that have nothing to do with controlling the outcome.

In the strategy tasks, he hunted for parallel situations, interviewed savvy insiders, and deduced some principles that he thought applied to the current situation. He analyzed the success and failure of similar situations to see what might work again. In the past, Ed said he would have read a book and formed a mental conclusion based on what he largely already knew. In this new situation, he held back and analyzed for three months before coming up with any conclusions.

For the problem with the direct report, Ed met with the person once a week and tried different techniques to improve the person's performance. He kept a journal of what he said and how the person reacted, which he then edited to pluses and minuses (what worked and what didn't). "When I looked at what I had done across time, I could see how I was messing up every time. It was all about what I wanted. I really wasn't doing anything to find out where the person was and what would play to his motivation. I was just making him feel worse." In the past, Ed would have just gone at the problem with no plan and wouldn't have changed his tactics much, if at all.

For the delegation efforts with his children and his direct reports, he did something he didn't recall having done before, except in a cursory way. He let them set the goals whenever possible and asked a lot of questions to help them think it through. In the past, everything for Ed was tell and sell. His questions were mostly to check understanding. He learned little consciously from other people. Once he opened up a bit, he learned a great deal. To his amazement, his preteen daughter was perfectly capable of masterminding a trip to Walt Disney World.

Learning in organizations

We are not suggesting that every person with a bit of potential go through a long soul-searching process in order to improve. It might be valuable but not very practical. Later we'll discuss smaller interventions to help people learn how to learn.

The learning promise is huge. It does seem to be the silver bullet of success. To make it work, though, several systems have to be in place. Organizations will have to hire differently, take another look at the people they already have, and distinguish types of learners. As we'll see, there are two kinds of superb learners. Developing learning agility can be done. It will be different for different people, and all people either do not need or cannot handle detailed, heavy learning interventions.

So if you are preparing for an uncertain future, knowing only that it will be different than it is now, bet on the learning agile to get you there.

Part III

Building talent
- a guide for
individuals

Chapter 7

Self-awareness: getting to know you

Knowing yourself better than anyone else does is step one to a successful career.

In Chapter 2, we showed you data on how adept managers are at developing people for the long-term. It's 67th out of 67 skills measured. Dead last among our competencies.

We showed you data on how good and comfortable managers are at giving critical feedback. Among the bottom 10 skills.

We showed you how good they are as coaches and mentors. Again, among the bottom 10 skills.

Managers are terminally busy in a fast-paced and changing global world. They are more focused on results, problems, and projects and less focused on managing and developing people. Developing staff for the long-term is not on their short list for completion this week.

Organizations are not following sound people-development processes. We have taken layers out of the organization, downsized, and now have fewer managers to do more work.

Wall Street is tactical and today. While they talk about long-term earnings, they buy and sell quarterly.

So who needs to pay the most attention to your development? Who is the most interested? Who has it as a high priority? Who has the most to gain or lose? *We believe it's you.*

If you wait for your manager, it will be too late. If you wait for the organization, it will be too late. If you also have to wait for you, then it's really too late.

What follows in this and the next four chapters is a protocol for managing your own career and reaching your personal work goals. While your manager and the organization you work for can and may be helpful, the burden is really on you.

The basic scheme is simple:

- Know yourself better than anyone else.
- Know what's required now and in the future.
- Learn how to get there and how to add the necessary skills.
- Do it now, don't wait.

Before we begin, here are some terms we will be using:

- Clear strengths – you are at standard or beyond in this skill; you are your best.
- Overdone strengths – you use a strength too often or at too high a pitch; you do too much of a good thing.
- Hidden strengths – you are better than you think you are; others rate you higher than you rate yourself.
- Blind spots – you think you're better than others do; you rate yourself higher than others rate you.
- Weaknesses – you're just not good at this; you don't do it well.
- Untested areas – you've never been exposed to this skill area.
- Compensators – skills you can use to work around a weakness or to neutralize the negative effects of overusing a strength.
- Career stallers and stoppers – negative characteristics or flameout factors that can derail a person's career.

A few things we know about self-awareness

- Self-awareness matters for performance. It is a key factor associated with performance and potential, especially for leadership roles.

- Leaders who are self-aware are open to feedback—even seek it out—and are willing to change.

- Self-awareness is the first step toward improvement.

- Low self-awareness increases the risk of derailment, especially at higher levels of leadership.

- The most common blind spots (areas where people overestimate their ability) include Making Tough People Calls, Demonstrating Personal Flexibility, and Creating the New and Different.

- The most common hidden strengths (areas where people underestimate their ability) include Managing Up, Understanding the Business, and Making Complex Decisions.

Observation | Liberation of self-knowledge

In our later careers, we've become enamored with the idea of self-awareness and self-knowledge. In study after study, the importance of self-awareness cannot be overstated. You can't be an effective manger or leader without self-awareness. You can't really work on your own self-development without self-awareness. Self-awareness facilitates success. The people we have seen who are legendarily successful have come to understand that total self-awareness is liberating. It should lead to a celebration. It is exciting to be at that day when you understand yourself and your impact on others completely. It is only at that point that you can be truly effective and grow to be as effective as you want to be. Because we know that people can make progress on all 67 skills in the Leadership Architect® Competency Library, and make progress on all 19 of the derailers, and can be truly successful with four to seven of the super strengths, and because people can work around their flat spots, true freedom is a complete understanding of self. People need to learn to enjoy and look forward to critical feedback. It's the only way you can grow.

7

| 125

A caution: How well do you think you know yourself?

You know your intentions and values and some of your behavior, but a lot of what you do is on autopilot. When asked to rate you, other people are more accurate because they are more likely to see your behavior from a fresh point of view and because your behavior has an impact on them. In several studies, all rater groups (bosses, peers, direct reports, customers) agreed more with each other than any agreed with self-ratings (you). More important, they are the more accurate raters when it comes to predicting performance. All rater groups (bosses, in- and out-of-unit peers, direct reports, customers) consistently show significant relationships between their ratings and the performance of the person rated (again, you). Self-ratings have a low relationship with performance and often don't relate at all. Put directly, self is the worst and least accurate rater of self. Not completely wrong, but least accurate. Ordinarily, your ratings won't agree exactly with those of others, and your ratings won't relate as closely to your actual performance.

In these days of empowerment and online self-ratings, it's tempting to go with the buzz and say, "I know myself," or "My self-assessment is better than nothing." According to much research, neither is true. Self-assessment is a well-meaning practice that doesn't work very well alone. More specifically, you (self) are most accurate on your strengths, less accurate on your weaknesses, and least accurate on interpersonal skills and the impressions you leave on people. This last point is very important because in Chapters 2 and 4, we pointed out that some of the skills missing in managers and executives were those very same skills that people are least accurate on.

So in order to manage your own career effectively, you first have to accept that your self-view is not adequate. You have to supplement it with information from knowledgeable others.

A second caution: Do others always give you accurate feedback? Do they truly tell you what they think?

Public feedback, as in an annual performance review, is usually sanitized to a degree. Giving bad news is not a preferred activity for many. Earlier, we pointed out that giving direct reports negative feedback as a skill was in the bottom 10 skills for managers and executives. Scores go up and accuracy goes down when the people doing the rating know they will be identified. (In a study of 58,000 appraisals, scores went up significantly in public appraisal processes.) So as a practical rule, you can't depend on formal appraisals alone. They are probably as much as .75 higher on a five-point scale than the raters would admit to under truth serum, and there will be less information about what the raters actually do think.

So, you have to look beyond formal appraisals to manage your career effectively.

Building self-awareness

With those two cautions in mind, the following is what you should and can do:

7

- *Know yourself well.* Without this, your chances of developing much are about nil. You must know what you are good, average, and bad at; what you're interested in; and what you overdo or overuse. Blind spots in skill areas that are important are the most dangerous thing. Your known weaknesses won't get you in as much trouble as your blind spots because you can work around weaknesses and compensate for them with other skills. With a blind spot, you think you are good at something that others know you aren't. The odds of your stumbling into a situation you won't handle well are strong. So your life goal should be to have no blind spots. Painful as it might be, find out all of the skills

| 127

that others would rate you as average or poor at and that you think yourself higher than average. The only other danger as great as this is to rely on your strengths so much that they go into overdrive.

- *To know yourself better, get confidential feedback beyond the formal appraisal processes.* Public feedback, as we said earlier, is of limited value. Discount your ratings and assume there is double the negative data that you receive.

- *A valuable source of feedback is private (to you) 360° assessment from people who know you well.* If your organization doesn't offer this service, most developmental courses you attend do, or you can arrange it on your own. Many 360s are now available online, so it is readily available. (We'll cover this topic in detail in Chapter 14.)

- *Use multiple sources.* Here is what is common: different people at different levels in different roles will see you differently. This doesn't mean you are a chameleon or two-faced. It is normal for a peer to rate your strengths and weaknesses differently than, say, a boss. They play different roles, are interested in different behaviors from you, and come up with different needs. If you don't use multiple sources, your feedback will be skewed. Bosses, for example, tend to focus on strategic grasp, selling-up skills, treatment of direct reports, presentation of problems, and the like. Due to this, the strengths and needs you will hear about are in the eye of the beholder. To hear the complete picture, you must have a complete jury.

- *The special case of having and using mentors.* Natural mentors (people who naturally select each other) are a rare find in organizations. Waiting for one can take a long time. Natural mentors can be a great source for original feedback and for confirming feedback from others. Realizing that not everyone has a natural mentor, some organizations have attempted to jump-start this process with formal mentoring programs that involve training on both sides, written expectations, and the like. Any mentor, if you're lucky enough to have one, can help greatly. If you don't have one or have not been assigned one, look for one on your own.

- *Pick carefully.* Two common questions are, "How many people should give me feedback?" and "Are more better?" Here's another way to think about this question. How many people have seen you in multiple work situations over one to five years? Your answer to this determines how many people should give you feedback. The reason is that beyond five years of knowing a person, ratings tend to go up and to be less related (or unrelated) to performance. The same is true for people who have known you for less than a year. We realize that work is not a laboratory and you may have to make do with who is available. Nevertheless, the best people to give you feedback are in the one-to-five-years-known range. If you need information on your first impression, look to people who have known you less than a year.

  As a general recommendation, we would say you, your boss, and three per response group. In a full 360°, this would be 11 (three each for peers, direct reports, and customers, your boss, and yourself).

- *Find out which skills are critical to improve or learn (short-term).* There are four areas where you must get feedback for short-term improvement:

  1. Which skills are the most important for success on your current job? Many organizations have success profiles for jobs, and you can also ask your boss or closest HR professional for that information.
  2. What are your strengths and weaknesses against this target?
  3. What are your hidden strengths and blind spots?
  4. What do you overdo and underdo?

  Finding out what is critical to learn long-term is a different question since any competency may matter at some point. If this is your interest, the most important for current success information is not as critical. All the competencies on all well-developed models are important for success in many places. That's how they got on the list to begin with. Look at Chapter 2 for a discussion of what, in general, is important for long-term success.

7

- *Analyze your results.* Most 360° systems come with various analyses already built into the reports. Our recommendation: focus on the highest and lowest competency results from each rater group. Note the highest and lowest quarter or highest and lowest third of your results from each group, and then look for patterns across groups. Do all groups have you as relatively high in some areas? Relatively low? Don't be distracted by the absolute scores. There are many reasons why ratings scores go up and down. (Scores tend to go up the longer a person has known you; people in tough jobs, like turnarounds, tend to get lower scores; Americans usually rate higher than Europeans.) For your development, it doesn't really matter what the raw scores are. High is nice, but it may not mean anything. Low is a concern but, again, it may not mean anything. What you should worry about is you relative to you. Your goal is simply to know yourself better. To do this, ask, "Why am I this way? How did my strengths get to be strengths? Do I overdo any of these strengths? Are my low scores areas I avoid, don't like, am not good at? Are some of them really just untested (I've never been in a formal negotiation)?"

- *Make deeper sense of your feedback results by confirming them.* Numbers don't tell the whole tale, even if the system you use has areas where raters can write in comments. While you are likely to be the least accurate rater, this doesn't mean the other raters are all-knowing. Often, there are only a few raters per category, and one person can skew the average score fairly dramatically. It is important to confirm your results in order to verify them and understand them better. A method that has worked well is to rely on the people who rated you. Select some specific areas from your feedback and get their opinions on the accuracy of your understanding. Make sure to send a clear message: "I heard you. You said I am strong at this and not so strong at that. Thanks for telling me. I intend to work hard on my development, but first I want to make sure I understood you correctly." Prepare a list of statements: "I think I focus too much on operations and miss the larger strategic connections. What do you think?" Ask them to respond anonymously in writing (in person if you know them

7

really well). Ask them what they would like to see you keep doing, start doing, and stop doing/do differently in order to improve.

- *Find out what you overdo at the same time.* As we showed in Chapter 4, strengths unharnessed and unexamined can lead to career derailment. Some feedback systems touch on this issue and some don't. As above, make a statement to the group: "I get the impression that I am viewed as being intelligent but make others feel less so."

- *Take a deep breath.* Development isn't the land of safety and comfort. You'll get some bad news and some new news. If you don't, you're either a person who really does know yourself, or you may be viewed as arrogant or defensive. If it's the former, your self-ratings should have agreed as much as possible with your rater groups. If it's the latter, you'll have to go back repeatedly to people to show them you take your development seriously. For most, you'll get some bad news. In dealing with this, remember that seeking negative feedback increases both the accuracy of your understanding and people's evaluations of your effectiveness. People know how hard it is to publicly admit needs; they are more likely to give you the benefit of the doubt going forward.

- *Categorize your results:*
  - Clear strengths – you are at standard or beyond in this skill; you are your best.
  - Overdone strengths – you use a strength too often or at too high a pitch; you do too much of a good thing.
  - Hidden strengths – you are better than you think you are; others rate you higher than you rate yourself.
  - Blind spots – you think you're better than others do; you rate yourself higher than others rate you.
  - Weaknesses – you're just not good at this; you don't do it well.
  - Untested areas – you've never been exposed to this skill area.

- Compensators – skills you can use to work around a weakness or to neutralize the negative effects of overusing a strength.

- Career stallers and stoppers – negative characteristics or flameout factors that can derail a person's career.

- *Be clear on what's important.* Are you primarily interested in your current job or future jobs? Does your firm have a success profile for this job (these jobs)? Although the weight of opinion from your raters is probably valuable for your current job, don't rely on just that source. They may be in no position to really understand the critical success factors since most of them are either not in the same kind of job (peers, customers) or may be a level down (reports). Go ask current and past incumbents. Consult with the wisest people in your organization. Become convinced about what is important. Development is hard enough without spending time building the wrong skills.

So development starts with the most accurate self-knowledge you can obtain. You are, unfortunately, at least at the beginning of this journey, the least informed about yourself. Bosses and formal appraisal processes are limited. Most informal feedback by the people around you will be sanitized. You have to work to get the feedback you need. You have to help the people who are capable of giving you career-enhancing feedback to give it to you. Read Chapter 16 on coaching for what it's like to be on the giving side. Please seek a coach if you tend toward defensiveness and resist feedback. To grow, you have to become a better receiver of constructive criticism. Take it in stride. Go with the flow. Remember the goal. You need to know the good and bad about yourself before you can accurately plan and pursue a career. Have no blind spots. Know all of your weaknesses. Know your excesses. Know your strengths. Then all there is left to do is make choices about your deployment and development.

Chapter 8

Development:
Challenge, feedback, learning loop

Development requires three things: (1) a challenging task (or person); (2) a way to get before, during, and after feedback; and (3) learning some new things to do.

Unless the three imperatives above are present, development either doesn't happen or it happens inconsistently by chance.

In the thousands of experiences reported by managers and executives and recorded in numerous studies, there are six key sources of growth. These are cited in their general order of power to bring about change:

1. A job change to a more challenging job.
2. A developmental task while in a current job.
3. Role models, coaches, and mentors.
4. Feedback.
5. Courses and reading.
6. Personal learning.

1 and 2 set the developmental challenge. Real-life, important job demands trigger the motivation to learn.

3 and 4 fuel continuous improvement. Without frequent, repeated feedback and coaching, change doesn't take.

5 and 6 provide the raw material of learning to do something different. Without some new to-dos, nothing meaningful can occur.

Alone, each of the sources of growth is incomplete. Combined together is where the power lies.

What does the research say about development?

As we discussed in Chapter 5, the research on development has come down pretty firmly around learning from all types of experiences like courses, readings, projects, feedback, assignments, or jobs. No one type does the job alone, but in concert they are powerful.

Development generally begins with a realization or being aware of a current or future need and the motivation to do something about it. This might come from feedback, a mistake, watching other people's reactions, a mentor, failing at or not being up to a task. In other words, it comes from experience. The odds are that development of the need will be about 70 percent from on-the-job experience or learning on-the-job, working on real tasks and problems; about 20 percent from feedback or working around good and bad examples or role models of the need; and 10 percent from courses and reading.

How you discover the need is less important than accepting that you have it. After that, what is critical is to go after the need with all the developmental remedies that you have access to.

Feedback alone won't do it; it only sets the stage.

Just trying it won't work. Experience by itself can be a lousy teacher— it's too involving and too fragmented. Few people set learning goals or benchmarks of success or stop to postmortem their experiences.

Neither courses nor reading will work alone. At best they involve knowing what to do better or differently and perhaps practicing in the safe environment of a course. Transfer of the new skill back to the job is difficult.

In short, the developmental remedies work best when orchestrated together. Alone, they are single instruments, each with its own limitations.

According to the studies we participated in at the Center for Creative Leadership, development specifically involves:

- Knowing what the target looks like – what the competency or skill looks like when done well (the after picture). What does a person do who is an acknowledged performer in this area?

- Knowing where you stand against the target (the before picture) – getting feedback. What do you do badly or not at all?

- Seeing some consequence or reason to develop – you have to be a motivated person in order to make progress on a need. This is the fulcrum of development. Motivated people can do amazing things. But if you don't really buy in, if fear or defensiveness or indifference gets in the way, nothing will happen. At best, you'll go through the motions. The question is, do you see a consequence that is unacceptable to you, one that spurs you to change?

- Having challenging experiences that test you in that area – not just practice, not just make-work, but stressful experiences where you get better at the area or you fail or don't cope well with the experience. Part of development is a demand pull on you to do something different or you fail or stumble. The task, say, running a task force where the members are experts and you are not, demands that you listen, learn from others, curb any defensiveness you may usually exhibit, etc. Not doing those things isn't a reasonable option.

- Hitting the need with every learning method available – seek out good and bad role models, get more feedback, analyze your mistakes, go to a course, whatever it takes to find some new, different, and better things to do.

- Making sense of it all – developing some new rules of thumb, guidelines, dos and don'ts so the new behaviors and attitudes can become part of your natural repertoire, not things you do once or twice and then forget to do going forward.

8

Chapter 9

Improvement planning:
Creating a plan that works

Take your time coming up with a development plan.
It will pay off greatly.

At this point, you have one or more needs and you are convinced (motivated) to do something about it. If this is not true, reading this chapter will not be of value to you.

First, you need to be sure about which category your need fits in. The reason is that the development plan will be different for each category. Once you know the category, you can form your developmental strategy. The possible categories are:

- A current strength that needs to be maintained or made stronger.

- An average skill that needs to be higher.

- An overdone strength – a strength that is in overdrive and causing noise.

- A hidden strength – an area where you may be better than you think.

- A blind spot – an area where you think you are better than others do.

- A weakness – you are not strong enough in an area that matters.

- An untested area – you are not skilled because you have never had to do this.

- A compensator skill – a skill you can use to offset the negative effects of any of the above.

Detailing the need

You have little chance of efficient development without a clear target. What are you like now? Look to the definition of the skill or skills you want to work on. Take a few minutes to detail your need. Which unskilled descriptors apply? How and why do they apply? With whom? In what situations? Next, ask about causes. Why do you do what you do related to this need? What drives the need? Is this something you haven't seen much reason to develop in previously? Why? Then, what does it look like when you are done developing the skill? Take each of your unskilled behaviors and list them on the left side of a sheet of paper, then write on the right side what they look like done well. What could a panel of 12 judges use to dispassionately evaluate when development has occurred? What skilled behaviors would they look to? Ask others more skilled than you for help in detailing.

How many needs do you recommend tackling at once?

You will often hear three, because this is what most people have learned to say. Actually, there is no set number. How many needs you should or can work on depends on:

- How difficult the need is to develop.
- How much support you will have.
- How similar the needs are.
- What you are willing to do.

9

Exercise 9.1 Developing the need

How difficult is the need to develop?

There are four considerations that answer the difficulty question: what type of need is it, how big is the gap from where you are to the target, how complex is the competency, and how emotionally involved or loaded is the competency.

1. What type of need is it?

The general order of difficulty—from hardest (5) to easiest (1)—of working on a need by type or category is:

5   Blind spot – You think you are good at something important that is really a weakness for you because you were convinced in the near past that you did this well.

5   Overdone strength – You use a strength too much or too often because this is what has brought you this far and it would be hard for you to throttle down.

4   Weakness – There is evidence that you don't do this well.

3   Average to better – It's just a matter of incrementally getting better at what you are already doing to some extent.

3   A compensator skill – A skill used to lessen the negative effects of a weakness or overdone strength. Just being a little bit better in these skills goes a long way toward decreasing the negative effects of more serious needs.

2   Untested – You aren't defensive about it since you haven't really tried it yet. You may even be reasonable at it right out of the box.

1   Maintaining a strength – You are already good at it.

1   Hidden strength – You are already better than you think you are.

Where do each of your needs fall? Using the five-point scale, how many points do you have? The higher the total (lots of 4s and/or 5s), the fewer you can work on at once. If you are working on multiple needs, it is useful to calculate an average. For each of your needs, record your scores on Worksheet 9.1.

9

Exercise 9.1 Developing the need–continued

2. How big is the gap from where you are to the target?

Use the following methods for determining the gap size:

- If you have 360° results on the need, look at your score on the need from all other raters (excluding yourself). Most 360s are reported on a five-point scale. Scores are generally inflated by about .75 and often the average item score is 3.8 or above. Unless you know the specific distribution of your items or scales, use the following scores as a rule of thumb: If your score on this need is 2.99 or below, that's scored a 5; 3.00 to 3.25 is a 4; 3.26 to 3.50 is a 3; 3.51 to 3.75 is a 2; and 3.76 or above is a 1. Again, an average is useful if you are working on more than one need.

- If you have a different scoring system on your 360° where your scores are rank ordered from highest to lowest, just look where this need is relative to your other skill ratings. If it is in the bottom 10 percent, score it a 5. If it's between the bottom 11 and 20 percent, then it's a 4. If it's between 21 and 40 percent, it's a 3. If it's between 41 and 50 percent, it's a 2. Anything over 51 percent, a 1.

- You may also have a percentile chart presented with 360° results. Percentile charts compare you with a norm group. Assuming you think this is a reasonable comparison group, the bottom 10 percent is scored a 5; the bottom 25 percent is a 4; the bottom 50 percent is a 3; up to 75 percent is a 2; and above this is a 1.

- If you have no 360°, then, from all of the people you know, think of the person who is best at this behavior you intend to work on—someone who is at or above the standard you are trying to reach. Then think about a person you know who is the worst at this. Add other

Exercise 9.1 Developing the need–continued

people (up to a total of 10) and record their names on a piece of paper, with the person who is the best at this behavior on top and the worst on the bottom. Line up the other eight people between the best and the worst. Now think of your own behavior. Where would you fall on that list of 10? Who are you most like? Toward the top? Toward the bottom? In the middle? The bigger the gap, the more time and resources will be required to close the gap. The bigger the gaps across your multiple needs, the fewer needs you can work on at once. Give the following point values to the gaps: a gap of 1 = 1; 2 or 3 = 2; 4 or 5 = 3; 6 or 7 = 4; and 8 or 9 = 5. How many gap points do you have? The more points you have, the less likely it is that you can work on multiple needs.

What is your gap average? The higher the average, the more difficult the development task. Record your scores on Worksheet 9.1.

3. How complex is the competency?

Not all competencies are the same size. Size is determined by things like complexity—how many things you would have to know to do this skill well and what the stakes are if this skill is done badly. Size is also determined by how much experience you would have to have to do this skill well. Examples of "big" competencies would be Strategic Agility, Understanding Others, Political Savvy, and Business Acumen. Smaller skills would be things like Action Oriented, Personal Disclosure, Patience, and *Timely* Decision Making.

If 5 is big and 1 is small, where do your needs fit? The bigger the number, the less likely it will be that you can work on multiple needs. If you are working on multiple needs, also calculate an average. Record your scores on Worksheet 9.1.

9

Exercise 9.1 Developing the need–continued

4. How emotionally involved or loaded is the competency?

It would be hard enough to work on building a skill if only skills were involved. But many skills also involve your emotions and beliefs. They are loaded with intensity and passion. Doing them creates conflict and tension within you and with others. Some competencies have more emotion and belief load than others. Generally, the higher the load, the harder they are to work on. Examples of higher-load competencies would be *Managing* Diversity, Composure, Managerial Courage, Political Savvy, *Dealing with* Ambiguity, and Conflict Management. All these competencies done well must include the ability to tolerate and manage your negative emotions and chilling beliefs as well as the emotions and beliefs of others. Examples of lower-load competencies would be Business Acumen, Functional/Technical Skills, Technical Learning, Written Communications, and Planning. Look at your needs. To what extent do they have strong emotional or belief components? The more loaded they are, the fewer you can work on at once. If 5 is highly loaded and 1 is not, where do your needs fit? If you are working on multiple needs, calculate an average. Record your scores on Worksheet 9.1.

Worksheet 9.1 How difficult is the need to develop

Name of need	Need 1	Need 2	Need 3	Need 4	Total (or average)
Consider:	Points 1–5	Points 1–5	Points 1–5	Points 1–5	
1. What type of need is it?					
2. How big is the gap from where you are to the target?					
3. How complex is the competency?					
4. How emotionally involved or loaded is the competency?					
Total (or Average)					

If you are using averages for multiple needs, then you will have a result between 1 and 5. The higher the average number, the more difficult the effort: 1 and 2 most people could do; 3 would be an average challenge for most; 4 would be challenging; and above 4.5 would be for the very motivated few.

If you are using totals, the range would be 4 to 20 per need, with 12 per need about average.

9

Exercise 9.1 Developing the need–continued

How much support will you have?

How many developmental resources (courses, a development library, tuition support, a development budget, etc.) do you have available to you? 5 is sparse, and 1 is unlimited. How supportive of development efforts are the people and the organization around you? 5 is not much, and 1 is total support.

How many total points out of 10 do you have? The more points you have, the more difficult the effort will be. The more points you have, the more you are on your own without much help. Calculate an average for each need. A need such as Planning may be widely supported, and a need like Approachability, little or not at all. Record your scores on Worksheet 9.2.

How similar are the needs?

Simply, the more similar the needs, the more you can work on at the same time because the developmental remedies and actions you choose will address more than one need at a time. So, if you are working on Listening, Interpersonal Savvy, and Negotiating, they are similar enough that you could probably work on all three in parallel. But if you are working on Listening, Strategic Agility, and being more Action Oriented, they have little in common.

List your multiple needs. How similar or how different are they? If you are not sure, ask an HR professional. If very similar is a 1, and completely different is a 5, what's your difference score? The higher the number, the more difficult it will be to work on multiple needs. Record your scores on Worksheet 9.2.

What are you willing to do?

Simply, the more ready you are to address your needs, the more you can handle at once. For each need, how motivated are you on a five-point scale?

9

Exercise 9.1 Developing the need–continued

1   I'm committed, eager, and frenetically ready.

2   I'm committed to working on this need; I take it personally.

3   I accept I have this need and am willing to give it a try.

4   I'm aware of this need but not very energized about it.

5   I'm pretty disinterested.

Unless you can answer 1 or 2 to any need, you need to divert to Chapter 16. A coach needs to help you decide if you really want to work on this. Record your ratings on Worksheet 9.2

Summarize your needs profile on a worksheet like the one below (using averages for multiple needs). Scoring note: For the "How difficult is the need to develop" category in Worksheet 9.2 below, insert your Total (or Average) scores from Worksheet 9.1.

Worksheet 9.2 Summary of your needs profile

Name of need	Need 1	Need 2	Need 3	Need 4	Total (or average)
Issues:	Points 1–5	Points 1–5	Points 1–5	Points 1–5	
How difficult is the need to develop?*					
How much support will you have?					
How similar are the needs?					
What are you willing to do?					
Total (or Average)					

* Record your scores from the last row in Worksheet 9.1.

How many needs do you recommend tackling at once? It depends.

The higher the average (or total), the more difficult working on the need or needs becomes.

If difficulty is moderate (3), support is high (1), your needs are somewhat similar (1), and your motivation is high (1), then you can work on as many needs as you can tackle on the job.

If difficulty is high (4-5), support is marginal (4-5), needs are quite different (4-5), and your motivation is average (3-4), then trim your needs down to the one that matters most.

So the simple answer is, work on three needs; the real answer is, it depends.

Forming your improvement strategy

Once you identify your need, focus on how you will address it. You may require a development plan, but maybe not. Maybe you would see improvement with a marketing plan, a substitution plan, or a workaround plan. Different categories of needs require different plans:

- **Clear strengths** – Build your strengths by testing them in new task assignments. If you're good at Conflict Management, use this strength on a cross-functional project while you learn about other functions. Or coach others in your strengths and ask for some help from them in their strengths.

- **Overdone strengths** – Cutting back on a strength is usually a failing strategy. After all, it's a primary reason for your success to date. The key here is to leave it alone and focus on neutralizing its unintended negative consequences (you're creative but others see you as disorganized) with your compensators. Figure out exactly how the dark side of your strength plays out and construct a plan for that (write a plan for getting more organized).

9

- **Hidden strengths** – Make sure you understand why others see you as more skilled in this area than you do. Try tasks that require this skill to confirm whether others are right about you.

- **Average in an important area** – Treat it like a weakness. The only difference is that you can start with tougher, more challenging tasks.

- **Blind spots** – Be cautious. Try to find a person who is a model of excellent behavior in this area and study what he or she does. Read, talk to people, and come to understand what excellence looks like before you try anything. Even then, start small and have a development buddy or monitor around. Try to understand why you were deluded about this. Why did you overrate yourself? Try first to understand yourself in this area before you start a skill-building program.

- **Weaknesses** – These are best handled with a development plan that focuses on the three imperatives of growth: challenging tasks, continued feedback, and building frameworks for new learning. Or, if you choose not to develop the skill directly, you can try an alternative approach. Substitute something or work around the weakness. (For more details on alternative plans, see our book *Paths to Improvement: Navigating Your Way to Success.*)

  - Substitute for the weakness. Can you trade something out? Lincoln managed a nasty temper by writing vitriolic letters, returning to them to extract the key points, then throwing the original letter away. He dealt with the key points once he regained his composure.

  - Work around the weakness. Are there others who can do this? People who have no affinity for strategy have worked around it by hiring experts and seeking help from strategic friends in and out of their firms.

- **Untested areas** – Since you haven't really been tested in this area, the plan would be to seek small opportunities to try out this skill. You could be pleasantly surprised to find out that you are already reasonable at this. If that is the case, follow the protocol for maintaining your strengths. If you find out early that you are not good at this, then follow the protocol on weaknesses.

9

Story

Development is not the only answer

A health care research organization hired Carol, a great hospital administrator, to lead the operations for the agency. With high hopes of immediate impact, the CEO felt frustrated after six months by a perceived lack of initiative and no results. "Was this the wrong person? Was this a bad hire? Did we err thinking someone could apply their experience from a hospital environment to a research and services environment?"

Before throwing in the towel, the CEO asked a development coach to help Carol. A 360° competency assessment was used to gather insight from both current and past associates of the new executive. Critical competencies were, indeed, rated lower. Action Oriented, Drive for Results, Organizing, Planning, Priority Setting— all skills you would expect a multi-hospital administrator to have. If Carol was weak at these, what then?

In the feedback and coaching dialogue, it became obvious that these were "phantom development needs." Her previous colleagues rated her high. The issue was not a lack of skill in these areas. Carol's issue was her approach to her new role. She knew she was an expert in hospital administration—she wanted to focus on learning the research side. This is why people perceived her as a neophyte in general.

Carol quickly realized she needed to shore up people's perceptions. She didn't need a development plan. She needed a marketing plan. Carol and her coach brainstormed ways to highlight her capabilities. She would focus on a few high-impact areas and deliver immediate results.

Taking a different path to improvement saved Carol's reputation and her job.

9

Tying your needs to developmental remedies

A development plan should be geared to your particular set of needs. Next is a table (9.1) combining the types of developmental needs down the left with the developmental remedies across the top that are most appropriate for that need. The sequence we suggest for the remedies is indicated numerically (1 = do first, 2 = do second, 3 = do last). Note that a job change is never recommended as a first option because some pre-development should take place prior to a new job. Taking a new job just to develop is too risky in most situations. Think and start small.

Table 9.1 Sequence of developmental remedies

Developmental needs	Developmental remedies					
	Job change	Task	Coach	Feedback	Course	Learn
Strength	2	2	1*		2	
Average in an important area	2	1	1	1	1	1
Overdone strength	2	1	1	1	1	1
Hidden strength	3	2	2	2	2	1
Blind spot	3	2	1	2	1	1
Weakness	2	1	1	1	1	1
Untested area	2	2	1	2	1	1
Weakness (compensate)			1		1	1

1 = Do first
2 = Do second
3 = Do last
*Coach Others

Learning from jobs

A lot of people pause at this recommendation. Why suggest a job change section here? I already have a job or I don't want to do this one or it would be risky for me to take such a job (a strategic planning job when I'm lousy at strategy). We develop competencies under moderate to high pressure, not under less-stressful conditions. If this is your last job or if you have no career ambition to do anything different or at a higher level, skip this section. Otherwise, read on.

This section on job changes is here because:

- The number one developer of competencies by far is stretching, challenging jobs—not feedback, not courses, not role models, but jobs where you develop and exercise significant and varied competencies. If you really want to grow, these are the best places to do it.

- If you are ambitious, the developmental jobs listed in Chapter 5 are those that matter most for long-term success. In the Center for Creative Leadership (CCL) studies, executives who remained successful had been tested in many of the jobs.

- No one is going to promote you to a significant role unless you prove you can perform under moderate to high pressure. Listening or Planning or Conflict Management for low stakes is not that impressive to most talent scouts. They want to know one thing: can you do it under high pressure? Developmental jobs are as high pressure as it gets.

- If you have a job that lacks some of the necessary elements for development, see if you can add to the job or enrich it with additional challenges.

- If you are already in one of the jobs suggested for development, you have a rich opportunity to use it to learn better from experience. What specifically is it about the job that demands you work on this need? Write down these challenges; focus your development plan on them.

- Use all other remedies to qualify yourself for one of these jobs. Particularly if you are ambitious, this is the best thing you can do. Use the other remedies to get ready, then show the decision makers you can handle a tough test. This will prove to them that you can handle different kinds of jobs and overcome a competency deficiency.

In one company, managers were asked to select a job from the developmental jobs list in Chapter 5 that they'd like to do, either because it seemed exciting, because it would take a lot of personal growth, or because they wanted to get noticed. Although none of them were qualified for their "dream" job at that time, 40 percent qualified themselves for and got this type of job within two years.

Many currently successful executives reported in various studies that they were coerced and dragged kicking and screaming into jobs they didn't want and couldn't see the importance of. Looking back, these jobs are often the ones they now report as having had the most lasting effect on their current skills portfolio. So be careful of being too judgmental about jobs that bosses, mentors, and concerned friends suggest you consider. Many times, you will not know ahead of time that this is the best developmental job you could take.

A last point is that it isn't just any new and challenging job that is valuable. It's a new and challenging job that requires the need you are working on.

Best developmental on-the-job assignments

Unless you have challenging job tasks where you either perform against the need or fail, not much development will occur. This is the essence of action learning or learning from experience— not practice, not trying things out, but getting better in order to perform. Take the example of listening skills, a common need. Everyone has had a million chances to listen better but often did not because they weren't motivated to listen and were able to get away with it. What if they were in a tough negotiation or

9

running a task force of experts where they were not an expert. Get the idea? It's listen or else you can't do the job. Any plan you write must have "perform this or else" tasks in it to work. Otherwise, you'll revert to your old ways.

To use these tasks, shape them to your job and organization. What tasks like these are available?

If you have a significant need (you are really weak or untested in this area), start with the smaller challenges and build up to the tougher ones.

Tips for learning from jobs

- What are the key challenges of the tasks you are doing? Start something up? Install a system? Deal with angry customers? Specify.
- What is a new or different task you could take on that needs doing? Do it.
- What are you learning from the challenges? What worked and didn't? Why?
- Who can check out your learning to provide you with a different perspective? Write it down so you won't forget it.

Key: Analyze successes to figure out what is repeatable for you.

Learning from other people

This is the order that these three types of resources are generally available in organizations:

1. Role models
2. Coaches
3. Mentors

1. Role models

Who exemplifies how to do whatever your need is? Who, for example, personifies Decision Quality or Compassion or Strategic Agility? Think more broadly than your current job and colleagues. For example, clergy, friends, spouses, or community leaders are also good sources for potential models. Select your models not on the basis of overall excellence or likeability, but on the basis of the one towering strength (or glaring weakness) you are interested in. Even people who are well-thought-of usually have only one or two towering strengths (or glaring weaknesses). Ordinarily, you won't learn as much from the whole person as you will from one characteristic. Role models, both good and bad, abound. Some tips:

- Go for multiple models.
- Pick single characteristics or skills, not people. Everything you are looking for is not likely to occur in a single person.
- Pick a person who is a bad example. You can not only learn some not-to-dos, you can learn them viscerally, by how they make you and others feel. Check yourself to see if you do any of these same behaviors around the need you are working on.
- Reduce what you see to rules of thumb, not generalities. For example, approachable people share something personal and ask open-ended questions (not the bland, "How are you?"). You should pick some, but not all, of their behaviors and adapt them to your own needs and style.
- You can interview the person. How do they view the need you are working on? What rules of thumb do they think they are following? Anything they've learned absolutely not to do? Where did they learn how to do this? How do they stay current? How do they monitor their impact on others?
- When you observe the person, compare him or her with what you do in similar situations. Many times, you will learn more by observing and noting. Your model may not be able to explain his or her behavior or may be an unwilling teacher.

|

2. Coaches

A coach is a person who is willing to help you directly with your need. In effect, you have a tutor. Ask a person to coach or tutor you directly. This has the additional benefit of skill building coupled with correcting feedback. Also observe the teacher teaching you. How does he or she teach? How does he or she adjust to you as a learner? After the process, ask for feedback about you as a learner. Some tips:

- Have you ever considered coaching someone yourself? What are you expert in and could help others with?

- Coaching others is a powerful way to learn about yourself. What gets a good reaction? A blank stare? How do you organize what you know to help someone else learn it? What are the key elements?

- Coaching is complex enough that we are including a chapter on this subject (see Chapter 16). Use it to help you help your coach or to coach someone else.

3. Mentors

Natural mentors have a special relationship with you and are interested in your success and your future. Since they are usually not in your direct chain of command, you can have more open, relaxed, and fruitful discussions about yourself and your career prospects. They can be a very important source for candid or critical feedback others may not give you. Natural mentors are a rare find in organizations; waiting for one can take a long time. Realizing this, some organizations have attempted to jump-start this process with assigned mentoring programs that involve training on both sides, written expectations, and the like. Any mentor, if you're lucky enough to have one, can help greatly. Some tips:

- They may tell you the pitfalls and land mines to avoid, but don't expect them to solve your career problems.

9

- The more specific you are, the more they can help. Most people are not natural coaches or teachers.
- Don't expect one mentor to know or be everything you need. Variety in all things wins long-term.

Studies have reported that natural or informal mentors have more impact. Those mentored have more satisfaction with the jobs and salaries. Formal mentors and mentoring programs are still nice to have, however. They help with recruitment, lowering turnover, and increasing commitment to the organization. Careful assignment, detailing the scope of the relationship, and regularly scheduled meetings are keys to success. Additionally, local autonomy helps mentors and mentees get more specific about the ropes of IT or careers in marketing.

Tips for learning from other people

- What does this person do well and how does he or she do it?
- What principles do you think are being followed? If you can ask why or get a step-by-step explanation, do so.
- What's different about how you go about this? What can you take directly from this person? What can you adapt?
- Could you either provide help to the person or ask for help from the person?

Key: Study the other person as a way to study yourself. Seek feedback from others.

Courses and readings

While learning from courses and reading may not be as effective as learning from experience, they remain an invaluable source of distilled wisdom. The research evidence is strong that a well-timed classroom or online learning experience can help build new competencies efficiently, and they can accelerate development dramatically when coupled with the other remedies. There are commercially available search engines to help you select the

9

best course for you in an area and, of course, a zillion books exist on all possible topics. Handbooks of tips, such as *FYI® For Your Improvement,* cover many competencies.

Tips for learning from courses and readings

- Courses that build management or leadership skills seem to require immediate application to work. What work tasks or projects will you apply the course learning to when you return? (There are courses that are generally valuable even if they have no specific application at the moment. Technical training, self-awareness, problem-solving methods, and perspective building are common examples. Still, if you want to get the maximum benefit from them, have a specific goal in mind when you attend.)

- If you don't have a specific purpose (goal) in mind, don't read improvement literature or take improvement courses.

- You should read and pay attention for tips and general rules of thumb to apply.

- Write down tips as a list of dos and don'ts or ideas.

- Take notes with your goal(s) in mind. Don't just take notes.

Key: Focus on what you want to learn that you can apply now. If you don't know, don't go to the course and don't pick up the book.

Personal learning

We dealt with this topic extensively in Chapter 6. What makes development last is a method to cement new learning. Keeping a learning journal, lists of rules of thumb, plus and minus lists, dos and don'ts is what makes learning repeatable.

There are three routes you can take, depending on your appetite for learning and your ambition:

1. Light (not to be confused with useless) – Commit to having one method of capturing learning. It might be as simple as discussing what you are learning with a buddy or keeping a written log.

2. Medium – Commit to trying different learning methods for different problems. Try visioning or mind mapping. Study successes to figure out what they have in common. Take a creative fantasy excursion, search history for parallels, go interview people, teach someone to do something, etc. Pick learning tactics you have never tried before to kick yourself out of your comfort zone. And, of course, have a method for capturing learning.

3. Heavy – Do a full analysis of yourself: 360° feedback, a personality instrument, an interest inventory, a time line of all significant events in your life and what you learned from them. Figure out what you like to do, like to overdo, and like to avoid—just as we described in Chapter 6. This isn't therapy; you are getting to know yourself as a learner. Then attack your flat sides with the goal of neutralizing your weaknesses and developing some new strengths. You won't know what you can do until you try.

Tips for learning from personal experience

- If you make a mistake, why did you make the mistake? Accepting that circumstances usually play a role, what part of the mistake is your problem?

- What would success look like? What would you be doing differently?

- What should you add to your behavior (it could be something you're not doing now)?

- Even if something just happened and is in no way your fault, what can you learn about how you could cope better?

Key: Focus on yourself, not on all the reasons why life should have been better. Avoid the traps of simply subtracting something from your behavior or doing the opposite. Neither are learning

| 157

strategies. The question is, what could you add or do differently that would remove the cause of the problem or help you cope better?

Unless your plan takes into account all the elements of development, don't expect much to happen. Remember what creates growth:

- A challenging, do-it-or-else task; a situation with high stakes.
- Some other people (good or bad) to help you (feedback, coaching, role models, maybe a mentor).
- Having some different to-dos and a method to make sense of what you are doing.

As a model, we have put together a general, or universal, plan protocol that will fit most needs. If you don't want to start from scratch on a plan, just follow the 10 steps below.

Universal ideas for developing any competency

1. **Choose wisely.** Figure out what is critically important to performance in your job or success in your career. This is a huge investment of your time and energy, so make sure that you're focused on something that matters to you and something that other people think is important too. Be realistic about what you can accomplish.

2. **Get specific.** Get more detailed and behavioral feedback on the need. Most of the time, people are weak in some aspect of a competency. It's almost never all interpersonal skills. It's usually something specific—for example, interpersonal skills with upper management under the pressure of tough questions from two of the seven on the management committee on topics you care deeply about. To find out more about what your need is specifically, go to a few

people who know and who will tell you if you ask. Accept that you have a need. Don't be defensive or try to rationalize away the need. Say you are concerned about the need and request more detailed information so you can focus on an efficient plan for growth and development. Ask them for specific examples. When? Where? With whom? In what settings? Under what conditions? How many times? Might anyone they know be of help? Get as specific as you can. Listen, don't rebut. Take notes. Thank them for the input.

3. **Create the plan.** If you have accepted the need as true and you are ready to do something about it, you need three kinds of action plans. You need to know what to stop doing, start doing, and keep doing. Since you have a need in this area (you don't do this well), you need to stop some things you are doing that aren't working. In their place, you need to start doing some things you either don't like doing, haven't ever done, or don't even know about. Even if you are bad at something, there are things you do in this area that you are probably good at. Send a form or e-mail to a number of people who would be willing to help you work on this skill. Tell them you have discovered and taken ownership of this need, want to do something about it, list the specific need you identified, and ask them for the things you should stop doing, start doing, and keep doing.

4. **Learn from others.** Research shows that we learn best from others when we: (a) Pick multiple models, each of whom excels at one thing rather than looking for the whole package in one person. Think more broadly than your current job for models; add some off-work models. (b) Take both the student and the teacher role. As a student, study other people—don't just admire or dislike what they do. Reduce what they do or don't do to a set of principles or rules of thumb to integrate into your behavior. As a teacher, it's one of the best ways to learn something as it forces you to think it through and be concise in your explanation. (c) Rely on multiple methods of learning—interview people, observe them without speaking with them, study remote models by reading books or watching films, get someone to tutor you,

9

or use a contrast strategy. Sometimes it's hard to see the effects of your behavior because you are too close to the problem. Pick two people, one who is much better than you are at your need and one who is much worse. Copy what the good model does that leads to good outcomes. Get rid of the behaviors that match what the bad model does. Or, get a partner. If you can find someone working on the same need, you can share learnings and support each other. Take turns teaching each other some to-dos, one of the best ways to cement your learning. Share books you've found. Courses you've attended. Models you've observed. You can give each other progress feedback.

5. **Read the "bible" on this need.** Almost every function and technology has a book people might call the "bible" in the area. It is the standard reference everyone looks to for knowledge. For example, how to negotiate to win. How to get along with bad bosses. How to win friends. How to be more creative. Go to a large business bookstore and buy at least two books covering your need. Take one hour and scan each book. Just read the first sentence of every paragraph. Don't read to learn. Just read to see the structure of the book. Pick the one that seems to be right for you and read it thoroughly. That book may reference or lead you to other books or articles on the skill. Use your reading to answer the following questions: What's the research on the skill? What are the 10 how-tos all the experts would agree to? How is this skill best learned?

6. **Learn from autobiographies and biographies.** Try to find books by or on two famous people who have the skill you are trying to build. Mother Teresa on compassion. Harry Truman on standing alone. Norman Schwarzkopf on leadership. Helen Keller on persistence. Try to see how they wove the skill you are working on into their fabric of skills. Was there a point in their lives when they weren't good at this skill? What was the turning point?

7. **Learn from a course.** Find the best course you have access to. It might be offered in your organization or, more likely,

it will be a public program. Find one that is taught by the author of a book or a series of articles on this need. Be sure to give it enough time. It usually takes three to five days to learn about any skill or competency. One- to two-day courses are usually not long enough. Find one where you learn the theory and have a lot of practice with the skill. Find one that videotapes if the skill lends itself to the lens. Take your detailed plan with you and take notes against your need. Don't just take notes following the course outline. For example, if you're attending a listening course and one of your needs statements is how to listen when people ramble, take notes against that specific statement; or if your need involves a task or project, write down action steps you can take immediately. Throw yourself into the course. No phone calls. Don't take any work with you. No sightseeing. Just do the course. Be the best student in the course and learn the most. Seldom will a course alone be sufficient to address a need. A course always has to be combined with the other remedies in this Universal Development Plan, especially stretching tasks, so you can perform against your need under pressure.

8. **Try some stretching tasks, but start small.** Seventy percent of skills development happens on the job. As you talk with others while building this skill, get them to brainstorm tasks and activities you can try. Write down five tasks you will commit to doing, tasks like: initiate three conversations, make peace with someone you've had problems with, write a business plan for your unit, negotiate a purchase, make a speech, find something to fix. You can try tasks off the job as well: teach someone to read, be a volunteer, join a study group, take up a new hobby—whatever will help you practice your need in a fairly low-risk way. After each task, write down the positive and negative aspects of your performance and note things you will try to do better or differently next time.

9. **Track your own progress.** You are going to need some extra motivation to get through this. You need to be able to reward yourself for progress you've made. Others may

not notice the subtle changes for a while. Set progress goals and benchmarks for yourself. If you were working on approachability, for instance, have a goal of initiating conversations with five new people a week. Keep a log. Make a chart. Celebrate incremental progress. Noting times you didn't interrupt others or made two strategy suggestions that people grabbed and discussed will reinforce your continued efforts.

10. **Get periodic feedback.** Get a group of people who haven't known you for long. They don't have a history of seeing you not do well in this skill over a long period of time. Get feedback from them a third of the way into your skill-building plan. Also, go back to the original group who helped you see and accept this need. Their ratings will lag behind the first group because they know your history in this skill. Use both groups to monitor your progress.

You know you are successful when you and a group of others who know you describe your behaviors in this skill area as matching the skills you outlined in your target at the beginning of this chapter.

Before you decide to rest on your laurels, it's better to select another need and continue the process. Go with the momentum.

Putting your plan to the test

Use the immutable laws of skill development to see how powerful your development plan is.

Once you have a plan constructed, put it to the test. Look at the eleven Laws of Development in Exercise 9.2 and see how your plan stacks up. Is there enough pressure or demand for it to work for you? What's your plan profile?

9

162 |

Exercise 9.2 Eleven laws of development

1. Variety beats repetition every time. People learn very little from repeating what they have already done. Similarly, they learn very little from a narrow circle of relationships. Multiple mentors or coaches are better than one. Different is better than the same.

   The same   **1**   **2**   **3**   **4**   **5**   **Very different**

2. Development is the world of the first time and the different. The varied and the adverse create a need to learn, and most learning occurs while we are in transition. Development is a demand pull—the experience demands that we learn to do something new or different, or we fear failure.

   Low stakes   **1**   **2**   **3**   **4**   **5**   **High stakes**

3. Development isn't away from work; development is work. Stretching jobs, real tasks, and first-time tasks set the stage for growth. People need to experience an optimum variety of job challenges. It's starting things and fixing things and forming strategies at an early point that eventually lead to skills growth.

   Make work   **1**   **2**   **3**   **4**   **5**   **Real work**

4. People feel there is a significant chance of failure. One of the truths of the human psyche is that we try hardest when there is between one-half and two-thirds chance of success. Moderately stretching goals motivate. Easy goals and too big a stretch don't.

   Safe   **1**   **2**   **3**   **4**   **5**   **At risk**

9

Exercise 9.2 Eleven laws of development–continued

5. What you do has to make an obvious, measurable difference. People don't learn much from situations they are caught in, that they didn't create, and where they couldn't influence the outcome. To learn to manage and lead, you have to manage and lead. The success or failure of something has to depend unambiguously on what you do.

    Indirect   1   2   3   4   5   Direct

6. There is a tremendous amount of pressure. Deadlines, people looking over your shoulder, travel, and an overwhelming workload show that when the stakes are highest is when we are also most motivated to learn.

    Relaxed   1   2   3   4   5   Stressful

7. Start small. The people who develop the most have had numerous small versions of what they faced later when the stakes were high. No one would have put them in the job if they had not already demonstrated they had the core skills.

    Large   1   2   3   4   5   Small

8. Without feedback and more feedback, people don't grow. Good people don't know; in fact, the most talented people also have a propensity not to ask for much feedback. They can't develop without an accurate portrait of who they are.

    No feedback   1   2   3   4   5   High feedback

9. Projects are the all-purpose developer of people. Multi-business or multi-functional projects are the safest and best mode for long-term development of many of the competencies.

    No projects   1   2   3   4   5   Many projects

Exercise 9.2 Eleven laws of development–continued

10. We love to overdo. It's the human condition. If more is good, a lot is great. Without feedback, our strengths may well tip over and become darkly hued. The key to this is heightened self-awareness, and the best tool to achieve this is private 360° feedback coupled with coaching, more 360°, and more coaching.

No 360°   **1   2   3   4   5**   **Repeated 360°**

11. Learning must be cemented. Unless people lock in what they have learned, not just what they have done, little long-term learning occurs. The feedback fades and the tasks are forgotten. Learning involves new strategies, seeing what works and what doesn't, and having a method for remembering. Without this, the learning isn't repeatable.

No methods   **1   2   3   4   5**   **Multiple**
to capture   **methods to**
learning   **capture learning**

What's your profile? 4s and 5s are great; 3s are OK; 1s and 2s require you to go back and tweak your plan.

Getting started

Assuming you're satisfied with your test profile (if not, choose again), the question becomes, how do you start?

Pick three things: a task (or job), a way to get further feedback (coach, buddy, etc.), and a new or different behavior to try. Capture what happened through the learning methods we previously discussed.

When you have completed any of the above, add one new task, feedback method, or to-do. Always have three needs on your developmental worksheet at any one time.

Either through the development planning process or the coaching process, you should have constructed some measures of success (see number 9 [Track your own progress] in the Universal Development Plan above). You alone, or with your boss or coach, will have to decide when enough is enough. You may only be trying to get to OK in an area or you may be angling to develop yourself for a promotion. Either case would dramatically affect the measures you choose.

Below are some general guidelines for when development has progressed enough on a need that you can put the need on a maintain basis and get on to a more pressing need.

How do you know when development is occurring (has occurred)?

You:

- Refer to the process as fixing "my need" and take ownership of the need.
- Are a motivated adult on a mission and show some passion about fixing the problem.
- Demonstrate a broad conceptual understanding of the need being worked on.
- Converse easily on the topic; your views are credible to more experienced people.
- Require less directive coaching and the coach's role is becoming more of a collegial one in this area.
- Deal with mistakes, unanticipated problems, and consequences of working on the need.
- Have repeatedly demonstrated the new skill across varied settings.
- Are working mostly on follow-through, checking, tidying up.
- Are looking actively for other needs to tackle.
- Are not asking nearly as many questions as before.
- Exude self-confidence in the area.

Observation

Workaround

During the first half of my career, I thought everybody needed to work on three things—that was the standard recommendation. Everyone had flat spots. In the early days, we were allowed to call them "weaknesses"; then, due to political correctness, "development opportunities." But everyone had some things they needed to work on, and based on the research of CCL and others, we know how to do that. That led to the ubiquitous 70:20:10. We were comfortable that we had the truth.

About midway through our careers, we began to interview and observe legacy leaders— truly outstanding leaders—which is one of the ways we found out two new truths of talent management and leadership development: the importance of self-awareness, and the prevalence of the workaround strategy.

We found two very interesting things. In the legacy leaders we worked with and interviewed and observed, they were more self-aware than their less-well-performing colleagues. What we found, to our surprise, was that after receiving confirming information through 360° and other information of their flat spots, they did not work on building those skills. They worked on working around those skills. We think they did this because they realized that they didn't have time to build skills they hadn't already built (up to around age 40) and that there was no need to.

In management and leadership roles, you are held accountable for outcomes—not that you do them yourself. So legacy managers and leaders are applying delegation skills to work around their flat spots.

I was presenting this information to a group of university presidents, and one of the presidents jumped up from the table and said, "You've just given me an insight. I want to introduce you to my weaknesses." He introduced two people sitting at his table. He said, "This is Joy. She has been with me at three colleges; I have brought her with me each time. She is my PR officer. I am not an articulate communicator, and I now

9

|

> realize that Joy is my workaround for that weakness." On his left he introduced us to Ralph, his CAO. "I am administratively challenged, and Ralph has also been with me at the last three colleges and universities. They are well paid and well taken care of because I realize I can't do the job of president of the university without them, and I am good at everything else I need to do my job well. If I had decided to become administratively agile and to become a good communicator, I would not have been here today."
>
> This is one of the best examples of this I have seen. Legacy leaders have people around them who are good at what they are not good at. And they give ample credit to those people for doing those things well.

Can you make it go faster?

A few months isn't realistic. One commonsense definition of a need is if you can become skilled in under six months, it's really not a broad-based need. Depending on the need, you might turn the corner on it in less than a year (Customer Focus), or it may take five to ten years (Strategic Agility, Creativity).

But you can turn the corner faster than ever before. Follow the developmental imperatives (a challenging task; a way to get before, during, and after feedback; and learning some new things to do) and learning will go as fast as it possibly can.

As you develop more quickly, you will undoubtedly have more opportunities come your way in the form of new job offers. In Chapter 10, we present our career ideas to help you make your decisions.

9

Chapter 10

Career planning: Managing your career for the long-term

By the way, what is your CFO account worth?

Let's test out some common career advice.

Many of our parents told us to go to college, learn a trade, get good at a specialty, join a big company with good benefits and stay until retirement with a good pension and lifelong health coverage. It sort of worked then, but doesn't so much now. The average executive works for five companies in a career, up from one or two 20 years ago.

Some of the current advice we read on careers isn't very compelling. One line of reasoning goes: find out what your strengths are, avoid your weaknesses (because they are hard to fix), and find a place where you fit. The problem with fit is that most of us fit best with people of similar personalities and interests. Studies show that personality/organization fit does not relate to success (salary increase and promotion).

Then there are the happiness missionaries and their cousins, the passion police. Find out what really makes you happy and comfortable and go find a place that fits your needs. Settle in. This is another pleasant-sounding argument with several holes in it. Personal motives change over time; happiness gets defined differently as we age and as we learn what are the real career opportunities. Want to take a chance you won't be downsized or whatever euphemism is used 10 years from now?

Here's the rub: we like to do what we're good at and comfortable with. The vast majority of us are nest-building, comfort-zone-seeking, return-to-the-middle, homeostatic, and habituated people. We tend to be more comfortable repeating. Even our bodies are designed to keep all of the needles (temperature, hormones, blood chemistry, etc.) centered in the green safe zone. In that sense, people are designed to find or build their physical and psychological comfort zone and fight to stay in it. That's probably why change is so scary and so unsettling. You love sales or California or France or the Internet or Java or building Web pages or being a stock broker. After you learn your trade and develop yourself a bit, you get less interested in further development and settle (or sink) into your niche. Your performance is still good, maybe just not quite as sharp. You get to where you can't imagine doing anything else. You are happy, fulfilled, and following your dream and passion and then...

...something changes. If you stay in the same role too long, you're blocking others, you're not growing, and you will not develop additional skills to any great degree. If you stay in the same company, you may get downsized during tough times. If you stay with the same skill set, it will get out of date. If you stay in the same geography, the area may deteriorate. Successful careers, as you'll recall, are a zigzag.

The first thing to get out of your mind is that you must follow your passion. It is well-meaning advice but the death knell for growth. Here we refer not to broad, technical passion (if you like cyberspace or salt mines, that's fine with us). Here we refer to the passion that makes us narrow—getting into a job type in a beloved area (supervising program designers or figuring out how to increase salt production) and staying there. Then you are violating the first law of development: variety beats repetition every time.

What if there were a law that you could only be happy, fulfilled, and follow your passion during one-third of your career? Either the first 15 years, the middle 15, or the last third. Which third would you pick?

10

Most of the advice to young people leads them to think they should pick the first third. Be happy now. Follow your dream and your passion from the get-go. The last two-thirds will take care of themselves.

We would suggest a different way to think about your total 45-year career. Assuming you are not going to invent something and sell it for millions of dollars before you are age 23, then you are like the rest of us. We have to work for 45 years.

What you should seek is maximizing your career freedom options (your CFO account). We would suggest that your happiness, fulfillment, and the extent to which you can follow your dream at any stage of your career is determined by your CFOs. The more you have, the happier you can be. The sooner you build up your CFO bank account, the sooner you can be happy and fulfilled a higher percentage of the time. Building CFOs is career enabling. Not building them is career chilling.

Here's how it works. A CFO is any time in your career where you can make a choice between jobs, companies, situations, geographies, or tasks because you have more than one skill or experience to sell. The more CFOs you have, the more things you will have to pick from and the happier you can be. For example, a person who speaks two languages has one more career freedom option than a person who speaks only one. Going forward, a person fluent in Spanish or Chinese has more language CFOs than a person fluent in French or German because more people use those languages in the world. A person who has lived and/or worked in two countries has one more CFO than a person who has been in one country. A person who has lived and worked in two countries speaking different languages has more CFOs than a person living in two countries, but speaking one language. A person who knows two programming languages has one more CFO than a person who knows only one. A person who has done both a start-up and a turnaround has more CFOs than a person who has only done one type of job. A person with a broader array of competencies has more CFOs than a person with a few. And so on.

10

The more CFOs you have in the bank, the more opportunities there are and the more choices you can make. The more choices you can make, the more likely it is that you can find and select the type of job, company, situation, industry, and geography that fits your current and future needs (passions, dreams, interests). The fewer CFOs you have, the more you will be at the whim of the economy, a bad boss, a changing industry, your health, or an aging skill.

We suggest you spend the first 15 years building up CFOs and putting them in your career bank. Then you can start spending them in the middle and last 15 years when salaries are higher, responsibilities are more challenging and interesting, and competition for the "good" jobs more intense. Or, simply, start spending them when you know more about yourself and how the world of work and opportunity works.

Or you can keep building CFOs all the way and have a wonderful endgame. Your choice. The more CFOs you have, the more confident you feel. The more confident you are, the better you will feel about what you do. Wouldn't you really rather have more control over your life?

We are all preparing for an unknown future. The half-life of job skills is decreasing. College degrees go out of date faster. It is said that engineering degrees last about four to five years. The half-life of companies is decreasing. We witnessed the failure rate of Internet start-ups within the first year.

Many more companies are struggling in the more competitive global market. The half-life of products is decreasing. Those people with large CFO accounts will be ready for whatever comes. They will be able to respond to opportunities. Those with impoverished accounts will have to do what's remaining or what's offered, most likely unhappily.

10

|

Observation

Conscious career planning

In the first issue of Fast Company, I got into trouble for saying that people shouldn't do what they want to do. Many times in life (particularly from parents), I have heard people say, you need to do what makes you happy. I personally don't think, based on 50 years of experience and looking at the research, that that is a very good career strategy. As in any other pursuit in life, you have to make investments before you can enjoy the fruits of your labor.

Because of the nature of my work and publications, I am frequently asked to work with the children of clients, executives, friends, and colleagues. The issue almost always comes down to the paradox of, should I do what I want to do and what makes me feel good and makes me happy, or should I do something that is not quite in the happy, makes-me-feel-good zone to improve my resume for the future.

During a recent fishing expedition, four people in their 60s were complaining about how hard it is to live in today's economic environment and how difficult life has become. All four had had difficult end-of-career experiences where they had been laid off or fired or experienced unplanned obsolescence. Because we had no place else to go since we were all out on a boat, I did a CFO (career freedom options) check. I asked them about their lives. What decisions had they made about their education? What had they done at various decision points in their lives? All four had chosen, at different points, things that made them happy and kept them in their comfort zone. They had all not invested in their careers. Each person had decided not to do something that would have been a stretch, a challenge, something out of their comfort zone—in retrospect, things that would have put them in a better position later in their careers. They didn't do scouting or make an attempt to be in student government because it wasn't cool; they didn't learn a second language because it was too hard. They didn't look for work that was career building. They looked for work that was convenient in their early days. They all made life convenient at the time. Decisions that, now, in the last third of their working careers, had made them unhappy, frustrated, mad at the system, blameful of others.

10

| 173

I am coaching two of their children. And they have passed on this same happiness-at-all-costs to the two children I am working with who are going to follow the same path. I'm happy to report that I have diverted one of the children onto the correct path. She had the choice of a comfortable summer—repeating a job she had done the previous summer, being with her friends, enjoying her parents' swimming pool—or going to China for six weeks on a humanitarian project. She chose China. She returned a new person— with a new perspective, with a new attitude about achieving in school, with plans to return to China next summer. I have seen case after case of kids making the current comfortable happiness decision and not basically building deposits in their career bank. What I would hope for people is if they make deposits in the first third of their careers, they can do what makes them happy in the next thirds of their careers. The conversations I do not look forward to anymore are people who are later in their careers who did not make career investments and now are beginning to understand and pay the price for not doing it. In most cases, it's too late.

Now that we are old, we can report on something too many of us don't know about until we're old, and then it's too late. We have seen the following sequence ad nauseam. Younger people say, "I don't want to...

- Move
- Change jobs
- Work in a foreign country
- Leave home
- Work for a big company
- Climb the corporate ladder
- Work for someone I don't like
- Work with people who are different
- Work on weekends
- Travel extensively
- Learn new skills

10

- Change functions
- Change companies
- Learn another language
- Do a different kind of job
- Play organizational politics

...right now."

All of the above build CFOs.

Then these same people in middle-to-late career, after they are passed over for promotions, laid off, slotted in dead-end jobs, can't find a job that pays enough, or can't find work in their preferred geography say, "I wish I had...

- Moved
- Changed jobs
- Worked in a foreign country
- Left home
- Worked for a big company
- Climbed the corporate ladder
- Worked for someone I didn't like
- Worked with more diverse people
- Worked on weekends
- Traveled extensively
- Learned new skills
- Changed functions
- Changed companies
- Learned another language
- Done a different kind of job
- Learned to play organizational politics

...when I had the chance."

10

The simple point is that younger people don't really know what they want to be doing later. They may know what feels good now. They may even think they know what climbing the corporate ladder means, but they usually don't. Another advantage of building up your CFO account is that with each CFO, you know more. Higher CFO people have a better likelihood of accurately knowing what they don't like before they make a career-limiting choice.

What you need to do is replace tactical happiness with strategic faith—faith that going into the unknown early actually makes sense for you and that there are wise people around you and in the organization who know this. Most successful executives recall how they were dragged kicking and screaming into jobs they didn't want, to countries in which they had no interest, into functions that they were not sure they could do well in, into strange side businesses that only became important a decade later, into situations they didn't want to face. Why? Because very few people leap up and ask to be thrown out of their comfort zone into something where they might fail.

Some years ago a colleague was running a workshop on learning to learn. In the room were 40 Human Resource professionals, all experts in helping others learn to do something new. Toward the end of one day, he announced that, just for fun, there would be a competition after hours—a track and field contest. He described the events, then had each person pick the event they would compete in. All 40 picked something they had done and were at least reasonably proficient at. No one picked something they had done once—the javelin, for example—or had never tried.

The objections to his metaphor began immediately: "You set us up. Of course we would pick something we know how to do. You said it was a competition. After all, we have to do it today."

"But there are no stakes," he countered. "This is just for fun. Why not learn something? The competition was to see who could learn to do something new. You ask the people you counsel to do this every day—go into the unknown."

10

Few bought his point, at least immediately, until he made an allied one. "Change makes us defensive. We pick defensive strategies so we can avoid embarrassment."

This is what you will have to fight against—you don't want to move to Kansas City, you don't want to work in a plant, you don't want to do sales, you don't want to fix or start up something. You just want to design software programs or manage salespeople.

Next, we repeat the developmental jobs we outlined in Chapter 5—the collective unknowns of development.

What are the most developmental jobs that add the most CFOs? (Listed alphabetically)

- Chair of projects/task forces – Leader of a group with an important and specific goal. One-time, short-term events usually lasting from a few weeks to a year. Much of the work in today's flatter, less hierarchical organizations can be classified as project work. Typical examples: implementing new ideas, product launches, systems development, acquisitions, joint ventures, one-time events like reorganizations.

- Change manager – Leader of a significant effort to change something or implement something of significance. Typical examples include: Total Work Systems like TQM, ISO, or Six Sigma; business restructurings; installing major systems and procedures for the first time; M&A integrations; responding to major competitor initiatives; extensive reorganizations; and long-term post-corporate scandal recovery.

- Crisis manager – Leader responsible for an unpredictable, unique crisis of significant proportion. Typical examples of crisis management would be: a product safety recall; product failure; unexpected death, termination, or scandal involving a CEO or senior corporate executive; trouble with a key customer or supplier; natural disasters; terrorist

10

attacks; kidnapping or arrest of employees; violent crime against employees.

- **Cross-moves** – Move to a very different set of challenges. Typical examples would be: changing divisions or functions, field/headquarters shifts, country switch, or changing lines of business.

- **Fix-Its/Turnarounds** – Cleaning up a mess where this is a last chance to fix it. Usually accompanied by serious people issues and morale problems. Typical examples: failed business/unit; disasters like mishandled labor negotiations, strikes, thefts, fraud, obsolete staff; restructuring; product liability events; system/process breakdowns.

- **Heavy strategic demands** – Requires new or significant strategic redirection; visible and watched by senior people. Typically part of a major job switch.

- **International assignments** – First time working in the country. Usually features new language, business rules, different cultural norms, and assigned for more than a year.

- **Line to staff switches** – Visible role in a staff function, often at headquarters. Typical examples: business/strategic planning role, heading a staff department, assistant to senior executive, head of a task force, Human Resources role.

- **Member of projects/task forces** – Member of a group with an important and specific goal. One-time, short-term events usually lasting from a few weeks to a year. Much of the work in today's flatter, less hierarchical organizations can be classified as project work. Typical examples: implementing new ideas, product launches, systems development, acquisitions, joint ventures, one-time events like reorganizations.

- **Scale (size shifts) assignments** – Jump in the size of a job in the same area for the person. Typically involves much more budget, volume of business, people, layers of the organization.

10

- **Scope (complexity) assignments –** Managing substantially more breadth. Typically involves new areas of business, increase in visibility, complexity. Typical scope jobs are: moving to a new organization, adding new products or functions or services, moving from staff to line, and numerous first-time jobs such as first-time manager, managing managers, executive, or team leader.

- **Significant people demands –** Involves a sizable increase in either the number of people managed or the complexity of the people-challenges faced. Typical examples are: going to a team-based management structure, changing to a quality format for work, and working with groups not worked with before.

- **Small entrepreneurial –** Founder or core team member of a company or brand. Typically, there is a personal financial stake in the business's success or failure. Typical examples include: being a small business owner, starting an incubator business or a new business line, launching a new brand or new product line.

- **Staff leadership (influencing without authority) –** Significant challenge where one has the responsibility but not the authority. Typical examples: planning project, installing new systems, troubleshooting systems problems, negotiating with outside parties, working in a staff group.

- **Staff to line shifts –** Moving to a job with an easily determined bottom line or results, managing bigger scope and/or scale, requires new skills/perspectives, unfamiliar aspects of the assignment.

- **Start-ups –** Starting something new for the organization. Typical examples are: building a team, creating new systems or facilities or products, heading something new, establishing a branch operation, and moving a successful program from one unit to another.

Each job requires somewhat different competencies—competencies you won't necessarily have. If you have done Start-Ups, you will probably wish to continue doing Start-Ups. A Fix-It/Turnaround or

10

a Line to Staff Switch will seem like anathema to you, but it's all really fear of embarrassment covering for the larger fear—that of failure.

This is the developmental rub. To make you feel at least a bit better, return to the events you listed in Exercise 5.1 – The Impact of Experience (see Chapter 5) and revisit them. They were the most developmental events in your life, the ones you selected above all others, yet you didn't know much about them going in. Most people will say, "I had 50 percent or less of the skills I needed." Yet you survived them. They made your short list, and why is that? Because you learned to do something different and became a higher CFO person in the process. You gained skills and CFOs that no one can ever take away from you. And you were scared, whether you admitted it or not. Only in retrospect do these events seem wonderful and freeing and career building. At the time, they were jolting.

Will your next job help your career?

Learning the new and different starts with fear. This is the true nature of growth. So take two deep breaths and use Exercise 10.1 to help you decide whether your next job is helpful for your career or will sink you deeper and deeper into running the same 400 meters you ran in high school. Does the job build your CFO account? Remember that it's the challenges in the job more than the technical content of the job that creates skill growth and builds CFOs.

10

Exercise 10.1 Jobs that build career freedom options (CFOs)

Answer "yes" or "no" to the following questions to determine whether a job will build career freedom options:

Part one

_____ Is there at least some element of trepidation in taking this job? Or am I scared (a little)?

_____ Am I missing significant skills that I will have to develop?

_____ Will my performance in this role make an obvious difference in the performance of the unit?

_____ Do I get the chance to be a big fish in a small pond?

_____ Will the role expose me to different types of people I have not worked with before?

_____ Do important people care what happens in this role?

_____ Is there something particularly adverse or contentious about this role?

_____ Is there a lot of variety in what I will have to do?

Part two

_____ Can I comfortably be successful?

_____ Do I have a strong track record doing this kind of job?

_____ Would I really like doing a job like this?

_____ Will I be working with many or most of the same people I now work with?

If many of your answers to Part one are yes (they build CFOs), and the answers to Part two are no (they don't build CFOs), take the job.

10

Many people are uncomfortable reading the above argument, and not because they are defensive. They don't want a promotion into a new area. They don't want to be CEO or an executive. They just want to be challenged and enjoy doing what they are doing. If this argument fits you, then the list in Exercise 10.1 isn't how you want to manage your career. You need a different list.

The Einstein question

If all of the above is true, then what about Albert Einstein? He was never even department head at Princeton. He didn't hold any patents. He wasn't rich. By these criteria, one of the great minds in history was a failure.

This is because Albert Einstein chose to be a deep professional. He wasn't interested in managing or leading large organizations. He was interested in depth in physics. And because he chose broadly, it happened that physics lasted his entire career. If instead he had specialized in buggy whips, we would be using someone else as an example.

Einstein was a pro—not interested in breadth, but depth—and there are many Einsteins out there. They may be motivated by newness, but it is newness in their chosen area. The area may be technical or functional, or it may be a certain type of challenge. They like to develop people or sell or fix broken businesses or are thrilled with working with a blank sheet of paper. It's what they do and all they want to do.

But they are taking a career risk. They are also giving up career options. If Albert all of a sudden wanted to make a lot of money, he would have been limited.

Which are you? Do you want to lead? Do you crave variety? Do you get bored easily and crave excitement? Or, do you like to delve deeper and deeper? Do you mostly like to be around others who share your interests? Do you like to work more independently than most? Consider the following questions in Exercise 10.2:

10

Exercise 10.2 High potential or high professional

I am seen more as someone who:

Likes to learn new functions/technologies.	or	Likes to be recognized as an expert.
Is strategic across areas.	or	Is strategic within an area.
Deals with politics as a matter of course.	or	Deals with politics reluctantly, if at all.
Has low tolerance for marginal people.	or	Is willing to lead marginal people by example or coaching.
Prefers to work with others.	or	Prefers to work more independently.
Prefers maximum diversity in others.	or	Prefers to be around those who share interests.
Is a poor developer of people.	or	Is good at developing others, either directly or by example.
Is creative and innovative.	or	Is steeped in expertise; may or may not be creative.
Is best under first-time conditions.	or	Is best under repeat conditions.
Is change driven.	or	Is product, technology, or relationship driven.

In Exercise 10.2, the list on the left refers to someone who is and should be a high potential—someone who is willing to take chances to grow and advance. The list on the right refers to someone who is and should be a high professional—someone who builds depth in a narrow area. Both are agile learners; neither is perfect. The former values variety and challenges more; the latter values depth of accomplishment in an area more.

Neither list may really fit you. You may be too inexperienced to know, or your career may not be an especially high priority for you. But for many of you, one of the lists fits you well.

If you are a high professional or a budding high professional, your development plans will be the same. Only your career goals will be different.

Say you are an employee relations (ER) person who is convinced you don't want to do anything else. You have zero desire to ever be a general anything. You don't want a line job. Your goal, then, is to become a subject-matter expert or leader in ER. To do this, ask yourself: What are the key challenges in the field of ER? What needs starting up, fixing? Where are the crises? What are the line-like elements and the staff-like elements, the political necessities, the projects that offer important perspective, the bodies of knowledge that are relevant, the team-building aspects, the labor relations hot spots, etc.? This is your world, and its leadership boundaries define your interests just as the physics of the universe bounded Einstein's.

You will need to ask some different questions about next jobs.

10

Exercise 10.3 Career-building jobs

Answer "yes" or "no" to the following questions to determine whether a job will build deep expertise in your profession:

_____ Is there at least some element of professional excitement in taking this job?

_____ Am I missing significant skills that I will get to develop?

_____ Will my performance in this role make an obvious difference in the performance of the unit?

_____ Will the role expose me to different types of people with expertise in my area?

_____ Will I get to pass on knowledge and skills, mentor or coach others somehow?

_____ Will this job further my mission and my vision?

_____ In two years, am I likely to be significantly more of an expert than I am now?

_____ Is there a missing piece of experience I will gain?

This brings our argument back to faith in others. In every organization we have ever dealt with, there are numerous wise people who truly understand how development works and have a nearly unerring sense of what good career moves look like. They can sense the future for both budding professionals and budding potentials. They are the ones who encourage young people to take dead-end-sounding jobs like building the Alaskan pipeline, or looking into this crazy idea called the Cloud. They understand what challenge and variety look like and know that straight-up promotions generally lead to narrowness.

10

These are the people you should listen to. Use the exercises for budding professionals and budding potentials to help you manage your career.

If you want to grow and be ready for all unknown challenges, build your CFOs.

If you don't know what you want to do, build your CFOs until you do.

If you know exactly what you want to do, build your CFOs in that specific area.

If you don't know what you don't know, build your CFOs to find out.

If you are just starting out, build CFOs.

CFOs will set you free. Free to be happier, more fulfilled, and able to follow your passions when you really know what they are.

By the way, what's your CFO account worth?

10

186 |

Part IV

Building talent
- a guide for
organizations

Chapter 11

A case for talent management

If most organizations are aware of the best practices,
why aren't they implementing them?

Ten years after *The Leadership Machine* was first published:

- We *still* have a gap in our bench strength.
- The war for talent hasn't subsided.
- Many organizations still don't get it.
- Those that did get it are reaping the benefits.

Almost 15 years ago, McKinsey & Company coined the term "the war for talent" to describe the forthcoming shortage of qualified labor. Research across industries, government agencies, and global regions all forecasted a similar, two-pronged assault on the qualified talent available to fill open jobs. First, there would be a mass exodus of Baby Boomers retiring from the workplace, leaving millions of jobs vacant. Second, the population replacing these Boomers would be only half as large and yet demand twice as much from their employers. Short in supply and tall in expectations, the cost for talent would be high. This gap between labor supply and demand was expected to worsen over the next two decades and companies would have to engage in war to fight over scarcer talent.

But that war for talent was never fought according to the widely predicted rules of engagement.

The U.S. economy slowed and eventually entered into a recession. Retirement funds shrank. Boomers didn't leave at the predicted rate because many could not afford to retire. Companies went lean and mean. They were not adding to payroll. Many roles that were vacated were not refilled. Unemployment saw its highest levels in the U.S. since the Great Depression. This, in turn, coincided with downward economic trends throughout the world. As a result, what materialized is a slightly different battle than the war for talent predicted.

Supply of labor was not the issue—quality of labor was—and still is. Today, the challenge is less about finding bodies to fill roles (a supply issue) and more about finding, developing, and retaining highly qualified talent that secures a competitive advantage. Sure, key talent was part of the original war, but today's talent issues are even more complex, more diversified, and more global.

The new talent challenge

We see at least five different talent challenges moving forward:

1. **The entry-level talent war.** There are not enough highly "skilled" people coming into the labor market to fill open jobs. Those that are available for work are not qualified for the jobs that are vacant. This is especially true in specialized fields like medical and technical professions. The need for qualified (more skilled than in the past) talent outstrips the supply. At one time, you had to make a decision whether to buy (select) or build (develop) your talent. Moving forward, that choice may already be made for you—companies will have to work with what they have because what they want is either not available or is out of reach. So the best strategy will be to buy the best you can find and build from there.

2. **The lack of qualified leadership in the U.S.** There is not enough talent on the bench to fill top management and senior jobs. This comes down to both a quantity and quality concern. Baby Boomers will eventually retire and

there are still only half as many Generation Xers to replace them. Those Gen Xers that wait in the wings do not all have the right skills or experiences. They must step into bigger, more complex, and more global roles faster—and with less experience—than their Boomer predecessors.

3. **The demand for global leadership.** You cannot simply assign or promote a talented domestic leader into a global role and expect him or her to be equally effective. Countless organizations make just this mistake, and do it repeatedly. Effectiveness in a global role as a leader demands different skills and a higher level of certain skills than those demanded of domestic leaders. The future need for qualified, global leaders greatly exceeds the supply.

4. **Your top talent is just waiting to jump ship.** Even in tough economic times, the top talent manages to find and keep a job. But that doesn't mean they are engaged and plan to stay with your company once the economy turns. From 2008 to 2010, 46 percent of organizations experienced decreased levels of employee engagement as opposed to the standard 15 percent in nonrecession times. Why? Because even the nonengaged will stay when they don't perceive there are a lot of alternatives. Once the economy improves and job alternatives are plentiful, organizations will experience increased turnover, especially of talented people.

5. **Talent in emerging markets wants more, and wants it faster.** Young, emerging talent, especially in developing regions in the world, are increasingly impatient to advance their careers. They readily jump to a new company when a bigger job is offered. And many are very mobile. Companies are no longer simply competing for talent within local pools—the talent pools themselves have become global.

Current state

Given the challenges faced, the current state of talent best practices in organizations should give us all heartburn.

We think most organizations know about best talent practices. There are countless books and articles and presentations everywhere you look. However, many, many more people know best practices than do best practices. There is a know-do gap. The evidence suggests that we are struggling to do what we know is best.

Observation | Knowing versus doing

After watching organizations struggle over the last 10 years trying to implement talent best practices, I have concluded that it is a do problem, not a know problem. Most, if not all, HR executives and the majority of C-suite officers know what the best practices are. They might even give the best practices lip service and include them in goose-bump speeches about leadership and talent management. On the other hand, actually implementing and doing best practices takes resources (time and money and staffing) and commitment. That's where the efforts falter. Over the past 10 years, evidence has accumulated on the ROI of best talent practices. Few disagree. Few contradict. You make more money by spending more money on talent management practices and processes. And you make more money than you spend. And it takes a few years starting from scratch to get best practices up and running before you see the payoff. That's probably the core of the problem. It is a longer-term payoff in a time of short-term focus. It also takes the courage to make tough calls on people. It requires creating categories of employees followed by differential treatment. It takes accepting that not all people are created equal from the standpoint of talent. Equal in many other ways, but not talent. People have different levels of talent to start with, and people develop at different speeds and in different ways. Some won't grow much at all and, for a few others, there is no boundary, given the right circumstances. So it is a short-term focus and the unwillingness to differentiate that's blocking process on talent best practices. It's not the science or the brain. It's the heart and the gut.

Consider that 40 percent of senior executives fail within the first 18 months and only 55 percent of new CEOs in the highest revenue-generating companies were filled with internal successors. These findings illustrate that leadership hiring and succession planning practices don't seem to be working very well.

Ten years later, are we better at developing leaders? *Nope.* Consider our current leaders. Among executives, the percent of respondents who said they have never:

- Had a position with P&L responsibility – 34 percent.
- Worked in an unfamiliar business unit – 40 percent.
- Made a cross-functional move – 42 percent.
- Had a leadership role in a start-up – 66 percent.

Ten years later, are we better at moving talent around the globe? *Not so much.*

Organizations lose repatriates after they return to their home country from an overseas assignment because the companies do not value the global experience gained and ignore input from these employees. Although the negative impact of loss to the organization may be felt if an employee leaves years after the return home, as many as 30 percent don't even make it through their first year.

Okay, but if our leaders and high potentials stay, then that means we've engaged them, right? Let's look at the research on high-potential employees:

- 1 in 4 of your high potentials plans to leave your company in the next 12 months, especially if the economy turns.
- 1 in 3 admits contributing less effort than is required to do the job effectively.
- 1 in 5 believes that his or her professional goals are not in alignment with those the organization has planned.

- 4 in 10 lack confidence in their coworkers and are even less optimistic about their senior leaders.

Oh, one more thing. Many of those strong performers that you labeled as "high potentials" are unlikely to become tomorrow's leaders. About 70 percent of high performers lack what is needed to be successful in future roles. Most of your high performers do not have the ability to move several levels higher in the organization and remain as successful.

If most organizations are aware of the best practices, why aren't they implementing them, knowing that best practices get measurable, demonstrated, and beneficial results?

a. Because most organizations are not convinced. They want more of the same evidence and more of the same data before they feel confident.

b. Because most organizations think they are unique and different and any number of best practices won't work for them. The organization is convinced they need to do it differently, their way, and build it from scratch.

c. Because it takes too much effort.

d. Because it requires courage.

Answer: All of the above.

There is pretty much common agreement among experts about best talent practices. We collectively know what they are. We know how to implement them. We know how to run them. But even the best systems won't work without courage, because what we advocate is measuring people and holding them accountable for performance and development. Systems can always be circumvented by the age-old practices of turkey trading, hoarding talent, special exceptions, and all the other sabotage tricks so widely practiced.

Making this all work is a case of:

- Blending the science and art of developing.
- Leveraging best practices.
- Executing with discipline.
- Demonstrating the courage to make tough calls.
- Holding people accountable.

In the remainder of this chapter, we will discuss the practices and systems that work—what they are, why you should follow them, and where courage is needed to make them work.

Best practices – The Leadership Machine design going forward

What do top companies do differently that improves their financial performance? Differential treatment. They know that treating people equally (the same) is outdated thinking. Treating people equitably (fairly) both drives results and is fair. Differential treatment of diversity leads to equality of opportunity and maximizing the contribution of all talent.

Whether you are attracting talent to the organization, keeping them engaged, or developing their potential, you have undoubtedly witnessed an unprecedented level of diversity of all kinds in the workplace. This diversity demands an individualized approach to enticing, motivating, growing, and keeping your talent. A one-size-fits-all approach is insufficient and ineffective. Consider these following eight best practice approaches to talent management:

11

1. Attracting talent

Organizations often have an employment brand, or employment value proposition (EVP). The more effective ones market or message different aspects of the EVP to various niches in the candidate pool. For instance, a consumer package goods company may market the EVP in slightly different ways to their employees at a manufacturing plant or distribution center than they do for those jobs at corporate. What drives people to select the same organization differs for these two groups of employees and what a career offers may differ as well.

Successful organizations create recruiting initiatives that target gender or ethnicity-specific professional organizations to reach specific candidate segments (like the Society of Women Engineers or the Association of Latino Professionals in Finance and Accounting, for starters).

Top companies visually feature minorities in corporate marketing and recruiting materials to increase attraction among minorities.

If you are targeting Millennials right out of college, you may want to prepare yourselves to market toward the "helicopter" parents and interact with them throughout the recruiting process.

The messaging alone is not enough. Best practice companies offer flexible, customizable benefits packages. This ensures that benefits are more likely to appeal to a broader range of candidates and meet the needs of the empty nester, the single parent, the college graduate, and everyone in between.

2. Assigning talent

Classify the jobs in your organization. Place your top players in the most strategic and impactful roles, and manage your average employees. Identify those roles that create critical experiences, shape key skills, or provide targeted exposure and reserve them for your high potentials. In other words, invest in groups of employees differentially. Don't leave blockers in strategic roles that prevent your high potentials from gaining the experiences they need to be effective in the long-term.

3. Competency models

Almost all organizations now have competency models. Defined competency models are used in approximately 53 percent of top organizations, and these organizations are 45 percent more likely to have models or profiles for critical roles.

Competency models create the foundation from which all talent practices are built upon and are used as a framework to align talent practices to organizational strategy.

Moreover, they are a verbal expression of the organization's culture. Competency models communicate what an organization stands for and what is expected of its employees.

A single, organization-wide competency model may need refinement to adequately capture requirements of a specific role. Job profiles can specify the combination of competencies needed to be effective in a job while using a common language across job families.

4. Engaging talent

Employees are motivated by different things in different ways and the key is tapping into that differential motivation. The same level of engagement that a single father finds from working split days might be achieved through a sabbatical for a married worker, or a shorter workweek for an employee that likes frequent, short travel. Other specific ideas for engagement include:

- Develop your leaders. We won't go into the how of it here, but both trust in senior leaders and relations with one's boss are key drivers of engagement.

- Create opportunities for individuals to make a difference. Give them a voice in a role that is part of a long-term career with your organization. Let them share what they want to do in the future and talk with them about the various paths to get there. Recognize and reward their accomplishments at each step along the way.

- Tailor messages about company strategy for high potentials to show how their development plans match the organizational strategy.

- Leverage your social networking to keep current employees and alumni in touch, and to benefit retirees who seem to use this outlet for applying to open jobs.

Observation | Engagement

We have lived through morale surveys, and then satisfaction surveys, and now, most currently, engagement surveys. There's been a substantive shift with engagement. In morale and satisfactions surveys, the assumption was that happy and satisfied people are more productive. That turns out not to be true. It is true that they stay longer and have fewer health problems. What has been captured by the more recent practice of engagement surveys is that engaged workers are, in fact, more productive. They stay longer and they have fewer health problems, though they may not be among the happiest of your employees.

The engagement concept centers on discretionary effort aligned with the mission of the organization. All employed individuals work and put in their eight hours. But few fully engage themselves in their job or role. The difference between an engaged and a less-engaged individual is the concept of discretionary effort—that is, do they bring their full skill set, passion, and enthusiasm to the job. An engaged individual goes above and beyond the average "full day's pay for a full day's work." It doesn't necessarily mean more hours, but it could. But what it really means is that they are fully dedicated to doing what they need to do to get things done.

We know there is a direct connection between leadership skills and style and employee engagement. Through the studies we and others have done, we know that leaders who produce engaged teams and employees are better listeners. They make deeper and more meaningful contacts with people. They look for ideas anywhere they can find them. They tend to not be elitist. They are accessible. They walk the talk—that is, they are good role models in what they expect in others. Engaged employees trust in their leadership and their vision. And they are other-centered more than self-centered.

We know from the research that engagement leads to increased productivity and increased retention. And that very specific leadership skills bring about increased engagement. Those skills are the ones we talk about in this book.

5. Compensation

You may not always get what you pay for, but you have to pay for what you get. Best practices dictate that you differentially recognize and compensate your high potentials. Top talent isn't cheap. Not differentiating talent well is very expensive.

6. Developing talent

Align your organization's development of its people with that of its business objectives. Determine what challenges will be faced in the future and identify where people can learn and practice skills in smaller but similar situations that evoke the same challenges.

Timing it right—create meaningful experiences at the right time (mentoring, feedback, etc.) and sequencing these experiences appropriately is important.

Talent must be developed at all levels, and organizations are looking for more effective ways to reach a wide range of learning styles and preferences. That's not exactly a news flash. Best practices in adult learning have been around for a long time. Many organizations are choosing to invest their resources in social networking to promote informal learning rather than in traditional classroom training programs. Others are pushing out just-in-time training through mobile devices (e-Learning) to increase speed of delivery, reduce costs, and keep people engaged.

The use of coaching is on the rise. We know that leaders do not learn as well in traditional classroom settings. Individualized feedback, custom approaches, and one-on-one time with a coach has documented positive results in the form of moderate to large skill and performance gains, as well as team performance, productivity, job satisfaction, and other business deliverables.

Regardless of the audience or media you use for learning, you must create a learning environment to see any transfer back to the organization, to the current job, or to future assignments. The use of mentorship, encouraged reflection, or thoughtful discussion of applications is quite effective.

The group graduating from college during the years of the recession struggled to find work. More graduates out of work means fewer people gained the skills and experience needed during those first few post-college years. This is an effect that will have long-lasting implications.

7. Managing performance

Successful companies embed performance management in their culture. Employees at all levels are held accountable and are fully engaged in an ongoing, continuous loop of performance feedback and improvement. That shouldn't be a surprise. But did you know that 81 percent of companies with executives that were highly engaged in the performance management process also had strong business results? Active and visible executive support drives real financial wins.

200 |

11

Are you tired of the criticism regarding your current performance management process? Very few organizations do it well. But, did you know that negative employee reactions result when managers focus more on the form and the process than the content of the review?

Employees don't react negatively merely because their performance is assessed. The process is broken because managers aren't comfortable delivering negative feedback. So they rarely (if ever) do it throughout the year. Instead, they save negative feedback for the end-of-the-year meeting where they try to hide behind the process, the form, and HR. It is in this formal review session where employees are caught off guard and surprised. If no one tells employees differently, they assume they are performing well. Remember, about 85 percent of us believe we are above average. If these employees are not told differently, an annual discussion where this feedback is shared and then blamed on outside factors is likely to have very negative effects.

8. Planning for talent succession

Organizations with mature talent management processes clearly and consistently differentiate performance and potential for advancement. Not all high performers are high potentials, and not all high professionals are high potentials. Best practice dictates different approaches for developing skills and creating the valuable experiences needed to further professional growth in employees of each category.

Excerpt

The talent challenge

In 2006, Avon Products, Inc. was 120 years old when it began the process of reinventing and turning around its business in order to build the foundation for future global growth. In addition to major restructuring, leaders took the opportunity to scrutinize existing talent management practices that were weak or counterproductive.

The Talent Challenge: After reviewing Avon's existing talent practices, the talent management group (TM) identified six overriding weaknesses that hurt their effectiveness. They found that existing talent practices were:

- *Opaque: Neither managers nor Associates knew how existing talent practices (that is, performance management, succession planning) worked or what they were intended to do. To the average employee, these processes were a black box.*

- *Egalitarian: While the Avon culture reinforced treating every Associate well, this behavior had morphed into treating every Associate in the same way. High performers weren't enjoying a fundamentally different work experience and low performers weren't being managed effectively.*

- *Complex: The performance management form was ten pages long, and the succession planning process required a full-time employee just to manage the data and assemble thick black binders of information for twice-yearly reviews. Complexity existed without commensurate value, and the effectiveness rate of the talent practices was low.*

- *Episodic: Employee surveys, talent reviews, development planning, and succession planning, when done at all, were done at a frequency determined by individual managers around the world.*

- *Emotional: Decisions on talent movement, promotions, and other key talent activities were often influenced as much by individual knowledge and emotion as by objective facts.*

- *Meaningless: No talent practice had "teeth." HR couldn't answer the most basic question a manager might ask about talent practices—"What will happen to me if I don't do this?"*

The Talent Turnaround: Over the initial turnaround period (twelve to eighteen months), Avon moved those talent processes from opaque to transparent, from egalitarian to differentiated, from complex to simple, from episodic to disciplined, from emotional to factual, and from meaningless to consequential, resulting in significant improvements in effectiveness.[†]

[†]From "Avon Products, Inc." Marc Effron in Marshall Goldsmith and Louis Carter (Eds.), Best Practices in Talent Management: How the World's Leading Corporations Manage, Develop, and Retain Top Talent. (2009). San Francisco, CA: Pfeiffer. Reprinted with permission of John Wiley & Sons, Inc.

Some return on investment (ROI) findings

"OK, let's say I do all of this, what can I expect in return? How can I measure whether all of this was worth it or not?" Great questions! Doing the things in this book will take time, resources, courage, and patience. It will bring about a lot of tension and conflict. And, for what, you ask? A lot of reward is our answer.

What's the business case for implementing talent best-practices?

Do top companies (based on 10-year total return to shareholders) manage talent differently than average- or low-performing companies? *Yes.*

Do top companies develop people differently? *Yes.*

Do talent practices make a difference? *Yes.*

Is this difference reflected in the bottom line? *Yes.*

In the 10 years since *The Leadership Machine* was released, numerous studies have quantified the benefit of following talent management best practices. The return on investment for organizations, teams, and individuals is compelling.

For organizations

- **Outcomes** – Let's start at the organization-wide level. Seven to ten years after you have put some or all of the best talent practices outlined in this book into effect, you would notice that goal achievement is better. Whatever your organization sees as important outcomes—like profit, cash flow, increased revenue, or even measures such as percentage of children passing achievement tests, lives saved, etc.—will improve in line with how many best practices you implement and how well they are done.

  There is a measurable and demonstrated relationship between company performance and talent management practices. Companies scoring in the top third on ratings of global dimensions of talent management earned more profit per employee than those in the bottom third.

  Companies that have exceptional talent management processes earn 15 percent more than their peers and have better stock performance and safety.

  Overall, the highest ROI for HR interventions includes (in descending order) performance management, training and development, and employee selection.

- **Engagement** – Since you would have better (more effective, more skilled, more prepared) managers and leaders than you did before, employees would report feeling better about the company, management, their bosses, and their jobs. Employees are engaged, committed, and place trust in their leaders.

Organizations with employees reporting high levels of trust outperformed organizations with employees reporting low levels of trust by nearly 3 to 1 in shareholder returns.

- **Retention** – Since bosses would, on average, be better managers and leaders, unwanted turnover would decrease. The research on retention shows that the top two causes of unwanted turnover are a poor relationship between the boss and the employee, and lack of opportunity to grow and develop. Top companies measure it: 94 percent of top companies participating in a recent study reported tracking retention of critical employees as a measure of leadership success.

  What can help?

  - Some recent studies have found that talent interventions have a positive effect on turnover.

  - The use of coaching among new hires reduced turnover in their first year and resulted in a 251 percent ROI.

  - Among a group of mid-level administrators in a public university, teamwork impacted engagement and had an indirect effect on intention to leave.

- **Recruiting** – Since your leadership brand on the street would proportionately improve, you would spend less time and money per head recruiting and get better people coming in. Your rank order among the firms you compete with as the preferred place to work would increase. That would also increase the flow of good candidates at less cost per head.

- **Commitment** – High levels of commitment to the organization are associated with improvements in turnover, customer experience, financial performance, and stakeholder value.

- **Safety** – After assessing the cost of safety incidents for committed and non-committed employees, Molson Coors was able to save $1.7 million in costs simply by improving the level of engagement in its employees.

- **Unnecessary distractions** – Since your managers and leaders would be on average more skilled, there would be less noise in the employment relationship. Fewer complaints. Less arbitration. Less litigation.

- **Fill time** – Open position time would decrease. Since the bench at all levels would be fuller, there would be quicker fill time for critical and key open positions. Positions would be filled faster and with better people.

- **Change management** – It would be easier for the organization to change. Since the average learning agility of talented people would be proportionately higher, collectively it would be easier to change directions. The organization would be less restricted by its past.

- **Innovation** – It would be easier for the organization to innovate. Since the average learning agility of talented people would be proportionately higher, collectively it would be easier to experiment, try new things, learn from others outside the organization, and easier to implement new, unique, and different ways of doing things.

- **Learning organization** – Because more talented managers and leaders would have proportionately higher learning agility, the entire organization would get better at being a self-renewing organization.

  After reviewing 18 organizational leadership development and change initiatives, companies received a return of 2 1/2 times their average approximately $500,000 investment.

- **International expansion** – Because managers' and leaders' knowledge and perspectives would be greatly increased due to broadening job experiences, the organization would be able to learn faster how to be effective in new countries and markets.

- **People development** – The organization would do a proportionately better job of developing all its people because the average skill level of managers and leaders would be higher on developing others, and they would have personally benefited by enhanced development. They, in turn, would return the favor. One common characteristic of legacy leaders is that they develop others better.

Pluzdrak (2007) reviewed changes in competency ratings before and after a leadership development program and found that improvements on key leadership competencies were positively related to important business outcomes like profits, turnover, and net. Being better at certain competencies can make as much difference as a million dollars per manager in increased sales and reduced turnover.

Help your managers learn how to coach and develop others. Data from 50,000 raters in 140 diverse organizations indicate that for managers, Developing Direct Reports and Others is the lowest-rated competency out of the 67 competencies.

For teams

- **Outcomes** – Seven to ten years after you have put the practices outlined in this book into effect, you would notice an increase in the rate at which the goals of the business units/functions/teams have been achieved has gone up proportionately to the number of practices you implement.

- **Team functioning** – Since the average quality of the managers and leaders would have increased, the quality of team functioning would go up proportionately. There would be more trust and cooperation, less noise and conflict, and better team-to-team and cross-boundary collaboration.

- **Team learning** – Since team members and team leaders would be better at learning agility, the learning capabilities of teams would go up as they learn faster.

For individuals

- **Outcomes** – Each person who is touched by the practices outlined in this book would proportionately increase in skills and perspectives. They would be better skilled at doing today's job and better prepared to take on tomorrow's challenges. They would feel more satisfied with themselves and better about the organization. They, in turn, would encourage others to join the organization.

Conclusion: invest in the future

The good news is that most of the above will happen if you do what this book outlines.

The bad news might be that if you do what this book outlines and reap all of the benefits listed in this chapter, your less-competent competitors and others will also raid you at a much higher rate. One dark measure of whether this is all working is whether others want to take your high-potential people. That means that as you get better, special treatment and retention planning is critical.

The best news is that your organization will be self-renewing, so they'll never catch you with this tactic. Many new organizations buy experience by hiring coaches and bringing in seasoned high professionals to bring young people along more quickly. This is a good thing—as long as it isn't used as a substitute for experience and as long as it plays its proper role as a piece of development.

Your competitors can't catch up because their Leadership Machine doesn't work as well. They may raid you for a few key people, but you have a developed bench they don't have. They may buy a few hundred years worth of learning from experience from your organization, but they can't afford the thousands or millions you have in your leadership bank account. With The Leadership Machine in place, you control your future.

Best talent practices pay.

Chapter 12

Competency modeling: setting a success target

A competency model will drive everything from selection and development to succession and performance.

You're sitting in your office frustrated or excited after reading the first 11 chapters. You know that, in many ways, we are talking about your organization—you're a bit spotty on selection, struggling on development, making a pass at succession planning, your systems creak. You're wondering where to start.

Start with a target—a competency model, a success profile. Why? Because the model will drive everything from selection and development to succession and performance. Without it, everything else will soon be unfocused and mosaic. You must know where you are going or...

What are your model building options?

In order of value from least to most, they are:

1. Executive declaration

There are a few cases where the CEO declares his or her model of leadership. They specify the values and competencies they believe are needed to win. It would be a rare CEO who doesn't have an opinion but, with due respect, it would be a very rare CEO who knows enough of the science to be close to right. The most right in our experience has been Jack Welch of GE, *Fortune's* manager of the century, who set the model for GE. Other models we have seen are underwhelming. In general, they are about one-half right. The good news is that the top manager believes in, endorses, and enforces the model. The bad news is that the models are generally full of competencies in high supply, such as Action Oriented, *Drive for* Results, and Integrity and Trust. They also usually lack any subtlety or texture. Remember that almost 20 percent of CEOs of the top 200 firms were replaced during the first 10 months of 2000. Also remember that the model might need to pass the legal test of being connected to actual results. Some lawyer is going to ask you where the model came from.

2. Values-driven models

Quite in favor currently. Someone or some group sets out the values the organization wants to practice. The competencies, policies, and practices are derived from the values model. If the values are aligned with the business necessities to win, then this process might work. But the values are almost always the same, organization to organization. They go something like this:

- We want to be the investment of choice for those investing in our industry or sector. We value shareholders. We want to be number one or a strong number two.
- We want to be the employer of choice for the talent we need to win. We value our people.
- We want to be the product or service of choice for the customer. We value our customers.
- We want to be a good citizen in the localities in which we operate. We value our communities.
- We want to be environmentally friendly. We value the environment.
- We promote team spirit in our organization.

All very good things. However, they are too general. And since everyone has about the same set of values, the resulting models look the same. If the models are the same, it will be hard for any one competitor to make progress over another. This is similar to every company in a sector having the same strategy and tactical plan. Then the only difference would be executional excellence.

3. External normative modeling

The third option would be to copy the model from an organization in the marketplace that is already what your organization aspires to be. If you want to be a fast and market-agile competitor who will be the first to market with new products and services across the globe, find a group of organizations that are like that now. Find out what their operating models are and copy them. Some vendors and some academic researchers offer this information. They benchmark or study target firms, deduce their operating models, and sell or publish the results.

There are also countless books written about single leaders. You could combine the traits and competencies of acknowledged leaders and use that model. For example, Neff and Citrin studied 50 consensus leaders and used another sample of 30 to test the model.

They concluded that collectively those leaders shared six skill sets:

1. Live with integrity and lead by example.
2. Develop a winning strategy.
3. Build a great management team.
4. Inspire employees to greatness.
5. Create responsive organizations.
6. Use the management systems to reinforce the values.

Good stuff. Hardly anything new. But confirming. There are countless books and articles like this through the years that study pools of great corporate, political, military, and humanitarian leaders.

Again, is this really aligned with your mission and will it be specific enough? Recall that in Chapters 2 and 3, we pointed out that most leader cluster studies describe very few leaders in the sample. Using these cluster studies may leave you chasing a phantom leader.

4. Internal modeling

We discussed this in Chapter 1. We find that reinventing the periodic table of the management and executive leadership elements is a waste of time and money. There are at least a dozen professionally done models that will serve as an excellent jumping-off place.

Some internal models use a start-from-scratch method where a number of successful people (and a comparison group of the less successful) are interviewed about critical incidents. Professionals then analyze and categorize what critical competencies define excellence. (There is also a weak, sister version of this technique where top management is simply asked what they think leads to success.) While the method itself is usually well done, the models produced necessarily have to look the same. Only the examples are different, as competencies are competencies.

Although the critical-incidents method is an established technique with 50 years of research and practice to back it up, it is quite expensive and time consuming. It can't really work unless you are number one or a strong competitor in your sector. Otherwise, this is akin to interviewing a last-place athletic team about what they think it takes to win a championship.

Such models also simply detail the present and near future. A dramatic business change would create a need for a brand-new, never-before-seen model, according to this way of thinking. While this is great for consulting firms, it's silly from a science point of view. While environments change, the competencies it takes to cope with them stay the same. Different ones matter at different times, but they all come from the same realm—that of human behavior at work.

Two of our clients independently collected more than 100 internally developed competency profiles from other organizations and determined from thorough content analysis that they were about 80 percent common and that all the concepts were contained in the commercial models. Hay-McBer found that jobs across 286 studies contained only 2 to 20 percent unique competencies.

Some firms acknowledge this and have reference models to cover other scenarios. When they do this, it's a tacit admission that the competencies are already known.

So why do we keep doing this? We are told that we do it because it eases implementation. The argument goes that by using participative and consensus techniques, the executives and the managers would buy into the model, making it easier to implement. "It has to be theirs to work," we are told. If this technique develops partial models (doesn't take into account all the competencies) or similar models (and many are very, very similar), then how could they be competitive-edge models? Is it worth all the time and resources to get buy-in on something that already exists? And if this is the main technique that has been used over the last 20 years, and it is, then why are we in the shape we are today? Why are so many CEOs failing? Why are we short on the leadership bench? Why do the majority of start-ups fail in the first 18 months? Why do only a few people really develop into leaders?

Although internal modeling is a much better practice than any of the preceding ones, it can be unnecessary and is certainly costly.

A better approach followed by some firms is to interview or assess against a standard set of competencies to see which ones differentiate superior from average performers. This is an excellent approach and is quite defensible legally. The drawback is that it's expensive.

Story

Reinventing the wheel

A multibillion-dollar pharmaceutical company wanted to focus on career planning and retention. They hired consultants to help. The company was claiming that functional professionals were leaving the organization in droves. After their high pros reached a vertical peak in their career, they could not advance any higher without taking a leadership role outside the function. To help create the perception of movement across departments within the function, it was important to display alternative career paths. But first, it was necessary to assess the degree of similarity required in skills and skill levels across roles.

They felt sure that job analyses and a customized competency model would solve their need. This required hours of interviews with dozens of subject-matter experts, hours of focus groups, and surveys sent to entire functions. Not to mention the review time and consensus building and wordsmithing!

In the end, they paid for an overly complex competency model. Stakeholders supported it, but the competencies were unusable. Managers couldn't make heads or tails of the competencies to help with development or performance. After investing more than half a million dollars, it was shelved when a new leader took over the function.

12

5. Alignment modeling

The best way to form your model is aligning the competencies to the specific mission, strategy, and goals of the organization. The more specific, the better. It is best to start with a research-based model that has definitions, support tools, development resources, etc., and determine which ones align with your strategy. That should get you 85 percent of the way there. You may have to wordsmith a few competencies to exactly fit your situation, combine others, and label a few with different titles. The rest of this chapter tells you how to do it.

12

Creating your model

Once you have selected a model or a competency library from which to develop your model, you will have a list of competencies—roughly 20 to 70 characteristics that have something to do with success at work. All the models measure the same thing under the hood. The only difference is chunking size. The models toward the low end put competency packets together to form larger competency statements. The models toward the high end keep packets more separate. And, of course, each model has different names for the same skills. You might also have a list of what causes failure (the career stallers and stoppers). Three well-known models have some form of derailers. In general, the more competencies, the better the model for development. The fewer, the better for selection.

How many competencies?

The popular notion today is to form a set of core competencies (usually 10 or fewer) that guides the entire organization toward success. That set of core competencies is used for recruiting, staffing, performance appraisal, and development. The reason given for 10 or fewer is that top management wants to focus on the critical few and that you can't really do a good job focusing on too many things.

| 215

Although we, too, like as few competencies as possible, the dream doesn't align with reality. For sizable organizations, there isn't a single set of competencies that would be reflective of performance across levels, business units, and business situations. The American Compensation Association did a survey of what was on these lists of core competencies. They found the following nine most used competencies:

1. Character/Integrity/Ethics
2. Communication Skills
3. Customer Focus
4. Functional/Technical Skills
5. Innovation
6. Leadership
7. Managing People
8. Results Orientation
9. Teamwork

Many of these core competencies are actually competency clusters, like leadership and managing people. These are higher-order concepts that are too general for selection and staffing and nearly useless for development. Would these collectively differentiate you from your best competitor? Five are in high supply and some don't differentiate much of anything (ethics, for example). Do most people at the management and executive level already have five of these? If yes, then why take up space on a list that is limited to 10 or fewer?

216 |

Excerpt

Competency success profiles

Although competency success profiles are created to be unique to a specific context, the uniqueness comes primarily from the particular combination of competencies, not from the competencies that comprise the profile. There are a number of commercially available, research-based leadership competency models available on the market. Because the good ones are based on research, they have a lot in common and they are able to describe the majority of skills and attributes that determine success for most contexts. Except for specific functional-technical skills, it rarely makes sense to develop homegrown competencies. Utilizing a research-based, commercially available competency set will save time and money, and will also provide normative data related to skill levels, supply in the workforce, and developmental difficulty. Several vendors have a variety of tools based on their competency set: 360° assessment instruments, interview guides, and developmental materials.[†]

[†]*From "Fundamentals of Competency Modeling." K. E. Ruyle and J. E. Orr in L. A. Berger and D. R. Berger (Eds.), The Talent Management Handbook (2nd ed.). (2011). New York, NY: McGraw-Hill. Reprinted with permission of McGraw-Hill.*

12

Five kinds of competencies

Another problem organizations have with the single-list approach is that a core competency list is not powerful enough to drive a winning strategy for the top of the house. If the list is a competitive-edge profile, it doesn't apply lower down in the organization.

As we argued in Chapter 2, there are five sets of competencies necessary to drive organizational success:

- There is a set of core competencies common to managing businesses, people, and change. That set of core competencies applies across levels.

- There is a second set of competencies that we would label the competitive-edge profile. These are the competencies that must ordinarily be developed because few people are naturally good at them. Almost all of these are related to performance and potential across levels as well. These are the ones that can really make the difference between you and your competitors.

- The third set, much smaller, are those that are fairly unique across levels.

- Fourth are competencies common to superior performers.

- Finally, there are the special competencies of functions, business units, and business situations. While they are all more the same than different, their differences matter. A business unit that is in a start-up phase will have a different profile than one that's in a turnaround stage. Marketing will have a different profile than manufacturing, and so on.

To say that you have a competency-driven system aligned with organizational success, you would have to have core competencies, competitive-edge competencies, level-driven competencies, competencies common to superior performers, and then a 15 percent adjustment for functions, business units, and business situations. Again, if you have selected a commercial model with a broad library of competencies, the same model can do all of the above. The advantage is that everyone is using the same library, albeit never the whole library. Sometimes you will need 5 competencies, sometimes 10, and sometimes 50.

Making your model work

Taking the model off the shelf and putting it into the hands of employees should be your goal. But for employees to adopt and embrace a competency model, it needs to be relevant and useful to them. Let's explore some key things to consider as you develop and implement your model.

Strategy

Tying competencies to your organizational strategy is a matter of knowing what challenges you face in the next two to five years. Start with challenges and business situations, not mission/vision/values or competency statements. This is because real challenges and jobs determine the competencies that must be emphasized. Are you in a start-up mode? Retrenchment? Rapid expansion? A lot of new projects?

12

Exercise 12.1 The 12 key challenge sources

This is a list of 12 key challenge sources we use that seems to work. For each, we have added a common example or two. Have a group of talented managers list the specific challenges related to each of these:

1. Aging of top management – average age of top 50 people.

2. Alliances and partnerships – international partners.

3. Business proposition – starting new businesses; low-cost producer, etc.

4. Competitor activity – mergers in your industry; foreign firms.

5. Customer trends and demographics – population aging; wants quick and simple.

6. Culture – diversity management.

7. Government trends – common currency; change retirement age; health care costs.

8. Labor market – war for specialized talent; unemployment.

9. Organization culture – hard to change; unionized.

10. Current and new markets – regions around the world.

11. Regulatory – environmental standards; right-to-work laws.

12. Resource supply – supply of raw materials.

Knowing how your strategy plays out in challenges is imperative. Is there a lot of negotiation, team building, cajoling, crisis management? Whatever is demanded is what you must model against. This notion is sometimes called results-based leadership since its focus is what competencies will drive the results you are trying to achieve.

12

To get to a list of competencies from the challenges, use common sense and science. You don't need a scientific study to figure out that Negotiation, *Building Effective* Teams, Interpersonal Savvy, and Command Skills would be critical for a typical start-up situation. You do need science to flesh out your model, however. What are the key skills that good team builders have? What about crisis managers? There are several studies that shed light on those questions, and you should use them as a benchmark to further refine a profile. Some models also come with various profiles attached to them for specific business propositions and strategic scenarios.

A number of model vendors have tools that help translate strategy and challenges into competencies. They have already aligned the major types of business propositions and key challenges to the competency model. So if you know the strategy and the key challenges, the mapping tools will guide you to the competencies.

Two cautions:

1. If you are going to emphasize 10 "new" competitive-edge competencies, you need to look for the skills in a textured way. Otherwise, you will fall into the trap of looking for people who don't exist. Good team builders are rarely high in Command Skills. A profile against your strategy and key challenges is a jumping-off place. Use it to model multiple jobs.

2. If you are going to emphasize 10 "new" competencies, you will have to de-emphasize others. Organizations abound with people who are results- and action-oriented but poor team builders and conflict managers. If your performance and compensation systems continue to reward the old behaviors, you won't get as much of the new behaviors.

Business units and major locations

Repeat the above procedures with each business unit or major location. After you have done all of the business units, you can see if there is a set of core competencies by looking across business units for commonality. Take it from us, there will be.

Jobs

Detail all key jobs in terms of competencies, either by working through job families or going job by job. This isn't as hard as it sounds. Most jobs have already been reviewed for compensation and performance purposes. To tailor your model to specific jobs or families:

1. Convene a panel of six or more experts—current successful incumbents, past incumbents, bosses, and job experts (two levels up from the job, job designers, senior HR).

2. Have them spend 30 minutes recording the major challenges the job faces now and in the foreseeable future (one to three years is common). Why? Because skills have more meaning if they're tied to work objectives and demands. Simply stating what skills are required to do a job introduces some biases: (a) pet theories of leadership/management, and (b) socially desirable skills like ethics and values. The outcome of this step should be a series of critical challenges/demands. You should not include any skills at this point. For example, don't say conflict resolution is important. Instead, list the major conflict situations (problems with unions, employees, customers, etc.).

3. Have each expert select no more than one-third of the skills in the model or competency library as critical to meeting these demands. Why? Because you can't measure or select for everything. Many skills would be nice and may even be important but, here, you are after the critical few.

4. Tally the list and initially accept any skills with a two-thirds majority vote.

5. Have each member suggest a skill that is not among the top skills. Discussion should focus on the challenge list and how this adds high value.

6. After discussion, the competency list tends to grow too large. One way to pare the list is by summarizing competencies into themes and selecting the most representative competency for that theme. This can be done with the factor structure of most models. In our experience, themes such as factors and clusters are useful for interviewing but may not be detailed enough for performance measurement.

7. To pare further, decide which competencies spell the difference between superior and average performance on the job. To be included in the superior list, competencies should meet these criteria:

   • The group should be able to name people who failed or performed poorly because they didn't have this competency at a high enough level.

   • The job should be a major test of the competency. This should either be the first time the competency comes into play or the demand for this competency must increase dramatically. An example of a first-time competency: below a certain level, people don't meaningfully participate in strategy in most organizations. An example of a quantum leap in demand: all jobs require some composure, but a job with heavy negotiations, customer service, or turnaround requirements demands much more.

8. This process results in two lists: price-of-admission skills to help set the candidate pool, and the critical skills this job demands.

9. Price-of-admission skills often dominate success profiles: Action Oriented, Integrity and Trust, Perseverance, and the like. As we showed earlier, these are in high supply already and muddy the waters in profiling. They set the baseline (without them, a person wouldn't be in the running for the job), but they don't spell the difference in performance

once you get there. Move them where they belong—to a knockout list.

10. Critical skills separate the average from the excellent, and they often seem odd. Consider this list:

- Approachability
- Presentation Skills
- Political Savvy
- Team Oriented

Do the above competencies describe a sales job in a team-organized business (teams of professionals who work with large clients)? Project manager who runs interference? Research job?

While the research job seems the least likely, it happens to be the answer in this case. In this firm, when the panel looked at people who hadn't succeeded, four reasons stood out. They liked to work alone, spoke in research jargon, didn't stay in the information loop, and committed faux pas with clients. People did not fail because they were not smart enough or lacked technical proficiency (this firm, like many, recruited high GPA students from respected universities).

Jobs are often not what they appear to be. While you still might think that the other two examples (sales job and project manager) are equally if not more likely, they in fact aren't. Both of these jobs are much more likely to attract people who already have these skills to begin with. The number of gregarious managers is far greater than the number of gregarious researchers.

Put another way, if the competencies are in high supply, then they cannot be critical differentiators of performance. They may describe it partly (price-of-admission skills), but if everyone has them, they can't be the difference between the superior and average or failed incumbents. And it is excellence we are after, not a raft of OK performers. Recall that excellent performers outperform the average by 40 to 100 percent or more.

Let's look at one other example. One of us sat through an expert-panel session for a beginning auditor job. The panel read through the job description (largely technical proficiencies), then one senior auditor asked, "Have we ever had an auditor who lacked any of these?" Silence.

"Then what use is this description?" he said. "Wouldn't we be better off just setting cutoffs for hiring from universities *X* and *Y*? To be interviewed, you have to be at a certain level of demonstrated skill."

The panel essentially agreed with this, which led to a lively discussion of what competencies made the difference and why. (They followed the procedure above.) Interestingly, most of the stories centered on auditors who didn't or did know what to do when they found an irregularity. "Bad auditors make people feel stupid. They don't fix the problem. People feel dirty, and we're not talking about anything unethical here." On the other hand, "Good auditors take an educational role. They explain, they don't judge, and aren't seen as executioners. A good auditor is like the best teacher you ever had. The one who told you the truth and made you feel stronger for knowing it."

The panel eventually decided there were only two critical differentiator skills: Interpersonal Savvy and Problem Solving.

Jobs seen this way look different.

How many competencies does such a method produce? While 4 to 6 would be sufficient for most jobs (just those that make a real difference), we usually see 10 to 15. This is because job profiles serve multiple purposes: they are used for description, selection, performance assessment, and to set interview dimensions. A typical profile ends up with a few price-of-admission skills, a technical skill or two, an aspect of the strategy that management wants emphasized (*Managing* Vision and Purpose, for example), and some competencies particular to a level as well as the critical differentiator skills.

224 |

Another way to model jobs

For those firms with more of an empirical bent, select a sample of high performers and average/low performers. Have people who know them well assess them on your competency model. This can be done through 360° assessment, an assessment center, or by a few trained raters.

Relate the results to organizational measures. (There are various statistical methods of relating competencies to performance or potential.) These are often performance ratings, stock options, bonuses, sales, profit indicators, turnover, and various potential measures.

The result will indicate what the key differences are between the superior and the average—the critical differentiators.

There are some problems with this approach. Numbers don't tell the whole tale. Many firms don't see this as sufficient. You may not get to Interpersonal Savvy for auditors this way. Discussion among experts is probably a better method for bringing out certain competencies, while empirical methods ensure that you don't miss anything.

Additionally, this method works best with jobs or families of jobs for which there are a large number of incumbents. Particularly with upper-level jobs, there are too few to model empirically.

Levels

See Chapter 2 and Appendix B for information on the competencies most correlated with performance at different levels.

Performance assessment

There are many cynical statements about performance assessment. Only 5 percent of people were below average in one of our studies. Everyone is good, so why bother? It can't be used for any true purpose. There's not enough money to differentiate performance, certainly not based on these sky-high ratings.

Rather than repeat the litany of failures in this area, we'll talk about practices that do work. There are three: Put everyone on the same metric. Focus on short-term performance and short-term competency development. Think about the future.

12

1. **Put everyone on the same metric.** If the job model actually makes sense—meaning that it has critical skills in it and these skills are communicated—it becomes hard to argue with performance in the job. Objectify as much as possible. It won't stop the complaining, but defending the model becomes easier.

2. **Focus performance on short-term performance and short-term competency development.** A common solution is to have a one-page performance appraisal. The front side of the page contains key result areas of the job, weighted to total 100 percent. These are often negotiated between boss and job incumbent. The back side of the page contains the critical competencies it takes to get those results, again weighted.

   People who are in a position to judge the incumbent's performance should complete the assessment. This list should be agreed to in advance. The boss serves as the arbiter and tiebreaker. There are many ways to do it, but we prefer the following: the boss rates separately and presents an average of what the other respondents said. Written comments are allowed, but no raters are identified. Performance ratings are dramatically inflated anyway. If raters are identified, they go even higher.

   For both sides of the page, focus on the most important variables with the highest ratings and the most important variables with the lowest ratings. The result will be what the person does best and what needs improvement.

The boss may have a different perspective than raters, but that is useful information. Recall that raters view different behaviors as important and don't always see eye-to-eye. What is admirable perseverance to the boss may be irritating to peers. The goal is intelligent discussion, not some mythical agreement.

Both the high and low ratings can be leveraged. For the high, how can the person build on this strength and deploy it in other areas? For the low, what can be done for immediate or short-term improvement? Returning to putting everyone on the same metric, in this system, everyone has highs and lows. They are relative to the only person that matters—the person doing the job. Any improvement, regardless of how the person compares with others, must necessarily start with that person's strengths and weaknesses.

For example, perhaps the person can serve as a coach or model for negotiations. Others can shadow him. For the developmental need (peers are irritated), what are three things the person can do immediately? He could explain better to peers why he is doing what he is doing. He could find something to trade or provide to peers to help the relationship. He could listen to their complaints and edit his behavior.

There are different points of view around how to tie this to compensation. Fifty percent for each side of the page? Fifty percent for results, 25 percent for competencies, 25 percent for demonstrated improvement on a low-competency or low-result area? Either of these can work with a well-developed model. In addition, some companies scrub the ratings (have a panel or bosses once-removed review them), or have a forced distribution from best to worst performers to differentiate for compensation purposes. More on that later, but for our purposes here, we focus on how to make the system meaningful for performance and development.

12

This approach puts together performance and development, and we are well aware that many people oppose this. We believe the two questions are inevitably tied together. How can a person sit through a performance appraisal that is other than vanilla and not immediately wonder, "What can I do?"

One of the reasons the state of development is so sorry is precisely this artificial splitting of performance and how to derive better performance through development. A common beef through the years has been, "My developmental goals seem to have little to do with my job or what I face each day." Well, no wonder. They've all too often been separated. While one is quite stressful (an imperfect appraisal), the other is safe, confidential, and often sort of "so what?"

Development is quite stressful; it is the furthest thing from safety and comfort. Short-term development that works must be placed where it has the greatest chance of success—directly affecting performance.

3. **Think about the future.** We spent most of Chapter 2 demonstrating that no one is developing much. The time to build skills for the future is by thinking a level up or next job up. What is most likely for this person? If he or she has plateaued, what would help him or her develop in the current job? The research says this person should be good at a maximum variety of projects and tasks. If he or she is a candidate for the next level, skills should be developed via project assignments or whatever is appropriate for those competencies. If he or she is on a specialist track, what is needed is high-professional development, as we talked about in Chapter 10. If he or she is in the bottom 10 to 20 percent, it's time for a final chance and then move the person on.

Hiring

Volumes are devoted to this topic. We are well aware that biodata and structured interviewing and certain test batteries can augment the hiring process. But this book is about development, not selection. As such, we will focus our argument on hiring with development in mind.

Looking for top talent is a losing strategy. The way we defined it in Chapter 6, there is only 5 percent to go around, and firms with big purses and new e-commerce start-ups snap up most of it.

It's time to get past the "grades in school" myth. Throughout our careers, the most enduring myth of all is that grades in school predict managerial success.

Us: *"Grades in school don't predict success as a manager. What's the GPA in this room?"*

Executives: *"Times have changed. Maybe GPA didn't matter before, but it does now."*

Us: *"What's the GPA in this room?"*

Answer after tallying: 2.8. (Many of these folks went to college before grade inflation; it's higher in firms with younger executives.)

Us: *"Even if it were true that times have changed, if everyone has a 3.5, then grades can't predict much. They are a price-of-admission skill, like showing up on time."*

Executives: *"Are you telling us to hire a 2.2 student? That grades don't matter?"*

Us: *"We're telling you grades matter for technical performance. Period. They are generally related zero to management success."*

Think about it. How much of your success is due to your grades in school? Would they be as important as your interpersonal skills or your perseverance or your business savvy or how you hold together in a crisis?

Generally, grades in school have little or nothing to do with managerial performance unless the job is highly intellectual in nature. Then intelligence would be a better predictor. The management job is one that calls for many attributes—interpersonal skills, drive, and tolerance for ambiguity—so no single variable will mean much. Grades have been much studied and generally have not predicted much other than intelligence and inner work standards. They indicate some degree of technical proficiency, some intelligence, and some amount of drive to complete work. That's about all.

It's the argument of who makes the best basketball coach or sales manager all over again. "Grades" indicate technical proficiency, and this is all they are intended to signal. The idea that they have more than the slightest relationship to managing anything won't stand up to examination.

The ranking of the college attended may not predict managerial performance either. Although recruiting profiles continue to feature it, there is only mixed evidence that it predicts anything beyond performance in the early years of employment.

It is much, much more the characteristics one brings to the job and what one learns than the college one attended or one's grades.

Are we arguing that grades don't matter? No. We are arguing that 3.5s and arbitrary cutoffs don't matter. While a few company internal studies have related grades to later success, generally it is just not so. The potential talent pool is far larger than most firms think it is.

Excerpt

Grades and managerial performance

"The overall results suggest that past research and past practices may have been aiming at the wrong college characteristics. Most researchers focused on college grades, and most results were disappointing. In fact, it has generally been difficult to demonstrate that grades in school are related to behaviors of importance other than doing well on aptitude tests.

It cannot be said that grades are unrelated to management performance, only that they are related to very specific components of management performance, namely, intellectual ability and inner work standards. Attempting to use grades to predict other managerial qualities, such as interpersonal skills, is misguided..."[†]

[†]From College Experiences and Managerial Performance. A. Howard. (1986). Journal of Applied Psychology Monograph.

12

So, what are we saying?

Bet on learners. Take a deep breath and hire some 3.0 students who are high in nonacademic learning. Expand your talent search beyond the so-called first-tier schools. Some companies recruit at different schools and consider this a competitive edge. Even when conducting confidential research for these companies, none would tell us what schools they looked at, only why. Through various special programs, these schools encouraged learning from experience. Their students were broader in many ways.

We have discussed learning agility extensively in Chapter 6 and elsewhere. Reviewing a few findings: A learning measure did better than IQ in predicting performance. Twice as many AT&T low-assessed people got to third-level management than did the high-assessed if their developmental opportunities were significantly better.

If there is a silver bullet, it's learning acumen (and, of course, intelligence)—not grades or the college attended.

To hire more learners, change how you interview. Sample interviewing questions:

- Tell me about three incidents in which you had trouble getting along with people. What did you learn from each? Did you change anything from one to the next? What do you think might be repeatable from these experiences?

- I see that you coached children's soccer. What were the biggest challenges in doing this, and what did you learn?

- You mention three marketing projects in your resume. What did you learn from number one that you used in number two, etc., and what do you think is common to all these projects?

The notion of learning interviews is not new, and many large companies use them in one fashion or another. We have licensed many companies to use our learning interview materials, and some, like GE, used such interviews before we began to work with the concept. Learning interviews sound difficult, but are not. Companies train line managers and tailor interviews to each job if need be, since any question can be turned into a learning question.

The difference is that learning interviews focus on conclusions we draw from having examined our experience. They tap into some facts about learners: they have more learnings, are more interested in learning from success, and have more rules of thumb, more repeatables, and fewer absolutes. They simply have better punctuation marks for their existence.

Typical remarks from companies are:

- *We hire more women and minorities.* Learning interviews focus on what a person gains from common experiences, not the experiences a person has had due to luck or social class or being male

- *Up to one-third of interviewees can't answer the questions at all.* Our hypothesis on this is, although they probably could have answered easily when they were kids, they are out of practice after fixating on right answers in school. Pure idea generation and invention drop dramatically after children start school.

- *Learners are more candid.* They are more willing to admit mistakes unequivocally and not cover them up with strengths described as weaknesses statements: "Yes, I failed at this project. My standards were too high for my coworkers, but I have to admit I was too pushy with them." Oh, gee, who wouldn't want to hire someone who is guilty of high standards?

12

- *We use fewer competencies; it's fairly obvious who can answer the questions and who can't.*

- *We're less interested in right answers, so the interviewees can't give socially desirable responses as easily.* Except for technical questions, we're less interested in what they respond and more interested in how they respond. Did they have many learnings? Have they thought a lot about their experiences? Was it interesting to listen to? Are they comfortable with not being perfect? Do they construct rules of thumb or at least have fairly specific learnings?

- *Once we hire more learners, we have to re-do our orientation programs.* They are more aggressive in their learning and require more variety.

- *Learners are much more successful from the beginning of their careers.* One company reported that at the end of its orientation program, young professionals had to be requested by a unit. There was no automatic job guarantee. The first time all trainees were requested was after the company switched to learning interviews.

- *Headhunters using learning interviews have reported up to a 95 percent success rate (successfully employed five years later) with learning interviews.* An internal interviewer made it to retirement with no failures after adopting the concept.

As we argued earlier, this is only a short-term strategy. Long-term, everyone will do this in some fashion. They may call it interviewing for emotional intelligence or street smarts, but the concepts are close enough in meaning that the "natural" learners will be snapped up each year by the firms with sophisticated hiring practices and deep pockets. There is only 1 percent to go around. (Top 10 percent of intelligence times the top 10 percent of learners equals 1 percent, as the two variables are not related.)

Or is there? Since learning skills can be developed for most of us, why not take the top 50 percent of learners who are also in the top 25 percent of GPA. Twelve and one-half percent is a much larger pool to work with and will be necessary anyway as the hiring age demographics shrink. Further, why not work with the people you have now. Even if you hire from the top 10 percent in intelligence (college graduates, typically), if you haven't assessed for learning acumen, you probably have 5 percent at random.

Finally, regardless of your hiring practices, developing the people you have is essential anyway. Later, we will talk about developing learning from the organizational point of view.

How many competencies do we need?

- For development – use all the competencies in the competency library
- For strategy – 20 to 30
- For job profiling – 10 to 15
- For hiring – 5 to 7

The courage to make it work

If you have a good model, you have accountability with it. People become accountable for delivering on a strategy, assessing people fairly, knowing what matters for job success, and hiring people able to push the organization forward. Opposition to this takes many forms, all of them understandable:

- *You can't describe people as a bunch of competencies—people are individuals.* Yes, but in this job, we want just these competencies, not their souls. People who don't have them can't do well. Then we don't do well, and the ramifications are enormous.

- *I've been doing this umpteen years; I know what superior performance looks like.* Fine, put it to the test. Compare the manager's model with a research-derived one. Have people rated using the models and see which one differentiates.

  We have to add that the evidence to support managerial assertion is nonexistent. In one study, the majority of factors managers named were related negatively to performance.

- *I'm going to interview my way.* Unstructured interviews are far and away the worst selection method. They have little or no relationship with performance, relying instead on chemistry and pet theories of success.

And now the more serious, darker objections:

- *These are my people. I'm going to determine what success is. I have my own model.* Ah, control and power. Here is where the real battle lies. Rational argument may not help any more than it has helped on the grades-in-school myth. The argument goes, of course, that they are not your people at all, they are their own people; but if they *are* anyone else's, they are the firm's—to develop, to pay, and to attempt to deploy to jobs where they can contribute. If your firm allows idiosyncratic models, you are only reinventing the wheel. Allowing this is the death knell to any human resource system. Remember the Romans—they were completely tolerant of religion (belief) and totally intolerant of language (competencies). They held this together for a thousand years.

- *This is all subjective.* Support for models usually holds together until the first person gets fired, and then the wildfire spreads—unfair, didn't have a chance to improve, etc.

12

Which brings us around to who performs this courage act. The answer is top management, the only ones who can signal a sea change and have any hope of having the clout to pull this off. Someone has to say, "We do our best to make the system objective, but unfortunately, sometimes we hire people who don't make the grade. When someone doesn't produce and doesn't improve, it's not fair to them to keep them on. They can't possibly enjoy not being successful, and it's arrogant on our part to believe they couldn't be successful doing something else. It's not fair to you for them not to carry their share of the load and, in so doing, get paid more than they are worth. This means you get paid less than your worth by definition. I think we are just afraid to step up to the plate. It's painful to give bad news, and none of us should enjoy it. But it has to be done."

Someone has to say, "We are not going to waste company resources by having a different competency model for every job, every function, and do-what-you-want interviewing practices. Just as we have one accounting system and one procurement system, we have to have one people system. Otherwise, we are simply medieval fiefdoms pretending to be a country."

Someone has to say, "Your job model is your job model. It's not negotiable. This is what we have determined, as rigorously as we could, to be the critical success factors. We will stick to it until we find evidence that the success factors have changed. In the meantime, each of you will have the opportunity to meet this model through assessment and development. If you don't want to do this, you can try to find another job within our firm that matches your skills. But I must tell you in all candor, that this will be a short-term fix. We can't afford to keep people who have limited skills and experience with little potential to grow. How can we deal with massive change with a workforce that isn't learning new skills?"

Courage begins the only place it can, with those in a position to do something about it. But courage only works when line managers step up as well—in performance reviews, in day-to-day standard-setting. To do this, they not only have to believe in the change, but all systems have to be aligned around accountability as well.

Accountability starts with candor. The discussion and arguments that need to happen for anything to change begin with discussing the heretofore undiscussables. We'll return to this notion of "discussing the undiscussables," pioneered by Chris Argyris, when we deal with organizational learning.

12

Chapter 13

Preventing derailment:
A priority for organizations

Stopping the talent waste must be an organizational priority.

In Chapter 4, we listed 12 well-meaning practices that derail more people than they help. When a critical mass of talented people derail or quit, the organization inevitably goes into a spiral from which it may not recover. Look at a Fortune 500 list from 1970. Many of those firms don't exist today as independent entities. While hardly the only reason why formerly robust organizations swoon, we've never heard of a case where companies with the best hiring and best development practices fail. Indeed, the typical arguments made by John Kotter, Tom Peters, the Center for Creative Leadership (CCL), Jay Conger, and many others point to such practices. Organizations with continuous talent continuously win.

From a systems viewpoint, derailment of previously well-thought-of people is the result of narrowness of development. There is too much emphasis on straight-up promotion and an absence of developmental strategies that develop the skills listed in Chapter 2. As you'll recall, most people are not good at these, and as they progress, what they don't have becomes critically important. It's not surprising that the list of derailment factors presented in Chapter 4 looks a lot like the skills most managers and executives don't have in Chapter 2.

Excerpt

Derailment

Strengths often carry a shadow side—a corollary weakness. A leader can be humming along through multiple jobs and assignments and find a point at which the strengths he or she was relying on for success no longer contribute to success. In fact, the strengths may become a liability and possibly contribute to derailment.

A strength's shift from asset to liability can happen as a leader is promoted to bigger jobs or as the context of the assignment changes—such as the global assignment in this example:

A highly regarded United States executive came to Asia in a senior position dealing with many cultures. He was very well qualified and very conscientious; he was very focused on getting the job done and had no hidden agendas. It sounds ideal. His focus should have been a strength, but he was too focused on getting the job done and had an acute lack of cultural sensitivity. To adjust to a different mode, you have to lay down your biases and hear. He couldn't do it. He was very effective in getting his message across, and on the surface he seemed to be getting respect. But the issues around his insensitivity got back to the home office. He failed miserably, was shipped back to the U.S., and has since left the company.[†]

This executive had been successful in one context, but something did not translate after the transition. Without taking stock of the leadership skills required in different contexts, competencies that were assets can flip to the negative, as in this example in which Drive for Results began as an asset but led to insensitive treatment of other people. When the executive's insensitivity affected results and he did not adjust, he was unable to recover from it.

Knowing that the skills required for success change depending on the job, the level, and the context can help leaders recognize the need for adaptability and self-awareness.

[†]From Developing Global Executives: The Lessons of International Experience. Morgan W. McCall Jr. and George P. Hollenbeck. (2002). Boston, MA: Harvard Business School Press. Reprinted with permission of Harvard Business School Publishing Corporation.

13

Prevent derailment by planning ahead

It's important that development on much-needed skills for the future not be delayed until the night before they are needed. To prevent derailment, you must plan ahead.

We present the 12 well-intentioned dark side practices again. Take a minute to reflect on the dream versus the reality.

The dream	The reality
1. We assign our best and highest-potential people to our best-performing units.	1. Promotes a narrow background; hard for a person to make a difference in the performance of the unit.
2. We promote almost entirely from within.	2. Being promoted into the boss's job or similar jobs is more of the same.
3. We promote broadness through job rotation.	3. "If it's Tuesday, it must be accounting" style programs have run off countless young people. They need real jobs.
4. We focus on real work. People stay in the core.	4. Cross-functional projects are the all-purpose developer.
5. We don't punish people for mistakes.	5. Airlifting people out of mistakes or failing to give feedback encourages learning nothing other than blame and denial.
6. We develop people fast.	6. People don't finish jobs and don't learn any deep problem-solving skills.

Continued

The dream	The reality
7. We ensure development through real-time performance feedback.	7. "What you did" feedback is half the story at best; "how you did it" can't be ignored.
8. We mentor the best with the best.	8. These people move too fast to develop others; high potentials rarely mentor or coach.
9. We develop experts.	9. If people rise through a silo, they'll never see the rest of the farm.
10. We reward performance with promotion.	10. The careers of successful people are zigzags; they are not straight up the line.
11. We develop collegial spirit among our high potentials.	11. Promotes arrogance and feeling anointed.
12. We accentuate the positive (build on strengths).	12. Feedback on strengths may do more harm than good. It leads to overdoing those strengths.

Many of these we have covered earlier. Here we will elaborate on a few of the 12, and summarize the others:

1. **Assignments.** People will develop best when you think variety. People do, in fact, need to be assigned to the best-performing units but also the worst, the start-ups, strategic assignments, and multifunctional projects. We'll discuss this in detail later. Overdoing any kind of assignment practice, no matter how much intuitive sense it makes, leads to

narrowness and subsequent stumbling when a person reaches a critical-breakpoint assignment.

2. **Promoting from within.** Excessive promoting from within generally leads to hiring senior leaders from the outside. Although this isn't always true, it typically happens because companies don't develop their people much; they simply promote the narrow achievers. As people rise, they get more narrow but more irreplaceable in their function or business unit as their expertise and experience deepen. The better they get, the more they serve to block others. When they plateau, retire, or get hired away, there are seldom good replacements for them. In support of that line of reasoning, a University of Michigan study found that the most profitable mix across businesses was 80 percent inside and 20 percent outside. Eighty percent for continuity and keeping promises to employees; 20 percent for freshness and unblocking paths.

3. **Job rotation.** In 1990, a major drug company told us how they hired 70 MBAs and sent them through a carefully designed two-year program to teach them all parts of the business. The name of this effort was "Fast-Tracking Young General Managers." No one ever completed this program; all left the company. In 2000, we heard exactly the same tale again, this time from a bank.

   Development is real work, and managers can't be developed through shallow make-work rotation programs. Knowing about the business and running businesses are two related but separate matters. Exposure assignments are usually a bust. They do more harm than good.

   By job rotation, we do not mean functional or business switches in real jobs. We mean assignments typically intended to teach new people all about the business in a short period of time. These are often cross-functional, but are sometimes within a single function.

   Many companies do not have such programs anymore because of the war for talent and the flattening of organizational structure, so you may wonder why we pause

| 243

to criticize a practice that, while common, is hardly universal. Our reason is that it exemplifies the core misconception in much of what is called "on-the-job" development.

A few years ago, we went to a Fortune 100 firm which hired only the best and brightest engineers and immediately put them in a two-year engineering rotation program. Two- or three-month stints in various aspects of the firm's technologies were common.

The complaints from managers who had to manage them were many:

- They're not that interested.
- They're not that helpful.
- They are just in the way.
- It takes up too much of my time.
- Some people start looking around for other projects to do. They meddle.
- We have a problem with turnover. Some of the better ones leave.

"Tell us about the assignments they work on," we said. Without going into detail that might compromise the identity of the company, the assignments were nothing to stir the heart of ambitious people with one or more engineering degrees. They were pieces of partial projects supervised by others in which the trainee was really a technical gofer.

After listening for a while, we handed them the Developmental Heat exercise (see Chapter 5, Exercise 5.2) and asked them to rate the assignments they had just outlined. Their average ratings are shown in Example 13.1.

Example 13.1 Developmental Heat: average ratings from engineers in a two-year engineering rotation program

Developmental Heat: rate each of the following on a five-point scale.

1 = Little challenge when compared to other jobs
2 = Some challenge
3 = Like other jobs
4 = More challenging than other jobs
5 = Much more challenging than other jobs

1. __2__ Success or failure are both possible and would be obvious to myself and others. I think I could fail or not perform well at this job.

2. __1__ Requires take-charge, aggressive, individual leadership.

3. __4__ Involves working with new people, a lot of people, or people with different skills.

4. __3__ High personal pressure (deadlines, high stakes, large shift in scope or scale, travel, long hours, work is viewed as critical).

5. __3__ Requires influencing people, activities, and factors over which I have no control (supervisors besides boss, lateral relations, partners, peers, outside parties, political situations, customers).

6. __1__ Involves high variety of tasks; doing something very different from what I've done in the past (line/staff switch, promotion to headquarters, changing functions or lines of business/technology).

7. __3__ Is closely watched and monitored by people whose opinions count.

8. __1__ Requires building a team or something from scratch, or fixing/turning around an operation in trouble (downsizing, restructuring, new product line, new business, establishing a new operation, poor-performing unit, major staffing issues, inheriting a failing unit).

9. __2__ Involves a tremendous intellectual/strategic/problem-solving challenge with little or no history for guidance.

10. __2__ Involves interacting with a significant boss (whether supportive or not, the boss's view is critical to success in this job).

11. __1__ Am missing something important (lack of management support, limited resources, not aligned with strategy or core of the business, poor legacy, missing key skills or technical knowledge, lack of credentials/credibility).

Adapted from Eighty-Eight Assignments for Development in Place: Enhancing the Developmental Challenge of Existing Jobs by Michael M. Lombardo and Robert W. Eichinger. © 1989 Center for Creative Leadership. Used by permission.

13

Twenty-three out of 55 points for the average assignment! The group quickly and easily restructured the assignments so that each assignment had a minimum of 35 (and preferably 40) points of developmental impact. They put people in charge of task assignments or teamed them on larger projects, gave everyone "succeed or fail" leadership opportunities, had high professionals available to instruct and oversee, combined smaller assignments, and upped the stakes by having teams report out to senior engineering teams who graded them on their solutions. This work restructuring, of course, cost nothing.

In this case, the company goal was clear—deep technical development of top-tier engineers. The problem is that you don't develop Albert Einsteins with itty-bitty assignments where it's hard to see the importance or how it fits in. If deep technical development is the goal, then doing an actual job in all its variety is what develops people. Augmenting this with coursework makes obvious sense as well.

If the goal is understanding the various functions (understanding engineering rather than being an engineer), then a project on a real business issue is the best vehicle. Assigning six to twelve young people with different backgrounds to a pressing issue can be powerful: there are high professionals around to teach and make sure nothing goes wrong; young people learn how the parts of the business relate; they add value with their fresh ideas and their backgrounds as well. GE is well known for doing this, and both John Kotter's studies and the CCL studies had the same finding. In the CCL studies, projects were the major source of learning technical/functional, as well as all about the business lessons. Job rotations were rarely cited. Why do projects work? Because the assignment is big and pressing, and people care about the outcome. Young people need the knowledge right now in order to contribute to a solution.

Another method that works is treating a rotation as a course. Say you have 20 young professionals, all of whom need to understand how the core technology of the business operates in order to do their jobs better. Then rotating people as a group of students makes sense. The classes are taught by the experts, there are tests, and the goal is technical understanding, not doing.

Simply put:

- If you want people to be experts, then they must do the jobs in all their completeness and variety. Dollops of learning don't work.

- If you want people to understand the areas, then projects and no-nonsense courses are best.

We have no opinion on whether people should rotate functions, businesses, or anything else. Development is development, but in an organization, the question is development *for what*? What must people understand to be effective in a function? In a business line? As a GM? What sort of background and experience is necessary in the top positions?

We know of companies that never rotate people across functions. They develop people thoroughly within functions and use projects and stints at corporate to gain broader understanding. We know of others who feel just as strongly that a person must have a job where he or she can contribute in multiple core functions or core businesses. The answer to this depends on the business proposition, not on the rules of development.

4. **Projects.** Projects are an organization's best shot at developing people and preventing derailment. A diet of jobs with no projects makes for narrowness. Even if a company decides to rotate people across functions or business lines, projects are critical in helping them develop so that once they are there, they can contribute.

Projects/Task forces

One-time, short-term events usually lasting from a few weeks to a year. Much of the work in today's flatter, less hierarchical organizations can be classified as project work. Typical examples: implementing new ideas, product launches, systems development, acquisitions, joint ventures, one-time events like reorganizations.

13

5. **Treatment of mistakes.** There are two errors made with mistakes: one is punishing people; the other is letting them off the hook through poor or namby-pamby feedback or simply airlifting them into another assignment.

    Successful executives and managers report more learning from mistakes and failures than do derailed managers. A likely reason for this is that successful people probably make more mistakes. In creativity studies, there's an interesting finding that points out why this may be. Eminent people conceive more inferior works as well as more superior works. Successful people have a lot of ideas, some of which are bad. They also have more chances to get it right and more chances to learn from what worked and what didn't.

    One of the unsettling things about working with derailers is that some of them will tell you they haven't made any mistakes or haven't made the same mistake twice.

    In a way this is true; it's unlikely they've been told much about their mistakes. If they have changed jobs often enough, their mistakes may not have caught up with them for quite a while. We have heard many managers justify this by saying that it's dangerous to come down too hard on people. They may get demoralized and quit. Yes, it's better to say nothing and wait for them to get fired.

    The typical derailer pattern is to have trouble admitting mistakes, shunt them off, be defensive, and look for others to blame. This not only leads to arrogance, it leads to blindsiding others because they are not warned of consequences.

Even if the person eventually realizes his or her mistakes, without intervention, two reactions are common—avoiding similar situations and trying to repeat the same behavior, only more diligently and harder. Neither is a learning strategy. Learning involves understanding the pattern of behavior that led to the mistake and adding new behaviors. It may or may not involve subtracting any.

Sometimes it's not what the person did, it's what he or she didn't do.

This needn't happen. Mistakes are like any other developmental opportunity. The person must understand the mistake (get timely and direct feedback), publicly acknowledge or take personal responsibility (willingness to grow), learn something new so that the mistake will not be repeated (development), and then move on. Dwelling on past mistakes invites caution in the future.

6. **Developing people fast.** Development doesn't respond well to business cycles or rapid change in the marketplace. In fact, it doesn't care one way or the other how fast organizations would like it to occur. The only way to develop people faster is to follow the principles we began outlining in Chapter 7. The only way to tell when people have developed is when their mistakes have caught up with them and they have fixed them. This is where deep problem solving takes place—when the person truly comes to understand the nuances of a job. It is true that almost any organization can speed up development compared with what they are doing now. But development goes as fast as development goes. There are no fast-track solutions.

"But our jobs need to be mastered in a year. That's the nature of our business." That may be, but no one is probably mastering them in that case. In any event, need for maximum speed calls for maximum development. Simply moving people in calendar time or according to the latest fad in some magazine or some primitive belief that "if I don't get promoted every year, my career will die" leads to derailment. Courage, salespersonship, and development are the answers.

7. **Performance feedback.** Without "how you did it" feedback, "what you did and what you accomplished" feedback alone sets people up for derailment.

8. **Mentor the best with the best.** Mentor the best with high professionals. They make the best mentors. Use multiple mentors rather than looking for one who is a star at everything. At best, there is a tiny percentage of those, and they are moving even faster than the mentees. Encourage learning from many.

9. **Develop the expertise of our people.** By all means, but avoid silo development (except for pure high professionals). The all-purpose derailer of talented people is the straight-up-the-line promotion until they hit the infamous T (terminal) job (multi-function, multi-business, multi-something they know nothing about). If you must operate this way for business reasons, then projects and more projects are your insurance policy against developing narrow, highly-likely-to-fail T managers.

10. **Reward performance with promotion.** Think promotion for what and into what. The careers of successful people are zigzags because of the variety of challenges they faced, not because zigzagging is inherently good. The best job for a successful young person is rarely the boss's job. Far preferred would be an overseas assignment, an important project, a job featuring new technical content, a job in a start-up, a turnaround, or a job featuring high strategic or team-building demands. None of these are necessarily promotions. Variety and adversity teach.

11. **We develop collegial spirit among our high potentials.** While on the surface this seems hard to argue with, anointing people early isn't a good idea. When young people are singled out, given special treatment through courses and visits with VIPs and the like, the confident, aggressive, independent syndrome can set in long before there are any real accomplishments to buttress it. Common sense indicates it takes five years or more to figure out who your high potentials are. Anointing at hire or in the first two years

can't be based on a track record of what matters most—performance under first-time conditions for that person. High potential lists are notably porous due to these early calls, and many actual high potentials get missed. It's better to hire for learning, develop learning, and consider jobs to be the developmental test where people show they can learn how to handle the new and different. Then anointing people is a fairer process. Others have less to grouse about if they had their chances as well.

12. **Accentuate the positive.** One more time—feedback that focuses overwhelmingly on strengths is a feel-good practice that encourages speeding violations later. If people come to believe that development is a nicety or that they have little to develop or all that's necessary is cloning strengths onto new jobs, look for them in outplacement soon.

13

Early warning systems

You get what you measure for. Earlier, we talked about the dynamics of derailment (see Chapter 4). Left alone or reinforced, strengths become weaknesses, and weaknesses that were there all along "suddenly" matter. A simple intervention that has paid dividends is a derailment profile. Based on the work of Jon Bentz at Sears and the Center for Creative Leadership, several commercial instruments such as VOICES® 360° feedback assessment and Benchmarks® now feature derailment scales. Some companies have developed internal profiles, published them in the company newsletter, given feedback on them, and used them in courses.

Repeating an example from Chapter 4, one company lost a lot of money with bad expatriate selections. Their selection profile, like most, concentrated on results in similar kinds of assignments. Yet they had 86 failures in one year alone, so they instituted derailment factor feedback. Their notion was that you had to neutralize the flaw before even being considered for an expatriate assignment. People were given feedback, coaching, and development plans. Those involved signed off that the flaw had been neutralized (e.g., they weren't warm and fuzzy, but they no longer made people feel stupid; they would never be confused with Douglas MacArthur, but they had some strategic skills). The result: the company saved more than $40 million the first year of the program in recruitment and relocation costs alone. No more people with stunning results histories who within two months cause an entire plant to quit—not strike, quit. No more arrogant types who can't adjust to other cultures. No more tacticians who can't spot business climate shifts.

13 An essential line of defense against derailment is straightforward, helpful feedback.

Vaccinate against career derailment. We presented how careers and development work to a group of high-potential bankers—25- to 30-year-olds, generally MBAs or master of finance degrees. They heard the arguments, did derailment exercises, and constructed a success profile for development. Then the majority roundly panned the day.

"That's not how it works. You do the job well, perform, make a lot of money."

"Developing these competencies won't help me make money for the bank."

"People don't derail for these things. They derail because they can't do the job anymore."

We had an ace in the hole. We had conducted the same course for senior executives the week before and had both their support and willingness to participate in this program. The second day, we brought in a group vice president who explained the facts to them.

He explained the following: "This is indeed how careers work. Let me tell you some stories." He then explained how demands change across careers, the need to develop new competencies, and how some people cling to old habits. He explained some of the tough transitions he had made and told about three people who had derailed within the past year. Although each derailed for different reasons, in all cases they failed to grow and clung to technical excellence as their salvation.

"You do need these competencies." He went back to his earlier examples and used our competencies to discuss what skills were necessary at each step.

And so on. It is hardly insulting to say that young people are naive. How could they be expected to know the pitfalls that await them, the job challenges they will face, or the skill shifts that will be needed if we don't tell them?

13

Career vaccination courses should include the following, at the very least:

- How careers are really built.
- How promising careers derail.
- The transitions people make across levels and the changes that occur in skill demands.
- What developmental jobs and tasks look like.
- How people develop.
- Why they must think of themselves as learners.
- The necessity of 360° feedback.

And...why they must have trust in the process. Most successful people report more than one time when they were cajoled or sold on taking a job that at best seemed odd and at worst seemed dead-end. One CEO told us of five such incidents in eight moves. At the time, he lacked the perspective to see how they fit in developmentally, but he was appreciative in retrospect.

In the remainder of the book, we will discuss a series of interventions through systems to prevent derailment and help people and their organizations succeed.

Chapter 14

360° Feedback:
options and best practices

It's the gift that keeps on giving value.

Nothing happens until career-minded people get direct, timely feedback on the things that matter. Critical feedback is a must in stimulating people toward self-improvement and job and career success.

We have learned so far that managers and executives are not very good at giving or taking feedback (Chapter 2). True mentors are rare. Most performance evaluations are inflated and are missing critical feedback. We learned in the McKinsey study that managers and executives know all this is true. Managers and executives, for the most part, are tactically focused and terminally busy. They do not have the time, interest, or facility to give critical feedback on the things that count.

So the burden is then on a system to deliver the necessary feedback to career-minded people. From a systems viewpoint, we have to get feedback:

- On strengths and weaknesses
- On the things that really matter, now and in the future
- To motivated people
- On a timely basis

...for anything meaningful to happen.

Options

The goal is quality feedback. There are many ways to get leaders the feedback they need. Here are a few options for you to consider as you begin to establish a feedback-rich culture in your organization.

1. Self-assessment

If self-assessment were more accurate, there wouldn't be a feedback problem. Everyone would know where they stood on the things that matter, and those who were career-minded would do something about the competencies where they didn't measure up. As we pointed out in Chapter 7, this unfortunately isn't the case. We can't create a winning, competitive-edge strategy based on self-assessment. At least not by itself.

2. Bosses

The next best, fastest, and cheapest method would be for all direct bosses to give their people continuous and comprehensive positive and corrective feedback on the things that matter now and, to some, on the things that matter in the future. That isn't happening now. And it won't likely happen. Your direct boss has important information about you, your performance, and your prospects. The challenge is to get this information. There are formal processes (e.g., performance appraisals). There are day-to-day opportunities. To help, signal your boss that you want and can handle direct and timely feedback. Many bosses have trouble giving feedback, so you will have to work at it over a period of time. Remember that giving direct reports tough feedback isn't just a little low, it's in the bottom 10 skills out of 67, and actually developing them is dead last. Waiting for this to happen wouldn't be a good strategy. Some managers and executives are good at giving feedback and many could improve with time and help. But this wouldn't be fast enough to win the war for talent.

3. Mentors

The next best way would be for each career-minded person to have a mentor who knows him or her intimately, knows how careers are built, and have the organizational clout to run interference. But good mentors are rare. Those who have them are very fortunate. To make up for the lack of true mentors, many organizations have assigned mentor programs. Studies to date show that assigned mentors have less impact than natural mentors. The impact increases when mentors are given training and orientation and when assigned mentors and learners have some input into the matching process. Since both natural and assigned mentors are terminally busy, this process won't add enough feedback to reach critical mass and win the war for talent.

4. Peers and colleagues

14

Next in line would be peers and colleagues giving accurate and timely face-to-face feedback. Peers and colleagues are the same people (managers and executives) in our sample who have difficulty giving others critical feedback.

Peers and colleagues have a special social and working relationship. They attend staff meetings together, share private views, get feedback from the same boss, travel together, and are knowledgeable about each other's work. You perhaps let your guard down more around peers and act more like yourself. They can be a valuable source of feedback.

However, your peers and colleagues may not be candid if they are in competition with you. Some may not be willing to be open with you out of fear of giving you an advantage. Some may give you exaggerated feedback to deliberately cause you undue concern. You have to set the tone and gauge the trust level of the relationship and the quality of the feedback.

5. Formal organization-wide systems

The next best way would be for the formal organization systems to be accurate, timely, and useful. Most organizations have performance appraisal systems. These are usually done annually and have some connection to pay management. In general, the usefulness of the formal performance appraisal system is marginal for development. Mostly, the ratings are inflated and what's measured is narrowly focused on today's job. Because bosses aren't good at giving critical feedback, they inflate their ratings and hold back negative opinions.

Because formal performance appraisal is many times tied to pay, that further complicates its accuracy. A low rating impacts pay (as it should). In the heyday of Total Quality Management, Edward Deming pronounced that performance appraisal was a failed system and should be dropped. He believed it was a fault-finding system and, for the most part, was demotivational. It also rarely differentiates levels of performance well. Typically, 95 percent or more are at or above average; only a few percent are below. So formal performance appraisal processes are only marginally useful for providing career development information. Whether many systems even measure actual performance on the job is up for grabs.

What's a person to do?

6. Assessment centers or 360° feedback for development

That leaves us with assessment centers and 360° feedback for development.

Assessment centers are usually accurate, assuming they are professionally designed and use well-trained assessors. They can be very expensive and very intrusive due to the tremendous amounts of resources they consume. We won't spend any time on them here, other than to say they can be very potent when used for selection, promotion, and/or feedback.

The tool of choice for now seems to be 360° data collection and feedback—360° refers to around-the-compass feedback from bosses, peers, direct reports, and customers. Numerous studies have shown that when properly designed and executed, 360° ratings relate to various organizational measures of profit, performance, and/or potential.

From a coverage standpoint, 360° makes sense because different constituencies have different viewpoints. So using multiple constituencies increases the richness of the feedback information.

We also know that some constituencies are in a better position to assess certain competencies. Delegation skills, for instance, would be best assessed by direct reports, strategic skills by bosses, and cross-boundary cooperation by peers. With multiple constituencies, you have a better chance of accurate ratings across different kinds of competencies.

14

From a personal standpoint, giving anonymous feedback is easier than face-to-face. That is, the same people who are reluctant to deliver critical feedback face-to-face will do it on a confidential 360° questionnaire. This may be because giving face-to-face critical feedback makes most of us feel badly, while giving critical feedback anonymously invites us to be honest. To knowingly give an inflated rating is, in effect, lying to ourselves and, more importantly, to the people who are trying to work on their development.

Also, since 360° comes from multiple raters, the chance of collective accuracy increases compared with relying on the single rating of a boss for the evaluation.

So after looking at the data and considering the alternatives, we strongly recommend that standardized, automated 360° feedback be used as your main developmental assessment system. It is the most cost-effective and accurate alternative for the purpose of development.

|

In the rest of this chapter, we will focus on the two types of 360° feedback systems—the 360° feedback process for development and 360° performance evaluation and feedback.

The 360° feedback process for development

After reviewing hundreds of homegrown 360s, running thousands of people through ours, and knowing generally what other vendors are providing, there are eight special issues revolving around 360° for development:

1. How many competencies
2. Item construction
3. 360° engines
4. Confidentiality
5. Feedback process
6. Use of norms
7. Use of narrative notes
8. Absolute or Relative results

The quick answers?

1. As many as it takes
2. Leave it to the professionals
3. Rent or buy, don't build
4. A mission-critical absolute.
5. See Chapter 16 for the six-step process
6. Not very useful
7. Carefully
8. Relative

Following is more detail on these and other issues.

Competencies to measure in the 360°

Unless the 360° process measures critical skills, nothing past that matters. Emphasize the competencies viewed as most important according to panels of experts or empirical studies (see Chapter 12). Tie the competencies measured to the short- and long-term business strategy, team effectiveness, and current job criteria.

How many competencies should you have

As with any tool, there are multiple purposes for 360° assessments. One of the biggest battles fought is over how many competencies to have in the model and on the questionnaire. There is a significant bias for simple. While we like simple if simple does the job, it doesn't for development. If development were simple, we wouldn't be writing a book about it, and McKinsey wouldn't report a 3 percent success rate in developing people.

One way to look at how many competencies from a system standpoint is to think about all of the competencies that make up a complete model of a person in a work setting. On how many competencies might one person differ from another that could make a difference in performance or potential? Many times, we find that organizations want a model with 10 or fewer competencies. "Keep it simple." "You can't focus on more than that." If you look at the major research-based commercial competency models, they have many more than 10 because success takes many forms. Development can't be based on 10. You can't create a competitive edge with 10. You can't win the war for talent with 10. People cannot be fairly evaluated on 10. Neither can a function or a strategy or a level be described that way. Why? Because it's a weak and limited diagnosis. It's the equivalent of saying there needs to be only 10 medical tests. Would you settle for 10 if you didn't know what was wrong with you, but some thought it should be kept simple?

Here is a way out of the "how many" dilemma. On the first and then every third administration of the 360°, use the full model of how people differ. It's like getting a complete physical every three years and having shorter ones in between. You get all of the general screening tests once every three years; more limited in between. People who will be called on in the future for significant growth and development especially need this full-model treatment. In the other two administrations, you can use fewer. You could just test the 10 most mission-critical competencies. You could use just the three needs a person is working on.

The answer to how many is "however many it takes to get the job done." If you want to focus the whole organization on a few mission-critical characteristics, use 10. If you want to help people develop over the short-term, use 20 to 30, depending on the model. If you want to help a person plan for long-term development, use them all.

Competency sizing

The most serious problem with many homegrown competency models and subsequent 360s is compound competencies. Wanting to have as few competencies as possible, people combine "clean" competency packets together in a way that renders the results unusable for development. A clean competency is a skill or characteristic you can assess clearly, and if people are not proficient at it, they know exactly what their problems are. It's actionable.

In contrast, we frequently find a compound competency that goes something like "needs to be smart, creative, and innovative." The problem with that competency cluster is that there are three right-sized packets, and in real people, they don't necessarily go together. There is no relationship between smarts or IQ and creativity beyond the threshold that is generally ensured by hiring college graduates (120 IQ). That means that although we know your IQ, we can't estimate your creativity. Additionally, being personally creative may be negatively related to innovation

262 |

management. Being personally creative brings with it a disregard for rules and order, which is many times what innovation management means. Innovation involves having the knowledge and the patience to herd an idea through the complex maze called the organization.

Let's say we consider one-third of the working population to be especially creative, one-third smart, and one-third innovative. It won't be the same one-third. Among real people, very few will be all three. The tacit admission of this in R&D organizations is moving research (creativity) off to a hill somewhere and having development (innovation) take over where research leaves off. If ratings were accurate on a compound competency cluster, most people would get a moderate rating because almost everyone will be low on one of the three and high on one of the three.

What about for development? If you get a low rating on this competency cluster, what does it mean developmentally? Do you need to work on being more creative, more innovative, or use your smarts more effectively?

That's the problem when organizations combine competency packets into larger compound clusters to get "fewer competencies" in the model.

Another common compound cluster example is "makes good and timely decisions." But making good decisions can't be closely related to making timely decisions. Those two competencies come from very different origins in the makeup of real people. One comes from complete analysis and reflective problem solving and the other comes from moving ahead in the face of uncertainty. Sounds good together, but it's really two different concepts which don't factor together in studies of people at work. Making good decisions clusters with resourceful and clever, while speed hangs out with guts and tolerance for ambiguity. What would you work on if your score was low?

A third example we see frequently is "attracts, develops, and retains good people." These sound good together but, again,

14

are very different skills. Attracting is partly having an exciting organizational vision or proposition, partly sales, and partly shrewd hiring and negotiating practices against a success model. Developing follows the rules of development outlined in this book and can be totally chilled by poor organizational policies. Retaining is certainly related to developing but involves other factors like treatment, caring, working conditions, and pay. Again, if you were rated low, what would you work on?

In order to measure and help someone develop, you have to stay at the right-sized competency packet level. You cannot put competency packets together into clusters to get fewer competencies or make them sound more appealing to nonexperts. Every compound cluster you make in a model decreases proportionately the good the model can do in development. Use experts to define the competency size. If you use one of the commercially available models, that work is mostly done, except for tailoring.

Competency item creation

Writing good competency items and definitions is, at the very least, a craft and probably approaches a science. Don't involve line people in the details of measurement and definition of the competencies. This is what messes up perfectly reasonable models. We have seen wordsmithing task forces decrease the value of otherwise good models. Once an agreement has been made to measure action orientation or strategy, leave the definitions and measurement to validated instruments and models or people trained in behavioral measurement.

The same is true of scales. Many years of research has resulted in the science of scaling and how scales work with real raters. Very popular now is the three-point scale. The script is compelling. You only need three points. Either they meet expectations, exceed expectations, or miss expectations. Sounds right. What could be easier? Simplicity achieved. Unfortunately, such a scale would not produce the kind of information needed for development or performance measurement. There would not be enough spread and differentiation. People would shy away from misses expectations and too many ratings would migrate up.

People generally use a three-point decision model, seeing people as high, low, or somewhere in between. But a five-point scale is needed to capture this. These additional points help raters express shades of meaning. The 2 needs to be there for people to be comfortable using the 1, and the 4 needs to be there for people to use the 5 choice. Misses expectations is stark—a 1, and very few people will use it. Misses some expectations is more believable—a 2 response. Very few employable people would miss expectations totally on any key result areas. Similarly, exceeds expectations is impossible anywhere the bar is set high and should be split into more conditional statements. Individuals simply don't have that kind of unilateral control at work. Very few people are comfortable giving such unrealistic ratings.

Better scales, in our opinion, are the tried-and-true five-point Likert scales, but we present this argument not to endorse this sort of scale or any other. Our point is that even good competency packets can be wrecked by bad scaling. Leave scaling to the experts. Line management should not get involved in decisions about scaling.

Gathering the feedback

It is critical to carefully think through the logistics involved in administering 360s. Gathering feedback that is useful and high quality depends upon thoughtful planning and execution.

360° Engines

For the same reasons we stated in Chapter 1, there is no need or excuse for creating a competency model from scratch. There is also no longer any need or excuse to create a 360° engine. There are now numerous 360° data collection and 360° management systems you can buy, rent, or pay as you go. All of the survey engines are basically the same. They all collect data electronically. Some may offer mobile capability. They are getting cheaper by the day. There are much better ways to spend money. Spend it in facilitation and development support. Find the engine that best suits your needs and buy it or pay as you use it. Don't create one.

How often

The most common practice seems to be an annual assessment, but most people don't change that rapidly. We think that for most people, an 18- to 30-month interval would work fine. An annual 360° for most would be demotivating. Nothing much would change.

For those in trouble with a fix-it-or-leave proposition, a more frequent assessment might be necessary. For those who are on a rapid development curve, more frequent administrations might be necessary. A 360° one year after a significant developmental job or role shift might be wise. So the answer is, "It depends on the question, but we don't recommend everybody annually."

Who

Those who need it and those whom you would expect would do something with the results. The common practice is everyone, or everyone at some level or in some location or organization. That practice is unsupportable from anything but an equal-treatment viewpoint. People are different. Needs are different. Some are career-minded and others are not. Readiness to learn and grow differs. Funds are limited. Rater time is limited. Developmental assignments are limited. Resources for development are limited.

So we have a triage situation. We have a relatively expensive, time-absorbing process. As budget allows and rater tolerance holds, you should set up a rank order of the types of people who should get a full-blown 360° on a set schedule. Maybe the high potentials—those you are counting on for future senior management jobs—might be the first to be served. Then perhaps high professionals, with special attention to women and minorities in the queue for management jobs. Next, people in key jobs who are in trouble. Seldom does it make much sense to use periodic 360° for everyone. While we believe it is mandatory for every organization to develop and help everyone, this doesn't mean everyone needs the most expensive tool.

Who should select the raters

There are usually heavy debates about how raters should be selected. Should people pick their own raters? What if they pick only people who they know will give them good ratings? This matters a lot less if the data is presented in terms of ranks (ordered ratings actually) rather than averages. Should we pick the raters for them? Should we make sure there are at least some raters who do not hold the person in high regard?

14

Our recommendation is to have people choose their own raters. While the average scores may go up or down depending on whom the person selects, the rank order will usually not be impacted much. If it is, it means that the groups genuinely see the person differently. Because acceptance of the data is key to the 360° process, it's best to have people select their own raters. This increases the chances they will accept the results. Have the learner pick raters using the following criteria:

- Direct boss and either an old boss or the boss's boss, up to five peers, five direct reports, and five customers. Why five? Because usually one or two will not participate, leaving three, which is the number usually recommended for anonymity.

- People who have seen them in multiple performance situations.

- People who have worked with them one to five years. Ratings go up beyond five years and were unrelated to performance in our studies. Less than one year's exposure isn't long enough to meet the second criterion, unless first impressions are the point of the feedback or this is a brief project or corporate assignment.

| 267

The constituency identification issue

Accurate constituency identification is a problem. There is always some small but steady portion of the constituency identification (a boss checks the direct report box) that is in error. We have looked at this for more than 40 years now and know that two-thirds of the problem is due to administrative snafus and badly designed constituency identification questions. Most typical is when a direct report who is rating a boss marks "boss" instead of "direct report" on the response form. The person interprets the question as "who are you rating?" instead of "who are you?" The remaining one-third of the problem is that people don't always want to be identified, even as a member of a group. They may have a poor relationship with the person rated or don't trust in the confidentiality of the ratings. Some solutions for intentional misclassification: color code the rating forms or fill out the relationship question and rater name in advance. Some electronic systems allow for this. But remember that any technique that's used to fix this problem causes another. The data may be less accurate if raters know (think) they are somehow being identified.

Air traffic control of questionnaire distribution

Don't overload raters with questionnaires. A commonsense method of doing this is to cascade by level or take a diagonal slice of the organization. Do one-third of the people each year. Use 360° sparingly according to some of the decision criteria we outlined earlier. Some companies collect the lists of raters and limit the number of questionnaires a person must fill out to three at a time. Some 360° engines allow raters to opt in or out of the process to control their rating load.

This is not always doable if the ratings are completed in preparation for a developmental course. We remember the launch of a 360° program for one of our clients when the COO received 29 questionnaires the first day of the process. It turned out this was also the last day for the 360° program! You need to especially protect the 20 top managers. Many will put them on their list of raters.

14

Delivering the feedback

If you don't deliver the feedback well, the whole system can break down. To minimize defensiveness and rationalization and to maximize absorption and acceptance, follow best practices for delivering 360° feedback.

Anonymity and confidentiality

Should 360s be confidential? Why are police tip lines anonymous? Why is there a curtain between the penitent and the priest in the confessional? Because confidentiality and anonymity increase the chances of honesty. 360° for development works best when the results are confidential, the raters are guaranteed anonymity, and the information is owned and controlled by the target person. Anything less than that will compromise accuracy. Our studies have shown that accuracy decreases as confidentiality is breached. When raters are easier to identify or the boss or others in the organization get a copy of the report or there are mandatory sharing requirements, the average scores go up and the spread (lowest to highest score) goes down. Yet in a survey conducted in 2000, almost one-half of the bosses had access to the reports and about one-third of the HR groups did.

Remember, the main reason we are using 360° is because it is difficult for peers, direct reports, managers, and executives to engage in straight talk with people about weaknesses. So any decrease in real or perceived confidentiality will be accompanied by a decrease in accuracy.

This leads to a tension. In some organizations, line managers don't understand why they can't have access to the data. They say, "I need the data to help manage and develop the person." "We have an open shop around here; my people would not be uncomfortable if I had a copy of the report." While no doubt there are some cases where that might be true, it isn't true in general. The majority of people do not want their bosses to have their actual data. If that is a requirement, they and their raters will inflate their ratings and not include as many critical notes. We'll deal with a solution for this issue later in the chapter.

Story

360S gone bad

It is a somewhat familiar story—and one that keeps some HR leaders up at night. The promise of confidentiality in the multi-rater process is breached. Hard-earned trust in HR deteriorates in a flash and the value of 360° feedback is compromised, perhaps indefinitely.

A large company in the hospitality industry experienced just this. The company had an established 360° program. Leaders were bought into the process. They appreciated the opportunity for candid feedback that would not negatively impact their career or performance ratings. Raters and learners were trained to provide honest feedback in order to avoid overly inflated scores which provide little useful information. HR promised confidentiality to respondents and to the learner.

All was well. Until the C-suite was in the process of deciding which leaders would be promoted into key positions and remembered that 360s had taken place. Leaders pressured HR into releasing results from the 360s to help assist with the promotion decisions. One C-suite member inadvertently told a participant that the 360° data was used, in part, to help with the decision-making process, and the learner went to HR and spread the word throughout the organization.

Leadership and HR lost face and, more importantly, employees' trust. Multi-rater feedback had to be abandoned for several years as a result. Even the engagement surveys suffered because of fear of breach in confidentiality and mistrust over how the data were to be used.

14

270 |

> *The same organization had to hire in a consulting organization to reengage and revive the 360° process. Once again, confidentiality was promised. To help ensure this, HR was not given copies of the reports or access to the data. Instead, it was kept off-site at the consulting firm. However, even three years later, the mean item rating was above 4 on a five-point scale with very little variance. Findings were not meaningful until trust could be rebuilt— something that was still a work-in-progress years later.*

The use of norms

Norms are popular. Most people like to compare themselves with others. But in the development arena, they *are* worse than nothing. In development, the main question is, which of my lowest skills are the ones that matter? How this compares with anyone else is interesting but not instructive and seldom motivating. Norms are relevant for selection, placement, and for performance, but are harmful for development.

In many cases, people look to norms to save them from negative results. Many times, we have heard the line, "Even though it's my lowest score, it's at the 38th percentile, so it really isn't that bad." Interpretation: "I don't think I need to work on that."

The lower the competency average is in the norm population, the better the excuse becomes. A person's lowest score might be, and often is, Developing Direct Reports and Others or Confronting Direct Reports. A middling norm makes the score look OK, when the truth is that this is the person's lowest score. All that really matters is how critical the competency is for the present job and the near future.

Norms also encourage people to work on the wrong things. For example, the norms for Integrity and Trust or Ethics and Values are sky-high on most questionnaires, above 4 on a five-point scale. They should be. People who aren't trustworthy get weeded out fairly efficiently in most organizations and those remaining are

14

an honest lot. Due to the vagaries of rating, a person may have direct reports who use a lot of 2s, 3s, and 4s and stay away from extreme ratings. A person gets a 4.0 on Integrity and Trust, when the normative average is 4.2: "What? I'm at the 35th percentile on Integrity and Trust. They must think I'm a snake." "No, of course not; 4.0 means you're talented and better than most." "Not here; it means 65 out of 100 people have more integrity than I do."

The only hope here is to have the person poll his or her direct reports and get a "you must be kidding" response. And even this won't help the person gain from feedback in the short-term. A conversation like the above usually destroys value. The person may not be able to think of anything developmental until this is resolved.

14

From an organizational perspective, the worst feature of encouraging people to work on the wrong things is that norms induce people to work on competencies that are already in high supply in the organization. Action Oriented is a commonly held skill, usually averaging around 4. A person with a 3.75 rating will look below average against norms and may interpret this to mean that he or she is too cautious. A plan is developed to work on something that (a) is not a problem, and (b) raters under Sodium Pentothal wouldn't endorse. How could they? They said the person was, on balance, above average in Action Oriented.

Norms used this way are alchemy. They transform straightforward ratings into something that raters often wouldn't endorse. If the raters said Jane is a 3.75 in Action Oriented, that is all they were asked to do. They were not asked if Jane is less Action Oriented than most or if this is something she should definitely work on.

From a human resource perspective, norms are a disaster. Would you rather have people working on the wrong things and on skills that are in high supply, or would you rather they worked on the most critical skills that are in low supply? Norms encourage exactly the wrong behavior.

Norms should be left to validated assessments (selection and placement tools where they actually mean what they say they do) in which a higher percentage of people with this score succeed than people with a lower score. In 360s, as generally untrained raters supply the results, percentile norms are a bad practice.

Relative norms are useful, however. Saying that Developing Direct Reports and Others is usually in the bottom 10 for people in your position and it is related to success in your role sends exactly the right developmental message. Norms are also useful in group audits—in assessing the general level of proficiency in a work unit to determine what is most in need of development. Similarly, they can be used to assess progress in year-to-year comparisons.

The use of narrative notes

14

Narrative notes are also popular, but we have seen them hurt almost as often as they help. Positive notes are double-edged. While those that buttress or explain strengths are all right, some learners use the positive notes to defend against any negative results. They place too high a value on a single note that counters negative data from eight raters!

A common situation is a low rating on, say, Approachability, but the only narrative note about this competency is glowing: "The warmest person I have ever worked with." In most cases, we would guess that the person writing the glowing note is very similar to the learner. In any event, the target person then uses that one statement to question the data, saying that the software program must have broken. "How could I get such a rating with this note? I got critical remarks elsewhere and none here. This doesn't make any sense." Pointing to the range data helps here, because to get a low score, the ratings must be all over the place.

Positive notes often create noise that only one-on-one feedback sessions can correct. Our recommendation is to ask that the raters restrict their narrative comments to helpful comments about how this person could improve. Of course, raters do not follow the directions all the time. At the very least, people need to know that one positive comment doesn't countervail low ratings by other raters. The actual meaning here is probably found by answering the question, "Why do people see you so differently on this competency?"

For the vast majority of learners, probably 90 percent or more, the task is to come to peace with a few weaknesses they have been avoiding or do not know about. We are seldom in the situation of trying to convince people of their strengths. For that reason, critical notes are more helpful than outlier (doesn't fit with the data) positive notes. They can help the person zero in on the specifics that are causing the problem.

14 Arithmetic averages or ranks

The format and data displays of the reports should guide the correct interpretation. The worst reports we see simply present arithmetic numbers, bar charts, percentages of people who said what ad nauseam, each item result, each scale result from the first to the last, and by each constituency. The learner often has about a thousand numbers with little guidance.

The next worst are those that do not provide Relative, or ranked, scores. The person's high and low skills are what is most important in determining developmental goals. Whether the lowest score is a 3.8, 2.8, or 1.8 makes no developmental difference, and since most ratings are inflated, even the Absolute average score may not mean a great deal. There are too many factors that can move average ratings up and down.

Functions, organizations, and nationalities rate (using a five-point scale) differently. Ratings vary by job type as well. People doing start-ups are rated higher than people doing turnarounds. Remember that the goal is to help people get in touch with their needs. Inflated or false averages do not help. A good report should present rank-ordered scores (ordered ratings) from highest to lowest in total and by each rater group so that the person can easily see relative strengths and weaknesses.

Finally, a good report should have some recommendation as to which competencies are most important, either predetermined (internal or external importance model) or by vote of the raters. Then, following the advice and procedures in Chapters 8–10, the learner can both make sense of the report and construct a reasonable development plan.

Direct, group, or one-on-one feedback

We have been involved in numerous programs over the years where, in a group session (generally a half day), everyone gets his or her report, an explanation of how to read and interpret the report, and an hour or more to fill out interpretation exercises. This has been followed by a shorter (one or two hours) one-on-one session with a trained facilitator. In some programs, the one-on-one is days after the group session. This is done mostly for cost-management reasons or as part of a training program that includes the 360° process.

In the past, we have received RFPs (requests for proposal) requesting an online survey system with target individuals ordering their own 360°, selecting their participants (OK so far), and getting their reports directly via e-mail with an online interpretation manual and a toll-free number to call for questions (not OK). Almost 30 percent of companies in a survey reported they did just this—sent out feedback reports without comment or coaching.

It's hard to imagine the ethics or wisdom of this, other than cost control. Our experience has been that regardless of how well the group session is designed, or how well it is supported by an interpretation manual, one-third to one-half of the people misinterpret the results, especially from their first 360°. They either miss the subtle meanings in the report, see it as more rosy than it is, or see it as worse than it actually is. Those who see it as worse get overwhelmed by all the data, fixate on one bad result, or focus on one group of raters to the exclusion of all others. We've found it all too common to sit down with someone who has spent two hours analyzing his or her results and hear, "My boss hates me." "But your boss gave you the highest ratings on 13 of 16 scales." "But he/she slammed me on the other three!" The problem with the one-on-one after the participant has had unguided use of the report is that much of the time is spent undoing the misinterpretation. The misinterpretation has had time to fester.

Of course, this is one of the reasons simple 360s are so popular. It's hard to argue that a report with 10 broad competencies needs a great deal of interpretation. But we will argue this, regardless. Unless the report is a single page, reporting the 10 competencies from high to low, most people will need help. (We would also argue that such a report is a waste of money.) The instant bosses, peers, direct reports, and customers are added, value goes up, complexity goes way up, and misinterpretation is likely.

Because of our experiences, we strongly believe that people in their first or second 360° on the same competencies should receive their report in a one-on-one session with a trained facilitator. The potential damage and wasted motion is significant if one-third to one-half of the people do not interpret the information properly.

Yes, it is time consuming to have one-on-one feedback sessions. It might cost a fair amount of money if the organization doesn't use inside people for the sessions. But we think you must commit to it. Frankly, we consider wishing this problem away a sign of not taking development seriously or, at the least, wishful thinking. People get so easily overwhelmed by all the data that we are tempted to ask, "Why bother going through this elaborate process if you don't care about the outcome enough to ensure correct interpretation?"

The idea that the learner knows best and should make his or her own interpretation is also fanciful. What qualifications does the learner have? Does he or she understand norms? Scaling?

Job success models? That different constituencies will see him or her differently? Even 360s with terrific reporting formats can be daunting. Here are the most important competencies, the highs and lows from bosses, peers, direct reports, and customers. Many have five to ten sections. We might as well say, "Here's your CAT scan. Why don't you just decide what you think it means? "

Starting with the third administration of a 360° with roughly the same competencies, then a more direct or group distribution method would be OK, but still not the best way. We still recommend one-on-one feedback first, followed by a group session emphasizing development planning. By this time, the learner has had a chance to analyze the report with a facilitator, to fill out exercises to aid in interpretation, and is ready to put together a development plan.

If you choose to ignore us for staffing or budget reasons and use group feedback first, we strongly recommend one-on-one feedback sessions as soon as possible after receiving the report— the same day if feasible. Don't let people sit on the data for too long.

If you use group sessions first, the goal is to help with the understanding necessary for action to occur as a result of feedback. One procedure that has worked well is to create a group report that combines data from all the participants. The reports will look exactly like the individual reports. This is followed by a guided walk-through of the reports, paying careful attention to common misinterpretations. Since their data is a part of the report, people pay attention. But since it is not their individual data, they are not threatened, listen better, and ask more questions.

After this session, the facilitator hands out the individual reports and calls a 30-minute break so that people have a chance to scan their results but not go too deeply into them. Each participant then meets with a trained feedback giver for 30–45 minutes. By holding the group session first, almost all the one-on-one time can be focused on helping learners understand their data. After

14

the one-on-one session, people are given exercises to further tease meaning from their data.

The day after these sessions, the group reconvenes to discuss and construct development plans and have additional one-on-one time if needed. Having slept on it, even people who received a lot of bad news are usually more receptive to thinking about development.

For special cases, one-on-one feedback is a must. People in sensitive positions (often executives), people in need of coaching, or people who are derailing should have one-on-one sessions. We will cover this in depth in Chapter 16.

14

Excerpt

360s

While 360° feedback is a powerful tool—a mirror that reveals a manager's effectiveness from the various points of view of those he or she works with closely—like the truth-telling magic mirror, it may give us information we did not expect and do not want to hear. That is why decisions concerning the forum for presenting and interpreting the feedback can be as important as choosing the method of data collection for the instrument.

While you may be gathering data on the right behaviors and ensuring that they are reliable, if the feedback is presented poorly and recipients are not able to make sense of it and use it to plan their development, the entire process will have been a waste of everyone's time. As a result, people may harbor ill feelings toward those who initiated the process and those who provided the feedback. And beyond that, they will learn nothing about themselves and how to improve their effectiveness within the organization.[†]

[†]From The Art and Science of 360° Feedback (2nd ed.). Richard Lespinger and Anntoinette Lucia. (2009). San Francisco, CA: Jossey-Bass. Reprinted with permission of John Wiley & Sons, Inc.

Introducing the 360° Process

1. Especially for first-timers, hold pre-questionnaire distribution orientations and discussions in small groups to answer objections and worries prior to collecting the data. Show a sample report. Discuss the logistics. Have people fill out a sample questionnaire. If written or typed-in comments will be used, show some samples and have people write a sample comment or two.

2. Discuss how the scales should be used. Average scores run as high as 4.0 on a 5.0 scale, severely limiting the usefulness of feedback. Convey to people that this is for development only; it is not a performance appraisal. A rating of 1 should indicate a pressing need; a 2, some work is needed; 3, skilled or at standard; 4, noticeably above standard; and 5, one of the best you've ever seen at this. The broader the ratings, the richer the data.

3. This is where people's anxieties come to the forefront and need to be addressed. The most common questions are:

   - *Is the feedback report confidential?* Describe the process in a straightforward fashion. Some people won't trust that feedback is confidential, but the more said the better. A typical policy for developmental feedback is that the actual report is confidential. Since almost all 360° instruments are now processed electronically, no one in the organization will have seen it. There is one copy, which the facilitator hands to the person at the feedback session.

   - *Is there any way raters can be identified?* We hope not, although we hear some sentiment for open ratings. Scores are already inflated (in a performance sense, more than 5 percent have to be below average) and open ratings really jack them up. Forty-three of our 67 competencies were rated significantly higher when people thought they could be identified. The themes are clear: when people rate under total anonymity, those rated (the learners) take a significant hit on most ratings—particularly Caring

14

About Direct Reports, Motivating Others, *Managing* Diversity, Self-Knowledge, and general interpersonal skills. They also get lower ratings on intelligence, *Managing* Vision and Purpose, Developing Direct Reports and Others, Composure, Conflict Management and, perhaps most important, Ethics and Values. This matters greatly because when raters thought they could be identified, their ratings were unrelated to the person's actual performance. Working on improving in what they recommended would be neutral, at best, and that is, no doubt, generous. Time is finite; use it to develop something that actually matters for performance or the future. Confidential ratings relate to performance; open ratings don't, or usually don't.

- *What will the results be used for?* To construct development plans. The covenant we recommend goes like this: "We're investing in your development through our 'feedback for development' system. The actual results (the numbers, the ratings, and comments) are private. The summary of your strengths and weaknesses should be discussed with your boss and HR. Developmental feedback, unlike a blood test, isn't truly private since the results come from your boss and coworkers in the first place. Your job is to continuously improve, and ours is to help you. Your direct boss will help with your short-term development (for performance), and top management and Human Resources will help with long-term development (projects, next job, anything outside the present scope of your responsibilities)."

- *Is this related to pay?* At first, no. Later, maybe.

- *What is the best approach to communicate with raters?* Design invitation letters and reminder notes for the raters. Reminder notes should be sent at intervals because if the survey isn't completed within a few days, it may be forgotten. Again, many electronic systems do this automatically. The best approach is to have the target person write a tailored note to the raters.

4. Don't present reports to the target person with inadequate numbers of responses. Set a minimum: usually boss, self, two to three peers, two to three direct reports, and two to three customers—and stick to it. Some companies allow boss, self, and one other rater group.

Used properly, 360° for development is a great tool. Used badly, it can do damage. Used too much, it can lose its bite.

A cautionary note: 360° feedback for performance

One survey said that one-half of Fortune 500 companies are using 360° for performance evaluation. But using 360° for performance has killed a lot of feedback interventions. Scores go up, raters make deals, people resist the data. In another survey, over one-half the companies surveyed had decided to stop using 360° feedback for performance purposes. The scores were high and meaningless. They received a lot of push back from raters who asked why they had to be the bearer of bad tales; why didn't bosses do what they were paid to do?

While this practice can work, there has to be comfort with multisource feedback, belief in the confidentiality of the system, and justified ratings for it to have a chance. The conditions we listed earlier have to be in place, plus some special modifications.

In performance measurement, determining the criteria and agreement on critical success factors is a major piece of the process. See Chapter 12 for our discussion of how to do this. More than 360° for development, 360° for performance has to be defendable in court. The competencies must have a demonstrable relationship to performance.

In addition, don't mix developmental 360° and performance 360°. Developmental 360° is written to indicate general levels of skill in an area, not all the ways a person might use that skill to get to their work goals. A 360° for an appraisal purpose has to focus on specific behaviors and outcomes that all raters can observe and rate. Raters should be trained in what to look for, and all ratings should be justified in writing. Technically, 360° for performance can only look at today's performance dimensions, whereas 360° for development can look to the future standards.

One company moved into 360° for performance after using 360s for development for some years. By then, multisource feedback had broad support. When the company decided to try 360° for performance, it did not tie performance to compensation at first because it assumed the results would be useless for that purpose.

Criteria were agreed upon (with multiple levels of performance defined for each result area and competency), raters were trained, people had a voice in selecting their raters, and each rater was required to back up ratings with narrative statements. For example, when Sally gave John a 3 rating on Negotiating skills, she both understood that this was an acceptable rating and that her written reply had to justify that level of proficiency against the criteria.

The boss collected the data electronically. Only he or she knew which ratings were whose. The data were presented as the average and range of the rater responses; the boss's ratings were separate and were done after reviewing all responses to get the most complete view of performance that he or she could.

Perhaps the critical feature of this system is that the raters get feedback on their ratings. The boss critiques each rater, even sending back rating forms for clarification and justification.

Whether a performance system can be used for compensation depends on whether the system distinguishes between high, medium, and low performance. 360° won't fix a bad appraisal system. In this case, the system evolved to a moderate weighting (50 percent is typical in survey data), with the remaining percentage accounted for by the boss's evaluations of how well workgroup performance targets were met. The total compensation pie was determined by how the unit performed against comparable units.

360° performance measurement can work and even be tied to compensation, but it seems all the factors above have to be in place.

Making feedback work

Feedback systems introduce accountability and increase work load. According to the McKinsey study, only 7 percent of firms hold managers accountable in any direct way for the development of their people. So without development, any such accountability system is doomed, even if flawlessly implemented. People won't grow; they won't perform any better; and the system, either development or performance, will be sabotaged.

14

Any feedback intervention must be accompanied with goal setting. There should never be feedback just for its own value. Tied to a goal or purpose, feedback helps people improve. Tied to nothing, it backfires.

In an analysis of numerous studies, feedback improved average performance. However, in one-third of the cases, it decreased performance. A review by Smither, London, and Reilly found that the magnitude of improvement was very small (about 0.10 standard deviation). Why wouldn't we expect large, across-the-board performance improvement after people receive multisource feedback? Because when feedback isn't tied to the tasks at hand, it becomes tied to the only other possibility—you. Getting better at X to achieve a goal and perform better can be quite motivating; simply getting better implies that something is wrong with you. Defensiveness and the need to maintain a positive self-image can quickly get in the way.

Any feedback intervention must also include positive and negative data. There is no evidence that accurate negative data

| 283

hurts people or that positive feedback helps them. The type of data is less important than tying it to criteria of importance.

Giving or receiving bad news is no fun, but it is as necessary for performance and growth as detailing strengths. Putting everyone in the same developmental or performance boat against carefully developed criteria takes away a lot of the sting. A fairly run system focuses people where it should—on continuous improvement.

So design and execute a system that delivers timely, packet-sized information about the competencies that matter.

14

Chapter 15

70:20:10 Development:
Jobs, coaches, and courses

How do we develop the people we have?

It has almost become a mantra: 70:20:10. Let's revisit the origins. The Center for Creative Leadership (CCL) conducted a series of studies in the 1980s looking at how successful executives learned the skills they needed to be successful. *The Lessons of Experience* highlights the findings from these studies. Executives were asked:

> When you think about your career as a manager, certain events or episodes probably stand out in your mind—things that led to a lasting change in you as a manager. Please identify at least three key events in your career—things that made a difference in the way you manage now. What happened? What did you learn from it (for better or worse)?

Since the original work, the studies have been replicated in Singapore, India, China, and with female executives. Guess what? These separate studies found very similar results. One small exception is that women may cite learning from other people more frequently than men. What were the key findings across all of these studies?

- Key events fell into four categories: hardships, on-the-job experience, people, and coursework.
- Sixteen full-time jobs and over 150 part-time assignments were identified as being the most developmental.

- Lessons learned from these developmental experiences showed a pattern. Certain types of experiences resulted in learning specific lessons.
- Some executives gleaned more lessons from their experiences than other executives.

When we take out hardships (because hardships are not something you put into a development plan), the remaining events cited by the executives were as follows: 70 percent were related to on-the-job experience, 20 percent were related to learning from others, and 10 percent were related to learning from courses. These executives were reflecting over the course of their careers on the events that had a lasting impact and changed how they manage now.

Learning from jobs

15

We were at a plant in a remote location. Turnover was nil, few people wanted to relocate there, and performance was flat. Their questions: "How do we develop the people we have? How do we even know who is worth developing?"

We started with the six supervisors and asked each of them to list on a flip chart the major tasks that were done in his or her area. We then asked them to star the ones that were toughest. Finally, we asked them to note how many they did, how many were done primarily by one person, and how many were done as a team. Not surprisingly, the supervisor did many of the toughest tasks, and one or two others did the remainder. Everyone else was in a more or less "do this please" role.

We asked if there was any particular reason the work had to be done this way. No, they said. OK, then, let's rethink the work. What would be best done as a team? What major tasks could you give responsibility for to each person? What are you doing that is no longer developmental for you but would be for someone else? What tasks could you trade? What tasks could be trained, and is there anyone else besides yourself who could do the training? What is some important work that is not getting done (it's not on your list)? What are some innovations you'd like to see explored?

In about two hours, the supervisors redesigned the work of their unit to be more developmental.

This is how you figure out who your budding high potentials and high professionals are—by thinking of all early jobs as 20 percent developmental. Many have reported back to us that thinking of jobs as a series of developmental tasks creates surprises: a geeky financial analyst who loved to explore new and arcane areas (little start-ups); a shy woman who excelled at resolving conflicts; a Ph.D. chemist who became a wonderful project manager. They (and we) will never know their capabilities unless the opportunity is there for them.

Enhancing learning has occupied much of the space in this book. We have discussed who learns best, how they learn it, and the details of how people can develop themselves better in Chapters 6 through 10. Here, we look at key topics from the organizational point of view.

Use the Developmental Heat checklist (Exercise 5.2) and/or the developmental jobs list from Chapter 5 to help you select. What are the little start-ups, fix-its, strategic moves, and common first-time tasks— first time learning a new technical area as you go, first negotiation, first project out of area?

By using real work to develop people, they learn what they like and don't like, they gain new competencies, and organizations begin to do what is necessary for survival—develop competencies a level before they are critical.

It's a two-fer. People begin to self-select. They love the new (may be a high potential someday) or they love depth (may be a high professional someday) or they really just want to be a jobholder (may be a solid contributor). The organization can measure how people respond to early challenges. Do they get defensive and balk? Do they love it? Do they go for breadth or depth? Do they perform better under first-time or repeat conditions? Does feedback help them improve?

New tasks are, of course, developmental at all levels. A CEO stood up on Friday afternoon and said to 1,000 employees, "By Monday morning, turn in to your boss two things: a task or responsibility that is no longer developmental for you but would be for someone else, and one new task you propose taking on in its place. The requirements are: you've never done it before, and you think it's important enough to our business for someone to do it. To kick off the process, here is what I am proposing to get rid of and here is my new task for Monday." Over the weekend, 2,000 developmental tasks were "created"—all real work, all important.

This last example is pivotal. We absolutely believe that all people should be developed all the time, regardless of whether they have no potential or no interest in doing anything else. Research and common sense inform us that employees will perform better, develop depth in their skills, and be more satisfied with their work because it is more interesting and challenging. And don't forget, some of them will surprise you. Once the challenge at work revs up, so will workers.

Observation | 70:20:10

I see this slide in PowerPoint presentations in almost every client I observe. And yet, it's one of the harder things to do because it requires taking a risk when you assign a person to a job that they are not yet qualified for. So the issue is not knowing that experience is the best teacher. In assignmentology, we can even tell you what kind of role or job that is. The issue comes down to a line officer willing to take the risk on someone who doesn't have all the skills to do the job.

|

Learning from people

Other people can be role models—mentors, spouses, good bosses, bad bosses. These people provide a model or an antimodel for key skills. Learning from other people also entails lots of feedback. Without before, during, after, or continued feedback, even the best plans usually fail, according to research studies. We roll along, think we're getting better, don't realize what impact we may be having on others, and pronounce the effort over. Or we think we've improved greatly, go on "autopilot," and six months later we're back to our old behavior. Getting further feedback keeps us growing. Help people identify the best sources of feedback for their particular need. A boss, a peer, a buddy working on the same need. Remember that multiple sources are always best. Encourage everyone to seek variety in feedback.

Learning from courses

15

Courses have been much maligned and unfairly so, partly because they remind adults of being in school and under someone else's schedule and control, and partly because they are often not designed with the rules of development in mind. Make courses more like assignments. New instructional design methods are doing this for you to some degree. Courses build in everything from simulation to action learning.

When we conducted research at CCL, courses were one of the more powerful events and a top-five developer of people. (Ahead of courses were various job types and developmental bosses.) Even though there are many forgettable courses, there are also many forgettable jobs and bosses. Considering how little time people spend in courses and how much time they spend on the job, courses could be considered even more powerful than they appear to be on the surface.

The research on the use of courses to increase productivity is impressive. Training in interpersonal, sales, and technical skills has been shown to have significant bottom-line impact. More general training in managerial skills has also been related to productivity increases, but the effect seems not to be as dramatic as for sales and technical skills. Regardless, anyone who, deep down, believes that people don't grow much should look at the results produced from well-designed courses. People do grow, and the growth results in real economic value (see Notes section).

Courses work for the same reason any developmental experience works. Whatever is in the course is needed right now. The content is urgent and real. For an organization, think of a developmental course in the same manner as a developmental job—40 points (see Chapter 5 for the Developmental Heat checklist).

One company scrapped its arrangement with a noted university for a strategy course and designed its own. It signed nondisclosure agreements with three noncompetitive businesses, and each brought their strategic issues to the table. The companies pulled in strategy experts as needed to guide them to their agreed outcome. Each would leave with a strategy that their respective firms would implement in the marketplace.

Participation in the course was restricted to about 20 people per organization—all high potentials and high professionals. The course met periodically during a one-year period.

Developmentally, this was dynamite. Success or failure was going to occur, important people were watching, and what the participants did made a huge difference. After the course, some of the participants were selected to implement the strategy. The company that dreamed this up, after attending our course on development, tripled its stock price in a year with the strategy it implemented. We, of course, don't know who the other firms were.

Other examples are less dramatic. Earlier, we mentioned using courses as technical training for young people. A group of young professionals rotated through technical aspects of the core business, were taught by practitioners, and took tests every week. If you failed one, you were out. If you failed to help your fellow trainees learn, you were out. No one failed.

All courses shouldn't be 40 points—only those designed to teach critical competencies that must be put to use immediately. The examples above demonstrate 40-point courses. Other examples would be a negotiation course as part of a project or the well-known GE course/job where teams of participants work on actual problems and make recommendations to senior management. The vast majority of these recommendations are accepted.

Self-awareness courses are an example of a course that shouldn't be as stressful. Personal examination is stressful enough. We'd hardly recommend that "people come back fixed or they would be fired."

Behavior-modeling courses have impressive research documenting their success in teaching some interpersonal skills like Listening. Although somewhat stressful (you're there for a reason), such courses rely on rehearsal, videotaping, and repeated feedback. They are not intended to be as today and assignment oriented as the other examples we have mentioned.

The key here is to go into any course with a specific goal in mind. Then the course becomes more actionable.

15

Excerpt

70:20:10 Learning from jobs, people, and courses

The Lessons of Experience study at the Center for Creative Leadership and subsequent global studies have asked leaders to cite key experiences that contributed to their ability and success as a leader. When you take out hardships (illness, injury, death in the family, etc.), 70 percent of the examples cited were on-the-job experiences, 20 percent involved learning from other people, and 10 percent from coursework.

70: The lessons learned from full-time jobs or part-time assignments are somewhat predictable. For example, handling a crisis is ripe with lessons in the areas of Problem Solving, Command Skills, Political Savvy, and Negotiating, as you can see from Brian's experience in Nigeria:

"Shortly after I arrived in January 1994, there was a problem. We were producing half the oil in Nigeria, and ours was on land rather than offshore.

"By June, the president-elect was in jail and one of the ethnic groups was threatening what looked to the government like secession. The unions decided to go on strike to shut us down and to put pressure on the government to install the elected president.

"The head of state called me in. He wanted to know why I shut down production. 'Very simple,' I answered. 'You can't control what will happen, and it will get out of hand if you send the army in. Give me six weeks, and I will get a settlement with the union.'

"He agreed, and with my knowing the people and the unions, I was able to negotiate an end to the strike, and they were back at work."[†]

20: Learning from other people (whether the person is a coach, a spouse, a good boss, a bad boss) can result in valuable lessons. In this case, Jean reflects on an early mentor who imparted the value of listening, team building, and communication.

15

"He was nearly a dozen years older than me, and he decided to coach me. We started taking trips together, and he shared everything. He taught me how to work in the U.S.; he was a kind of sponsor who introduced me to a lot of our business partners whom I could not have gotten to know. I learned about people and about business. He had the ability to criticize positively. He taught me the importance of pushing people to talk, to overdialogue in order to understand. The second learning was the power of teamwork—we worked together and built a strong team across the organization. I saw the importance of other people who had different strengths than you. I learned that by talking and listening that you can always build a team. You must put yourself in the other person's shoes, then you can understand and build a team."[†]

10: *Carefully timed courses can provide the foundation for flashes of insight back on the job. Take this example in which Brian (whom you met earlier) had coursework under his belt that informed how he transformed the culture of a company.*

"Suddenly, I grasped some key things about management. We had the challenge of changing an old company embedded in an old-fashioned society. I learned how to transform a company without destroying the people, how to work with a complicated system. This was a long and complex process, not just one single event.

"A key in my doing this was that I had spent nine weeks at MIT (Massachusetts Institute of Technology) where, among other things, I learned about systems thinking. This provided an extremely useful set of tools. We were able to use these tools in the transformation."[†]

Harvesting lessons from jobs or assignments, other people, and courses can happen during the experiences or later when reflecting upon the experiences. It's never too late to learn from experience.

[†]From Developing Global Executives: The Lessons of International Experience. Morgan W. McCall Jr. and George P. Hollenbeck. (2002). Boston, MA: Harvard Business School Press. Reprinted with permission of Harvard Business School Publishing Corporation.

15

| 293

Development plans

Everyone should have a development plan. Everyone has something they could improve upon. Please do not misinterpret this as us saying that every weakness needs to be developed. Only mission-critical skills for which there are no substitutes or workarounds must be developed. The failure rates at all levels are unacceptable in most organizations due to people not being developed. The plans will range from a simple job-improvement plan to a 10-year career plan ending up in the CEO spot. Each plan should have 40 or more bulleted menu options for the person to pursue so that the plan doesn't have to be redone often.

An operating plan for a need consists of three imperatives:

1. A challenging task (or person).
2. A way to get before, during, and after feedback.
3. Learning some new things to do.

In practice, a person should work on three things at once, not 40. As these are completed or somewhat mastered, more options should be added from the menu.

Except for short-term performance improvement plans, which should go with the performance appraisal cycle, development plans should be keyed to the job cycle. For high potentials and high professionals, they should be keyed to succession planning as well. We'll discuss this topic in Chapters 17 and 18.

Development plans should be keyed to the job cycle because this is where the demand pull of development lies. As we've argued repeatedly, development doesn't happen until people try some actions, make mistakes, immerse themselves deeply in the job issues, come up with a fine-grained map of the problems faced, and deal with underlying causes (deep problem solving). We have summarized this point as "your mistakes catch up with you, and you've fixed them." This is where development and performance peak. It's in the best interest of the organization and

15

the person. The process, according to Jack Gabarro's research, is predictable. People go through these phases, whether they know it or not, unless the sequence is interrupted with a hasty move.

With high-powered development plans, the process can go faster, but no one is sure how long it takes. Without intervention, it took more than three years for the general managers in Gabarro's study. With intervention, we postulate 2.5 to 3 years at executive levels and 18 months to 2 years at lower levels.

Development works best when seen as a triangle:

- The person – who indicates willingness and energy to grow.
- The boss – who handles performance-improvement planning and on-the-job development.
- Human Resources – who handles anything out of current job. This may be part of succession planning and involves projects and other activities that the boss can't access.

15

Creating an organization of learners

We discussed learning to learn in Chapter 6. From an organizational point of view, what is critical is to provide punctuation marks and reinforcements for learning.

Punctuation marks. Hold regular postmortems after significant work assignments or projects are finished. What did we do well? What turned out not so well? What have we learned that we can use in the future? One company adopted the interesting practice of having each member of the senior management team present one success and one failure each year, with the CEO going first. Each was analyzed and lessons drawn by the entire group. Similar meetings were held down the line.

Another company decided to discuss the undiscussables that were getting in the way of performance. The senior executive wrote a letter to the chairman, then met to discuss the issues.

Others use the technique pioneered by Chris Argyris, where a meeting scenario is written down on the right side of a piece of paper. On this side, a person describes an issue and how people are likely to respond. On the left side, the person writes down thoughts and feelings he or she would likely have during the meeting but wouldn't express. But instead of holding the meeting, the person meets with the people involved to analyze this scenario.

One company held weekly phone chats in basic work units to discuss major problems people had encountered and how they had solved them. Particularly clever solutions ("Here's how someone dealt with an irate customer...") were passed on electronically each week. Other companies do this electronically, sharing everything from soft tips to technical tips—like use of raw materials.

And then there is reading. Books of tips can be very helpful to a motivated person with a need. Some companies provide standard sources in all units and some have tailored their own and shared them electronically.

We have found more general reading to be helpful in three areas:

1. Some people don't respond well to disembodied tips but relate to biographies of people who faced similar situations.

2. Some people need to read about role models more like themselves to convince themselves that if this person could do it, so can I. We recall a shy man who was extremely uncomfortable with rah-rah team-building tactics. As part of his developmental plan, he read about a famous basketball coach who spent very little time praising or criticizing players. Most of his coaching was strictly informational. This approach gave the shy man hope that he could build a team using similar techniques and let others take care of the rah-rah.

3. Much of strategy involves parallels from history, whether in business or political areas. Many strategic notions have come from seeing a distant parallel with what was done 500 years ago in a similar situation. Many people report their "ahas!" came from realizing that a pattern was repeating itself.

Other punctuation marks simply ask people regularly: "What have you learned this week about...?" or "What have you learned this week that you think is repeatable in other situations?" The point is basic: without punctuation marks, life goes by, we perform tasks, we succeed and make mistakes, and we may learn nothing.

Reinforcement. Learning is probably best done for its own sake, for the improvement that comes with it. Reinforcement should be a matter of helping people learn and encouraging a learning attitude, especially when mistakes are made.

Building talent for any future

Five basic developmental systems help organizations build talent:

1. Measure what really matters through success profiling.
2. Know how to prevent the derailment of your people.
3. Provide actionable, useful feedback for growth.
4. Use coaches to spur growth.
5. Consider all jobs as developmental.

If you do the above, you will have a more competent workforce, you will have a more motivated workforce, you will find out who is a candidate for more responsibility, and you will make people calls more objectively. In the next chapter we outline a method for coaching people to address needs and spur growth.

Chapter 16

Coaching for 70:20:10 development

It can be as easy as ABC.

There is an orderly process people go through from becoming aware of a need to cementing a new skill into their day-to-day repertoire to getting rewarded for the effort. That process has six steps. Each step requires coaches to apply a different set of skills, use different tools, play different roles, and accomplish different tasks. The six steps must be accomplished in order. You can't skip steps. People can and do get blocked at any step and stay blocked for a long time, possibly forever. They can even move backwards to a previous step.

The ABC Model

For ease of remembering, we call the skill-building process the ABC Growth and Coaching Model.

The first goal is creating a motivated adult with a need. A learner with a recognized need and ready to do something about it, a learner with no defensiveness and having the confidence that something can be done. The learner becomes aware of the need, takes ownership of the need, and becomes motivated to act.

A

1 **Aware** – The coach helps the learner become aware of the need.

2 **Accept** – The coach helps the learner accept and take personal responsibility for the need.

3 **Act** – The coach helps the learner become motivated to address the need.

The second goal is establishing a development support system that works. A system or process that helps the learner build and execute a plan that works and then supports using those new skills back on the job. The learner builds a plan and blends it into the workplace

B

4 **Build** - The coach helps the learner build a plan to improve skills.

5 **Blend** - The coach helps the learner blend the new learnings and skills back into the workplace.

The third goal is creating a recognition and reward system that works. A learner is recognized for the effort and success of addressing the need and then rewarded with tangible and intangible consequences. Accomplishment is rewarded and celebrated through positive consequences.

C

6 **Consequences** - The coach helps the organization recognize the learner for the effort and success in addressing the need.

We see the ABC Model—three goals and the six steps—as the fundamental framework for all coaching, mentoring, 360° facilitation, and adult skill building.

A manager or coach or mentor has six different jobs or tasks to do and roles to play. These six phases of coaching or mentoring have to be accomplished in roughly linear order to work. Each phase builds a foundation for the next stage to build on. People will not benefit from a training course on a need they do not accept they have.

A1 Aware – help the learner become aware of the need

From: "I am not aware of any critical needs."

To: "I can see that others think I have a critical need I should be working on to improve."

Why?

- No one will or can work on a need which they are not aware of.
- People are more right about their strengths and less right about their weaknesses, especially interpersonal weaknesses.
- Self-assessment is the least accurate source when evaluating "soft" weaknesses.
- Most learners need help in understanding themselves.
- Many people are unaware they have a specific need, or any needs for that matter.

Essentials

16

- Atmosphere of truth, trust, and honesty.
- Credible, understandable feedback from trusted sources.
- Drill down to the behaviors.
- Repeated use of multisource, formal feedback (from bosses, peers, direct reports, customers, friends, spouses, etc.) for overwhelming evidence.
- Use of multimethod feedback (daily feedback, informal conversations, formal performance reviews, career assessments, and 360°).
- Coach and mentor availability, if needed.
- Availability of professional facilitation.
- Receptive, nondefensive learner.

Coaching notes

Here are a few things to keep in mind as you coach a learner at this step in the process:

Skills needed

- Understanding competencies (needs).
- Diagnosis of needs.
- Feedback skills, sometimes very directive.
- Convincing and influencing skills.
- Proof of evidence skills.

Tips

Most people don't know themselves well enough to efficiently and effectively improve their current job performance. They need help. If a 35-year-old doesn't yet know his or her weaknesses, he or she needs outside help to discover them.

This first step (awareness) is simply to help learners realize what others think they need to work on. In many cases, they will have a general notion, so the goal is to get behaviorally specific. In other cases, they know some of the issues, so the goal is to help them understand the nuances. In some cases, they know one issue but not the others.

The awareness step can be as simple as, "Did you know you don't present well in front of top management?" To which the learner replies, "No, I didn't. I thought I was doing OK, but I know that's an important skill, so I will get on it immediately." It can be as difficult as, "That's not true. I'm the best presenter in the organization. They don't know what they're talking about. I'm not interested in hearing anything they have to say about it."

16

The difficulty of getting through this step depends upon what kind of need is being surfaced. (See Chapter 9 for a discussion of the types of needs.)

For all needs, learners need a before-and-after picture so they can set a target, gauge the gap, and move to close it. Past feedback may need to be detailed further.

From your *FYI® For Your Improvement* book, find the skilled definition of the competency to form how the person should look, and an unskilled definition to outline how the person looks now. Note the nature and the size of the gap between them for each need. (See Chapter 9 for the discussion on determining gap size.) Add examples—the more the better, the more specific the better.

Check the person's five greatest strengths. See if any of them are in overuse. Do those overuses relate to the unskilled needs in any way? Are there any common themes? For example, do they overuse *Drive for* Results and have a need in Caring About Direct Reports?

Don't skimp on time defining the need(s). Much effort is lost if people try to work on a wrong or ill-defined need. Engage the learner in extensive dialogue and reflection to define the need(s). Use the before-and-after process.

16

Figure 16.1 Types of needs

EASIEST

Ease of development

Strengths: The task is to help make learners aware that even though they are already good at this, they need to be even better.

Average skills: The task is to confirm and validate behaviors and skills that are acceptable, just OK, with the goal of improving those behaviors and skills.

Hidden strengths: The task is to help learners become more confident that others around them think they have skills they are not aware of, with the goal of leveraging the skills and using them more often.

Untested: The task is to help learners understand that a behavior or skill they have never used before is or will be important. The goal is to test the skill under live fire.

Weaknesses: Since learners already have a notion they are weak in this area, the task is to add detail and confirming evidence. The goal is for them to see the need in very specific behavioral detail.

Overdone strengths: The task is to help learners understand a strength done to excess has a dark side. To some extent, the current troubles they are having are due less to weaknesses and more to a revved-up strength. The goal is to understand that doing something too much has negative consequences.

Career stallers and stoppers: The task is to help learners understand that they have one or more of the 19 Career Stallers and Stoppers that frequently derail otherwise promising careers.

Blind spots (the most difficult): The task, and this is the hardest, is to help learners understand they have a significant weakness in an area they believe is OK or even strong. This is where the skills of the facilitator and quality of the evidence come into play the most. People can go years and even decades not knowing they have a need in a mission-critical area.

HARDEST

Style and approach

Coaching styles range from passive to active, soft to hard, indirect to direct, and aide to expert. We have found that all styles have a chance to be successful, but breakthroughs in awareness and acceptance generally require a more aggressive, direct approach. Remember, you are working with an adult who has 20 to 50 or more years of life experience who doesn't recognize a need. The chances of a soft self-discovery method being successful are slim. When dealing with the more difficult types of needs, especially with blind spots, the coach has to be more active, expert, directive, and forceful. Very few learners break through alone. Otherwise, they wouldn't have blind spots. Steps A3 through C6 can be managed in a more participative, self-discovery manner.

A2 Accept – help the learner accept and take ownership of the need

From: "I know that others think I have a need that ought to be fixed, but I'm not sure it's real."

To: "I have a need."

16

Why?

- More people are aware of what others think are their weaknesses than there are people who accept them as true.
- Taking ownership, becoming a shareholder, accepting is the first step to real change.
- The need must belong to the learner for any progress to be made.

Essentials

- Once you have a motivated adult with a need, fixing the problem becomes much, much easier.

- There are a multitude of remedies available—from simple to complex, from quick to long-term, from free to expensive—to help motivated people with a need to build skills.
- The facilitator needs to assure the learner that progress can be made.
- The facilitator must be able to assure the learner that acknowledging the need is a strength, not a weakness.
- The facilitator must be able to handle the 24 defense scripts learners bring up while trying to get out from under negative feedback.

Coaching notes

Here are a few things to keep in mind as you coach a learner at this step in the process:

Skills needed

- Conflict management and coolness.
- Counseling skills.
- Giving good examples.
- The rules of evidence and proof sourcing.

Tips

Only motivated adults with a need can make progress building competencies and improving performance. A coach should help the learner accept the need. That's where examples and critical incidents come in. Share personal stories about your own needs from the problems you have had to face. Share stories about people you both know who did or did not take ownership of their needs. Talk about the consequences of being defensive or trying to rationalize away the need.

In extreme cases, send the person to talk to another respected person who is several levels higher in the organization. Have this more senior person reinforce the need and explain why it is critical to rise above it. Also, ask the person to make self-observations of situations where this need plays out and describe to you the consequences of not being skilled in this area. Until the person says, "This need plays out in ways that are unacceptable for me and for my performance," nothing much will happen.

So show some patience. Some people have a hard time acknowledging flaws or admitting that they matter. Many times, people never get by this second step. They are forever blocked at knowing others think they have a need but denying it's true.

We have been collecting "defense scripts" people use when defending themselves against negative feedback. In the past 30+ years, we have each facilitated thousands of feedback sessions. All of the following are real things people said (and continue to say) in the face of negative information coming from multisource assessments:

1. My raters really don't know me that well (and therefore the feedback is not true).
2. The wrong people evaluated me (and therefore the feedback might be true, but isn't important).
3. My job makes me act this way; I'm really not like this (and therefore the feedback is about a condition and not really about me).
4. Some of my raters have it in for me (and therefore they falsified their feedback to hurt me).
5. The computer must have scored this wrong.
6. My raters don't understand the situation I'm in.
7. All my strengths are all right, but my weaknesses aren't.
8. The norms really don't apply to me.
9. I used to be this way, but I've since changed.
10. Nobody really understands me.
11. This must be someone else's report.

16

12. My boss doesn't like me and marked me low because of it.

13. My raters didn't understand the questions.

14. My raters don't speak English very well.

15. This was a bad time to do this assessment.

16. I actually filled out all the surveys myself, but apparently I did it incorrectly.

17. This can't be my report because I'm perfect.

18. I wasn't like this in my last job.

19. My boss asked me to be this way; actually, I'm quite different.

20. My raters are just jealous of my success.

21. I purposely picked people who didn't like me.

22. It's all accurate, but I just don't care.

23. I've changed since the assessment was completed.

24. This is just what I expected, but it's not me.

We have also been honing responses to defense scripts people use when defending themselves against negative feedback. Here are some approaches that have worked for us:

- Typical reactions to feedback: up to one-third are deniers, devastated, or hostile; one-third are basically OK—they know they have the need but aren't really motivated to do much; and one-third are energized by finally figuring out what it was that wasn't working for them and how to fix it. One half of these are usually good performers who want to get better, and the other half are people scared they will not get the next promotion or will be fired.

- For the true deniers, ask them to consider why they might make the same statement about someone else. Get a commitment that they will have a discussion about the need with someone who has their best interest at heart. Recite your view (and that of others) and what people mean by saying it. Ask what the consequences of people believing it are.

- If someone is really down, say, "People don't keep doing things that don't pay off. How has doing that worked for you in the past?" Explain how strengths left ungoverned sometimes tip over to weaknesses. Turn the negative energy into a positive by getting the person to see his or her downsides as consequences of strengths.

- When people are hostile, let them talk. Reflect calmness to them. Then take whatever is said and restate it in an exaggerated way: "So there's absolutely no truth to this evaluation." "So this is totally unfair." Often, this will get the person to acknowledge the issue.

- Go after the toughest issue first unless the person is really hurting. Pick what the person is most likely to remember.

- In dealing with overused strengths, try to sell the person on a balanced strategy. Refrain from advising a person to demonstrate less skill when it's being overused. It usually doesn't make much sense to say, "hide your intelligence" or "hide your creativity." Ordinarily, we will fall back on our strengths under pressure anyway. A more productive strategy is to leave strengths alone and develop a counterbalance, as in a seesaw. An intelligent person might work on listening skills to be seen as more open; a creative person might work on follow-through so that he or she won't run off and leave loose ends and confused people in the wake.

- When someone is clearly poor at something like team building or strategy, ask, "What's getting in the way?" Find out what the person doesn't like to do and how he or she understands the issue. You will generally find the person has a poor understanding and needs a fresh mental map before much progress can be made. For example, poor team builders usually lack not only skill, they lack attitude, may not see the value of teams, don't think like team builders think, and aren't tuned in to reading and learning from other people.

- Have the person describe tough situations that are stumbling blocks. "Take me inside a meeting where that

16

happened. What did you say? When did you first notice..? What triggers you? What are your hot buttons?" Work with the person to identify what is getting in the way and what hits hot buttons. Have the person focus on triggers that lead to loss of control or frustration and devise simple countermeasures for those triggers.

- The essence of acceptance is when the person can vividly describe consequences that are personally unacceptable and is able to take the coach inside situations to describe poor behaviors and the undesirable consequences.

Style and approach

This is the most difficult and critical step. If you can't pull a learner through the acceptance step, you are dead in the water. Remember, you are working with a person who has 20 to 50 or more years of life experience who doesn't accept a documented need. Again, as in the awareness step, the chances of a soft self-discovery method being successful are slim. When dealing with the more difficult types of needs, especially with blind spots, the coach has to be more active, expert, directive, and forceful. Very few break through to acceptance alone. The 24 defense mechanisms are in full force. Otherwise, they wouldn't have blind spots. Steps A3 through C6 can be managed in a more participative, self-discovery manner.

Nothing happens until the learner owns the need.

A3 Act – help the learner see the value in working on the need

From: "I have a need but I'm not sure I want to do anything about it. I wonder if it's worth it to work on this need."

To: "I have a need I want to work on."

Why?

- More people accept that they have weaknesses than there are people who commit to taking action to fix the problem.
- Nothing happens until a person wants something to happen.
- Motivation to work on the problem is the elixir for real change.

Essentials

- Success profiles that illustrate why this need is important.
- Proof stories that describe what has happened to others with this need.
- Consequence management that defines what will happen if the need is not addressed and, alternatively, what will happen if there is success.
- Modeling the skill.
- Creditably demonstrating that the need can be successfully addressed and telling stories about others doing so.
- Mentoring.
- Atmosphere of optimism and hope.

Coaching notes

Here are a few things to keep in mind as you coach a learner at this step in the process:

Skills needed

- Influencing.
- Proof skills.
- Success storytelling (implying you would have to know some).
- Negotiating.

16

- Visioning what would happen if the person improves at something.
- Relating history of people who did and did not do something about this need.

Tips

As we did above for acceptance, we have been collecting reasons why people who admit and accept they have a need still don't think they should work on it. Again, all real.

1. No one above me is good at this (and therefore why should I work on this?).
2. I've done well enough thus far without it (and therefore I can make it all the way with this need unaddressed).
3. I don't think I could really change enough to make a difference.
4. I don't think this is a real requirement for success around here.
5. This would be too hard to do.
6. This would take too long to do me any good.
7. "They" (the organization, top management, my bosses) don't support fixing this here.
8. I don't understand why this is important for me.
9. I am what I am; they just need to accept me for what I am.
10. I like the way I am.
11. It's too late for me to change.
12. I've decided to leave, so this is no longer important.
13. Even if I fixed this, it really wouldn't help me that much.
14. Fixing this will make me less effective.
15. Fixing this is not worth the effort.
16. I'm not ready to fix this yet; I'm too busy.

17. I just got done fixing something else; now you want me to fix this too.

18. No one else around me is working on fixing this or anything else.

19. I've never seen anyone like me change this.

20. I don't see the payoff to me going through the effort to fix this.

The task in Step A3 is to convince the learners that the need they admit to is important enough to work on. The time to act is now.

What the facilitator must do is to find out what drives the person, what gets the person out of bed in the morning. Legacy? Promotion? Job satisfaction? Pleasing others? Power? Being liked? Being respected? Somewhere in the person's motivation hierarchy is the key to moving from knowing and admitting to acting.

This is usually accomplished by a series of positive or negative what-ifs. What if you were better at presenting? What if you were better at listening? What if you were an above-average strategist? What would that do for you? What would it lead to? Is there a payoff for you somewhere in there?

16

The more drastic process is a series of negative consequence what-ifs. What if you don't learn to be a better strategist? What if you don't learn to work more smoothly with direct reports? What has happened to others you or we know who didn't get better in these areas? Are you willing to live with the possible consequences of never fixing this?

Remember, nothing happens until the learner wants something to happen.

The task is to move from knowing (A1) to acceptance (A2) to commitment to act (A3).

Story

Awareness – Acceptance – Action

It was a standard question at the start of facilitated feedback: "So what did you think of this process?" Jack's answer was less standard: "Do you really want to know what I think? I think this process was a load of crap." Fortunately for the coach, he was being honest. Unfortunately for the coach, she had two hours scheduled to discuss this "crap." Probably not enough time for Jack to have any personal breakthroughs.

But he wasn't defensive, so the coach stayed on course. She asked him about his role. He described being an entrepreneur who had started his own business, was bought out by a large national organization, and went inside to manage for them in the same geographical area. "I hate the organizational structure and the hoops they make me jump through, but I know I do a good job and exceed my business goals; what else can I do?"

The coach suggested they crack open the report to see how he was viewed from different perspectives. He grew more interested, studying the pages, and became aware of a few critical interpersonal skills his boss and peers felt he could improve upon. As he reflected on the feedback, he made a connection, "I have two children, and one I understand and get along with great, but the other one I don't understand at all." Almost suddenly, Jack acknowledged and accepted that the feedback had merit and that he had some work to do.

It became clear that he really wanted to improve his relationship with his daughter, and he quickly made the leap that self-understanding (even if it was through a tool at work) could help him do that. He was committed to taking action on a couple of critical interpersonal skills that would help him have a breakthrough at work and at home.

16

B4 Build – help the learner create a plan to build the skill

From: "I have a need to work on and I want to work on it, but I don't know how. I need help building a plan that will work for me."

To: "I have a plan that will fix the problem and I am happily working on it and I am making progress."

Why?

- Once you have a motivated adult with a need, fixing the problem and building the skills become much easier.
- But most people don't know how skills and careers are built. They have had this need for years and have not done anything much to fix it.
- There are a multitude of remedies available—from simple to complex, from quick to long-term, from free to expensive—to help people build skills.

Essentials

- Effective support system.
- Efficient use of resources.
- Multifaceted approach.
- Safe-haven practice.
- In-process/in-progress feedback.
- Action learning.
- Atmosphere of support.

16

315

Coaching notes

Here are a few things to keep in mind as you coach a learner at this step in the process:

Skills needed

- Knowledge of skill-building technology.
- Knowledge of the Paths to Improvement system.
- Access to resources.
- Willingness to commit and execute resources.
- Teacher/coach/role model.

Tips

When you have motivated learners with a need, they usually want to launch into fixing the need in a hurry. Yes, even after 10 years of not doing anything.

Look first at the Universal Development Plan in Chapter 9 that lists 10 ways to develop in any area and pick any that fit for the learner. This universal plan can be used as a basic core for any coaching session.

Then look through and select tips and tasks from your developmental source materials. Please seriously consider all sections. Remember that developmental remedies are much more powerful in concert than by themselves. Follow the guidelines laid out in Part III, especially Chapters 8 and 9.

In addition to working directly on the need, however, what if there were other kinds of plans that successfully "address the need"?

The traditional path of creating a "fix-it" development plan is not always the most effective route to a learner's improvement. While this approach works for most people, focusing exclusively on fixing weaknesses can be challenging and discouraging.

Depending on the skill level, the need, and the situation, we have developed several approaches for getting better results at work. *Paths to Improvement: Navigating Your Way to Success* reviews 14 different paths to improvement for learners who are seeking alternative routes to improve their performance and potential.

Whether you are working on the skill directly or using an alternative path to address the need, you should lay out a plan and a schedule with the person. His or her action plan should include at least three items to be worked on immediately and refreshed every time one task gets completed. Agree on measures for the number of times the person did this or didn't do that and a method of recording these efforts so improvement can be tracked. Set a specific time frame of no more than one month to try these items repeatedly; if the person's time frame is longer or indefinite, he or she will be less likely to do anything.

In selecting specific steps, consider:

- The energy of the learner.
- How much time the learner has to spend on development.
- How practical each selected step is in the context and culture of the organization.
- Start small and build up strategies.
- Build in some early successes.

16

Help the learner with resources. Development and job improvement take time and money. The learner needs access to tasks, projects, and assignments. The need may call for expensive courses or time off work for parallel tasks (such as working on listening by serving on community projects). You can help by running interference in the organization and helping the learner negotiate with the organization and arranging for the learner to work with others in the organization who can be helpful.

The learner will need continuous feedback, emotional support, and reinforcement. When developing any skill, most actually get worse before they get better. It can be a real emotional struggle. In order to work on any need with a big gap, the person has to let go of one trapeze—the past—and grab for the other trapeze—the future—before any progress is possible. In between the two trapezes is nothing but air with no safety net. Many never let go of the first trapeze. You have to help the person realize that forgetting past habits is just as important as learning new ones.

Many times, all that's necessary is that you listen and provide a friendly sounding board, but don't make yourself the sole source of feedback or comfort. Developmental remedies work best in multiples. Encourage the learner to get the maximum number of perspectives, not just yours.

People who have made a negative appraisal of the learner's skills will be slow to recognize incremental differences. The person may get demoralized when others don't recognize early progress. You may have to chart and mark off progress on the gap ruler to keep spirits up. Use suggestion 10 (Get periodic feedback) in the Universal Development Plan. Have the learner get feedback from people who aren't so familiar and don't have strongly formed negative opinions.

16

B5 Blend – help the learner integrate the new skills back into the workplace

From: "I have learned some new skills and behaviors and addressed the need successfully. Now I need a plan to integrate the new behaviors back into the workplace."

To: "I have integrated the new skills and behaviors I have learned into my daily portfolio of skills."

318 |

Why?

- Many change efforts fail because integrating the new skills back into the workplace is not planned or supported.
- Support must extend beyond the fix for the effort to work.
- The job is not done until the job is done right.
- Bosses and coworkers prefer that people stay the same and sometimes resist accepting new and changed behaviors.

Essentials

- Back-in-the-workplace support from the boss and coworkers.
- Educated boss/mentor.
- No-fault practice.
- In-process/in-progress feedback.
- Confirming feedback.
- Atmosphere of finishing the job.

Coaching notes

Here are a few things to keep in mind as you coach a learner at this step in the process:

16

Skills Needed

- Understanding of the blending process.
- Patience.
- Affirmation.
- Team coaching.
- Working behind the scenes.
- Influence in the workplace.

Tips

Many people get to the point where they have learned some new skills and behaviors only to have them chilled when they try to apply them to the terminally busy and insensitive workplace. Say the need was to talk less and listen more, a common first step for those seen as arrogant. Sara volunteers for a task force assignment featuring an unfamiliar segment of the business. From this, she picks up on new skills—how to listen between the lines and ask questions to pick the brains of the more knowledgeable members. She learns how to best contribute and impress others with a willingness to work, not just to learn.

But back with her regular workgroup, no one notices any change in Sara. When she listens and asks questions, gives others the benefit of the doubt, and tries to appreciate others' perspectives, no one seems to notice or they assume the interest is insincere. They suspect she is trying a new tactic that is driven by personal agenda. Some ask if she feels all right because they don't see Sara's previous aggressive, impatient behavior.

What is actually happening is that Sara has changed, and it can take up to eight positive instances of a new behavior before people begin to alter their views and question the previous negative behavior.

This is the critical blending point. The boss has to be an active party in helping the person blend back into the work environment with new behaviors and skills. The solution might be to have Sara meet with her coworkers and explain the need, her attempts to fix the problem, and what she needs in support of the new behaviors. And Sara should explain what she will do differently to support the work team. Research indicates that this is usually the best way to turn around a negative situation. The learner admits the need, asks for help, and provides help. Then people are more prepared to give the benefit of the doubt. They know how tough it is to change.

16

C6 Consequences – help the organization respond to the successful effort the person has gone through by delivering the promised rewards and consequences

From: "I have worked hard and successfully learned and integrated new skills and behaviors into my portfolio; I now want the promised reward."

To: "I have been fairly rewarded for my efforts, and I am willing to get to work on my next need."

Why?

- The successful development effort must be properly and fairly rewarded for any future attempts to be effective on the part of this individual and indirectly for anyone else.
- Promised or implied consequences have to come true.
- Essentials.
- Workplace response to changes.
- Staffing/succession actions.
- Pay change.

Coaching notes

Here are a few things to keep in mind as you coach a learner at this step in the process:

Skills needed

- Assurance that effort leads to reward.
- Helping the organization deliver on promises.
- Managing the reward system.

16

|

Tips

Many times, the proposition for change is the following two scripts:

1. If you don't change (build this skill, address this need, adopt this new behavior), the following bad things will happen:

   - You won't get promoted.
   - You won't get a choice assignment.
   - You may get terminated.
   - You may not have the impact you desire.

2. If you do change (build this skill, address this need, adopt this new behavior), the following good things will happen:

   - You will get the promotion you've been waiting for.
   - You will get the pay raise you've been waiting for.
   - You will get back on your career track.
   - You can keep your job.
   - You will be included as a real member of the team.

What is at stake is the credibility of the development or improvement process for:

   - This one learner. Will he or she ever work on anything again?
   - All learners in the organization. Will anyone work on anything?

If the predicted consequences do not occur, this learner will probably not work on any other needs. If this happens frequently, others in the organization will come to believe that this development stuff is a sham and that there is no real payoff for going through the painful process of exploring and working on needs.

It is up to all the combined coaches, mentors, bosses, HR, and top management to ensure that the projected good and bad consequences happen. If they don't do this regularly, then no development or performance improvement process or system will do anyone any good.

Some possible rewards include:

- Recognition by boss.
- Recognition by coworkers.
- A team celebration.
- A roast, applauding changes by parodying past behavior.
- Merit pay or bonuses.
- A special assignment as a developmental project.
- Being placed in the queue for more challenging jobs.
- Increase in base pay.

You may be the only person who really knows what the learner has gone through. Find ways for the learner to demonstrate newly developed skills and behaviors. Take the measurements and milestones the two of you have established seriously. When one is met or exceeded, celebrate it!

16

More general coaching tips

If you are the coach:

- Being an expert is a matter of theme and pattern recognition and applying insights from that recognition. It is not just giving answers. What are you an expert in? What keys do you look at? How can you pass those on?
- Always explain your thinking. The role of a coach is to teach someone how to think/act in new ways. Giving the person solutions won't help unless he or she knows why and how you came up with them.
- Before you give advice, ask yourself why this is a strength for you or others you know. What are the first items (keys) you

would teach as the keys to help the person form umbrellas for understanding? How did you learn to do this? What were your key experiences? Who helped you? Use these insights and the skilled definition of the competencies to write a list of key behaviors that the person can use as targets.

If you are the person being coached:

- Remember that it is the coach's role to help you grow. Your coach may be an expert in the developmental process and/or an expert in your need area. You will gain most if you focus less on the coach's solutions and more on why and how the coach arrived at the solution. Ask him or her to explain—many people won't do this unless asked.

- How does your coach teach? What adjustments does he or she make for you? Ask for feedback on how you're doing.

- Set projects for yourself that give you feedback on how well you are gaining expertise in an area. If you are working on active listening, set five specific situations in which you actively listen. With your coach, set results in advance that will be evidence of your effectiveness.

- In the case of a boss/mentor as a coach, distance your feelings from the relationship and try to study things that work for this person. Focus on what the person does well.

- More effective learners reduce insights to rules of thumb. If your coach is an expert, what five things does the coach do that you think you could do? What five rules of thumb are you learning from your own efforts? If you have a developmental coach, what have you learned about how to learn and develop that you could use again?

- Unresolved defensiveness will kill any coaching effort. Resolve to accept whatever you are told and at least consider giving it a try. After all, you're the one with the need.

324 |

The bottom line

How would we know if any given person has changed? Added skills? Gained perspective?

At the 500-foot level, is this person doing his or her job better? Are performance ratings better? Is he or she prepared for more future jobs? Do more raters endorse this person as a high potential?

You could measure the change using a 360° process. In most organizations, people believe changes could be measured by repeated administrations of a 360° instrument. They reason that if a person works on something—say, listening skills—then their scores would go up the next time. Unfortunately, that's probably not true.

Let's pose two cases for listening skills:

Listening skills – example 1

1. First 360°: Listening gets a 1.93 out of 5 points, the lowest score
2. Selects listening to work on
3. Does something: Goes to a course on listening
4. Second 360°: Scores 2.23 on listening; still last but a higher score
5. Measure change: +.30

Listening skills – example 2

1. First 360°: Listening gets a 1.93 out of 5 points, the lowest score
2. Selects listening to work on
3. Does something: Goes to a course on listening
4. Second 360°: Scores 1.83 on listening, which is the third-lowest score
5. Measure change: -.10

16

Which of the above demonstrates that the course on listening skills was effective? All but the most educated skeptic would answer number one. But the fact is, we don't know. There are valid reasons to argue either way.

In a study on retaking 360°, the authors point out that change (or non-change) in 360° scores from before and after do not relate much to other, more direct observations of change. They point to three potential influences that may make the scores go down:

- Different people rating: they might use different points on the scale which has nothing to do with personal change.
- Different job/role for the person where standards are higher.
- Different expectations: you said you were working on listening; we expected more.

They conclude that most 360° assessment for development tools are not designed to measure small changes in skills and behaviors.

Other factors that could make a test/retest format unworkable are:

- Score inflation: the scores on most 360s are inflated.
- Range restriction: people don't use the bottom score.
- Repeated administration: there is some evidence that the average scores go down in repeated administrations because people get more comfortable with the process and use more of the scale.
- Psychometric sensitivity: most 360s are not sensitive enough to pick up small gains in listening skills.
- Personal disclosure: in the darkest of possibilities, if the person acknowledges that he or she is working on listening skills, the scores next time might even go down because the person has given people permission to rate more honestly.

Since being able to measure change is so important to the whole process, we suggest a specific personal change survey. It is along the lines of the mini-survey suggested at several conferences by Marshall Goldsmith of Keilty Goldsmith.

There would be six questions for every competency the person is working on. The questions would be something like the following:

A1 Aware:

To what extent do you think this person is aware that others think he or she needs to work on or has a problem, a weakness, needs to get better, or has a development need in listening skills?

- ☐ 5 Fully aware/100 percent.
- ☐ 4 Mostly aware/80 percent.
- ☐ 3 More aware than not/60 percent.
- ☐ 2 Somewhat aware/40 percent.
- ☐ 1 Just starting to be aware/20 percent.
- ☐ 0 Clueless/0 percent.

A2 Accept:

To what extent do you think this person has taken ownership, taken this need personally, or taken personal responsibility for his or her need for better listening skills?

- ☐ 5 Has taken full ownership/100 percent.
- ☐ 4 Has mostly taken ownership/80 percent.
- ☐ 3 More ownership than not/60 percent.
- ☐ 2 Has taken some ownership/40 percent.
- ☐ 1 Just showing beginning signs of ownership/20 percent.
- ☐ 0 Doesn't accept/doesn't show ownership/0 percent.

16

A3 Act:

To what extent do you think this person is willing to make the effort to work on listening skills?

- ☐ 5 Full effort/100 percent.
- ☐ 4 Major effort/80 percent.
- ☐ 3 Moderate effort/60 percent.
- ☐ 2 Some effort/40 percent.
- ☐ 1 A little effort/20 percent.
- ☐ 0 Won't do anything/0 percent.

B4 Build:

Do you think this person has a development or action plan for improving listening skills that you think, if executed, would work to effectively address this need?

- ☐ 5 Yes/100 percent.
- ☐ 4 Pretty sure/80 percent.
- ☐ 3 Somewhat sure/60 percent.
- ☐ 2 Maybe/40 percent.
- ☐ 1 Not sure/20 percent.
- ☐ 0 No/0 percent.

16

B5 Blend:

Now that person *X* has successfully addressed his or her listening skills and behaves and acts differently, to what extent will this be supported and accepted back in the workplace?

- ☐ 5 Fully supported/100 percent.
- ☐ 4 Mostly supported/80 percent.
- ☐ 3 More supported than not/60 percent.
- ☐ 2 Somewhat supported/40 percent.
- ☐ 1 A little support/20 percent.
- ☐ 0 No support/0 percent.

C6 Consequences:

Now that person *X* has successfully integrated his or her improved listening skills back into the workplace, has the organization responded with the expected/promised consequences?

- ☐ 5 Fully responded/100 percent.
- ☐ 4 Mostly responded/80 percent.
- ☐ 3 More responded than not/60 percent.
- ☐ 2 Somewhat responded/40 percent.
- ☐ 1 A little response/20 percent.
- ☐ 0 No response/0 percent.

16

If you used such a survey process across people, then a group report will provide the organization with some progress measures about skill-building successes and failures. You could also test out the developmental power of jobs, assignments, courses, and even mentors and bosses by aggregating the results across people.

The special case of those about to derail

Although the coaching process is the same, people in trouble require some special emphasis. Those about to derail are typically quite defensive, steadfastly cling to strengths, see them as strengths, and view the weakness side as illusory. "It's all jealousy or low standards or the glass ceiling" or any of the other defense scripts we have listed. After receiving feedback of their precarious state, they need:

- Vaccination, vaccination, and more vaccination. They should read Chapter 4, take the exercises, attend a vaccination course if available, and be able to explain their own situation to the coach in these terms.

- Outside help. If they are in this kind of trouble, the organization needs to provide them with out-of-unit help such as a coach, people higher up who can explain the facts to them, projects from outside the unit. No one inside is likely to want to help them.

- The awareness and action steps can take a long time. Even if the person is on an "improve in six months or you're out" probation, be prepared to spend two or three of the months on A1, A2, and A3. Nothing will happen until a motivated learner with a need is present.

- Remember that for most potential derailers, what is crippling them now are the very strengths that have propelled them this far. Threatening those strengths only produces consternation and backlash. Follow a balance strategy and work on compensators such as Listening to compensate for Arrogance or Problem Solving to compensate for overdone Interpersonal Savvy.

- Don't give up too soon. Some of the best talent you have may be among the most likely to derail. Fifteen percent of successful executives in the original Center for Creative Leadership study volunteered (they weren't asked) that they had derailed at one time (one got fired twice before he got the message). Many future leaders have big strengths and corollary big weaknesses. They are great at strategy but not that interested in people, or they are great at building systems but are confused by ambiguity and change. They also tend to be curious, so mistakes and blunders may happen as well. For a more detailed version of this argument, see Chapters 2 and 4.

- Potential derailers may have to be placed in another part of the organization, even after they have changed. Too many bridges may have been burned.

- Saving potential derailers is much cheaper than replacing them. We mentioned in Chapter 4 that one company saved more than $40 million in replacement and relocation costs in a one-year period.

- Rescued derailers typically become developmental advocates and often go on to develop others well. We would hope the reasons for this would be obvious by now.

So we're almost done. After reviewing competency modeling, derailment, feedback and development, and coaching—you have the ability to help people improve. All these ensure that we will do what we do today better. Only The Leadership Machine drives the future and this is what we will address in the final section.

16

Part V

The
Leadership
Machine

Chapter 17

Driving The Leadership Machine

You cannot reap what you do not sow.

The output of The Leadership Machine is producing waves of take-your-breath-away managers and leaders who are ready when needed. Those take-your-breath-away managers and leaders have to be better than the managers and leaders they replace because the challenges are greater, the speed faster, the competition tougher, and the marketplace increasingly global.

The strategic pundits tell us that the only real restriction to growth is people. Typically, there is abundant financing for promising business propositions, there are markets opening up around the world, and there are technologies to exploit. The restriction is the managers and leaders necessary to fuel growth.

The McKinsey *War for Talent* study and other studies, including our own, tell us that current leaders give themselves poor grades for developing people and keeping the bench full of aspiring talent. Studies report that leaders are chronically short of the specialized talent they need to succeed. The outcome of this is shown in a study in which only 15 percent of executive selections came from the succession plan. That is good news for headhunters, tragic news for organizations.

So we have a dilemma. It is basically known how to keep the bench or the farm team full of exciting candidates for fueling future growth. It is a relatively well-researched and documented process. We also know that many leaders in organizations generally know how to do this...but they don't. We know that many more in the HR function know...but they can't get the organization to execute it.

So the issue is not so much what to do, it's doing it—consistently—over a long period of time.

Observation | Succession

If there's anything we know about, it's how to do good talent management and succession planning. Best practices have been honed and are well known. And there is proof that the most successful companies are the ones that do a better job at talent management. Yet still today, boards of directors and companies do not prepare adequately for CEO succession. The business press is full of examples of both failing CEOs and the lack of adequate successors. This is good news for major search companies who are in the business of finding replacement CEOs, but it doesn't say much for companies who have thousands and thousands of employees and decades of history who can't find internal fills for C-suite jobs.

More recently, boards have started to pay more attention to succession, which has always been their responsibility, but even more so given current legislation. But the Catch-22 is that individual board members are not selected for their talent management expertise as much as their financial acumen or political connections. I have met few board members who, in my opinion, could actually add value to the issue of senior talent management.

17

336 |

You know what to do

What to do is covered in this book, but we can only be of marginal help in getting it done. That's pretty much a local issue related to managing the tensions we will outline, dealing with the conflicts that arise, and having the managerial courage to act in the face of resistance.

What to do is conceptually simple. You have to:

- Hire the best you can at entry, balancing the short-term demands of the first few jobs with the long-term needs of The Leadership Machine.

- From time to time, supplement entry hiring with experienced hiring to get today's job done, as well as being on the lookout for speculative future talent.

- Give people good jobs early and skip the rotational programs and the make-work jobs.

- After people have had two successful job experiences, begin to identify those with special talent who have the foundation skills, the motivation, and the eagerness to learn that will keep them moving on to greater responsibility.

- Within this pool of in-the-pipeline talent, identify the consensus high potentials that you will need for the top jobs in the future.

- Design and execute a treatment and management process for those special people. Make sure you retain the best. As we have said before, the best way to do that is by moving them through a series of challenging assignments and making sure they feel someone in top management is paying attention to their development. Make sure their pay remains competitive with a similar top talent group out in the marketplace. Human nature being what it is, many high potentials won't take a sure-fire developmental job unless it offers more money as well as more opportunity.

17

| 337

- Design and execute a development plan that will center around a series of challenging and expanding jobs.

- Have top management take ownership of the process and allot the time and resources necessary to get it executed. They also need to clear the path and remove people who are blocking the talent pipeline.

So it's easy to think about, but hard to do.

What makes it hard? There are a few issues and tensions involved in driving The Leadership Machine.

- **Elitism.** The Leadership Machine is by its very nature an exercise in elitism. Yes, some people are better than others. Not in the eyes of a deity or in the eyes of the law, but in the eyes of the talent judges. For reasons we can't know completely, people are different. They have varying talents and skills. They have different motives and values. They have different levels of ambition. A few win the gold, some the silver, more the bronze, and most win nothing. For The Leadership Machine to work, everyone must accept the basic fact that people are different. In some of the ways in which people differ, future leadership potential lurks. Managers have to be able and willing to judge talent. They have to come to peace with the fact that some of their people have it and others don't. More extremely, they have to be able to communicate both of those messages clearly and courageously.

  The Leadership Machine requires differential treatment. Some are going to get more development than others and some will get different kinds of development than others.

  We are always asked, "Shouldn't we be developing all of our people?" Our answer is always yes. Yes, yes, yes. All organizations should develop all of their people all of the time. All people should have things like developmental tasks to enrich their skill set, tuition support, and access to a development library of books, tapes, and other development material. If the organization has internal training, all people

17

should have access to skills improvement and orientation opportunities. If the organization uses outside training, all people ought to have access to it as appropriate. Every boss in the organization should be spending time with all of his or her employees—working on improving their performance in their current assignments. All employees in the organization with the potential to do more and move higher should be given the chance to prove they can do it.

That said, some will and should have more resources applied to them than others. Some are given additional development and enhanced opportunities. Some will succeed and others will stumble. Those who succeed will be advanced to filling the bench for future leadership responsibilities.

It is culling the herd. It is separating the wheat from the chaff. It is finding and nurturing the special people. It is an elite practice. Not everyone can or wants to play.

- **States' rights.** In multidivision or business unit organizations, there is always tension around whether an employee belongs to corporate or to the units. We are in an era of decentralization where the most effective businesses decentralize operations so that the people closest to the opportunities run the business. In many organizations, corporate has become something like a holding company— basically, the banker. The power is in the divisions or strategic business units.

The Leadership Machine requires central coordination of jobs and people. It can't be run in a decentralized mode. We will show later why that is.

- **Customers.** Who are the customers for The Leadership Machine? Actually, they are future shareholders, future employees, future pensioners, and future customers. Therein lies a basic conflict of interest or a share-of-mind problem. The Leadership Machine contributes to the future success of the organization. In a pure sense, it is neutral to current success. It neither harms nor greatly helps the present if done right. Current shareholders, for the most part, want results today, this quarter. Current managers

17

and leaders are primarily interested in performance today. Current customers want what they want today. We have right-sized the organization for today. We have taken layers out of the organization to be effective today. We are paying special attention to cost management to produce results today.

The Leadership Machine invests today for the benefit of the future. The bind is that for it to work, tactically oriented decentralized managers have to surface and probably lose their best people to move to other divisions and business units. In return, those managers will receive people not fully ready for their open jobs, all for the benefit of a future where they will be gone.

When we lay out the succession process later, it will become clearer that a small number of employees in the organization are owned by a future that has no present owner in residence. Therefore, it is always the future that loses to the present under the pressure of today.

And that's why we do not have enough leadership talent on the bench. If you are short on the bench today, that means your predecessors were asleep at the wheel 10 to 15 years ago, tending exclusively to the business of that day. They didn't do what this chapter outlines. If today, you do not do what this chapter outlines, your successors will not have adequate bench strength to succeed.

17

- **Who's driving?** The next tension is who should be driving The Leadership Machine. In the ideal world, it would be the person closest to the person with the potential—his or her boss. Direct bosses would assess their people and identify those with longer-term potential. They would spend extra time with those people discussing their future, giving feedback, and making time available for development. When the time comes, and it's always sooner than most managers would like, they would surface that person for new and challenging experiences and lose them to the future.

That isn't happening, much.

Why?

- Most managers are tactical. They need people who can do jobs now. Their share-of-mind for the future is small.
- Most managers are terminally busy. They are putting out fires, responding to unanticipated crises, and trying to make this quarter's numbers.
- Most managers haven't been developed either.
- Most managers are not good at giving feedback.
- Most managers are not good at coaching.
- Most managers are not skilled at long-term career development.
- Most managers are not rewarded for these kinds of activities.
- Most organizations have weak development support systems.
- The leaders of most organizations don't take the lead.

That's why.

So there is a technology that's known by many. There is time, which is short. There is long-term interest, which almost always gives way to the here and now. There is a set of feedback, coaching, and career management skills, which is in low supply. There is unselfish courage that is hard to come by. And there is territory protection that is natural to the species.

Easy to explain, hard to do.

Making The Leadership Machine run

The Leadership Machine only runs when there is four-part harmony:

1. The target person being developed – Target people must want to learn and grow, have a hand in their personal development, and trust the system.

2. The direct boss of that person – The direct boss has to assess, give feedback, coach, and be unselfish.

3. Management above the direct boss, all the way to the top – Top management has to lead the effort, make the resources available, and manage the assignment process centrally.

4. HR – The HR function has to design the simplest process possible to do the job and must be an active player in the process.

1. Target people

For target people in this select population to "run" properly, the major hurdles to jump are:

- Career information – How do people really get ahead, why do careers flame out, what actually develops people?

- Accurate feedback – Get them the best 360° feedback the organization can provide. Read Chapter 14 for the whats and the hows.

- Trusting the process – Most currently successful leaders can tell you stories about the number of times they initially turned down assignments that turned out to be the most valuable. Most young people don't know what they really want or how to get to where they think they want to go. Organizations have to help this special population understand the long-term career process. Self-management of careers works about as well as being your own doctor.

2. Direct boss

Managers have to make the time, get more courageous about giving tough feedback, and have to improve their skills at assessing and coaching. See Chapter 16. They also must be the organization's day-to-day spokespeople for the future. If they can't explain to young people why all this development is necessary, the machine won't run as well.

3. Top management

Top management has to be the stand-in stakeholder for the future. They have to be worried about their legacy in equipping their successors. What good does it do to build a great company if you leave it in the hands of a group of ill-prepared and less-skilled leaders to run it? Remember that today's shortages were born 10 to 15 years ago.

4. Human resources

HR has to embrace the science of long-term development, design practical systems, and take a more active role in the process. HR has to be able to influence current leaders and managers on behalf of the future. HR has to resolve all of the tensions by facilitating the process.

The parts of The Leadership Machine

17

The Leadership Machine relies on two main components: (1) recruiting and selecting the right people, and (2) identifying and developing high potentials. Getting those two things right will get the machine humming. Flub those two things up and the machine will stall.

Recruiting – where it all starts

The process starts with recruiting for entry employees with one eye on the present and one on the future. In order to fuel the present, you need to hire people who can do the work. They need to have the technical and personal competencies required by the first few jobs. In order to fuel the future, you want to hire those who are also the best learners. Read Chapter 6 for our discussion of the silver bullet of learning. Remember that college grades, albeit helpful for other predictions, do not tell you anything about the person's ability to learn from experience. So at entry, add a learning to learn assessment to what you are already doing.

High potentials

As we argued in Chapter 6, those with potential for future growth tend to be good at learning agility:

- A major characteristic of successful people at any level and at any age is seeing oneself as a learner, actively making sense of work and personal experiences, and striving to get better.

- A growing body of research indicates that learning agility may be more important for identification of potential than intelligence and technical skill, which is more likely to explain why someone got hired or placed into a job. Learning agility keeps skills fresh and provides the fuel for learning new skills and behaviors. It is related to both current success and future potential.

- Why is learning agility so important? Because we're creatures of habit. We rely on successful habits from the past, and under the pressure of change or new situations, we stick to our comfort zone and repeat what has worked for us previously. Learning agility helps us get out of our ruts, learn something new, do something different, respond to change instead of just responding to demands.

- People who learn faster aren't any smarter. They simply have more learning strategies in their arsenal to help them learn what to do when what they've been doing isn't working as well.

People high in learning agility do four things well:

1. They are excellent critical thinkers who are comfortable with complexity and ambiguity, examine problems carefully, and make fresh connections. These individuals can clearly explain their logic and thinking to others.

2. They know themselves and can readily deal with a wide variety of people and tough situations. They are cool and resilient under the pressures of change.

3. They are curious, like to experiment, and can effectively deal with the discomfort of change. These individuals have a passion for ideas and are highly interested in continuous improvement.

4. They deliver results in first-time situations by inspiring teams and having significant presence. They exhibit the sort of presence that builds confidence in themselves and others.

No one ever has all these attributes, but people with strong potential for personal growth and development have more of these than others do, and they can be spotted early in a career. Such people learn as they go, adapt as the situation changes, and build new skills needed for success. They also bore easily and don't have much tolerance for a lack of opportunity to show their stuff and perform. The higher the person is in learning agility, the harder it may be to manage and retain him or her.

So The Leadership Machine, or the succession planning system, needs to not only identify and track these high potentials, but it has to make sure that they have a series of challenging assignments and that their treatment in terms of pay and perceived opportunity for growth keeps up with their ambitions.

A typical sequence should go something like this:

1. After hiring, look for those who do well with the unfamiliar during their first two jobs. Focus on their performance under first-time conditions for them. This is much more telling than how they do under repeat conditions or in their area of specialty.

2. After first identification as a possible high potential, provide a more challenging assignment, see how much the person learns and changes, assess again, give another stretching assignment, assess again and only then consider them for key jobs.

3. In addition, use:

   - Projects, especially multifunctional ones.
   - Developmental tasks on current job.
   - Multiple assessments by different people.
   - Encouragement to experiment, some of which will fail.
   - Off-job developmental experiences.
   - Feedback/self-awareness activities.

How The Leadership Machine Works

As far as the actual succession planning system is concerned, there are many fine books and articles written just on that subject. There is a global professional organization—the Human Resource Planning Society—whose members design and manage succession systems. There are conferences on the topic. There are collections of best practices. There are several journals devoted to the topic. There are consulting firms and consultants who specialize in this field.

We will restrict our discussion to those aspects of succession planning that directly relate to oiling The Leadership Machine.

The succession planning system

Making the calls: Who judges potential?

There needs to be a periodic assessment process where direct bosses, the boss's boss, and close-in HR identify the talent pool. Most organizations do this annually. We think that because this subjective judgment is so critical to running The Leadership Machine, the assessment should come from three assessors and should be uniform—checklist or instrument-driven—following the findings listed above. Single-judge systems are fatally flawed. Not everyone is a good judge of talent, even with a list of criteria in hand. Multiple assessors are pivotal to the process. (We will detail a method for doing this in Chapter 18.)

Observation | High potential identification

Among the things that line managers hate doing (annual performance management being one of them), identifying high potentials is probably their second most resisted activity. As I've watched this, there are three fundamental barriers. One is a general feeling of anti-elitism—that is, to many companies, their basic value systems would stand in the way of labeling a subset of employees as high potentials, meaning the rest of the population doesn't have potential. I have watched many companies struggle with the high potential nomination system because of the company's values. The values idea that everyone is equal and that everyone should be treated fairly (and the same) stands in the way of the basic tenet of succession planning—looking for a few good people (high potentials).

The second blockage is the issue of how does one recognize high potential. Since the normal distribution applies to almost everything, probably only a third of managers are even capable of assessing potential. One of the major efforts of our tool development over the decades has been to help line managers identify high potentials through tools like Choices Architect®, Learning From Experience™, and viaEDGE™.

17

| 347

> *The third blockage is an interesting one. Since very few of the population are truly high potentials, that would mean the majority of people making the nominations for high potentials are not themselves high potentials. So the existential question is, can someone who is not a high potential recognize someone who is? And from an elitism standpoint, how do I feel about putting people forward who will eventually be higher in the hierarchy than I am? More people think they are high potentials than actually are. Therefore, since they are wrong about their own potential, how could they possibly be correct about other people's potential? Moving over to sometimes much-hated and sometimes much-loved sports metaphors—could a person who has never pitched in the major leagues identify pitching prospects in high school and college? I would think it would be difficult. That is why we've developed tools. We know managers don't like it and have difficulty doing it because it's an advanced evaluation that a minority of line mangers would be able to do. We have empathy for these managers.*

Essentially, to qualify as a high potential, there should be evidence of things like:

- Solid performance in the current assignment, better than most.
- New behavioral skills acquired.
- Increase in technical and business savvy.
- A willingness to take on first-time challenges.
- Openness to feedback.
- Key challenges/tasks/assignments they have handled that were different or first time for them.
- An analysis of these accomplishments so that high performance isn't credited in situations where almost anyone would have done well.

An accomplishment analysis must demonstrate what the person did that was different from what others have done. (It goes without saying that only those with reasonably good performance would even be discussed.)

Here are types of errors to watch out for:

- People identified who are not people with potential. These are often technically proficient people or those who do one thing extremely well (get results, build a team). The question here is, are these people seasoned professionals or simply not quite high potentials yet?

- There will be people with potential who will be missed. They may be stuck in a dead-end job where they have little opportunity to learn new skills, or they may have some personal problem blocking superior performance at the moment. They may also have people assessing them who are not good at it.

There are three myths that affect the quality of the calls made on potential:

1. **Many mistake being brilliant with being learning agile, but there is essentially no connection between the two.** In the population from which organizations recruit (college graduates, 120+ IQ), the two are unrelated. While being smart is a very good thing, being learning agile may be even more important. In one study, learning agility was much more related to performance than intellect. But managers have a better chance to be accurate on their assessment of intelligence than on learning agility. Intelligence is easier to assess and more familiar to them. In addition, many look for it and tend to overvalue smarts in making potential calls.

2. **There is a general belief that high performance is a prerequisite to having high potential.** More accurate is that good performance across varied assignments is the precursor, not high performance in any specific assignment and especially not high performance in a repeat assignment.

17

The strongest performers today in any job are probably the seasoned professionals, not the high potentials. Seasoned professionals stay longer in jobs, know the technology better, and probably perform better. The high potentials move through jobs faster, learn less about the technologies, and spend less time in any one area of the organization. It's important to not confuse performance today with a time line of performance record across varied jobs. What you are looking for is high potentials (ambitious learning agiles) who have performed acceptably to well across varied jobs. Those are the people who will make good general managers later. They know something about a lot of things rather than a lot about a few things.

3. **Many naturally believe that the best performer should be given the promotion as a reward.** If you did that, then the seasoned professionals would get the promotions and the high potentials would be left behind. The reward for being a strong performer should be rewards and recognition in the form of pay and other hard and soft benefits. Being the best at today's job is no guarantee of performance in the next, especially if the next job has new requirements and unique challenges. We discussed this in Chapter 4, where we recounted how organizations derail careers with this practice—good salespeople become sales managers, good basketball players become coaches. But the jobs aren't similar. Being promoted to the next job because they deserved the chance has crashed countless careers. The element that will determine whether any person can perform in a job different from today's will be learning agility, not current performance.

Creating the record of high potentials

Once high potentials are identified, there needs to be a central record of who (name of person) from where (name of unit) for what (jobs for which the person is a candidate). At the most basic level, you need to keep a record of how many open jobs there will be and how many candidates exist to fill them.

Succession management is just actuarial math. Without much work, you can determine how many high potentials need to be in the pipeline to fuel growth. So if you turn more than 50 percent of top management every 10 years, you need that many take-your-breath-away candidates one layer down on the bench. Once selected, they will need to be replaced at every level of the organization. So if you have five levels and you replace 10 executives a decade, you will need 50 high potentials moving through the five-layered system.

Historically, 50 percent or so of job placements don't work. (If you use most of what we've recommended in this book, maybe 15 percent will still not work out for various reasons.) Starting where you are now, take the number of failed calls (we'll use 50 percent) and double that—100 to yield 50. Then you have turnover. Your organization has a predictable level of turnover. You need to replace those people. Let's say you turn more than 5 percent a year. That means you need to add 5 percent of your employee population each year, mostly at entry. Some of those need to be high potentials. Then you have to figure in growth needs. Are the number of products, businesses, countries, or divisions going to increase? The increase will require additional people in the pipeline. Then there is the special case of losing people from your high potential list. How many high potentials do you lose per year? Add that in. So, plus or minus something, you can actually figure out how many high potentials it will take to keep the pipeline and the bench full. In many companies, the ratio has been 3 to 1.

17

Succession planning software is making the record-keeping task simpler. Major systems like PeopleSoft and SAP® have succession planning applications, and there are specialized packages just for succession management.

The assessment (judgment) question

We have a best-practice suggestion on assessment. The questions typically asked are, "Who can make it to the top?" or "Who has the ability to make it two or more levels?" We think a better practice is to ask who has performed well and has the behaviors of someone with learning agility as outlined above. Remember that these judgments are coming from direct bosses whose people-assessment skills are marginal. Asking them who could be an executive someday is probably beyond the reach of two-thirds of managers. Some of the managers you are asking to make that judgment are themselves not very self-aware and are not going to grow beyond the job they are in. One-half of them are below average. That's why you need multiple assessors. We think that with checklist or instrumented assessment of learning agility, we can get much more accurate judgments of potential. Whether they make it all the way or not, only time will tell.

The talent pools

The question of high potential is actually *high potential for what*? In practice, there should be a number of pools of high potentials. There is the enterprise-wide top-management pool. These are usually directors or VPs who have been tested across many different assignments and have received the endorsement of many assessors. They are in the process of fine-tuning their skills and are in waiting for the open top-management job. They are one job away from executive management.

Remember, this pool usually needs to be twice (or even three times) the number of jobs you need to fill because of bad calls, attrition, and other dropout factors. Most of the talent on this bench will be slated to be general managers of multiple businesses.

There are functional pools—people in line for the CFO job, the senior IT officer, head of marketing, etc. Since the heads of functions rely a little more on technology than general managers, it sometimes takes a special background and credentials to fill these spots. Some of the same people can, of course, be in multiple pools.

There are business unit, division, and sometimes country-specific pools. These pools are made up of people with at least the potential to have significant jobs at that level. Some from these pools move on up to the general management or functional pools.

In layered organizations, there are or should be feeder pools to all of the pools above. You will have as many pools and feeder pools as you have layers and functions. Some also have special diversity and gender pools.

Diversity pools are cropping up outside the United States as well. In meetings recently, we talked with clients about diversity pools in South Africa, Australia, and the United Kingdom. In this larger context, diversity means any population that has been underrepresented, underdeveloped, or disadvantaged unfairly in the past. In many cases, laws and litigation are the motivators, along with the feeling that it's the right thing to do. From a research standpoint, it could probably be demonstrated that everyone wins as a workforce becomes more diverse.

Replacement planning

Replacement planning (also called Position Specific Succession Planning) asks the question, do we have someone specific in the queue for CFO? Business unit president? CEO? Generally, the board will ask to see replacement charts on what are considered to be the key jobs. The CEO will ask to see replacement charts for key jobs in the business units and the functions.

In the early days of succession planning, the process was virtually all replacement planning. For each high potential, managers reported which job or jobs they were likely to move to and when they would be ready. Typically, the data were presented as an organization chart with the name of the incumbent; the date of the most likely turnover of that position; the first, second, and third candidates for that role; and when they would be ready.

There were many problems with this practice. Managers doing replacement planning were very likely to just list people they knew or people from their unit, but the best person might be from outside the unit. You'll recall that the careers of successful senior managers tend to be zigzag, so this is and has been a common occurrence. Often, more senior managers wouldn't accept that any of the candidates listed were legitimate candidates. They were often seen as doing well in a current job but not necessarily having potential for the next level. Also, the manager proffering the nominations might not have been highly regarded.

Replacements generally followed the list less than 50 percent of the time, leaving behind disappointed managers and number one candidates, many of whom would be unofficially told they were in line.

We recommend that a few key officers and HR should do periodic replacement planning. That group looks at each key job, looks at the pool of available talent, and audits what jobs are reasonably covered and which aren't. Those data are generally for the board and for the small group that runs the centralized talent pool system. The data shouldn't be shared back down into the organization since this sets up an implied contract that is broken more times than it is followed using today's typical practices. If you actually followed the practices outlined in this book and became more accurate, then disclosure would make more sense. When some particular key job is not covered in the pool, then either an accelerated program of development must occur with a few likely but distant candidates and/or outside hiring must be considered.

The treatment (retention) plan

People repeatedly nominated for pools, and especially those on key replacement lists, are the ones you don't want to lose. For each person, the system should assign a retention manager. The manager is seldom the direct boss because the role changes too often. It should usually be a mentor if there is one, a boss two levels higher in the organization, or a senior HR development specialist.

The retention manager keeps up-to-date with the key person's career goals and satisfaction with current assignment and is knowledgeable about future opportunities for the person. We recommend the manager work with a checklist which might contain these questions: Is compensation competitive? What would a competitor pay to have this person? How marketable is this person? How visible is he or she to the outside world? Is his or her current boss an enabling, neutral, or chilling influence? What's going on in the immediate family? Does he or she have children with special educational needs? Extended family? Elder care? Illness in the family? What does this person want to do eventually? What drives him or her? What jobs are available for this person? And so on. The result is a treatment plan for each person which should be executed one level higher by the direct boss's boss.

The meetings

Succession meetings range from a couple of hours to a full day each. Frequency varies from biweekly to annually, the most popular choice. The formats are pretty standard. Books are prepared. Many times, they are given out ahead of time. In some organizations, they are very heavy books.

Attending would typically be the heads of the functions and the heads of the businesses and sometimes heads of the larger country operations.

17

Since the stakeholders for the future aren't around, their stand-in has to be the CPO—the Chief People Officer—usually the CEO. In some cases, it's the COO. In rare cases it's a committee of senior managers. The CPO has to have a CTO—a Chief Talent Officer. Sometimes it's the VP of HR but more often it's a development specialist either reporting directly to the VP of HR or sometimes directly to the CPO. The CPO (CEO or COO) has to lead with aggressive support from the CTO.

The agenda? What did you say you were going to do last year and what did you actually do? What does your organization look like today? Who are your seasoned high professionals and who are your high potentials? What are your plans for the high potentials? What are your backup plans for key positions? Do you foresee likely or planned turnover? Did you lose any high potentials and why? Are there people issues you plan to move on, and how will you fill in those positions? (In Chapter 18, we'll help provide answers to this question.)

In some larger organizations, these meetings could take up to 10 to 20 days for the CPO and the CTO. A noteworthy finding from some of Kotter's research was that in the best-managed firms, CEOs spent more time on personnel matters than any other issue. For example, Jack Welch has said, and others have verified, that he spent about 20 percent of his time on these filling-the-bench issues (about 44 days per year).

A few process suggestions:

- The meetings are not so much to create the record as they are to set the model. The CPO should ask good questions. The presenters get to showcase their people-calling and management skills. Problems surface and are sometimes solved. Moves are negotiated. Rewards are dispensed. We feel that putting the burden on that meeting to create the official record will chill the potential of the meeting. The actual record of who is and isn't on the list can be completed off-line and after the meetings. It's more important to have a lively interchange than to finalize the record. The CPO has to be able to ask the right questions. Why do you think this person is a high potential? What accomplishments does he or she have that most others do not? Is that the right next job? What is he or she missing that we need to build next? When are you going to act on that person? How are you doing with minorities and women in the talent pools?

- There is always a debate about who should be in the meetings. Sometimes it turns out to be a cast of dozens, which chills the debate. Most CPOs/CEOs prefer smaller groups, but the problem with this is that the more junior people don't learn about their role in producing future leaders. A compromise practice we like is to have the direct reports of the head of the unit attend the first half of the review. They present with their peers in the room, talk about their high professionals and high potentials, and respond to questions. The purpose of this is four-fold: (1) They are seen and further evaluated by the CPO and the CTO. (2) The presenters observe the process when others are presenting. (3) Valuable information is produced. (4) The more junior people learn more about the operational definitions of talent and how to think through what it means in their units. The second half of the meeting is trimmed down to the head of the unit and his or her HR head, the CPO, and the CTO. In this second part of the meeting, the people who just presented are reviewed and a more open and frank discussion can occur.

- The team from corporate is usually the CPO, the CTO, and the head of HR, if different from the CTO. We also recommend that all unit heads who present attend one other presentation as an observer. That helps set calibration and further models the right behaviors. Sometimes it might also be useful if some of the board members attend one session.

- If the organization has a sector set up for divisions or countries, then the final meeting might be all of the sector heads sitting together for a day to review the rolled-up results of the previous meetings. At that meeting, only high potentials ready for a move are reviewed. This might be the place for deciding on the year's final list.

- To trim down the time all of this takes, we recommend that only a few people each year be reviewed in depth. One way to do this is to list the high professionals but don't review them. The reason is that most in the room know them intimately, and they have been reviewed several times before. This in no way is meant to signal less worth, only that there is usually no new information. Then, list the high potentials, but only cover those who are due for a new challenge in the next reporting cycle. That means high potentials who have been in their jobs for a year or more.

The development plan

Since development value follows the 70:20:10 rule, 70 percent from assignments, 20 percent from people, and 10 percent from courses (see Chapter 15), then the time in the review should be spent the same way. Seventy percent of the time should be allotted to next best job assignments; 20 percent on the next best boss, role models, or seasoned professionals; however, 10 percent of the time should not be spent on courses. It doesn't add much value to review potential courses. That should be automatic. If the person has a need in strategic planning, then the CTO should determine the best place to go. Spend the last 10 percent on any special needs of the person. Particularly important are any derailing tendencies that may prevent the person from reaching his or her potential.

Assignment management – the big mission-critical point

(We will cover assignmentology in detail in Chapter 19. Here, we will only cover how assignments play in the succession planning process.)

Since 70 percent of the development of critical leadership competencies comes from jobs—that's where the payoff is. It's people with talent being put in challenging jobs. The process is simple:

- You have an identified pool of talent.
- Each person in the pool has some documented needs.
- You have jobs that are created or that come open during the year.
- Each of those jobs has key elements, challenges, or required skills.
- All you have to do is match the needs of the pool to the challenges of the open jobs.

But it often doesn't happen this way.

Why?

States' rights again, tactical focus, and not knowing how good a replacement might be. Also, the candidate may not be willing.

- Managers with the open jobs want to fill those jobs themselves. After all, in their minds, the open jobs are their jobs. Managers generally want to fill open jobs with people they know well, usually from their own work unit and, most importantly, with a person who can "hit the ground running." All understandable. Any manager worth his or her salt would want to do that. These open jobs are mission critical to getting results in their units. They are being held accountable for results this year, this quarter, this month, not for results 10 years from now. They are just doing what good mammals do, protecting their territory. What they say is, "Although I really believe in all this development stuff, I have to fill this particular job with someone who can hit the ground running." Then they list why. What's amusing is that, eventually, they list all possible situations: It's because we are expanding. Cutting back. In the middle of a merger. Divesting a business. A new product or service launch. A critical project. A problem with a key customer. In other words, there is no good time.

- Managers with high potentials as candidates for open jobs outside their own units don't want to lose them. Since they are high potentials, they are very valuable where they are. Those high potentials are helping a manager get the numbers. They say, "Although I really believe in this development stuff, he or she isn't really ready, is in the middle of a very important project and doesn't want to move. I can take care of that person in my unit or I need him/her for one more year." They also end up listing all possible situations. Again, there is no good time.

- If managers of high potential candidates lose them, then they have an open job. Even if offered a high potential in return, this person certainly can't hit the ground running.

- Even high potentials have limits to how many times they will move for development. They also may get picky about what kinds of assignments they will take. Since the high potential is one of the four key participants in the process, concerns need to be heard. On the other hand, they are not always right. A fine balance must be struck between the next best consensus opportunity and the high potential's willingness to take it. Some combination of the direct boss, a mentor, the CTO, and the CPO may have to be called on to tip the scale in the right direction.

Divine intervention

This is where "divine intervention" comes in. If the succession process were left to the managers with open jobs, the managers with high-potential candidates, and the high potentials themselves, not much would happen. The managers would fight to put people in jobs they have already done and hold on to every piece of talent they have. This is where leadership courage and divine intervention apply. The CPO and the CTO have to collect all of the data, listen to the objections with both an open and a critical ear, and then make the call. They must either agree and release the job, or disagree, and override a key executive or two in the process. This phase of filling the leadership bench is not a participative consensus process. It is unresolvable at the local level. If the organization does not have a CPO who will from time to time overrule line officers for the sake of the future of the enterprise, then all is lost. Then it's better to fill open jobs from the outside in those many cases where there are no viable internal candidates. Straight-up-the-line manager development doesn't work well. The best person for a job is not necessarily, and quite often isn't, a person who can basically already do it.

The test of whether these decisions were right or not will probably come long after all of the protagonists are retired and gone. This is a 10- to 20-year proposition. It's even unlikely the board will reward the efforts to fill the future leadership bench. It almost has to be the self-satisfaction of the legacy of leaving better leaders behind than what existed when you came. It's like the political question, "Are you better off now than you were before?" Is the bench fuller when you left than when you came? Maybe there's a special reward in the afterlife! The organization cannot reap 10 to 15 years from now what you don't sow today.

Centralized job clearinghouse

Because putting people with potential into challenging jobs is the key, all open jobs that are possible developmental jobs for people in the pools need to be centrally managed.

Central management of the candidate slate

An open job notice is forwarded to the CTO. The CTO looks at the demands of the job and searches the pool mechanically or electronically for anyone who would greatly benefit from that job. A slate of one or more candidates is prepared. If there are no viable candidates, the open job is returned to the manager to fill as he or she wishes. The slate is reviewed and edited by the CPO. The final slate is offered to the manager with the open job. The CPO and the CTO listen to the 10 reasons this isn't the time and how it won't work. In some cases, they will agree and the job is returned to the manager. In rare cases, the manager is excited about the slate and actually is happy with the process.

Since the high potential candidates are generally well known to most managers with open jobs, interviewing multiple candidates is usually not necessary. It just creates losers in those who are not selected. The manager with the open job might want to meet with the best candidate. Even that step requires divine intervention because the manager of the candidate will give 10 reasons why this isn't the time and how it won't work. Again, the CPO and the CTO listen, sometimes agree, sometimes override. Then there is the candidate who will be curious about the peculiar zigzag move. Remember, many future effective leaders will initially turn down the very assignments that build them into leaders. It's one big negotiation where almost no one is left happy, except the future.

17

So, simply put, for all this to work, there has to be a central clearinghouse for open jobs and for candidates, with no exceptions. The major reason is that the best development turns out to be zigzagging through and across boundaries, between business units, functions, and countries, and between corporate and the field. This has to be centralized. But remember, only a minority of the jobs will be filled by high potentials for development. In most cases, the open jobs will be passed back to the managers to fill as they see fit.

In most cases, for this system to work, the CPO has to apply divine intervention for development moves to happen. It just doesn't work without it.

Air cover

After the move occurs, the CPO has to make it clear to the manager with the job that the success of the person from the talent pool is now his or her responsibility. The new boss has to run air cover and be especially helpful the first three to six months.

The boss has to ensure a good start, prevent early trouble, and provide time and resources to learn.

Safety net

After the move occurs, the CTO has to track the person's progress the first three to six months to make sure he or she succeeds. The CTO has to detect early signs of trouble and intervene. By definition, you are putting people at risk by putting them in jobs they have not done before. Not everyone will make it. There is also a special problem in going outside the person's home country. There is a script in many companies that says, "If I go offshore, I'll be lost and out of the flow." The CTO has to make sure that doesn't happen.

The biggest secret of all...

If:

- The assessment of potential is accurate.
- The candidates for development moves are strong learners.
- They have several successful jobs under their belts.
- Multiple assessors agree.

Then:

The current business is not at risk if the job does not require being a technical expert in order to succeed. Some jobs simply require seasoned professionals or heavy technical people. Generally, these jobs wouldn't be used for development anyway.

For other jobs, an ambitious, resourceful learner will outperform a safe fill in the long-term. This is why the person is a high potential—he or she is versatile and clever. This is how successful people get to be that way—by succeeding at jobs for which they are "not quite ready." By doing the jobs you listed in Chapter 5 that you really didn't know how to do (or so you thought). Maybe in the first three months a safe fill would be better, but surely the organization can run air cover during the break-in period. Since this resourceful learner hasn't exactly done this specific job before, he or she will find someone who has and ask questions. The learner will find seasoned professionals to lean on, see things in a fresh way, and be more likely to innovate than a safe fill who has basically done this job before.

True high potentials will add value because they have fewer preconceived notions of how things work. They bring a broader perspective and will listen carefully until they find the essence. They will figure out how to perform well. If new skills are needed, they will either develop them or find ways to compensate.

This is the nature of high learners. It is indistinguishable from who they are.

17

The seasoned professionals

We have spent this chapter talking mostly about high potentials, the leadership bench, and the feeder pools. There is another group that is equally important for the development of future leaders. It is the seasoned professionals, the master performers, the irreplaceable high professionals, the solid citizens, the master sergeants, and chief petty officers of organizations. These are the people who keep the ship running. They do most of the work. They manage most of the people. They stay in jobs the longest. They make most of the profit. They train the junior officers.

The safety net for developmental moves is the seasoned professionals. They will help prevent the green high potential from damaging the business. Remember that real high potentials will search out, befriend, and listen intently to seasoned professionals. Since high potentials are more self-aware of their strengths and weaknesses, they know that they are marginally qualified to do these jobs. They are naturally going to find and use the seasoned professionals to learn what they need to learn.

So in that sense, it is important to identify and reward the high professionals as well. They are essential to running The Leadership Machine. Some also make good mentors. If you know where the high professionals are, you will know where you can place the high potentials.

17

The CTO (Chief Talent Officer)

The role of the Chief Talent Officer is a special one. It is a difficult role to do well, somewhat akin to the Chief Internal Auditor or the Head of Quality. All are responsible for getting things done the right way. The CTO has to, of course, know the technology of The Leadership Machine, be a respected confidant to the CPO, and be in the top 10 percent of people assessors in the organization. The role is to be the keeper of the secrets, privy to the most sensitive information in the organization. Anyone doing it has to be comfortable around the board and has to be a respected person of the utmost integrity.

|

Watching CTOs across many organizations, we have come to the conclusion that it is best when this person is a seasoned professional and not a high potential. Being a high potential would be a conflict of interest. We also think this person ought to be in their role for 10 years or more. In order to do this job well, the CTO would have to know the top high-potential people personally, attend division and functional off-sites to meet and observe them, and be at all of the business and strategic meetings, both to learn the people and to know where the business is going.

Most critical of all, the CTO should be a heavy contributor to making people decisions for the long-term. He or she may be one of the few people around to help those 10- and 15-year efforts pay off. The CTO has to have the courage to speak up and, when necessary, challenge the system, the managers with open jobs and favorite candidates and, especially, keep the CPO looking forward.

In this sense, the CTO is the key representative for the future stakeholders of The Leadership Machine. Because of the above, we have noticed that many times an effective CTO can be a converted line manager with about 15 years left to go in his or her career. These converted line officers can learn the technology of The Leadership Machine to complement their knowledge of how the business works. The only absolutes are unquestioned integrity, being learning agile, and being a good judge of people going in.

17

To tell or not to tell

There is a continuing debate about whether the organization should inform people that they are on the high potential list. It generally comes from the "let's be open and honest with all of our people" value or script. Yet a major survey found that 70 percent don't disclose the list and 30 percent do.

We come down on the don't disclose side. While we certainly believe in openness and honesty in all of our dealings with employees, there is a limit. The list is only accurate at a point in time. People come and go; even the best lists will have errors and omissions. The people helping to create the list are fallible judges, and their people-calling skills are not in their top 10 skills ordinarily. They are also not good at giving negative feedback to their people.

The high potential list is created to help manage the organization. It is a piece of proprietary information. It is just like the organization's merger and acquisition plans that are generally not disclosed to all employees until something is afoot. Surely mergers and acquisitions are just as important for people to know about as being on the list.

Now the fact is, most of the people on the list know they are on the list. They notice special treatment. They get to go to special seminars. The CPO talks to them when he or she is in town. Someone who is not their boss (the retention manager) drifts in and asks them questions about now and later. The CTO has struck up a dialog with them. They are given zigzag job offers. They are asked to pick up VIPs from the airport. They give the tours. So official informing doesn't add much value. But what if they fall off the list? What will you tell them then? Will it be motivating to hear that they used to be well-thought-of but aren't anymore? We think it is better, even in this case, to work with the person on growth. Fifteen percent of the successful executives in the original Center for Creative Leadership study were derailed at one point in their careers. They didn't just fall off the list; they were let go. The obvious case is that life and development is not a steady progression for most people as they roll to victory after victory. It's fits and starts.

It is also a fact that many people not on the list think they are. For them, informing would mean telling people who think they are on the list that they are not. For that disclosure to be value-adding, each boss would have to be able to explain clearly why they are not on the list, what they are missing, and coach them on a plan to get on the list. It is unlikely that all of those discussions would go smoothly. They are more likely to be painful for both parties.

That said, the organization owes every employee information about how they are doing and what their prospects are. For the high potentials, they need to be told they are doing well and that they are well-thought-of and discussed from time to time. But leave this just short of "you're on the official list." The seasoned professionals need to be told they are crucial to the organization and that they need to keep on doing what they are doing. Other aspiring employees need to be told what they are missing and what to do about it. Many of them may make the list eventually.

Until you are ready to rank order your children in terms of long-term potential and hang the list on the refrigerator once a year, don't tell people whether they are on the list or not.

Clearing the path

There is one last task to be done. Every organization has people in key jobs who are no longer contributing at a high enough level. Those people are blocking learning and performing opportunities for the people in the pools and on the bench. As Ram Charan's study of CEOs in *Fortune* found, CEOs who fail don't deal with problem people quickly enough. They don't make decisions about the people on their team who are no longer a positive influence on the business. The McKinsey *War for Talent* study observed that average companies in particular have a tremendous ability to rationalize the existence of low and OK performers.

17

Doing nothing creates a cascade that ends in poor business results, impoverished development, and good people leaving. High potentials and budding high professionals don't have enough good bosses to work for; they block positions and, inevitably, poor to OK performers end up surrounded by performers just like them. Who else do you think is going to work for them across time?

Creating future leaders also involves removing past leaders from blocking the paths for the next generation.

Simply put, all key jobs should have either a high potential or a high professional in them. Nothing else will help you succeed.

What's going to be your legacy?

If you are short on the bench today, it's the fault of your predecessors.

If you are short on the bench in the future, the responsibility is yours.

17

368 |

Story

Reap what you sow

A brilliant high-tech entrepreneur started a local company in Silicon Valley in the 1980s. Over several years of intensive engineering focus, the company grew. In the late 1990s and early 2000s, the company grew by acquisition into a multinational corporation with manufacturing and R&D in almost a hundred locations around the world. In his late 40s, before his company's exponential growth, he first became acquainted with and experienced the power of multi-rater feedback. It changed how he thought about building leaders.

It also changed how he approached acquisition. As new companies joined the now-parent company, they weren't just brought up to speed on technology integration, engineering, and marketing—they brought organizational development to the table, even for organizations who hadn't been familiar with the term.

People at headquarters who had integrated people development into their work started spending several months in Japan, Spain, Germany, or India to explain, train, and introduce the concept of people development to a new line of business in a new part of the world. OD professionals, some newly hired in the wake of the acquisition, were helped with new systems, new tools, and new priorities in their positions. Every leader in every part of the organization was expected to plan on receiving facilitated multi-rater feedback over the next few years.

In multiple languages in multiple time zones, people received feedback, created development plans, and learned it wasn't just what work they did, but how they did it, that mattered. The right CEO had learned that growing the right people wasn't just technological—it meant an investment in people all along the way.

17

369

Chapter 18

Succession planning:
the Performance Potential Matrix

The Performance Potential Matrix is used for managing human capital. It's an efficient way to find out who and where your high potentials and high performers are.

The term *human capital* has become more than buzz. A common statement is "Our key assets leave the building each day." Some organizations are beginning to use human capital accounting, the balanced scorecard, or measuring managers on how well they develop the people assigned to them. Some large consulting firms have created human capital practices. Wall Street looks at the "intangibles" when evaluating businesses. Such intangibles include the quality of leadership. As we discussed in Chapter 11, hard evidence now exists about how much value leaders, people, and specific competencies contribute to an organization.

As we pointed out in Chapters 10 and 17, there are three special-value populations in organizations—high potentials, high professionals, and those moving toward those two categories. Those three groups return the best value for the human capital dollar. The high potentials are preparing to lead in the future, the high professionals are leading now, and the "to be's" will play those roles in the future.

In Chapter 6, we made the case for learning agility as one of the keys to producing future leaders. We have tools that measure learning agility. As we pointed out, people high in learning agility learn more rapidly, apply past learnings in creative ways to first-time problems, and add skills to be more effective. When people high in learning agility are given unfamiliar assignments, they learn to cope with them quickly and build additional skills and perspectives. Successful senior managers are generally former high potentials who have had diverse backgrounds and have an impressive array of skills picked up along the way.

Seasoned professionals (solid citizens, master performers, journeymen, irreplaceable high professionals, etc.) are people who are doing very well where they are, like doing what they are doing, tend to stay in jobs a long time, and consistently produce superior results. Either by choice or by skill set, they probably won't move much beyond where they are now. Their value is today and into the near-term future. In many ways, these professionals season and coach the high potentials.

In terms of value to the organization, you need seasoned professionals and leaders, the high-potential people who will become seasoned professionals and leaders, and the people who will become high potentials.

Story

Succession best practices

Every organization has some process for assessing talent, identifying high potentials, and facilitating talent reviews with the leadership team. Names are plotted on a nine-cell matrix. Managers discuss their people.

Such was the case with a regional bank. However, the leadership team was also frustrated with the fact that each year the same people were discussed, tough people decisions skirted, and little or no action ever followed the review meeting.

Three new ideas were added to their process that made all the difference in attitudes and results:

The first idea: Introduce a science-based definition for potential. Learning agility replaced a gut-level feeling that someone had the "right stuff." The conversation shifted to who could best learn in first-time situations.

18

The second idea: Future C-suite candidates need broad, across-the-business experience and had to have succeeded in each of these roles. Learning agility provided the language for reviewing incumbents and potential successors more objectively for evidence of such experience.

The third idea: Recognize that talent review meetings are not about opinions. Talent review conversations take the subjective and make it objective by differentiating talent in the performance and potential grid.

The CEO dealt with a key C-suite staffing decision he had been avoiding for years. He recognized that changes required could not be made by the current, long-tenured—but low learning-agile—incumbent. A more junior executive had both the experience and agility to affect the changes required in the role.

Coming out of the talent review session, the CEO said, "That was the most enlightening conversation about talent that we have ever had. There was no way to talk around the obvious changes that needed to be made. It was an epiphany."

The Performance Potential Matrix in succession planning: determining long-term value to the organization

There is an inventory or value-tracking tool called the Performance Potential Matrix (PPM) that can aid in placing both short-term and long-term value on employees. This tool can be a valuable addition to the other pieces of The Leadership Machine outlined previously. The tool can be used for making job assignments and for making "build or buy" decisions.

The PPM is a tool used in the '70s at PepsiCo by one of the authors as a method of looking at the relationship between performance and potential in the context of the succession planning process.

18

It is used to help managers select and nominate high potentials and to evaluate the overall short- and long-term value of each employee to the organization. It can also be used to inventory people at similar levels across the organization to calibrate the talent reserve.

Several research findings and observations underlie the creation and use of this matrix:

- Current performance (the past year's formal performance appraisal evaluation and rating) is overused as a criterion or verification in succession planning. Current performance and future potential are only somewhat related. Many people are high performers but only in a single area or in a current job. Others may be high performers due to the situation (it's a high-performing unit or the job is too easy or they've done virtually the same job before). So a high, medium, or low performer might or might not do well in a totally different type of job or a job at a different level. While strong performance might be a threshold requirement for being labeled a high potential, it alone is not a sufficient indicator of potential. It's a comfortable notion, because performance is more known and certain than potential.

- Research has shown most people can accurately differentiate about three points when rating others—higher than all the others or highest, lower than all the others or lowest, and somewhere in the middle or between the two. The PPM tool asks managers or other raters (see Chapter 17 on who should make the call) to divide people into thirds—as highest third, middle third, or lowest third—in performance and potential. The important point is the "est." It's a Relative assessment, not Absolute. There have to be highests and lowests for the tool to work.

- Performance for the PPM tool is measured in terms of long-term past performance. Not just the last year, but the ability to consistently deliver results over time. The focus is on an employee's sustained performance over the past three to five years, not on one specific accomplishment or performance period.

- Estimations of potential have to do with capability to handle different kinds of jobs that will be first-time challenges for most people. Performance data can be somewhat known. Potential is a bet that someone can quickly respond to diverse, intense, varied, and adverse assignments; demonstrate superior performance under first-time or different, not repeat, conditions; eagerly learn new competencies in order to perform; and learn to handle different challenges in the future based upon evidence that they have done so in the past.

The Performance Potential Matrix is a three-by-three table as depicted in figure 18.1.

Figure 18.1

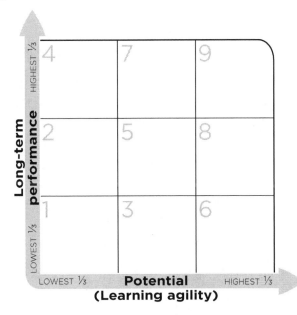

The numbering of the nine cells in the matrix is weighted in favor of or toward long-term potential or learning agility. The general rule driving the table is the higher the number, the greater the long-term potential benefit or value for the organization. Therefore the 6 is one better than the 5 because the 6 is a higher number

| 375

and to the right in potential. The 7 is better than the 6 because it is two levels higher (up) on long-term performance but still middle in potential. The 9 is better than the 8 because it is one level higher on performance and at the same level in potential.

The PPM can be used by one manager looking at the collection of people who directly report to him or her. It can also be used to look at all people in one category, like directors or regional sales managers, for example. It can be used to inventory entire organizations. We will describe the tool using one manager and nine direct reports (team one).

How to use the Performance Potential Matrix

1. To use the PPM, have managers, alone or with assistance (see Chapter 17), assess all of their direct reports on performance over the long-term—defined as the ability to consistently deliver results over time in multiple jobs. Some organizations put more specific criteria around what performance looks like for them over the long-term.

   The assessment task is Relative (forced distribution of 1/3, 1/3, 1/3), not Absolute (placing as many candidates in each cell as appropriate). There have to be winners or bests (highests) and losers or leasts (lowests). The matrix and the PPM process will not work unless the group is divided into even thirds. If the number of people in the group cannot be divided into thirds, the excess goes into the middle category if there is only one person, and into the middle and bottom categories if there are two people.

   Almost all managers will resist this arbitrary division of people into thirds on performance. They feel they can accurately and fairly categorize their people against Absolute categories (high, middle, and low performance). Most of the time, they can't. If left free to place people without restriction, managers tend to place too many people in the high category. If they could, performance appraisals would be accurate rather than inflated. Although managers will resist this, letting managers place their people in any box they want on the left-hand side of the matrix is the biggest mistake in the use of the PPM. Later in the process, there is a follow-on step where a panel of people might be able to convert this Relative (1/3, 1/3, 1/3) sort into a more Absolute categorization. We will speak of that later.

Display the results down the left-hand side of the nine-cell Performance Potential Matrix (see Figure 18.2).

Figure 18.2

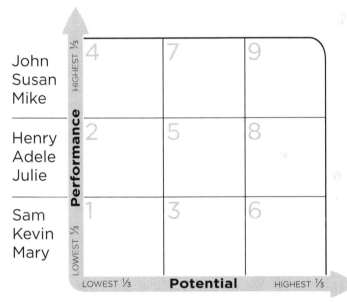

2. There are three ways to sort potential or learning agility (see Figure 18.3):

- **Method 1:** If you have only manager or manager-assisted assessments, then the manager divides the group into thirds, as before. These judgments will be debated and possibly changed later in the succession planning sessions.

- **Method 2:** If you have more formal psychometrically proven assessment tools like the Choices Architect® online

18

survey, viaEDGE™ self-assessment, or Learning From Experience™ interviews, the people would be arranged in rank order from highest to lowest (total) average score and then be divided into thirds before being entered into the matrix. We are not suggesting using score as the sole criterion but only for initial placement. Any score must be vetted by showing repeated evidence of performance under first-time conditions and learning new skills.

- Method 3: If you are totally confident in your scored instrument (you believe the scores are accurate—they have been completed by multiple raters who know the people well), then you can enter people into the table by their scores. If you were using the Choices Architect® online survey as an example, scores of 258 and below identify the lowest group; 259–293 the middle; and 294+ the highest group. It is rare that a direct score method (Method 3) would be used, and it is the only time that the 1/3, 1/3, 1/3 rule does not apply. Theoretically, an organization could have many high potentials or few.

Figure 18.3

Performance (HIGHEST ⅓ to LOWEST ⅓) / Potential →	LOWEST ⅓		HIGHEST ⅓	
HIGHEST ⅓	Lowest ⅓ nomination	Middle ⅓ nomination	Highest ⅓ nomination	Method 1: judgment
	Lowest ⅓ scores	Middle ⅓ scores	Highest ⅓ scores	Method 2: Scoring
LOWEST ⅓	Research 81-258	Research 259-293	Research 294-405	Method 3: Valid

Some organizations first have managers make the nominations by themselves and then affirm or conform the ratings with an instrumented measure of learning agility.

Put the names above the correct columns on top of the matrix (see Figure 18.4).

Figure 18.4

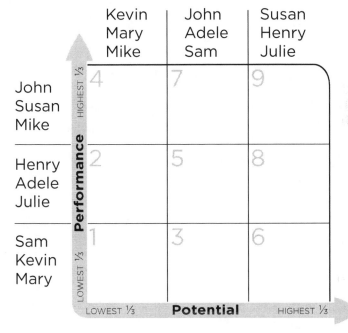

3. Locate the common intersection cell on the matrix (where the name on the side row and the same name on the top column match) in order to place the person's name in the matrix (see Figure 18.5).

Figure 18.5

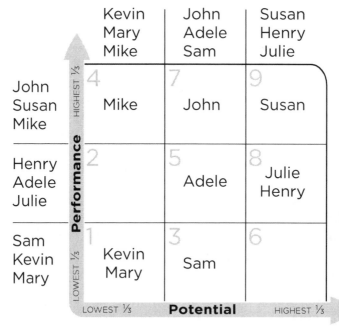

4. The resulting PPM yields an ordered list (from 1 – lowest Relative value, to 9 – highest Relative value) that can be used for selection, development, or succession planning according to priority needs. Among high potentials, the 9s are better bets than the 8s to handle a new job; but the 8s may be the top priority developmental candidates (future 9s). Among high professionals, the 7s are more valuable today than the 4s and the 3s, and 5s may have more potential to be high professionals than the 2s. Ordinarily, we would recommend that high professionals and budding high professionals not be on the high potential list and be on a list of their own. Depending upon the need for high potentials, a number of cells could be candidates for the list. Surely 9s and 8s. If those don't produce the numbers you need, you would next

18

add the 6s, then the 5s, and finally the 3s. The 7s tend to be needed as deep professionals but could also be considered.

5. Another way to look at the resulting matrix is to use some guiding labels (see Figure 18.6). The following labels are suggestions. Some organizations choose other titles that are more acceptable in their culture. Some organizations also do not use the nine numbers because people focus too much on them.

Figure 18.6

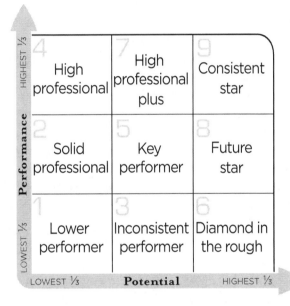

Cell 1   Lower performer

Is not delivering results as expected and cannot effectively adapt to new and different situations. This cell returns the least value for development effort and resources. People in this cell may require performance action.

Cell 2   Solid professional

Consistently meets and may occasionally exceed expectations. Knows current job well. Does not effectively adapt to new situations. Has a narrow bandwidth in terms of professional interests.

381

Cell 3   Inconsistent performer

Has some potential to do more but has not yet fully demonstrated it. Is not meeting performance standards applied to others in the organization and, as a result, is struggling. May be new to the job or to the company. May be in the wrong job or function.

Cell 4   High professional

Consistently produces exceptional results and high performance ratings in a defined but focused area. Knows current job extremely well. Does not always easily adapt to new situations, particularly those outside of their functional area. High Professionals are very valuable to the organization. May be promotable within functional/technical area.

Cell 5   Key performer

Meets the expectations of the role. Understands and knows the current job well and enhances skills for their current job as well as the near-term future. Can adapt to new situations and challenges as necessary. Comfortably assumes new jobs and roles and performs well in them in time. Probably promotable a level vertically or able to move laterally within the organization.

Cell 6   Diamond in the rough

Diamonds in the Rough are truly high potentials. Most would agree that they have the potential to perform and do great things for the organization. They have potential, but as the title suggests, the actual playing out of the potential is in the future. They have either not had sufficient time or opportunities to demonstrate what they can do or have been inconsistent in the past. Some may have had one or more significant stumbles recently but people still think they have the potential to break out and be a significant contributor. May be in the wrong job or a poor fit for the current situation.

18

|

Cell 7   High professional plus
Consistently produces exceptional results and receives high performance ratings. Is particularly good in one or more areas, businesses, geographies, functions, or specialized skills. Can adapt to new situations and learn new areas. May be promotable in multiple functional/technical areas or general management.

Cell 8   Future star
Consistently meets and sometimes exceeds expectations and has the capacity to take on new and different challenges on a consistent basis. Addresses new challenges and issues with ease. Quickly gets up to speed when taking on a new assignment. Has the potential to make career changes into different situations.

Cell 9   Consistent star
Typically in low supply but in high demand. Performs well in almost everything they take on. Learns fast. Transfers learning from one area to another. Resourceful. Gets things done under tight deadlines and resources. Has the ability to take on major stretch assignments in new areas with promotions and lateral movement into just about any situation.

Matrix tectonics (movement within cells)

The rules for movement in the matrix are:

1. To move vertically (up), develop deeper job skills.
2. To move horizontally (right), enhance learning skills and give new assignments.
3. One cell moves vertically are very doable—move from 3 to 5.
4. One cell moves horizontally are doable but a bit harder—move from 5 to 8—you have to become more learning agile and have diverse experiences.

18

5. One rank diagonal moves are more rare—a move from 5 to 9 or 2 to 7.

6. Two cell moves vertically could happen with lots of job skill development and lots of time—3 to 7.

7. Two cell moves diagonally happen but are very rare—a person would have to have a really significant life experience and commit to change course permanently—from 1 to 9.

8. People can move backward as technologies, strategies, and challenges change.

9. The PPM vertical (performance) can be situational. A person might be a 1 in one environment, company, division, geography, or industry and a 2 or 4 in another.

10. The PPM horizontal (potential) is a bit more permanent. It's unlikely for someone to be a 2 in one environment and an 8 in another. A one cell difference might occur but a two cell jump would be rare.

11. Significant life events and changes can have an effect on cell placement, either up or down.

12. In general, most managers—without the discipline of the PPM—would estimate a cell or two higher (both up and right) placement for their people than might be real for either dimension. That's why the 1/3, 1/3, 1/3 works best.

13. In general, lower ratings on potential mean that people aren't as adaptable to new/first-time situations, but that doesn't mean they can't be promoted a level in their specialty. Middle ratings on potential mean that they could be promoted in their specialty and, with further development, into first-time assignments. The highest third are those who thrive on first-time assignments, get bored more quickly with routine, and will seek a new assignment every 18 to 24 months if the organization isn't doing this for them. As a result, these are the people most likely to move outside their area of technical expertise or functionality, move multiple levels, or have the potential to move into general management jobs.

Advanced uses of the Performance Potential Matrix

You can use multiple matrixes to compare two or more similar units, teams, or groups. If you wanted to roughly compare team one and team two, you could take the two completed matrixes and basically overlay them. The following matrix might be used (Figure 18.7).

Figure 18.7

Cell	Team One	Team Two	Comparison
9	Susan	Hank	Team two is better
8	Julie Henry	Charles	Team two is better
7	John	Renee	Equivalent
6		Peter	
5	Adele	Kevin S.	Equivalent
4	Mike	Margaret	Equivalent
3	Sam	Amy	Equivalent
2		Terry	
1	Kevin H. Mary	Mark	Team one is better

18

For each category, a judgment by a panel of people would be made on the relative value of people in the same cell across teams. You can determine if different bosses use the same criteria when rating talent by comparing matrixes. As in performance appraisal, some bosses will be more strict/lenient than others. Matrix overlays can help to calibrate talent across the organization (Figure 18.7). In cell 9, is Susan equal to, greater than, or less than Hank? Using this method, you could conclude that team two is net better than team one. It is also possible that Charles (an 8) from team two is better than Susan (a 9) from team one. You could slide the column for team two up or down until the benchmarked people line up across. You might find that cell 6 (Peter) is equivalent to cell 8 (Julie and Henry) across the two teams.

Better, equivalent, or less than is a judgment about the people in the same cell across the two teams. Better means better performers and/or better potential and/or better experience.

You could add another team to the comparison (see Figure 18.8).

386 |

Figure 18.8

Cell	Team One	Team Two	Team Three
9	Susan	Hank	Adrienne
8	Julie Henry	Charles	Jim
7	John	Renee	Sharon
6		Peter	Harold
5	Adele	Kevin S.	Sid
4	Mike	Margaret	Russ
3	Sam	Amy	Nellie
2		Terry	Ivan
1	Kevin H. Mary	Mark	Bill

| 387

You could then combine the data into a single matrix to get a summary picture of the whole group. Let's say all of the people in the group picture in Figure 18.8 were at the same level—all Regional Sales Managers.

Figure 18.9

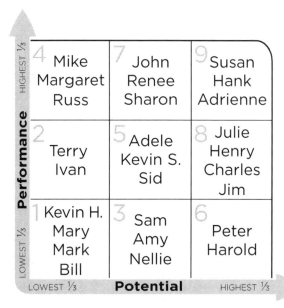

This summary picture (Figure 18.9) will be instructive as to the general potential bench strength of the total unit. You can then use the data for making the build or buy decision. Looking at current and near-term needs, are there sufficient high-numbered-cell people to fill future jobs? The summary will also help make the assignment decisions—who should get the next job?

18

Movement analysis

In the most advanced use of the PPM tool, you can compare summary matrixes across levels, functions, units, and/or geography. Let's say we have another matrix of District Sales Managers (see Figure 18.10) who are one level below the Regional Sales Managers.

Figure 18.10

You now have a basis for comparing people across levels. In a visual sense, if the two summary matrixes were on transparency film, you would overlay them (see Figure 18.11) so that cell 9 from the District Sales Managers matrix (the lower level) would overlay cell 1 on the Regional Sales Managers matrix (the higher level).

Figure 18.11

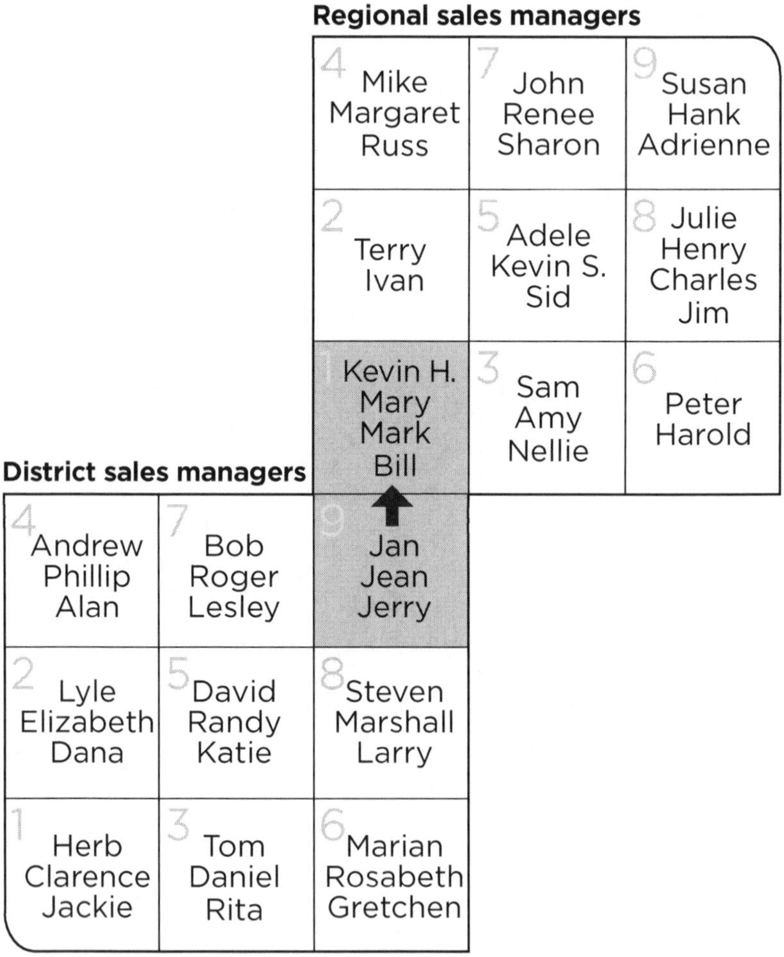

Regional sales managers

4 Mike Margaret Russ	7 John Renee Sharon	9 Susan Hank Adrienne
2 Terry Ivan	5 Adele Kevin S. Sid	8 Julie Henry Charles Jim
Kevin H. Mary Mark Bill	3 Sam Amy Nellie	6 Peter Harold

District sales managers

4 Andrew Phillip Alan	7 Bob Roger Lesley	9 Jan Jean Jerry
2 Lyle Elizabeth Dana	5 David Randy Katie	8 Steven Marshall Larry
1 Herb Clarence Jackie	3 Tom Daniel Rita	6 Marian Rosabeth Gretchen

18

Figure 18.12

Cell	Regional sales managers	District sales managers
9	Susan Hank Adrienne	
8	Julie Henry Charles Jim	
7	John Renee Sharon	
6	Peter Harold	
5	Adele Kevin S. Sid	
4	Mike Margaret Russ	
3	Sam Amy Nellie	
2	Terry Ivan	
1	Kevin H. Mary Mark Bill	Jan Jean Jerry

It's easier to show in a matrix like the one in Figure 18.12. The first step is to compare the cell 9 (best) District Sales Managers to the cell 1 (worst) Regional Sales Managers.

This is the value and movement question (see Figure 18.12): are Jan, Jean, and/or Jerry (District Sales Managers) better (would or could do a better job at the regional level) today than Kevin H., Mary, Mark, and/or Bill (Regional Sales Managers) individually or collectively? If the answer is yes, you should move Kevin H., Mary, Mark, and/or Bill out of the organization and promote Jan, Jean, and/or Jerry. Another perspective is what would be the more serious loss to the organization? If Kevin H., Mary, Mark, or Bill left the organization, or Jan, Jean, or Jerry? If it's Jan, Jean, or Jerry, it's time to take action.

If you don't, you risk losing Jan, Jean, and/or Jerry who will become impatient with their progress.

Let's say that the decision is that all of the high-potential District Sales Managers (cell 9s) are better than the current cell 1 Regional Sales Managers. Then you go on to test the next cell.

Are Jan, Jean, and/or Jerry better today than Terry and/or Ivan (Figure 18.13)? If yes, move Terry and Ivan out of the organization. And so on. You keep sliding the District Sales Managers column up until Jan, Jean, and Jerry are no longer better than the Regional Sales Managers column. Then apply the same reasoning to the 8s who are District Sales Managers—Steven, Marshall, and Larry. Are they also better than Kevin H., Mary, Mark, or Bill (the cell 1 Regional Sales Managers)?

The group summary overlap process keeps the high potentials moving and developing, gets the deadwood out, reduces the turnover of people you need to keep, and fields the best multilevel team possible.

Figure 18.13

Cell	Regional sales managers	District sales managers
9	Susan Hank Adrienne	
8	Julie Henry Charles Jim	
7	John Renee Sharon	
6	Peter Harold	
5	Adele Kevin S. Sid	
4	Mike Margaret Russ	
3	Sam Amy Nellie	
2	Terry Ivan	Jan Jean Jerry
1	Kevin H. Mary Mark Bill	Steven Marshall Larry

Matrix conversion

Some organizations convert the Relative matrix into an Absolute one. That is, after the reviews of the individual Relative matrixes, a panel (more than one decision maker) decides to reassign people to Absolute cells. Usually the reassignment is limited to a one cell shift up or down and/or a one cell shift sideways (so it could be two cells in total). This is done to get a truer picture of the talent inventory. Some organizations may feel that even though many people ended up in cell 9, there are no truly high-potential stars to fuel future growth. The panel may decide that one unit has better people generally than another. They may choose to move everyone down a notch from a less-than-stellar unit and up a notch in a particularly high-performing unit. This is usually best done after the total review process. Some organizations keep this resulting Absolute calibrated matrix private to the people-management team.

Once the individual matrixes have been calibrated, they can be combined into summary matrixes. Top management can then have a simple and convenient way to examine levels, functions, units, and locations to see where the talent is stored.

Many organizations also color code the summary matrixes on special issues like gender, race, and age to track numbers, location, and progress. Some also color code key technologies, language skills, and international depth.

18   Benefits of the Performance Potential Matrix

The overall benefit of the PPM is to keep your best people by moving out people who are not performing up to standard. As a result, your best people can be deployed to where they are needed and developed further.

- **Discipline** – The PPM puts more discipline to the people-value proposition. In Chapter 2, we outlined the strengths and weaknesses of typical managers and executives. One of the findings was that typical managers and executives have a hard time making tough people decisions and moving people out of the organization on a timely basis. The PPM makes those necessary decisions and actions a little easier and more rigorous.

- **Reason** – In actual use, all managers have to make the hard calls to prepare for the succession planning discussions. They have to support and defend their thirds. They have to make comparisons between levels in the organization they manage. They have to defend not taking action. They have to explain when cell 8 or 9 people leave the organization for better opportunities. The PPM teaches managers how to assess people.

- **Courage** – In time, using the PPM tool strengthens managers' resolve to act. They are more comfortable making the tough calls.

- **Turnover** – Organizationally, all of the PPMs together can be used to keep an inventory. Turnover statistics should be tracked against the cells. High turnover of lower cells is generally good. Low or no turnover of higher cells is very good.

- **Developmental assignments** – Assignment actions should also be tracked by the cells. Are the 6s, 8s, and 9s being given the most appropriate opportunities? Are the 2s and 4s being given job-skill-enhancement opportunities? In talent review meetings, some organizations report on the developmental progress of the top cells and the terminations/movement of lower cells as a method of measuring results from the process.

- **High potential tracking** – Do we have enough high potentials (8s and 9s)? Are they spread around the organization or are they concentrated? Do we need to go out and get some more or can we build what we need from the inside?

- **Performance matters** – Part of performance in a balanced scorecard approach can be tracked by seeing what happens to the people in the various cells.

18

So, first, get the people inventoried and into the correct cells.

Then have an action and treatment plan for each cell.

Track the results.

The payoff will come in time.

Excerpt

Succession at its best

There are organizations in which succession planning is working well. What do they do differently? Since everyone has roughly the same processes, programs, templates, forms, and requirements, what is the distinguishing characteristic driving their ability to attract, retain, and develop high-performing and high-potential talent?

Top executives have a talent management mind-set.

In 2001, while visiting with the chief executive officer of a multibillion-dollar diversified company, we were asked, "How does GE do it?" The CEO was referring to the recent naming of Jeffrey Immelt as the successor to Jack Welch, but the primary focus of his question was about the GE succession process, "...the most closely watched, highly anticipated, and frequently second-guessed corporate succession drama ever." This CEO was perplexed by the following characteristics of the GE process:

- *Jeffrey Immelt, the ultimate successor to Jack Welch, was actually identified as a potential successor in 1982, shortly after Jack was named CEO. In the subsequent years, Immelt was carefully guided through a series of developmental assignments designed to test and prepare him for a senior executive officer position, within or outside GE.*

- *In 1995, Jack Welch and the Board of Directors reviewed and scrubbed a potential successor list numbering approximately*

18

5,000. Three were deemed worthy of intense consideration and scrutiny: Immelt, Bob Nardelli, and Jim McNerney. Each was given an enhanced assignment of responsibility, and Jack's Board of Directors carefully observed the progress of each during the ensuing three years.

- *Within 48 hours of Immelt being named the final choice, McNerney and Nardelli were named CEOs elsewhere. Nardelli went to Home Depot and McNerney went to 3M.*

How can this be? How can Jack Welch have three world-class executives as backups? How does GE have the ability to scrub a list of 5,000 potential candidates for the backup to the CEO? How is it that GE can lose superior talent to other companies without batting an eye?[†]

Succession planning works well in organizations when the executive ranks think that way. They understand the need for a talent management mind-set.

[†]From Succession Architect®: Best Practices for Building and Executing a Succession Planning Program. (2011). Lominger International: A Korn/Ferry Company.

18

Chapter 19

Assignmentology: The art of assignment management

The 70 percent solution. Not to be confused with the 85 percent solution.

Remember the 70:20:10 solution to development from Chapter 15? Seventy percent comes from jobs and assignments, 20 percent from people, and 10 percent from self-development and courseware.

The number one developer of the skills necessary to be an effective manager and leader is job assignments. While it's tempting to say enrich all jobs, make them all more developmental, and all people will grow, that isn't a practical suggestion. Some research indicates that one-half or more of jobs aren't especially developmental. They provide continuity, promote stability, and make sure the organizational train runs on time. Similarly, there are a large number of people who aren't particularly career oriented. They are jobholders who believe in a fair day's work for a fair day's pay, or they are high professionals, happy to do what they do.

Job assignments can do triple duty. Jobs help develop skills, they add to a person's experience and exposure bank account, and they help a person become more learning agile—able to do new and different things well.

Leaders are effective to the extent that they:

- Have the requisite skills needed to be successful or compensate for the ones they don't have.

- Have had the requisite exposures to the key leverage points of the business to apply past lessons to future challenges.

- Learn from experience and apply those learnings to new situations.

Think of jobs and assignments like task forces and study groups or even courses in three ways:

1. What does it require and, therefore, teach in the way of skills?
2. What does it allow the person to learn about the business?
3. What new challenges does it provide?

Story

Assignmentology at work

What do you do when your high potentials are not up to the task? A privately held, thousand-employee medical device manufacturer found that high-potential employees were not as well rounded and versatile as they needed to be when promoted into challenging new assignments. The talent needle needed to be moved from "not quite there yet" to "ready now."

In order to provide high potentials with the skills and experiences they needed before the big promotion, the company decided to invest in building an assignmentology-based system of development. A side benefit to assignmentology would be a breakdown of the siloed and stagnant relationships between functions.

After a successful pilot in which a high-potential employee from manufacturing was placed into an 18-month assignment designed to provide broad exposure to the HR function, the CEO cleared the way for more up-and-coming employees to participate in similar assignments. The HR exposure assignment became a permanent developmental role within the organization. The organization also chose to focus on project-based assignments as the means to give high potentials needed on-the-job exposure to development. On occasion, elements of other developmental jobs such as international exposure or managing a turnaround effort were also present in the assignment. Most projects were designed to last three to six months. The position of the person transferring to the new assignment was usually backfilled by a temporary employee.

Assignmentology has given multiple employees exposure to powerful on-the-job experiences that have left them with stronger skills and greater readiness to tackle new challenges. Many have successfully gone on to more significant roles in the organization. The individual involved in the pilot assignment in HR has completed a number of subsequent development assignments and is now being called upon to lead a strategically important international start-up operation.

Jobs as deposits in the experience bank account

Here is a way we help the CPO (Chief People Officer), the CTO (Chief Talent Officer), and top management understand what jobs high potentials need to go through on their way to the top. We ask them to imagine a meeting of top management 10 years from now. The team is facing a mission-critical crisis. Depending on the quality of the problem solving of this group, the organization will go on and be more successful, or this day will be pilloried in *Bloomberg Businessweek* as the beginning of the death spiral.

Who would you want in the room? What skills would you like them to have? What experiences and exposures would be helpful and contribute to the right decision? What do you need people to know and do? What modes of business must they understand? What do they need to be experts in? Which functional skills will be needed the most? What is the proper mix of background and experience in the top positions?

In brief, begin with the end in mind.

19

In order to complete the exercise, you need to have some idea about what the issues and challenges are. What's the strategic plan? What businesses will you be in? What resources will you be dependent on? Which locations will be dominant? What regulations might challenge your business proposition? What labor market or customer demographic trends might chill your business? What are likely to be the key leverage points of the business? Where are the markets? What products and services will you be offering?

The answers to those questions will determine what experiences you would want around the table.

For example, let's say you project a dramatic increase in percentage of business coming from outside your home country. You go on to strategize that the biggest opportunities for you will be in Eastern Europe. You also know that in order to penetrate those markets, you will have to partner with governments in Eastern Europe as well as have joint venture partners in those countries. Additionally, your business depends on an uninterrupted supply of iron ore and rough industrial diamonds, both of which have to come from Russia.

So what and whom do you want around the table? You would want one or more people who have had experience in, exposure to, and knowledge of:

- International law in Eastern Europe.
- Doing business in Russia.
- Running joint ventures.
- Barter trade for raw materials in difficult situations.
- Negotiating with difficult governments.
- Hiring good people in marginal labor environments.
- Getting laws passed favorable to your business.
- Converting multiple currencies into U.S. or Euro dollars.
- Acquisition of foreign assets.
- Maintaining expatriates in difficult locations.

19

Given the above requirements, what jobs, task forces, study groups, or prolonged tours would you want the people in the room to have been exposed to?

- Obviously, you would want someone who has personally worked in one or more of those Eastern Bloc countries for 18 months or more.
- You would want someone who has negotiated with the Russians on raw product contracts.
- You would want someone who has negotiated with difficult governments.
- You would want someone who has managed joint ventures in those countries or somewhere else.
- You would want someone who has dealt with the legal system in Eastern Europe.
- You would want someone familiar with employment law and practices.
- You would want someone with experience in converting profits from one currency to another.
- You would also want to hold top management off-sites in those countries.
- You may even want to hire one or more high potentials from those countries as a backup plan.
- You may want teams of high potentials to spend significant time in those countries on various study missions as part of a course.
- You may want one or two people to concentrate on forming relationships with the ambassadors to the key countries.

This gives you the assignment dance card or punch list or checklist for high potentials who you believe will someday be sitting at that table making death-defying decisions about the business.

Not everyone has to do everything, but one or two around the table will have to have done them all. Yes, the group can bring in experts, use consultants, or depend on staff, but there is no real substitute for experience.

An additional discussion we have with top management is about which of the newer design strategies is being considered:

- Small corporate or head office.
- Creation of start-up ventures designed by business teams at all levels.
- Strategic alliances with suppliers/vendors/customers.
- Continuous improvement techniques.
- More accountability/responsibility within the unit (implying fewer layers, more autonomous work).
- More project-based workflow.
- Work accountabilities linked more horizontally.
- Self-directed work teams.
- Contracting out or outsourcing professional-level services.
- Design manufacturing and sales serving as staff of business units.
- Staff services converted into profit centers.

What are your key jobs and assignments?

The answers to the above questions produce one-third of the assignmentology puzzle. Think of a large Assignment Management Matrix (see Figure 19.1). Down the left side you will have the general and specific types of jobs and assignments people need to go through to fill their experience and exposure bank account.

19

Assignments:

- Country manager
- Joint venture head
- International HR director
- Raw materials task force
- Foreign government liaison
- Joint venture board
- Etc.

Across the top of the assignment management matrix, you would have a list of the key skills that you project you will need in the future. We have outlined that approach in chapters 2 and 12.

Figure 19.1

Assignments:	Strategy	Vision	Innovation	Political savvy	Develop people	Etc.
Country manager						
Joint venture head						
International HR director						
Raw materials task force						
Foreign government liaison						
Joint venture board						
Etc.						

19

You now have the jobs that incumbents need for exposure and skill building. Now for the exciting part. You can get a two-fer from a single job. You can kill two birds with one stone. Look at the jobs down the left and see what challenges and skill-building opportunities they offer the incumbent. What are the major skills that make up those jobs? What are the core challenges, and what is the core knowledge for each? What do incumbents have to be experts in versus having an understanding of how to manage?

The assignment matrix in Figure 19.2 is as an example only. Many of these jobs have research-based profiles that would indicate up to 85 percent of the skills most likely to be tested/developed by such jobs. Even if the job is "unique," it can be described by its core elements that we discussed in Chapter 5 and a reasonably accurate profile can be developed. In other words, if the job type is that of a project requiring formal negotiations, the skill demands of such a job are mostly known. Or if it is a start-up in a foreign country, the basic skill demands of that are known as well.

19

Figure 19.2

Assignments:	Strategy	Vision	Innovation	Political savvy	Develop people	Etc.
Country manager	✓			✓		
Joint venture head		✓		✓		
International hr director					✓	
Raw materials task force			✓			
Foreign government liaison				✓		
Joint venture board	✓	✓		✓		
Etc.						

Where there is a checkmark, the job serves double duty. It builds the needed skills—apart from the content and context of the job—and it provides the experiences and exposures needed to learn how key things run. You now have two-thirds of the assignmentology puzzle. You have the skills and the jobs.

Finally, there are the people—the high potentials you are preparing for the future. You have selected them on track record and learning agility and ambition (Chapter 18). Each person has needs to work on before he or she will be truly ready for significant duty.

The needs have been discussed before: experience needs and skill needs. The real trick is to try to combine the two needs in

19

two-fer jobs. Let's say you have a high potential two moves away from the meeting where catastrophe awaits and this person's significant needs are international exposure and visioning and strategic skills. You have two jobs left to get the high potential ramped up to serve.

The assignment matrix (Figure 19.3) would tell you that the best-bet assignment for this high potential would be a Country Manager in Eastern Europe, while at the same time serving as the organization representative on the Joint Venture Board overseeing the raw materials operation in Russia.

You decide to do this and, as a bonus, you also decide to give this person some finishing-school experience at INSEAD on international political skills.

Figure 19.3

Assignments:	Strategy	Vision	Innovation	Political savvy	Develop people	Etc.
Country manager	✓			✓		
Joint venture head		✓		✓		
International hr director					✓	
Raw materials task force			✓			
Foreign government liaison				✓		
Joint venture board	✓	✓		✓		
Etc.						

Now you have the basics of the assignmentology cube. It's exposures, skills, and high potentials—3D development.

In considering high potentials, a job assignment has no value in itself until you have a person in mind. Some organizations set aside so-called key jobs, but other than jobs for high professionals only, they are not really key until you have a person with that need. On the other hand, if you have a full assignment management matrix for your organization, listing all of the exposures down the left and all the key skills across the top, the checkmarks show key jobs. If you have someone with the double need, it is the most efficient assignment you can make.

While jobs have inherent value in terms of the challenges they offer and the skill-building opportunities they present, until you have a person in mind, none of this really matters.

Adding to the matrix

Only some jobs are suitable for high potentials. Others require high professionals or solid performers. How should you determine the nature of the jobs? Lay out your jobs, determine what the key challenges are, and rate them on developmental impact. Decide which are high potential jobs, which are high professional jobs, and which jobs are for continuity. Use performance data, and don't assume a "new job" is really new. It is similar to other jobs. Use the matrix technique above coupled with your success profile for the job.

Determining key challenges

Some firms prefer to list developmental challenges rather than rate jobs. The advantage of this is that it forms a nice history of the challenges people face, can be made particular to the organization (your language), and is useful in personal career planning.

19

We recommend you do both. Rating key challenges illuminates what is developmentally hot within the organization. Rating jobs gives you a useful metric to compare jobs. Both challenges and jobs help you see where the future challenges lie. Both can be summarized on the Developmental Heat checklist we presented in Chapter 5 and repeat later in this chapter.

Following might be a typical list of developmental job demands. For young people, their best jobs are often found in small units that offer some of the following:

- Starkly different activities (cross-functional/divisional, different business, country).
- Major changes (smaller corporate staff, delayering, outsourcing, shift accountability downward, link accountabilities horizontally, self-directed work units, staff as profit centers).
- Major projects (continuous improvement methods, new ideas, products, services, systems, design/redesign of existing systems).
- Formal negotiations (customers, acquisitions, partners, divestitures, unions, governments).
- One-time events (crisis).
- One-time events (major presentations to boards, Wall Street, stockholders).
- Troubleshooting (crises, product service failures, shutdowns, PR problems).
- Fix-it (turnaround, losing money, people problems).
- Fix-it (reorganization, restructuring).
- Fix-it (systems, process breakdown).
- Heavy strategic (major innovation, repositioning, harvesting, failure of previous strategy).
- Influencing change without authority to make it happen (change systems across units).

19

- Line to staff switch (field to headquarters, business/strategic planning, analyst, task force head).

- International assignment (away from home country, many new languages, cultural/business differences).

- International assignment (international responsibilities but stay in home country).

- Jump in size (people, layers, budget, location, activities, deadlines).

- Jump in complexity (unfamiliar function, technology, business, products, people, teams, explosive growth).

- Heavy people demands (more people, different skill levels, different specialties, problem performers, antiquated skill sets, major team building, diversity issues, conflict resolution, nonexpert manager, new groups not worked with before).

- Staff to line shifts (bottom-line responsibility, new technical and leadership skills required).

- Start-up from nothing (creating, hiring, building).

- External roles (lobbying, working with civic or government leaders, representing organization externally).

19

So the matrix we started above with specific jobs and assignments (see Figure 19.3) is expanded to account for types of assignments. Again, the skills listed in the matrix are as an example only (see Figure 19.4).

Figure 19.4

Assignments:	Strategy	Vision	Innovation	Political savvy	Develop people	Etc.
Start-ups		✓	✓			
Fix-its	✓					
Large projects			✓	✓		
Install systems			✓			
International assignments				✓	✓	
Scope job (complexity)	✓					
Scale job (size)					✓	
Etc.						

When you have added the appropriate types and classes of job experiences to the specific experience and exposure people need, then the left-hand side of the matrix is almost complete. The last addition will be mission-critical functions and specific business units and locations (see Figure 19.5).

19

Figure 19.5

Assignments:	Strategy	Vision	Innovation	Political savvy	Develop people	Etc.
Marketing	✓		✓			
Foreign exchange				✓		
Geneva				✓	✓	
Computer chip business	✓		✓			
Largest plant					✓	
Corporate assignment	✓	✓		✓		
Etc.						

The last thing you have to do is determine the degree of difference between job assignments. Remember that one of the aspects of learning agility is the ability to perform well in new, unique, and different situations. We know that a major source of this learning comes from going through a series of jobs and assignments that are different in challenge, location, culture, business proposition, etc. The more different, the better.

One way to judge similarity is to find jobs that demand many of the same competencies. Jobs that have few or no checkmarks in common are different. You'll notice in our example (Figure 19.4) that Start-Ups and Scale Assignments have nothing in common. This could form a two-job sequence with quite different lessons to learn. On the other hand, a Corporate Assignment and being

19

on a Joint Venture Board are similar. Those two jobs would not be that different.

In summary, there are five things you must do to form and use the Assignment Management Matrix, the chassis upon which The Leadership Machine sits. You must be able to:

1. Project the most likely future in terms of issues, challenges, and leverage points. What are you getting people ready for?

2. Project which skills will be the most mission critical? What will the people have to be able to do?

3. Diagnose the developmental value of jobs and assignments. What jobs deliver what skills?

4. Assess the needs of the high potentials. Who needs what in terms of skill development?

5. Match up all of the data to get the most time- and resource-effective assignments where you get two-fers, three-fers, and more-fers.

Again, all jobs can't be key. Some jobs are much broader than others. Many of your jobs will involve the managing and implementing of systems and policies. They may be important but they are not terribly developmental. They demand leadership with a small "/." To help all employees learn to perform better in those jobs, refer back to Chapter 15.

There are three axioms implied in using jobs for development:

1. If you know your key jobs, you can develop people more effectively. Recalling the AT&T studies, the low-assessed dramatically outperformed the high-assessed if they had more challenging jobs and more supportive bosses. This means that to know who is really good, we have to put them to a fair test.

2. If you know the nature of your jobs, you'll move and promote the right people. Disasters abound in organizations when

jobs are not critically analyzed. High potentials try to run an HR function or research group. Or high professionals are thrown into strategy situations in unfamiliar areas. Knowing the jobs helps you move people intelligently. One company decided that assistant restaurant manager was a good pass-through job for high potentials. Why? Because it taught them the business, and they often had to serve as acting manager. Restaurant manager was for high professionals only. There were frequent crises, and managers who performed better had extensive networks in their community. Whenever the company had tried a high potential in the job, performance dipped. For high potentials, they learned there was much more to running a chain restaurant than counting pickles, and their fresh ideas improved performance yet further.

3. If you know how developmental your jobs are, you can design a job sequence that makes sense for the person and the business. The toughest jobs should have a high potential or a high professional in them. Sequences can be determined by thinking through the mix of jobs in any unit. Decide which jobs are most similar and dissimilar and place them in a matrix with the columns indicating level and the rows indicating different jobs. Define similarity along two lines: how challenging the jobs are and the technical demand of the job (be an expert or understand how to use/manage experts).

The point of knowing your jobs is performance; development is a fortunate by-product. Done better, as in the example above, development improves performance. It is not a particularly risky business.

Always remember that the goal is to have people in the catastrophe meeting who can solve the future equations. Even if they haven't solved exactly that specific problem before and if they are all learning agile, then they will attack the problem through the lens of their relevant experiences and learning. Assignmentology ensures their experiences will equip them to do that.

19

Story

Mis-assignmentology

Matching people to challenging assignments can accelerate development. But watch out. Do you know how the talent will be redeployed when the project is completed or abandoned by the company?

Start up

A large retail company initiated a start-up—a new brand reaching a new market. Top talent was tapped from all over the company. These high-potential employees were relocated and worked diligently on the start-up brand. However, after just a couple of years, the start-up was deemed a failure. The company took a loss on its balance sheet and also took a loss in terms of talent. With all of the high-potential employees' previous positions backfilled, there was nowhere for them to be placed when the start-up was shut down and their jobs were eliminated.

Special task force

A multinational energy company organized a special task force—a strategic initiative that took three years to complete. A few dozen high-caliber employees were identified for the roles on the project. The project was successfully implemented, one department at a time, until the entire company adopted the new system. At the successful close of the project, the high-potential employees were responsible for finding a new home. A few employees found open positions that matched their skills and interests. Many employees did not. Again, when the positions were eliminated, many highly gifted people were exited from the company.

In these cases and others like them, employees are likely to no longer view a full-time stretch assignment as an opportunity to develop their skills and advance their careers. They may view the assignment as a dead end where there are no guarantees of their being reabsorbed back into the business when the assignment is complete. Assignmentology as a practice needs to have an eye on the endgame—to grow and retain top talent for key positions.

19

Another general tool for determining the value of jobs and assignments

Many companies have used the Developmental Jobs list from Chapter 5 to audit their jobs and determine to what degree they are developmental. (Or they may use a formal measure such as the Center for Creative Leadership's Developmental Challenge Profile.) Many times, they have found that the more developmental jobs (people had a greater chance of success or failure, individual leadership made a difference, etc.) were not the ones they would have expected. This is generally because something in the business situation changed—advertising became critical, management of a particular product line became an exercise in saving a crashing loser, or a change in organizational structure turned a job into either a bottleneck for others or a helpful expediter for problem solving. Job challenge ebbs and flows with changes in the business. What makes them developmental does not.

Key jobs are where your high potentials and high professionals should be. Any job they visit for a while should be worth 40 or more developmental points on the Developmental Heat Exercise (19.1).

Within any business unit, a number of jobs will stand out as most critical. Some will be best done by high potentials, some by high professionals, and some by solid performers without high career aspirations or whom the organization for one reason or another doesn't see as especially promotable.

19

Exercise 19.1 Developmental heat

Developmental heat: Rate each of the following on a five-point scale.

1 = Little challenge when compared to other jobs
2 = Some challenge
3 = Like other jobs
4 = More challenging than other jobs
5 = Much more challenging than other jobs

1. _____ Success or failure are both possible and would be obvious to myself and others. I think I could fail or not perform well at this job.

2. _____ Requires take-charge, aggressive, individual leadership.

3. _____ Involves working with new people, a lot of people, or people with different skills.

4. _____ High personal pressure (deadlines, high stakes, large shift in scope or scale, travel, long hours, work is viewed as critical).

5. _____ Requires influencing people, activities, and factors over which I have no control (supervisors besides boss, lateral relations, partners, peers, outside parties, political situations, customers).

6. _____ Involves high variety of tasks; doing something very different from what I've done in the past (line/staff switch, promotion to headquarters, changing functions or lines of business/technology).

7. _____ Is closely watched and monitored by people whose opinions count.

8. _____ Requires building a team or something from scratch, or fixing/turning around an operation in trouble (downsizing, restructuring, new product line, new business, establishing a new operation, poor-performing unit, major staffing issues, inheriting a failing unit).

9. _____ Involves a tremendous intellectual/strategic/problem-solving challenge with little or no history for guidance.

10. _____ Involves interacting with a significant boss (whether supportive or not, the boss's view is critical to success in this job).

11. _____ Am missing something important (lack of management support, limited resources, not aligned with strategy or core of the business, poor legacy, missing key skills or technical knowledge, lack of credentials/credibility).

19

Adapted from Eighty-Eight Assignments for Development in Place: Enhancing the Developmental Challenge of Existing Jobs by Michael M. Lombardo and Robert W. Eichinger. © 1989 Center for Creative Leadership. Used by permission.

Putting the best person in every job

Who could argue with that? The best person for the job is always a debatable topic. We recommend to organizations that they do not use that phrase in their value statements. Why? Is the best person someone who can do the job day one, someone who would bring fresh thinking to a job (and would not be seen as the best person by many), or is it a seasoned professional who will do the job for a long time? When PepsiCo looked at this question some years ago, it found the answer by looking at the performance of those who performed the best in key roles. Here's what they found:

Table 19.1 Who performs best in key roles

High potentials perform best (little or no previous experience in this type of job)	High professionals perform best (extensive experience in this type of job)
Requires fresh ideas, new ways of thinking.	Requires considerable experience in area, depth of knowledge.
Is in a quick-changing field, area of business where future is undefined.	Requires understanding of the past in order to address current situations.
High strategy component to job.	Requires tactical skills.
Needs to manage experts.	Needs to be an expert.
Is in an area with chronic problems, most/all previous incumbents have failed.	Is in an area where crises are common.
Requires political savvy.	Requires continuity of relationships.

19

While it is always dangerous to generalize about jobs as they are somewhat fluid, "typical" jobs where a high professional does best are customer oriented, involved in negotiations, or deeply technical such as controller, auditor, plant manager, salesperson, or restaurant manager. Typical jobs where a high potential does best are a bit harder to categorize but tend to be in new areas of a business such as start-up ventures, strategic alliances, new product lines where there is no history, or in older parts of the business with chronic problems where many have tried but none have fixed it.

But jobs will fool you. A few years ago we challenged an old-line, seasoned, high-professional-dominated engineering firm to put the concept to the test: check out 20 key jobs and see who performed best in them—high professionals steeped in experience or high potentials who blew in from somewhere else. To our and their surprise, most of the superior performers were high potentials. They were engineers but not experts in the kind of engineering problems the unit faced. They had few relationships and no continuity with customers. What they did have, however, was fresh thinking, knowledge of how to manage and appreciate experts, and an experimental demeanor. They shook things up, and the unit improved. This is reminiscent of Jack Welch bringing in an executive to run Lighting who had no background in the area. When asked why, he said something like, "I have 80,000 lighting experts. What we need is leadership and team-building skills."

We make this point because, as it is evident that there is more change, more rapid change, and more complex change, then more jobs will become jobs best done by high potentials. However, without high professionals, all organizations would collapse. They run the technology and systems, develop most of the people, and make most of the money. They are the best performers year after year. In response to any feeling you may have that we are labeling them as somehow second-rate, we are not. Think about Albert Einstein again. High professionals are pros by choice. They are the best at depth; high potentials are best with the unfamiliar.

Coda

Chapter 20

A universal approach: the global Leadership Machine

Development is development. With a few wrinkles, its rules apply across groups, organization types, and national boundaries.

Over the years, we have presented various pieces of the research, findings, and practices contained in this book. At the end of the presentation, we are inevitably asked at least one of these seven questions:

Since much of this research comes from studying male Caucasian managers and executives working in the old North American and European economy, do all of these things apply to:

1. Women?
2. Minorities?
3. Staff groups?
4. Other countries?
5. Individual contributors?
6. Nonprofits?
7. E-business or the new economy?

The general answer is yes to all of those. To this point, we have focused on the men and women who should lead organizations today or any day—high potentials and high professionals. But what about high-potential or high-professional women? Don't they have special issues? How about high-potential and high-professional minorities? Staff groups? Are we making our arguments just for the United States or do they hold internationally as well? Individual contributors? Nonprofits? And what about the wave of the future, e-companies?

In this chapter, we highlight some of the similarities and differences in development for these groups.

Women and minorities

We realize that the term *minorities* rankles some, but we find that the term *people of color* sometimes rankles others and may not apply internationally. We chose minorities because our interest here is the development of people who can lead, and females and non-Caucasians are definitely distinct minorities among incumbents of major roles in U.S. organizations. In other places around the world, the term minorities refers to various "out-groups," not part of the dominant group. Color may not be the issue. It is as likely to be religion, sect, geography, or even occupational status.

Anytime the topic of women or minorities comes up, it's usually necessary to deal with claims of prejudice and discrimination up front. And, of course, it exists even in our politically correct age. We've heard such prejudicial comments many times and will counter with some research-based assertions of our own.

So what appears to be the truth?

Are men and women equally skilled? Men and women, in fact, don't differ much in skills. As almost everyone knows without studying it, women are, in fact, somewhat better on average at most interpersonal skills, and men are somewhat better on average at business problem-solving skills. These small differences tell us little about a group and nothing about individuals. Any specific female may be better at business decisions or any specific male may be better at interpersonal skills.

20

Do women and minorities have to perform better to get ahead? Women and African Americans may, in fact, have to perform better to get ahead than Caucasian men do. There is probably a double standard. This would be typical of any out-group working its way into the dominant culture. Some studies show that among women and men at the same level, women have higher-assessed skills. Similarly, a Center for Creative Leadership study showed that African Americans had higher scores on a 360° instrument versus a Caucasian comparison sample.

But doesn't this mean that women are more effective than men? While some say this is so, studies that look at men and women in the same companies, in the same jobs, at the same level, with the same amount of managerial experience find that effectiveness is about equal. Many of the findings that tout the female edge have a major flaw: they are comparing people holding very different kinds of jobs (women are often in HR or public relations). They also make too much of small differences between the two sexes. Again, small differences tell us little about a group and absolutely nothing about an individual.

Since a lot of your recommendations hinge on feedback, wouldn't bias show up in 360° and performance ratings and be quite unfair to women and minorities? What's the evidence? What we should be most concerned about in this case is if there are systematic rating distortions when rating competencies. In a fairly large study we did, women and men rated their opposite gender the same on 84 percent of our competencies. Neither gender rated its own gender higher than it rated the other overall, and male and female raters agreed much more with each other on people of either gender than with the person rated. For example, male and female raters agreed on the ratings of a competency called Interpersonal Savvy, and their ratings correlated with performance (higher performers received higher ratings from both groups and lower performers received lower ratings). Neither group agreed with the self-ratings of either gender. We concluded that both genders are largely rating competence, not gender. So while there is some evidence of rating bias between men and women, the effects are generally small.

20

Similarly, while there is some evidence of rating bias between African Americans and Caucasians, people largely rate competence, not race. It does appear, however, that African Americans rate themselves higher than they do Caucasians, and that at least Caucasian bosses rate Caucasians higher.

Our point here is not that bias doesn't exist, but that people primarily seem to be rating competence. Nevertheless, we should be aware that bias exists when looking at feedback results.

Aren't some groups simply smarter than others? Color presumes difference to many, and indeed there are some differences in performance on ability tests. African Americans score about a standard deviation lower on IQ tests than do Caucasians; Hispanics about half that; Asians score as well or better.

But we and many others question this contention. These arguments are discussed in detail elsewhere, but IQ is at least somewhat malleable. It can be affected positively by adoption, for example. More important, it seems to be affected by cultural beliefs. If African Americans are told a test they are taking is for research purposes, they score the same as Caucasians, although the test is, in fact, an IQ test. If told the same test is an ability test, they score significantly lower.

While we are aware that the findings listed above are more complex than we have acknowledged here, the essence of them is fact. Our view is that while we need science, science can never do justice to the complexities of life. There are many reasons why a person may score lower. Poverty, malnutrition, and broken families are obvious reasons. Perhaps less obvious is living down to expectations—learned inferiority. This argument has three parts: (1) When the larger society projects an image of inferiority to a group long enough, that group internalizes it. (2) When that inferiority is attributed largely to genetic causes, the group's fears increase even more. (3) The group learns to live down to expectations and actively avoids intellectual competition.

20

We're reminded of the chilling story a teacher once told us. She had a minority student who seemed quite bright but performed poorly on tests. The teacher, for no reason she can recall, said to the girl, "Why don't you fill out the tests the way an admired person would, someone you think is really smart." The girl scored 100 on the next test, but when the teacher congratulated her, she replied, "Yes, but that wasn't me."

We find it hard to explain how a person's score can differ dramatically simply from a test instruction. Changing one's score significantly on an ability measure should be impossible. We also find it hard to explain why adoption would create a dramatic increase if intelligence is basically immutable. It makes far more sense to us that the ability was there all along but had been suppressed by many factors, including feelings of inferiority.

Can women and minorities get a fair shake in organizations? While we certainly believe so, the evidence so far is fairly bleak.

In the original study of female executives, *Breaking the Glass Ceiling:*

- Men were three times more likely to report the major developmental jobs that season managers most: start-ups, fix-its/turnarounds, and having a large jump in scope assignments (moving into a complex, well-functioning organization). In a follow-up study, the results were no different.
- No female executive ever reported a start-up. In the follow-up study, one reported a start-up.
- Women had their first management job nine years later than men. Time is, of course, finite in a career. People who start off at a nine-year deficit are far behind in facing the transition from professional to manager and far behind in learning lessons of delegation and leadership of direct reports.
- Lyness and Thompson show that women have fewer moves, narrower experiences, and jobs with less authority.

20

- Similarly, Hurley and Sonnenfeld report that women have had jobs in fewer departments and have less functional breadth.
- Lyness and Thompson show that women are less likely to say that mentoring facilitated their advancement.
- Of the top wage earners in businesses, only 2 percent are women.
- In an unpublished study, the Center for Creative Leadership looked at the experiences of African American male and female managers and executives (compared with a Caucasian sample). The results are to be expected but are depressing, nevertheless. All the following are statistically significant:
  - Caucasians had more challenging assignments than African Americans.
  - Men had more challenging assignments than women.
  - Caucasian men had more challenging assignments than African American men.
  - Caucasian men had more challenging assignments than Caucasian women.
  - African American men had more challenging assignments than African American women.
  - Among women, there was no difference by race in challenging assignments.
  - Like women, African Americans were less likely to have start-ups and fix-its/turnarounds. They were also less likely to have experienced the all-purpose developer projects.
  - Not surprisingly, African Americans report more hardships. It was by far the largest event category reported and included an experience called "Race Matters."
  - As you can't learn from experiences you're not having, Caucasian men learned more lessons about managing the work than either African American males or females of both races.
  - African Americans report more learning dealing with their racial identity and cynicism and less about managing direct reports and developing their skills.

20

- While racism is undoubtedly a large factor in the above, there is even more to the story. In a confidential conversation with one of the authors, a large media company admitted that it had derailed African American journalists with its fast-track program. The company had been so intent on ensuring the success of its young African American journalists that it gave them jobs at which they couldn't fail. Unfortunately, they couldn't grow much either. Whether outright discrimination, myths and prejudices, or well-meaning protectionism, lack of challenging jobs is a huge problem.

- Additionally, many women and minorities are in staff roles, and they are typically impoverished developmentally. Line jobs have about twice the variety in job assignments as do staff jobs. They are often removed from the business core and lack any true bottom-line responsibility.

We must conclude that women and minorities typically work in a developmentally impoverished environment. Sexism, in job assignments at least, appears to be more pervasive than racism. Both appear to be deep problems.

Some best practices in combating racism and sexism

Education. Stereotyping and prejudice are real. Overt prejudice is rare these days, as it should be. Yet it does exist. In one study, Caucasians reported that people of other ethnic backgrounds are less intelligent and less hardworking. In another, African American managers gave African American direct reports higher ratings. In another, women received lower ratings when they were a small proportion of the workgroup. In another, identical resumes were sent with different photographs. Executives selected the women for administrative tasks, the men for line assignments. When the experiment was repeated with minority women, the results were identical! They also picked the men for the line assignments. In another, female recruiters saw male applicants as more similar to them and more qualified than female applicants.

20

Prejudice and stereotyping are more complex than the old saying, "Birds of a feather flock together." As we've seen, expectations can lead same-group members to be biased against their own ethnic or racial group as well. Some biases are conscious, but many of them appear to be unconscious as well.

Whatever stereotypes and prejudices may exist, most of us have them and don't know it. Some success has been reported in diversity courses where conscious and unconscious prejudices are exposed and explored. At their root is what we discussed earlier—differing expectations. Such courses backfire, however, when they become exercises in bashing old Caucasian guys. To work, no one should be bashed. Everyone should face whatever conscious and unconscious prejudices they may have, including prejudices against their own nominal group.

Removing barriers to effectiveness through information and support. A central problem for out-groups is they're not in the know. They lack the information and support, the water cooler, the golf games, all the mechanisms where tidbits of information and how to get things done get passed around. Information or support groups sponsored by senior management have helped here. The idea of these groups is to find out what's getting in the way of peak performance, how to get timely information, and how to remove barriers so the playing field becomes more level.

Giving diversity efforts teeth. Just like the company with the brand-new success profile, diversity efforts need systems behind them. Including diversity goals in performance appraisals and bonuses and having diversity candidates automatically considered on job slates are common examples. Some firms create a separate list of diversity candidates in the succession planning system to further ensure that they are considered for challenging jobs.

It's jobs, jobs, jobs and development, development, development. Consider the previous three recommendations as zeros. Without jobs and development, they will remain zero in any real sense. Jobs add a one before the zeroes. Then each subsequent zero makes development richer.

20

430 |

Job challenge is the key that makes development possible. Fill jobs in the same old way, and neither your developmental system nor your diversity efforts will amount to much.

Staff groups

Let's use the example of staff managers and professionals. Staff, from bottom to top, has had far fewer of the high-powered assignments that teach. The most common experiences reported by line executives are turnarounds, leaps in scope or scale, and start-ups. For staff executives, the most common experiences reported are projects, incidents revealing the values of others, role models (usually direct bosses), and early nonmanagement jobs.

Limited experiences create limited learning as well. On 360° results collected as part of this study, line executives were rated significantly higher on 11 of the 16 competencies. On the remaining 5, there was no difference.

But there is little reason for this to be. Staff jobs are more similar in challenge than they are different from line jobs, if the jobs are thought about differently.

While many people are content to remain in professional jobs, for high-potential staff, those with a chance to lead:

- Find ways for staff to work on line issues. Use projects to teach staff about the technical business core. The goal here is to understand and contribute, not to actually do core jobs in most cases.
- Look for line-like jobs in staff units. Examples are payroll, compensation and benefits processing, or hardware and report generation.
- Think small. Make heavy use of developmental tasks to see who shows an inclination toward management. Look

20

for line-like components: little start-ups and fix-its, bottom lines, and deadlines.

- Look to make early, permanent staff-to-line switches.
- Consider a charge-back system, where the line can make choices between inside and outside sources of staff services.
- Use line executives on temporary staff assignments as coaches and mentors.

We do believe that women and minorities will eventually get their fair due in organizations. While we are not naive enough to think that change will be easy, change is inevitable because this time it is being forced by global competition.

Most organizations do a poor job of developing anyone. Talent is short and is becoming shorter. Any organization that doesn't cast its net broadly and try to develop everyone it can, will lose. Bill Cosby once said that as soon as someone figures out how to make a profit from better race relations, the problem will be solved. That time has come, at least for educated and marketable people. Global business and economic wars won't be won by relying on one-third of the population who are Caucasian males.

As far as women and minorities are concerned, they have a tougher time getting to the upper ranks, but they get there the same way. Once there, they look the same and are rated the same (or slightly higher). If anything, they might be a bit better because of the additional hardships required getting there. They develop the same competencies and use the same competencies to lead.

20

Internationally speaking

If competencies and learning acumen are universal, then our argument should apply to other parts of the world as well. The case is fairly strong that this is true.

- Development Dimensions International (DDI), the international assessment firm, uses the same 70 competencies for all jobs worldwide.

- Many 360s have been validated internationally. Similarly, a study at the University of Pennsylvania of 18,000 managers in 65 countries produced a single measure of competencies.

- Countless multinationals use their competency models worldwide.

- Studies of a learning agility measure found that it related to performance or potential just as well for German or British managers as it did for United States managers.

- One company reported that its success rate on international placements went from 50 to 95 percent once it instituted learning agility as its primary selection criterion.

- A study of derailment in the United States and Europe found that "there are not great differences in factors related to derailment when United States and European managers are compared."

- Expatriate studies have shown that the same competencies can be used to describe success essentially anywhere. One firm had international operations in more than 100 countries. It used the same model and the same derailment-prevention techniques everywhere with no problems. In an empirical study of successful versus failed international managers, the competency factors that differentiated the two groups were:
  – Handling business complexity
  – Directing, motivating and developing direct reports
  – Integrity
  – Drive for excellence

20

| 433

- Organizational savvy
- Composure
- Sensitivity to others
- Staffing

There was nothing unusual or different about any of these competency findings.

This is not to argue that nothing is different anywhere or that what becomes emphasized or de-emphasized doesn't shift. Of course it does.

Perhaps the Center for Creative Leadership summed this point best in discussing its revision of Benchmarks®, a 360° instrument designed originally in the 1980s. The revision was aimed at making the instrument more applicable to a global environment. "While our research found that many of the factors that go into effective leadership haven't changed, there are some notable differences in the way organizations and successful leaders operate today. Factors like strong interpersonal skills, meeting business objectives, and building a strong team are just as important as they were when the original research was done. Other factors such as leveraging differences, having a participative management style, managing change, and possessing career self-management skills are growing in importance."

What is dramatically different internationally is, of course, culture. Much research has shown that culture has a dramatic effect on the values one brings to the job. Agreeableness (caring and concern for others) has been shown to matter more internationally. People identify with different kinds of leadership internationally. Japanese employees are reported to prefer people who are profound as their leaders; Indonesians prefer an authoritative bearing.

What contributes to success or failure remains the same—interpersonal savvy, ability to read cultural differences and adapt, propensity to learn. A manager air-dropped into another country would face significant problems figuring out what to do, what

20

drives people, what is "good" behavior and what is a turnoff. But the mechanisms (competencies) he or she would use are the same. Different ones might be emphasized (reading subtle differences for example), but they are hardly unique to a setting.

The other possible difference is that the competencies internationally are somehow different. We've never seen any evidence that this is the case. The need for competencies is rooted in organizational structure and business demands, not culture. Studies show that accountability hierarchies and organizational cultures are more alike than different in Europe and the United States, for example.

Most international companies are much the same, regardless of home country. International executives accomplish their objectives using the same competencies around the world. What would look somewhat different would be a company that primarily services its home country. Its culture and way of operating would mirror more closely the national culture and political system.

Individual contributors

All of the people studied across all of the research used for this book were at one time individual contributors. They all started with some foundation skills that lead to their first management job. Development is development. Even if a person wanted to or just remained an individual contributor his or her whole life, some adjustments in skill would be necessary. Adjusting old skills or building new ones follows all the development logic laid out in this book. A target. Feedback. Development plan. Skill building. Practice. Blending.

An individual contributor will benefit when jobs are developmental, especially early in a career. Developmental tasks help everyone. They give individuals a sense of what's challenging and exciting and what isn't, and they help organizations make calls on people with more objective criteria. Some research indicates that even

20

for people who are plateaued, job enrichment, in the form of varied tasks in their specialty area, is beneficial. Other research shows that as we age, we become more interested in autonomy and achievement. Calling our own shots is, of course, directly related to the breadth and depth of the skill set we have.

Some individual contributors will grow to be seasoned professionals in very valuable technologies. Although they may never manage anyone, both they and the organization benefit when jobs are seen as sets of challenges requiring competencies as well as sets of challenges requiring technical proficiencies. Unless nothing changes over a 45-year career, the developmental imperatives apply to them.

Not-for-profit/government

We have looked at the research on the competencies necessary to be effective in the nonprofit world. Our conclusions are twofold:

1. As far as running the business side of a nonprofit, the competencies, issues, and challenges are the same. So the business of the United Way, the Red Cross, a hospital, a school district, or a branch of government is all the same. They require the same individual contributor, supervisory, management, and executive skills as any other business. It's a business with a budget, products, services, and customers.

2. There are differences that are significant:

   - Pursuit of funding/raising money.

   - The acquisition and retention of volunteers: the management of volunteers is similar but more difficult than managing employees since you don't have money or authority as tools.

   - Compliance with regulations, laws, and rules (many times conflicting).

20

- External political relations (a lot more than most private firms have to deal with—external boards, many political jurisdictions, citizen oversight, media access, etc.).

Even in the case of the differences, there are no new competencies. It's a matter of emphasis.

E-companies

We have presented to many e-businesses, dot-coms, B2Bs, and high-tech start-ups. Many say that competency modeling is the old way, appropriate for the old economy and very large organizations. They claim that modern, hip organizations act differently and, in fact, have different models of success.

Whether it's new or old economy. Low-tech or high. A start-up is a start-up and always has been. HP® was a start-up. Microsoft® was a start-up. Xerox® was a start-up. Walmart was a start-up. Southwest Airlines was a start-up. They looked the same during their first year or two of operations as any Silicon Valley start-up looks. Maybe speed is faster, but we doubt it. E-businesses look no different from a competency point of view than start-ups from the past. The challenge is order from chaos, fast response time, learning from successes and mistakes, and living with lack of control.

Think of George Washington and the start-up of the Continental Army—enlistment was for a year, people shielded deserters (we weren't a real country yet), the commanders largely acted on their own, a common problem was gunplay in the camps, discipline was shoddy. Anyone who thinks Washington had any real control of the army for the first few years is unfamiliar with his monumental achievement. He indeed made something from nothing, just as start-ups of today must. Vision, team building, motivating, and getting it 80 percent right is the nature of the job.

20

Summing It Up

We started this chapter with the question, "Do all of these things apply to...?" and the answer is yes. We listed additional best practices for women, minorities, and staff managers. Certainly if you're running a start-up or your business is truly international, you may want one of the models more specifically geared (degree of emphasis) toward those environments. But competencies are competencies, learning is learning, development is development. Don't expect to see anything new or different.

20

Appendix A

Rationale for the 85 percent solution

Think of a career as a staircase: each platform represents the core skills of that level; each riser represents the jump to the next.

At the base of the staircase is what most people should be selected for at entry. Following are the competencies that are generally related to success as an individual contributor and which people usually perform well on. These are the entry competencies to select for:

- Action oriented
- Decision quality
- Functional/Technical skills
- Intellectual horsepower
- Learning on the fly
- Perseverance
- Problem solving
- Process management
- *Drive for* results
- Standing alone
- Technical learning

These knockout factors are skills that most people do quite well at already. These could be used as a "quality check" rather than a formal selection mechanism. To be considered as a hire or for promotion, one would have to show strength in most of these areas. The rest should at least be at an average skill level.

All would not have to be looked at directly, especially for hires into the individual contributor ranks. Many competencies, although titled and defined somewhat differently, are related to one another at the core. Grades in school are a pretty good measure of functional/technical skills and intelligence, for example. Also, each falls into a statistical factor (all Leadership Architect® competencies lie in one of six factors), meaning that they are closely related. High on one will often relate to being high on another within a factor. In selection, it's fairly rare to look at more than five to eight competencies, so we suggest a subset of the competencies above to be looked at for selection:

- Action oriented
- Functional/Technical skills
- Learning on the fly
- Problem solving
- Process management
- *Drive for* results
- Standing alone

Others could be selected from the list of the most common competencies relating to performance at this level. (These are listed in Appendix B, Table B.1.) Again, we emphasize the logic of our argument, not a specific list of competencies.

Why we selected what we did

Individual contributors

Select for: What is needed later is also important now in individual contributor roles. People who are not Action Oriented and who are passive don't fare well across time. Similarly, those who work on 97 things at once rather than making sense of their work and focusing on key problems, who don't learn from their job tasks, and who don't develop a distinctive competence are among the first to be weeded out of organizations. A consistent research finding illustrates this: more successful people in any field (from math to tennis to management) build their skills from the ground up. They don't jump all about. They spend their early career developing a true competence. If they're accountants, they sweat every line; if they are oil engineers, they drill for oil. The selection factors for individual contributors are also the foundation for a successful career.

Most likely weaknesses (competitive-edge competencies that must be developed):

- Motivating others
- Personal learning
- Strategic agility
- *Managing* vision and purpose

Interest in development drops dramatically across time. The place to emphasize it is where it does the most good—with the group that is most oriented toward it to begin with—early-in-career people. Across time, priorities change. Need for advancement goes down inexorably, while need for achievement and autonomy goes up. The right moment to work on growth is when we are at our most open and when the stakes are low. This also is a bonus because many entry jobs are technical and not that interesting because they lack breadth. People can get away with all kinds of interpersonal follies at this level, but the problems will come back to haunt them later (see Chapter 4). Early is the best time to work on chronic weaknesses like Motivating Others and Personal Learning. Early is also the time to begin to work on long-term developmental propositions like Strategic Agility and *Managing* Vision and Purpose, both among the competencies it takes the longest to become proficient at. They are also prime indicators of early breadth. At this level, they are more likely to mean thinking ahead, seeing beyond one's immediate job, and inspiring others on behalf of the organization. The time to begin to work on these is when the consequences are minimal (but not zero), then emphasize them for those who make it to manager.

Measure and reinforce (competitive-edge competencies emphasized at this level):

- Creativity
- Informing
- Interpersonal savvy
- Listening
- Organizing
- Peer relationships
- Planning
- Total work systems

Many of these skills provide a hedge against future derailment. All are in moderate supply. All are correlated with high performance across multiple studies. Listening is a special case. Listening is one of the eight "saving grace" competencies that differentiate superior from average performing managers and executives. Listening serves as a balance so other strengths don't shift into overuse later. As we point out throughout the book, what you can get away with early does you in later.

Any competency that characterizes a level essentially means that high performers are much better at it, and any increment in performance pays off for the organization today. People who flounder at these may be strong technical performers on solitary projects. If they are really talented, some misguided person might make them managers, but they can't be effective at either level. They will run out of people to work with, won't be able to run projects, and their skills will begin to have that stale aroma to them. The special emphases of a level should be handled through the short-term performance appraisal process—feedback and improvement plans should be immediate. (Again, we could have picked others from our list of the top 22 competencies (see Appendix B, Table B.1). In our opinion, the competencies listed above are most critical in general. For your organization, you decide.)

442 |

Develop early for high potentials:

- Command skills
- Conflict management
- Creativity
- Managing and measuring work
- Motivating others
- Perspective
- Planning

The main differences between management and individual contributor roles are embodied in the competencies above. They reflect the need for tactical skills, dealing effectively with conflict, and learning to create something new. Managers typically run both the processes of the organization and are on the front line of innovation. First among equals in the need for development is Command Skills (dealing with crises). It is essential for managers and executives.

Managers

Select For: The next step in a career is supervisor or manager, and it is the greatest leap by far in organizations. Here are the "select for" competencies we suggest:

- Action oriented
- Comfort around higher management
- Customer focus
- Functional/Technical skills
- Integrity and trust
- Intellectual horsepower
- Organizing
- Perseverance
- Problem solving
- *Drive for* results
- Standing alone

These may seem an odd list, when we have made the case that the management level basically involves day-to-day management, innovation, and conflict-resolution skills. The problem, unfortunately, is these skills are ordinarily in very low supply, and we recommend that you select for what is available. These skills emphasize the ability to build trust and have integrity, a strong focus on the customer, being resourceful, and being comfortable with and responsive to senior managers in the implementation of organizational plans.

Most likely weaknesses (competitive-edge competencies that must be developed):

- *Dealing with* ambiguity
- Command skills
- Conflict management
- Confronting direct reports
- Creativity
- Developing direct reports and others
- Directing others
- Hiring and staffing
- Informing
- Innovation management
- Managing and measuring work
- Motivating others
- Perspective
- Political savvy
- Self-knowledge
- *Building effective* teams
- *Managing* vision and purpose

Unfortunately, this is a long list due to weak developmental efforts and very complex jobs. The core of the managerial job is running the organization's processes through its people. There is a load of natural conflict built into the job of being in the middle and too much work for the individual contributor with an

A

"I will control all" mentality. This is where all the developmental needs of individual contributors come into play: 90 percent of the problems managers deal with are ambiguous, their time is not their own, and here is where efficient managers and team builders can really make a difference once they have competent people to manage. Being the boss and having a boss means that, for the first time, the person has to manage up and down and deal with the inevitable conflicts that occur.

While it would be ideal to work on everything a manager needs in advance, this is not always possible, although you can begin the job by starting development a level early. A person can work on individual creativity while an individual contributor, and this helps greatly in managing innovation later. But some things can only be done when they are demanded. In the studies at the Center for Creative Leadership, developing direct reports doesn't happen until one has full-time direct reports (if then). The same is true for measuring work and managing work processes and making actual staffing decisions. The real development at this level occurs through managing others when it counts. Forward development is more strategic in nature. Here the broader scope of a management job can be leveraged to help a person grow in perspective.

Measure and reinforce (competitive-edge competencies emphasized at this level):

- Command skills
- *Timely* decision making
- Decision quality
- Managing and measuring work
- Presentation skills
- Priority setting
- Process management
- Self-development
- Time management

Because managers run the processes of the organization, they have more competencies emphasized at their level than any other. The job is part political and part work process. Again, those who flounder at the basic demands of the job, such as Presentation Skills or Organizing, run into trouble sooner or later.

Develop early for high potentials:

Here is where development gets tough for managers. For those few who are picked as high potentials, they must do double duty. Once these few reach executive roles, the game is basically over. It's too expensive, the time too valuable, and the incumbents are least interested (or maybe too exhausted) for much personal growth. It's also much too late. At the executive level is where all the 10- to 20-year developmental propositions pay off.

- *Dealing with* ambiguity
- Creativity
- Innovation management
- Motivating others
- Negotiating
- Perspective
- Political savvy
- Strategic agility
- *Managing* vision and purpose

Note: For some organizations where the operations are very decentralized, *Managing Through* Systems may need to be added to this list.

The chronic complaints in most organizations are exemplified in the list above. Where are the visionaries? The strategists? The change masters? The answer is that they are wherever the people are who have these skills. Very few do. The portrait painted is bleak. Development is a must, as these competencies are in very low supply.

446 |

Executives

Select For: If there has been little development in the past or if your organization has downsized and delayered as most have, then you can expect a lot of executives to fail. Estimates from research have varied, but 50 to 70 percent failure rates are typically cited. And little wonder: Strategic Agility, *Dealing with* Ambiguity, Perspective, etc., aren't built in a year or two. Mastery studies in any area talk about the 10-year-rule to truly master any skill. Perhaps we can speed it up a bit faster with maximum intervention, but probably not by much.

The selection factors for executives are then double-edged. They are real, yet few people in the feeder pool of middle managers are good at most of them. As one very funny executive said, "On Friday, I was a regional manager who sold cars. On Monday, I'm an international strategist. Now what does that mean?" Brought up in functional or SBU silos, few executives have had the opportunity to really learn or even think about most of what they must do in the role. Previous development is the only way to make The Leadership Machine operate at this level.

Because we strongly contend that it is much too late for major skill development at this level, we can only present an ordered list of probabilities in selection.

High supply:

- Business acumen
- Comfort around higher management
- Command skills
- Customer focus
- Decision quality
- Functional/technical skills
- Intellectual horsepower
- Learning on the fly
- Organizing

- Problem solving
- *Drive for* results

Moderate supply:

- *Dealing with* ambiguity
- Negotiating
- Perspective
- Political savvy
- Priority setting
- Process management
- Strategic agility

Low supply:

- Creativity
- Innovation management
- Motivating others
- *Managing* vision and purpose

For many organizations, to approximate this profile is all that can be done. Pick those who come closest to fitting the essential skills. Or select an executive team with complementary skills. Or split the office of the CEO into two or three positions. In the average organization, it's hard to get excited about a candidate pool where Strategic Agility, arguably the number one skill for an executive, is 37th out of 67 competencies. In other words, it is a mediocre skill. Most of the managing change skills such as *Managing* Vision and Purpose or Motivating Others hover near the 50s.

Our argument boils down to this: develop individual contributors and managers, but select executives. Without having built teams (that can lead to *Managing Through* Systems later) and unless they have had to think creatively, been a major part of change efforts or strategy task forces, or have had something to command earlier, it's unrealistic to expect anything beyond the current failure rates. If first-time executives don't have these skills, there probably isn't enough time to significantly develop them, given the time demands, the high stakes, and the low interest in self-development. The vast majority of skills on this list are hardly amenable to short-term development.

A

449

Appendix B

Below are the competencies most correlated with high performance at the individual contributor, manager, and executive levels across multiple studies.

Table B.1 The top 22 competencies by level

Individual contributors	Managers	Executives
■ Action oriented	■ Action oriented	■ *Dealing with* ambiguity
■ Creativity	■ Comfort around higher management	■ Business acumen
■ Decision quality	■ Command skills	■ Comfort around higher management
■ Functional/technical skills	■ Conflict management	■ Command skills
■ Informing	■ Creativity	■ Creativity
■ Intellectual horsepower	■ Customer focus	■ Customer focus
■ Interpersonal savvy	■ *Timely* decision making	■ Decision quality
■ Learning on the fly	■ Decision quality	■ Functional/technical skills
■ Motivating others	■ Functional/technical skills	■ Innovation management
■ Organizing	■ Integrity and trust	■ Intellectual horsepower
■ Peer relationships	■ Intellectual horsepower	■ Learning on the fly
■ Perseverance	■ Managing and measuring work	■ Motivating others
■ Planning	■ Motivating others	■ Negotiating
■ Problem solving	■ Organizing	■ Organizing
■ Process management	■ Perseverance	■ Perspective
■ *Drive for* results	■ Perspective	■ Political savvy
■ Sizing up people	■ Presentation skills	■ Priority setting
■ Standing alone	■ Priority setting	■ Problem solving
■ Strategic agility	■ Problem solving	■ Process management
■ Technical learning	■ Process management	■ *Drive for* results
■ Total work systems	■ *Drive for* results	■ Strategic agility
■ *Managing* vision and purpose	■ Self-development	■ *Managing* vision and purpose
	■ Standing alone	
	■ Strategic agility	
	■ Time management	
	■ Total work systems	

Note: managers list has 26 competencies due to ties.

Appendix C

The leadership machine quiz

Take this quiz to check your knowledge. Or, test someone else's knowledge of *The Leadership Machine.*

1. What percentage of competencies is shared in common by different models of management and leadership success?

   a. 35%

   b. 50%

   c. 85%

   d. 100%

2. When putting a competency model in place in an organization, it is most important to make sure that:

   a. the model reflects the competencies unique to your organization

   b. buy-in is obtained from key people and departments

   c. the model is based on sound research

   d. the model can be changed easily as the organizational culture changes

3. The three primary reasons why organizations avoid best practices for development are:

   a. ignorance, arrogance, and poor execution skills

   b. insufficient resources, time pressure, and internal conflict

   c. conflicting research, lack of commitment from line management, and competing priorities

   d. time lag, false prophets, and (lack of) courage

4. The Leadership Machine refers to:

   a. perfectly aligning the organization's culture to drive leadership performance

   b. how to use succession planning to develop people to meet future demands and how to make calls on who gets the jobs

   c. balancing EQ and IQ for superior results

   d. the schools and companies that are the most common sources of talented business leaders

5. The most fundamental need in developing effective leadership is:

   a. being able to identify and measure the competencies critical for job success

   b. having support from top leadership

   c. a generous and consistent budget for funding leadership development efforts

   d. hiring the best talent to begin with

454 |

6. How many competencies are included in the Leadership Architect®?

   a. 15

   b. 29

   c. 46

   d. 67

7. Development efforts should be targeted on which set of competencies?

   a. price-of-admission competencies

   b. competitive-edge competencies

   c. hidden competencies

   d. dynamic competencies

8. The root cause for most derailment is:

   a. poor boss relationships

   b. patterns of behavior reinforced by previous successes

   c. lack of technical skills

   d. excessive risk taking

9. Which category of employees tends to be more critical than others when rating their own skills and their flaws?

   a. derailed

   b. plateaued

   c. key player

   d. high potential

10. Two foundations of long-term career success are:

    a. technical skills and intelligence

    b. interpersonal savvy and political skills

    c. self-awareness and learning agility

    d. strategic agility and decision quality

11. Dead last in skill ratings of different competencies is:

    a. Listening

    b. Strategic Agility

    c. Developing Direct Reports and Others

    d. Conflict Management

12. You are likely to find the highest proportion of low-performing employees in:

    a. individual contributor roles

    b. managerial roles

    c. executive roles

    d. none of the above; poor performers are found in the same proportion across different levels of the organization

13. The type of experience that tends to have the most impact on learning and development is:

    a. key jobs

    b. important other people

    c. hardships

    d. courses

14. Development is more likely to occur when:

    a. you have previous experience to build on

    b. you feel your chances for success are relatively good

    c. you have less accountability for producing results

    d. you feel a tremendous amount of pressure

15. Which of the following is not a characteristic of learning-agile people:

    a. verbal agility

    b. mental agility

    c. people agility

    d. change agility

16. The silver bullet of success is:

    a. ambition

    b. learning agility

    c. intelligence

    d. being in the right place at the right time

17. The foundation for a successful HR system is:

    a. a competency model that profiles the skills critical for success

    b. incorporating Six Sigma practices

    c. balancing centralization and decentralization

    d. establishing sound ROI metrics

18. An effective process for coaching others is the:

    a. ABC Model

    b. do as I say, not as I do model

    c. sink or swim model

    d. go for the brass ring model

19. A development plan should include:

    a. a challenging task (or person)

    b. a way to get before, during, and after feedback

    c. learning some new things to do

    d. all of the above

20. Which of the following is not a key element in making The Leadership Machine run:

    a. the target person being developed

    b. peers

    c. the direct boss

    d. HR

21. The relationship between intelligence and learning agility is:

    a. strongly negative

    b. strongly positive

    c. curvilinear

    d. essentially nonexistent; they are unrelated

22. The value of developmental experiences is identified using what rule:

    a. 80:15:5

    b. 70:20:10

    c. 60:20:20

    d. 40:35:25

23. The appropriate matrix to use for succession planning is the:

    a. value-fit matrix

    b. drive-adaptability matrix

    c. skill-will matrix

    d. Performance Potential Matrix

24. The practice of placing individuals in job roles that will provide the most developmental value is called:

    a. box filling

    b. assignmentology

    c. crystal ball HR

    d. strategic career mapping

25. Which of the following is not a characteristic of a situation where high potentials perform best:

    a. requires fresh ideas, new ways of thinking

    b. high strategy component to job

    c. requires continuity of relationships

    d. is change-driven

26. Which of the following is not a characteristic of a situation where high professionals perform best:

    a. requires considerable experience in area, depth of knowledge

    b. requires political savvy

    c. requires tactical skills

    d. is technology-, product-, or relationship-driven

27. Leadership competencies tend to differ for which group:

    a. women and minorities

    b. non-U.S. companies

    c. nonprofits

    d. none of the above

Answer key

1. c. 85%

2. d. the model can be changed easily as the organizational culture changes

3. d. time lag, false prophets, and (lack of) courage

4. b. how to use succession planning to develop people to meet future demands and how to make calls on who gets the jobs

5. a. being able to identify and measure the competencies critical for job success

6. d. 67

7. b. competitive-edge competencies

8. b. patterns of behavior reinforced by previous successes

9. d. high potential

10. c. self-awareness and learning agility

11. c. Developing Direct Reports and Others

12. d. none of the above; poor performers are found in the same proportion across different levels of the organization

13. a. key jobs

14. d. you feel a tremendous amount of pressure

15. a. verbal agility

16. b. learning agility

17. a. a competency model that profiles the skills critical for success

18. a. ABC Model

19. d. all of the above

20. b. peers

21. d. essentially nonexistent; they are unrelated

22. b. 70:20:10

23. d. Performance Potential Matrix

24. b. assignmentology

25. c. requires continuity of relationships

26. b. requires political savvy

27. d. none of the above

C

Notes

Chapter 1. The change vaccine: developing leaders for any future

See Bennis and O'Toole (2000) and Charan and Colvin (1999) for discussions of CEO failures.

See Sessa and Campbell (1997) for executive failure rates and a review of broader issues around executive selection.

A brief discussion of the McKinsey *War for Talent* study is contained in Chambers et al. (1998). A book on the continuing studies appeared in 2001, see Michaels et al.

Twelve percent of AT&T managers were able to cope effectively with ambiguity. See Moses and Lyness (1990).

The 1997 merger study is Sirower (1997). The A. T. Kearney study is Habeck et al. (2000).

Executive impact of 15 percent or $25 million after-tax comes from Barrick et al. (1991). Goleman (2000) reports that top performers exceed revenue targets by 15 to 20 percent.

The percent impact numbers come from Hunter et al. (1990). People who were one standard deviation more productive outperformed average performers by a wide margin: unskilled jobs (19 percent), skilled (32 percent), managers (48 percent).

Data on sales jobs comes from Spencer and Spencer (1993).

Data on computer programmers and account managers comes from Spencer (2001).

Bottom-line data on return to shareholders is contained in the update to McKinsey's *War for Talent* study. See Axelrod et al. (2001). A book on the continuing studies appeared in 2001, see Michaels et al.

Findings on Gen Xers vs. Baby Boomers are contained in Bond et al. (1998). Another study of worker motivations from twenty years before appears in Rewick and Lawler (1978).

Surveys of the motivations of graduating college students are Poe (2000) and NACE (2001).

The reference to Development Dimensions International's taxonomy of 70 generic competencies is from Wusteman (2000).

N
O
T
E
S

The reference to competency models being 85 percent the same comes from the Hay-McBer studies, which can be found in Spencer and Spencer (1993). An internal company review of dozens of models reached the same conclusion. Similarly, we developed a software program to analyze competency models because we are often asked to "translate" or map one model into another. The designer of the program reported to us that the total competency library of 50,000–100,000 competency statements can be reduced to 1,800 root words that are combined in various ways to produce those statements. Research referring to generic or "universal" competencies can be found in Schippmann et al. (2000) and Wusteman (2000).

Competency models are truly a dime a dozen. Pick up any journal, popular or scientific, and you will see the competencies of e-company presidents or public sector employers. Research-based models are another matter. The Center for Creative Leadership periodically issues a report, see Leslie and Fleenor (1998), which reviews research-based models used for feedback purposes. For a broader view of competency research, see Bass and Stogdill's (1990) summary of thousands of empirical studies.

464 |

A 1999 Linkage survey found that 60 percent of 360° assessments were custom developed and overwhelmingly based on a competency model. Only 21 percent were tailored from generic models (Linkage 360° Feedback Conference, 1999).

There are countless books and articles around selection issues. For executive selection, see Sessa and Campbell (1997) and Sessa et al. (1998). For some research articles on what works best in selection, see Schmidt and Hunter's (1998) review of 85 years of selection research; Cortina et al. (2000); Mount et al. (2000).

Chapter 2. Leadership competencies: what effective leadership looks like

The first edition of *The Leadership Machine* listed fourteen competencies as important to performance but in short supply. Now we list but eight. There are several reasons for this. First, our database is much larger and includes information on promotions and terminations, so we have a fuller picture of what happens at different stages of a career. Second, all fourteen are still there. Three of the remaining six now appear on the "most likely weaknesses" list for managers (Developing Direct Reports and Others, Directing Others, and Managing and Measuring Work). One of the remaining six now appears on the "most likely weaknesses" list for individual contributors (Personal Learning).The fifth appears as a "measure and reinforce" for managers (Self-Development). And the sixth is listed as both a "most likely weakness" for managers and a "develop early" skill for high-potential individual contributors (Conflict Management). As we have analyzed more research data, it appears these six are more level-specific than general. Finally, we present these as a probability and a way of thinking, not as truth. The question for any organization is, what competencies are critical across levels (or for managers and executives) and in short supply?

Find more on the Big 8 in *the Leadership Architect® Technical Manual* (2010), Lominger International: A Korn/Ferry Company.

The reference to Lyle Spencer's research on the value of increasing average skill levels in specific competencies is Spencer (2001).

The reference to the democratization of strategy comes from Hamel and Prahalad (1994). For later work, see Hamel (2000, rev. 2002).

Chapter 3. Leadership types: The effectiveness patterns of real people

N
O
T
E
S

A wonderfully thorough review of the research on genius, see Simonton (1987), shows that few geniuses have or could ever have all or even most of the characteristics associated with such eminence. Craig and Smith (2000) applied the same logic to integrity tests and found that virtually no one in their samples matched the hypothetical high-integrity and low-integrity individuals. Kaiser and Kaplan (2000) found that maybe 5 percent of the executives in their study could be described as balanced— being versatile at both forceful and enabling behaviors, for example.

Chapter 4. Derailment:
The failure on the other side of success

That human beings have strong drives is an axiom of personality theory stretching to the dawn of human commentary. Research on the Myers-Briggs® Type Indicator (a summary of 345 type studies appears in Carskadon, 1999) indicates the preferences certain types have for accounting or law, for example. Kaplan et al. (1991) and Kaiser and Kaplan (2000) apply this argument to managers and executives.

Interest research looks at the patterns of activities preferred by those who select into various occupations. For example, see the Campbell™ Interest and Skill Survey. Hogan et al. (1996) discusses the uses of personality instruments in determining occupational interest and success.

Derailment research began with Jon Bentz at Sears (1985a, 1985b). Based on his ideas, we began a series of studies at the Center for Creative Leadership: McCall and Lombardo (1983), Lombardo and McCauley (1988), Lombardo and Eichinger (1989), and Leslie and Van Velsor (1996) are examples of this work. These studies looked respectively at the basic arguments for derailment with male executives, the empirical evidence for derailment, preventing derailment, and a comparison of European and U.S. managers. The Leslie and Van Velsor piece includes an update of derailment factors as the economy becomes more global. The topic of derailment is also extensively covered in the original books on male and female executives, see McCall et al. (1988) and Morrison et al. (1987, rev. 1992).

Successful people are more likely to report failures and mistakes than the derailed, see McCall et al. (1988). Successful women are more likely to report them than successful men, see Van Velsor and Hughes (1990).

Jack Gabarro (1987) describes the five learning phases managers go through when taking charge of a new job. He also describes how long it takes to truly learn to do a job well—at least three years at more senior levels. In a similar vein, Schmidt and Hunter (1998) found that up to five years, job experience increases performance; after that, it trails off.

Although it may seem mildly counterintuitive, high potentials and especially executives get less feedback. They are more likely to be told how wonderfully they are doing; specific feedback or even formal performance appraisals can be rare. See Kaplan et al. (1985) and Kaplan et al. (1991) for discussion of this. Also see Howard and Bray (1988) for a similar discussion.

N O T E S

Chapter 5. Learning from experience: Experience is still the best teacher

To our knowledge, the first empirical evidence of how much development adds to success came from the initial report on the long-term AT&T studies, see Bray et al. (1974). Shortly after that, we attended an American Psychological Association symposium where none of the presenters had anything good to say about the argument that one should just select for talent and that development doesn't matter much. The best will simply get better sounds good, but the truth is much more complex than that.

Following this came the original Center for Creative Leadership studies, see McCall et al. (1988), Morrison et al. (1987, rev. 1992), Lombardo (1986), many internal corporate studies, and studies in other fields (principals, sports). For a summary of more studies on development through job experiences, see McCauley and Brutus (1998) and Brutus et al. (2000).

Both Mumford et al. (2000) and Lyness and Thompson (2000) show how skills develop through experience. In the Lyness article, the authors show how level and compensation is related to breadth of experience, and developmental assignments are strongly related to career success.

See the Notes on Chapter 6 for our discussion of learning agility.

Research on the core elements of developmental experience was reported in the Center for Creative Leadership studies above, and in the detailed technical summary of the research. See Lindsey et al. (1987). Later, these core elements were codified into an instrument—the Developmental Challenge Profile. See McCauley et al. (1994, 1995).

Evidence for the effectiveness of courses can be found in Spencer (2001), Morrow et al. (1997), and Burke and Day (1986).

For sources on talent, refer to Appendix A.

The topic of this book is development in organizations. Other writings we recommend are Conger and Benjamin (1999), McCall (1998), Hollenbeck and McCall (1999), and Charan et al. (2001) or any of our updated references.

Chapter 6. Learning agility:
The silver bullet

See the Notes on Chapter 12 for our discussion of grades in school.

While IQ certainly matters, see Herrnstein and Murray (1994) and Howard and Bray (1988), it's effects aren't simple. As Simonton (1987) observed, "Intelligence is a necessary but not sufficient cause of adulthood success in careers that demand creativity or leadership." While certainly related, excessive intelligence seems to hurt; the most effective people are somewhat smarter than the average for their group, but not too much smarter, see Simonton (1987) and Most (1990).

Research explicitly on measuring and developing learning from experience can be found in Sternberg and Wagner (1990), Sternberg et al. (1995), Spreitzer et al. (1997), Goleman (1998, 2000), and Lombardo and Eichinger (2000). These studies respectively looked at measuring learning and its independence from intelligence (Sternberg), its use in identifying international executive potential, the measurement and development of emotional intelligence, and the measurement and application of learning in U.S. and Canadian organizations as a prime indicator of potential.

In Sternberg et al. (1995), the correlations reported in all these studies rival those of IQ in relating to performance, potential, or a number of other organizational measures, such as salary. Their measure of practical intelligence (which they also refer to as learning from experience) added 32 percent to the variance explained by IQ alone, and was the single best predictor of managerial performance. In our studies, the best predictors of actual promotion were learning agility and drive for results.

Similarly, the correlations reported in other studies above are comparable to that of IQ and performance measures.

As Sternberg points out (1995, p. 924), "The most viable approach to increasing the variance accounted for in real-world phenomena (e.g., job performance) is to supplement existing intelligence and aptitude tests with selection of additional measures based on new constructs, such as practical intelligence."

Learning agility appears to make as much difference as IQ in success in a number of areas, including management.

Additional confirmation of this contention comes from the research on training effectiveness. Obviously, if IQ were essentially all that mattered, training could have little effect beyond educating people in unknown areas, such as a technical skill. This is not the case at all—training can have powerful effects in improving performance and bottom-line measures. An excellent meta-analysis of the effectiveness of training across 70 studies is contained in Burke and Day (1986). For a meta-analysis, see Morrow et al. (1997).

Learning agility's normal distribution in the employee population is from De Meuse, Dai, Hallenbeck, and Tang (2008).

Learning agility scores and the relationship to gender is De Meuse et al. (2008) and Lombardo and Eichinger (2003).

Learning agility scores and the relationship to age is De Meuse et al. (2008).

The reference to younger individuals tend to score slightly higher than older ones on the Change Agility subscale is Lombardo and Eichinger (2003).

The reference to ethnic background doesn't matter is Church and Desrosiers (2006) and De Meuse et al. (2008).

Learning agility and the relationship to global regions is from De Meuse et al. (2008).

The reference to people scoring relatively higher on Results Agility and Mental Agility than on People Agility and Change Agility is Lombardo and Eichinger (2003).

That this scoring pattern is consistent across the five international regions we looked at is De Meuse et al. (2008).

The point about self-awareness and learning agility scores is from De Meuse (2008).

Overrating and underrating on learning agility mirrors the findings for other self-assessments, see Atwater and Yammarino (1992) and Eichinger and Lombardo (2004).

Several excellent sources of practical learning strategies are Bunker and Webb (1992), Daudelin (1996), Dechant (1994), and Siebert (1999). For a look at learning strategies in children, see Pressley et al. (1987).

The reference to low-performing executives having almost random learning patterns from job assignments comes from Lombardo (1986).

Interest research looks at the patterns of activities preferred by those who select into various occupations. For example, see the Campbell™ Interest and Skill Survey. Hogan et al. (1996) discusses the uses of personality instruments in determining occupational interest and success.

Chapter 7. Self-awareness: Getting to know you

For how self-awareness matters for performance, see Church (1997) and Sala (2003).

The assertion that leaders who are self-aware are open to feedback is from Lombardo and Eichinger (2009).

The reference to self-awareness as the first step toward improvement is Ruyle, Hallenbeck, Orr, and Swisher (2010).

The finding that low self-awareness increases the risk of derailment, especially at higher levels of leadership is Tang, Dai, and De Meuse (2010).

The reference to the most common blind spots (areas where people overestimate their ability) is Orr, Swisher, Tang, and De Meuse (2010).

The reference to the most common hidden strengths (areas where people underestimate their ability) is Orr et al. (2010).

That raters agree more with one another than they agree with self-ratings is well documented; similarly, they are more accurate. For readable discussion on this and all other important feedback topics, see two excellent books: *Maximizing the Value of 360 Degree Feedback*, Tornow et al. (1998) and *The Art and Science of 360 Degree Feedback,* Lepsinger and Lucia (2009). Two excellent articles on the issues surrounding 360° feedback are Bracken et al. (2001) and Peiperl (2001). Other empirical evidence can be found in Harris and Schaubroeck (1988) and Murphy and Cleveland (1995, see pages 137–140 for their discussion of self-ratings).

We and others have concluded that knowing or believing that one's ratings will not be anonymous drives ratings up. See the sources above and Lombardo and Eichinger (2003).

The reference to a study of 58,000 appraisals is Jawahar and Williams (1997).

For a review of the research on mentors, see Douglas (1997) and Higgin and Kram (2001). For one of the few empirical studies on the effects of informal vs. formal mentors, see Chao et al. (1992); for a review of the literature from a female perspective, see Ragin (1997). Lyness and Thompson (2000) show that women are less likely to say that mentoring facilitated their advancement. A discussion of race and mentoring appears in Thomas (2001). The pitfalls of mentoring are discussed in *BusinessWeek Online* (April 17, 2001). (This magazine is now *Bloomberg Businessweek.*) Some best practices in mentoring are contained in Michaels et al. (2001), pp. 116–121.

For the difference it makes in how long someone has known the learner, see Lombardo and Eichinger (2003).

Ashford and Tsui (1991) conducted a fascinating study which shows that when managers sought negative feedback, this increased accuracy of understanding, and it enhanced superiors', direct reports', and peers' opinions of the managers' overall effectiveness! In contrast, seeking positive feedback decreased constituents' opinions of their effectiveness!

Chapter 8. Development:
Challenge, feedback, learning loop

The imperatives of development come from the Center for Creative Leadership studies and are summarized in Lombardo and Eichinger (1989) and formed the basis for the "Tools for Developing Successful Executives" course at CCL.

Chapter 9. Improvement planning:
Creating a plan that works

The reference to alternative plans is from Eichinger, Lombardo, Stiber, and Orr (2011).

For a review of the research on mentors, see Douglas (1997) and Higgin and Kram (2001). For one of the few empirical studies on the effects of informal vs. formal mentors, see Chao et al. (1992); for a review of the literature from a female perspective, see Ragin (1997). Lyness and Thompson (2000) show that women are less likely to say that mentoring facilitated their advancement. A discussion of race and mentoring appears in Thomas (2001). The pitfalls of mentoring are discussed in *BusinessWeek Online* (April 17, 2001). (This magazine is now *Bloomberg Businessweek.*) Some best practices in mentoring are contained in Michaels et al. (2001), pp. 116–121.

The evidence that carefully constructed courses can improve productivity, particularly in sales and technical jobs, is extensive. See Spencer (2001), Morrow et al. (1997), and Burke and Day (1986) for the results of many studies in this area.

Chapter 10. Career planning: Managing your career for the long-term

The finding about personality/organization fit is from Carskadon (1999).

Chapter 11. A case for talent management

A brief discussion of the McKinsey *War for Talent* study is contained in Chambers et al. (1998). A book on the continuing studies appeared in 2001, see Michaels et al.

See McCall and Hollenbeck (2002) for research on leadership effectiveness for global executives.

The reference to 46 percent of organizations studied experienced decreased levels of employee engagement as opposed to the standard 15 percent in nonrecession times is Hewitt (2010).

Executive failure rate research is Davis (2005). Percentage of internal successors is Miles (2009).

Repatriate attrition is a McKinsey study (Guthridge, 2008).

Lack of what is needed for success is Martin and Schmidt (May 2010).

Tactics for attracting minority candidates is Avery et al. (2004).

For a discussion on placing A players in strategic positions, see Huselid, Beatty, and Becker (2005; HBR OnPoint 2009).

For the prevalence of competency models in organizations, see Aberdeen (2007).

NOTES

For a discussion on how competency models create the foundation from which all talent practices are built upon and are used as a framework to link talent practices with organizational strategy, see Hollenbeck (2009).

For competency models as a method for communicating organization expectations, see Hayton and McEvoy (2006).

For communicating to high potentials how their development plans match the organizational strategy, see Martin and Schmidt (May 2010).

For use of social networking to engage and retain talent, see Phillips and Edwards (2009).

The reference on differentially recognizing and compensating your high potentials is from Martin and Schmidt (May 2010).

Finding the right challenges and meaningful experiences at the right time and providing the right support is from McCall (2009), Giber (2007), and McCall and Hollenbeck (2008).

For a discussion on informal learning versus traditional learning, see Mallon (July 2009).

For a review of the results associated with coaching, see De Meuse, Dai, and Lee (2009).

For a review of the use and benefits of mentorship, see Giber (2007).

The assertion that 81 percent of companies with executives that were highly engaged in the performance management process also had strong business results is from Bersin (July 2011).

Employee reactions to managers' focus on the performance evaluation form is Lounsberry (2008).

The assertion that not all high performers are high potentials, and not all high professionals are high potentials is backed up by Corporate Leadership Council (2005).

Better financial performance associated with companies employing best talent management practices is from Guthridge and Komm (2008), Hackett Group Study (2007), and McBassi and Co. (2006).

Rank order of ROI for HR interventions is from Spencer (2001).

Organizations with employees reporting high levels of trust outperformed organizations with employees reporting low levels of trust by nearly 3 to 1 in shareholder returns is from Watson Wyatt & Company (2002).

The focus on retention of critical employees as a measure of leadership success is from Hewitt (2007).

The use of coaching among new hires reduced turnover in their first year and resulted in a 251 percent ROI is from Edwards and Lounsberry (2008).

Teamwork impact on morale and retention is from Edwards (2001).

The benefits associated with high levels of commitment to the organization is from Lockwood (2007).

For relationship between engagement and safety, see Lockwood (2007).

For ROI on organizational leadership development and change initiatives, see Carter, Ulrich, and Goldsmith (2005).

For relationship between improvements on key leadership competencies and business outcomes, see Pluzdrak (2007).

For the study on the ROI of competency development, see Clark and Weitzman (2008).

Data from 50,000 raters in 140 diverse organizations indicate that developing others is the lowest-rated competency out of 67 is from Lombardo and Eichinger (2002) and has since been updated in Dai, Tang, and De Meuse (2009).

Chapter 12. Competency modeling: Setting a success target

See Neff and Citrin (1999) for detail on the six winning strategies of corporate stars.

For an excellent discussion of results-based leadership, see Ulrich et al. (1999).

Performance ratings are indeed inflated. A major study is titled *Where All the Children Are Above Average.* See Jawahar and Williams (1997).

For a review of the issues in performance appraisal, see Murphy and Cleveland (1995). An interesting Web site features a free newsletter, how-to information, case studies, and the latest research on issues of performance measurement, performance management, and 360° applications. The address is www. zigonperf.com.

Structured interviewing has been long established as an excellent selection method. For empirical studies, see Schmidt and Rader (1999) and Cortina et al. (2000). Cognitive measures, biodata, and reference checks also have strong support. See Schmidt and Hunter (1998) and Mount et al. (2000). Assessment centers are another expensive but valuable selection method. For a description of one of the best-known assessment centers, see Howard and Bray (1988).

478 |

An extensive discussion of grades in school and what they relate and don't relate to for managerial performance can be found in Howard (1986). In *The Bell Curve* by Herrnstein and Murray (1994), they report an overall relationship of .11 between college grades and general job performance, making it the sixth-best predictor of performance. Cognitive test scores (such as IQ) did much better. A study of consensus famous leaders concluded that formal education was *inversely* related to achieving eminence in leadership positions. See Simonton (1987).

Grades in school were not even included in some meta-analytic studies we reviewed, although some authors such as Bobko et al. (1999) called for them to be included, as they are so widely used by organizations. Even a relatively favorable study, Roth et al. (1996), reported only a correlation of .14 with performance in business jobs (managerial or not was not specified). As a comparison, Schmidt and Hunter (1998) report a correlation of .58 with general mental ability measures and managerial performance. To be fair, grades are related to general mental ability and conscientiousness, so the practice at least makes some sense. But the establishment of arbitrary cutoffs and specific cutoffs can't be justified.

The jury is still out on college quality. The McKinsey studies support it as a hiring criteria, but a large empirical study, see Howard (1986), did not. See Chambers et al. (1998) and Axelrod et al. (2001).

For "discussing the undiscussables," see Argyris (1991).

Chapter 13. Preventing derailment: A priority for organizations

See Notes on Chapter 4 for derailment sources.

The most profitable mix of inside to outside staffing is 80/20 according to Ulrich and Lake (1990).

See Kotter (1988) for further evidence of the power of projects in development.

The finding that creative people produce both more inferior and more superior creations comes from Simonton (1987).

No one really knows how long it takes to spot potential. Past estimates have ranged from two to ten years of experience, with five being a common number. With better measures of learning potential, we can move this number down, but potential is and always will be evidenced by performance under first-time conditions for the person. It will ordinarily take a couple of jobs and first-time tasks for this to be seen.

N
O
T
E
S

For a review of the research on mentors, see Douglas (1997) and Higgin and Kram (2001). For one of the few empirical studies on the effects of informal vs. formal mentors, see Chao et al. (1992); for a review of the literature from a female perspective, see Ragin (1997). Lyness and Thompson (2000) show that women are less likely to say that mentoring facilitated their advancement. A discussion of race and mentoring appears in Thomas (2001). The pitfalls of mentoring are discussed in *BusinessWeek Online* (April 17, 2001). (This magazine is now *Bloomberg Businessweek.*) Some best practices in mentoring are contained in Michaels et al. (2001), pp. 116–121.

Chapter 14. 360° Feedback: Options and best practices

See Notes on Chapter 7 for our discussion on feedback.

The survey cited throughout the chapter is Rogers et al. (2000).

For the reference to the 360° performance survey and an excellent review of the issues surrounding 360° performance appraisal, see Lepsinger and Lucia (2009).

The reference to the study of the conditions where feedback can backfire without goal setting (or help with it) is Kluger and DeNisi (1996).

Feedback typically improves average performance; however, in some cases it decreases performance. See Kluger and DeNisi (1996).

For a discussion on the magnitude of performance improvement, see Smither, London, and Reilly (2005).

Chapter 15. 70:20:10 Development: Jobs, coaches, and courses

Jack Gabarro (1987) describes the five learning phases managers go through when taking charge of a new job.

Evidence for the effectiveness of courses can be found in Spencer (2001), Morrow et al. (1997), and Burke and Day (1986).

For "discussing the undiscussables," see Argyris (1991).

The reference to the origin of 70:20:10 is McCall, Lombardo, and Morrison (1988).

Since the original *Lessons of Experience* studies, the research has been replicated in Singapore, India, China, and with female executives and global executives. For more details see Wilson (2008), Zhang et al. (2009),Yip and Wilson (2008), Center for Creative Leadership (2008), McCall and Hollenbeck (2002), and Van Velsor and Hughes (1990).

The reference to women may cite learning from other people more frequently than men is Van Velsor and Hughes (1990). The general findings about female vs. male executives are contained in Morrison et al. (1987, rev. 1992).

The reference to 16 full-time jobs and over 150 part-time assignments were identified as being the most developmental is Lombardo and Eichinger (2010).

Chapter 16. Coaching for 70:20:10 development

Other sources we recommend on coaching are Goldsmith et al. (2000) and Hargrove (1995, rev. 2002). For an annotated bibliography on coaching, see Douglas and Morley (2000).

See Notes on Chapter 7 for our discussion on mentoring.

The study on the pitfalls of retaking 360° is Howland and Martineau (Fall 1998).

Chapter 17. Driving the Leadership Machine

See Notes on Chapter 6 for our discussion on learning agility.

Only 15 percent of executive selections came from the succession plan in Sessa et al. (1998).

Succession planning has a significant body of knowledge for readers to refer to. First, we recommend membership in the Human Resource Planning Society and Senior Human Resource Management Association to keep up-to-date. Next, there are many excellent sources to refer to. Rothwell (2001) covers the topic from A to Z. Eastman (1995) contains an annotated bibliography of major sources. Bishop (2000) contains a number of practical suggestions on making succession systems work more smoothly.

Kotter's finding on time spent by CEOs on succession and development is in Kotter (1988).

Chapter 18. Succession planning:
The Performance Potential Matrix

Charan et al. (2001) also makes use of the Performance Potential Matrix.

Chapter 19. Assignmentology:
The art of assignment management

No notes.

Chapter 20. A universal approach:
The global leadership machine

Well-known assessment center studies such as AT&T, see Howard and Bray (1988); 360° feedback studies, see Lombardo and Eichinger (Spring 2003); and studies of learning agility, see Lombardo and Eichinger (2000) have found few differences that make a difference in male/female skill levels. This case is also well made by Morrison et al. (1987, rev. 1992). Eagly et al. (1995) reports no overall difference in skills, but notes that men do better in stereotypically masculine jobs and vice versa. A report on numerous research findings is in the November 20, 2000 issue of *BusinessWeek Online. (This magazine is now Bloomberg Businessweek.)*

Among women and men at the same level, women had higher-assessed skills. See Howard and Bray (1988) and Lombardo and McCauley (1993). See also the November 20, 2000 issue of *BusinessWeek Online. (This magazine is now Bloomberg Businessweek.)*

In a matched sample of African American and Caucasian middle managers, African Americans had higher-assessed skills from peers and direct reports. See *Center for Creative Leadership* (1995).

The findings about male and female raters comes from Lombardo and Eichinger (2003).

Evidence on African American and Caucasian bias comes from Mount et al. (1997).

The research on ethnic differences in IQ and in raising cognitive ability is reviewed in Herrnstein and Murray (1994). Dickens and Flynn (2001) cite evidence of increase in IQ scores in their introduction.

The research on African American scores on ability tests varying significantly when test instructions are changed is reported in Gladwell (2000). For the empirical study upon which this part of the Gladwell article is based, see Steele and Aronson (1995).

The general findings about female vs. male executives are contained in Morrison et al. (1987, rev. 1992) and Van Velsor and Hughes (1990). Lyness and Thompson (1997, 2000) show that women have fewer moves, narrower experiences, and jobs with less authority. Similarly, Hurley and Sonnenfeld (1998) report that women have had jobs in fewer departments and have less functional breadth. Lyness and Thompson (2000) show that women are less likely to say that mentoring facilitated their advancement. That only 2 percent of top wage earners are women was reported in *Catalyst* (1996).

The findings concerning African American managers is Douglas (2003).

Caucasians report other ethnic backgrounds less intelligent. See Morrison (1992).

African American managers rate African Americans higher. See Mount et al. (1997).

Women receive lower ratings when they are a small percentage of the work group. See Sackett et al. (1991).

Even with identical resumes, men are favored over women. See Morrison (1992).

Female recruiters saw male applicants as more similar to them and more qualified than female applicants. See Graves and Powell (1995).

Many excellent recommendations for increasing diversity in the workforce may be found in Morrison (1992) and *Catalyst* (1998).

The findings on staff and line differences in development are in Eichinger and Lombardo (1990). The finding that line jobs are more important than staff jobs comes from Hurley and Sonnenfeld (1998).

The reference to Development Dimensions International's use of the same 70 competencies worldwide is Wusteman (2000).

The GLOBE project (House et al., 2004) at the University of Pennsylvania produced a single list of competencies from a study of 18,000 international managers.

The Center for Creative Leadership periodically reviews 360° instruments. See Leslie and Fleenor (1998). Some of these have been validated internationally.

The learning agility measure validated against international samples is described in Spreitzer et al. (1997).

The United States–Europe derailment study is Leslie and Van Velsor (1996).

The expatriate study referred to is Lombardo et al. (1988).

The quotation about the Benchmarks® revisions is Craig and Raju (1999).

N
O
T
E
S

A discussion of values differences internationally and extensive references can be found in Leslie and Van Velsor (1996, 1998).

The finding about agreeableness mattering more internationally is from Wilson and Dalton (1998). The examples of Japanese and Indonesian employees come from Tornow et al. (1998, Chapter 8).

References to George Washington are Bobrick (1997) and Royster (1979).

Appendix A. Rationale for the 85 percent solution

NOTES

One of the first major studies to demonstrate how talent is built from the ground up is Bloom (1985). Sports psychology has added to this contention. For a research analysis, see Ericsson et al. (1993). For an excellent and very readable account of the growth of talent, see Hurst (2002, Chapters 6-10).

There is little doubt that as we mature, our interests and motives change. Howard and Bray (1988) describes how this process plays out through adulthood, as do the popular books *Seasons of a Man's Life* (1978) and *Seasons of a Woman's Life* (1996) by Daniel Levinson.

For a complete list of the eight "saving grace" skills, see *Paths to Improvement: Navigating Your Way to Success* (2011), p. 41.

That 90 percent of problems dealt with are ambiguous (neither the problem nor the solution is clear) seems self-evident and is commonly contended by researchers and the popular press alike. For thoughtful discussion of dealing with ambiguity, see White et al. (1996) and Moses and Lyness (1990).

That some competencies can only be developed as they occur or as they are demanded under stress also seems fairly self-evident to most. For a discussion of this, see *The Lessons of Experience,*

McCall et al. (1988) and *Breaking the Glass Ceiling,* Morrison et al. (1987, rev. 1992). These are the two original Center for Creative Leadership studies of executive men and women.

The 10 years to develop mastery is often called the 10-year-rule. It refers to a general finding of 1,000 hours of practice for 10 years to master the violin or to develop a complete tennis game. We observed the same phenomenon at work in executive development, see Lombardo (1986). Hurst (2002) has an extensive discussion in Chapters 6 to 10. For research findings on the 10-year-rule, see Ericsson et al. (1993) and Bloom et al. (1985).

N
O
T
E
S

| 487

References

Abel, A. L. (2011, June). *It's about trust and training: Examining your organization's internal coaching practice.* New York, NY: The Conference Board Executive Action Series.

Aberdeen Group. (2007). *Competency management: The link between talent management and optimum business results.* Retrieved September 20, 2011, from http://www.assess.co.nz/pages/AberdeenStudy.pdf

Aon Hewitt. (2010). *Trends in global employee engagement* [White Paper]. Retrieved from http://www.aon.com/attachments/thought-leadership/Trends_Global_Employee_Engagement_Final.pdf

Argyris, C. (1991, May–June; HBR OnPoint Enhanced Edition, February 1, 2000). Teaching smart people how to learn. *Harvard Business Review.*

Ashford, S. J., & Tsui, A. S. (1991, June). Self-regulation for managerial effectiveness: The role of active feedback seeking. *Academy of Management Journal, 34*(2), 251–280.

Atwater, L. E., & Yammarino, F. J. (1992). Does self-other agreement on leadership perceptions moderate the validity of leadership and performance predictions? *Personnel Psychology, 45,* 141–164.

Avery, D. R., Hernandez, M., & Hebl, M. R. (2004, January). Who's watching the race? Racial salience in recruitment advertising. *Journal of Applied Social Psychology, 34*(1), 146-161.

Axelrod, E. L., Handfield-Jones, H., & Welsh, T. A. (2001). The war for talent: Part two. *The McKinsey Quarterly, 2,* 9-11.

Barrick, M. R., Day, D. V., Lord, R. G., & Alexander, R. A. (1991). Assessing the utility of executive leadership. *Leadership Quarterly, 2*(1), 9–22.

Bass, B. M., & Bass, R. (2008). *The Bass handbook of leadership: Theory, research and managerial applications* (4th ed.). New York, NY: Free Press.

Bass, B. M., & Stogdill, M. (1990). *Handbook of leadership: Theory, research, and managerial applications* (3rd ed.). New York, NY: Free Press.

Bennis, W., & O'Toole, J. (2000, May–June; HBR OnPoint Enhanced Edition, February 1, 2002). Don't hire the wrong CEO. *Harvard Business Review, 78*(3), 170-176.

Bentz, V. J. (1985a). Research findings from personality assessment of executives. In J. H. Bernardin & D. A. Bowdas (Eds.), *Personality Assessment in Organizations* (pp. 82–144). New York, NY: Praeger Publishers.

Bentz, V. J. (1985b). *A view of the top: A thirty-year perspective of research devoted to the discovery, description, and prediction of executive behavior.* Paper presented at the annual convention of the American Psychological Association, Los Angeles, CA.

Bersin & Associates. (2011, July). *High-impact leadership development for the 21st century: Key findings, trends, and analytics* [Executive Summary]. Oakland, CA: Author.

Bishop, C. H., Jr. (2000). *Making change happen one person at a time: Assessing change capacity within your organization.* New York, NY: AMACOM.

Bloom, B. S. (Ed.). (1985). *Developing talent in young people.* New York, NY: Ballantine Books.

Bobko, P., Roth, P. L., & Potosky, D. (1999). Derivation and implications of a meta-analytic matrix incorporating cognitive ability, alternative predictors, and job performance. *Personnel Psychology, 52,* 561–589.

Bobrick, B. (1997). *Angel in the whirlwind.* New York, NY: Simon and Schuster.

Bond, J., Galinsky, E., & Swanberg, J. (1998). *The 1997 national study of the changing workforce.* New York, NY: Families and Work Institute. www.familiesandwork.org

Bond, J., Thompson, C., Galinsky, E., & Prottas, D. (2003). *Highlights of the 2002 national study of the changing workforce.* New York, NY: Families and Work Institute. www.familiesandwork.org

Bracken, D. W., Timmreck, C. W., Fleenor, J. W., & Summers, L. (2001, Spring). 360° feedback from another angle. *Human Resource Management, 40*(1), 3–20.

Bray, D., Campbell, R., & Grant, D. (1974). *Formative years in business: A long-term AT&T study of managerial lives.* New York, NY: John Wiley & Sons, Inc.

Brutus, S., Ruderman, M. N., Ohlott, P. J., & McCauley, C. D. (2000, Winter). Developing from job experiences: The role of organizational-based self-esteem. *Human Resource Development Quarterly, 11*(4), 367–380.

Bunker, K. A., & Webb, A. D. (1992). *Learning how to learn from experience: Impact of stress and coping* (Report No. 154). Greensboro, NC: Center for Creative Leadership.

Burke, M., & Day, R. (1986). A cumulative study of the effectiveness of managerial training. *Journal of Applied Psychology, 71*(2), 232–245.

BusinessWeek Online. (2001, April 17). The hidden pitfalls of mentoring. New York, NY: Author. (This magazine is now *Bloomberg Businessweek.*)

Carskadon, T. G. (Ed.). (1999). A grand synopsis of 345 studies in psychological type, 1979–1999. *Journal of Psychological Type, 50.*

Carter, L., Ulrich, D., & Goldsmith, M. (Eds.). (2005). *Best practices in leadership development and organization change.* San Francisco, CA: Pfeiffer.

Catalyst. (1996; updated 2002). *Catalyst census of women corporate officers and top earners.* New York, NY: Author.

Catalyst. (1998). *Advancing women in business: The Catalyst guide.* San Francisco, CA: Jossey-Bass.

R
E
F
E
R
E
N
C
E
S

Center for Creative Leadership. (1995). Benchmarks®: Are African American managers rated differently from White managers? *Issues and Observations,15*(4). Greensboro, NC: Author.

Chambers, E. G., Foulon, M., Handfield-Jones, H., Hankin, S. M., & Michaels, E. G. (1998). The war for talent. *The McKinsey Quarterly, 3,* 44–57.

Chao, G. T., Walz, P. M., & Gardner, P. D. (1992, Autumn). Formal and informal mentorships: A comparison of mentoring functions and contrast with nonmentored counterparts. *Personnel Psychology, 45,* 619–636.

Charan, R., & Colvin, G. (1999, June 21). Why CEOs fail. *Fortune, 139*(12), 69–78.

Charan, R., Drotter, S., & Noel, J. (2011). *The leadership pipeline: How to build the leadership powered company* (2nd ed.). San Francisco, CA: Jossey-Bass.

Church, A. H. (1997). Managerial self-awareness in high-performing individuals in organizations. *Journal of Applied Psychology, 82,* 281–292.

Church, A. H., & Desrosiers, E. I. (2006). *Talent management: Will the high potentials please stand up?* Symposium presented at the annual conference for the Society for Industrial and Organizational Psychology, Dallas, TX.

Clark, L. P., & Weitzman, M. (2008). *Making millions by mining management competency data* [White Paper]. Minneapolis, MN: Korn/Ferry International.

Cohen, S. (1994). Designing effective self-managing work teams. In M. M. Beyerlein & D. A. Johnson (Eds.), *Advances in interdisciplinary studies of work teams* (pp. 67–103). Greenwich, CT: JAI Press.

Colvin, G. (2001, January 8). Changing of the guard. *Fortune, 143*(1), 84–99.

Conference Board. (2011, April). *CEO challenge 2011: Fueling business growth with innovation and talent development* (Report No. R-1474-11-RR). New York, NY: Author.

Conger, J. A., & Benjamin, B. (1999). *Building leaders: How successful companies develop the next generation.* San Francisco, CA: Jossey-Bass.

Corporate Leadership Council. (2005a). *Realizing the full potential of rising talent (Volume I): A quantitative analysis of the identification and development of high-potential employees.* Washington, DC: Corporate Executive Board.

Corporate Leadership Council. (2005b). *Realizing the full potential of rising talent (Volume II): Strategies for supporting the development of high-potential employees.* Washington, DC: Corporate Executive Board.

Cortina, J. M., Goldstein, N. B., Payne, S. C., Davison, H. K., & Gilliland, S.W. (2000). The incremental validity of interview scores over and above cognitive ability and conscientiousness scores. *Personnel Psychology, 53*(2), 325–352.

Craig, S. B., & Smith, J. A. (2000, April). *Integrity and personality: A person-oriented investigation.* Presented at the 15th annual conference of the Society for Industrial and Organizational Psychology, New Orleans, LA.

Craig, S. B., & Raju, N. S. (1999, April). Using item response theory to update Benchmarks®. In D. McDonald-Mann (Chair), *Revising a 360 degree feedback instrument: Integrating quantitative and qualitative data.* Symposium presented at the annual conference of the Society for Industrial and Organizational Psychology, Atlanta, GA.

Dai, G., Tang, K. Y., & De Meuse, K. P. (2009). *The Leadership Architect® 2009 global norms report 1: Competency norms and analysis technical report.* Minneapolis, MN: Lominger International: A Korn/Ferry Company.

Daudelin, M. W. (1996). Learning from experience through reflection. *Organizational Dynamics, 24*(3), 36–48.

Davis, S. H. (2005). Should a 60 percent success rate be acceptable? *Industrial and Commercial Training, 37*(7), 331–335.

REFERENCES

Dechant, K. (1994). Making the most of job assignments: An exercise in planning for learning. *Journal of Management Education, 18*(2), 198–211.

De Meuse, K. P. (2008). *Learning agility: A new construct whose time has come.* In R. B. Kaiser (Chair), *The importance, assessment, and development of flexible leadership.* Symposium presented at the annual conference for the Society for Industrial and Organizational Psychology, San Francisco, CA.

De Meuse, K. P., Dai, G., Hallenbeck, G. S., Jr., & Tang, K. Y. (2008). *Global talent management: Using learning agility to identify high potentials around the world* [White Paper]. Minneapolis, MN: Korn/Ferry International.

De Meuse, K. P., Dai, G., & Lee, R. (2009, September). Evaluating the effectiveness of executive coaching: Beyond ROI? *Coaching: An International Journal of Theory, Research and Practice, 2*(2), 117–134). doi: 10.1080/17521880902882413

Dickens, W. T., & Flynn, J. R. (2001, April). Heritability estimates versus large environmental effects: The IQ paradox resolved. *Psychological Review, 108*(2), 346–369.

Douglas, C. A. (1997). *Formal mentoring programs in organizations: An annotated bibliography.* Greensboro, NC: Center for Creative Leadership.

Douglas, C. A. (2003). *Key events and lessons for managers in a diverse workforce: A report on research and findings.* Greensboro, NC: Center for Creative Leadership.

Douglas, C. A., & Morley, W. H. (2000). *Executive coaching: An annotated bibliography.* Greensboro, NC: Center for Creative Leadership.

Eagly, A., Karau, S. J., & Makhijana, M. G. (1995). Gender and the effectiveness of leaders: A meta-analysis. *Psychological Bulletin, 117*(1), 125–145.

Eastman, L. J. (1995). *Succession planning: An annotated bibliography.* Greensboro, NC: Center for Creative Leadership.

REFERENCES

Edwards, L., & Lounsberry, C. (2008). Measuring ROI in coaching for new-hire employee retention: A global media company. In P. Phillips & J. Phillips (Eds.), *ROI in action casebook*. San Francisco, CA: Pfeiffer.

Edwards, R. L. R. (2001, August). The morale and satisfaction of midlevel administrators: Differentiating the constructs and their impact on intent to leave. *Dissertation Abstracts International, 62*(2-A), 482. Section A: Humanities and Social Sciences.

Effron, M. (2010). Avon Products, Inc. The talent challenge. In M. Goldsmith & L. Carter (Eds.), *Best practices in talent management: How the world's leading corporations manage, develop, and retain top talent*. San Francisco, CA: Pfeiffer.

Eichinger, R. W., & Lombardo, M. M. (1990). *Twenty-two ways to develop leadership in staff managers* (Report No. 144). Greensboro, NC: Center for Creative Leadership.

Eichinger, R. W., & Lombardo, M. M. (2004). Patterns of rater accuracy in 360-degree feedback. *Human Resource Planning, 27*(4), 23–25.

Eichinger, R. W., Lombardo, M. M., Stiber, A. J., & Orr, J. E. (2011). *Paths to improvement: Navigating your way to success.* Minneapolis, MN: Lominger International: A Korn/Ferry Company.

Ericsson, K., Krampe, R., & Tesch-Romer, C. (1993). The role of deliberate practice in the acquisition of expert performance. *Psychological Review, 100*(3), 363–406.

Gabarro, J. J. (1987). *The dynamics of taking charge.* Boston, MA: Harvard Business School Press.

Gates, S. (2011). *Measuring more than efficiency: The new role of human capital metrics* (Report No. R-1356-04-RR). New York, NY: The Conference Board.

Giber, D. (2007). *Improving ROI: Three leadership development best practices.* Burlington, MA: Linkage. Retrieved from http://www.linkageinc.com/thinking/linkageleader/Documents/David_Giber_Improving_ROI_Three_Best_Practices.pdf

R
E
F
E
R
E
N
C
E
S

Gladwell, M. (2000, August 21 & 28). The art of failure. *The New Yorker,* 84–93.

Goldsmith, M. (2007). *What got you here won't get you there.* New York, NY: Hyperion.

Goldsmith, M., & Lyons, L. S. (Eds.). (2006). *Coaching for leadership, second edition: The practice of leadership coaching from the world's greatest coaches* (2nd ed.). San Francisco, CA: Pfeiffer.

Goleman, D. (1998). *Working with emotional intelligence.* New York, NY: Bantam Books.

Goleman, D. (2000, March–April; HBR OnPoint Enhanced Edition, August 1, 2000). Leadership that gets results. *Harvard Business Review.*

Graves, L. M., & Powell, G. N. (1995). The effect of sex similarity on recruiters' evaluations of actual applicants: A test of the similarity-attraction paradigm. *Personnel Psychology, 48,* 85–98.

Guthridge, M., & Komm, A. B. (2008, May). Why multinationals struggle to manage talent. *McKinsey Quarterly.* Retrieved September 22, 2011, from www.mckinseyquarterly.com/Why_multinationals_struggle_to_manage_talent_2140

Habeck, M. M., Kröger, F., & Träm, M. R. (2000). *After the merger: Seven rules for successful post-merger integration.* London: Financial Times Prentice Hall.

Hackett Group. (2007). *Companies can improve earnings nearly 15% by improving talent management function* [Press Release]. Retrieved from http://www.thehackettgroup.com/about/alerts/alerts_2007/alert_07242007.jsp

Hamel, G. (2000; rev. 2002). *Leading the revolution.* Boston, MA: Harvard Business School Press.

Hamel, G., & Prahalad, C. K. (1994). *Competing for the future.* Boston, MA: Harvard Business School Press.

Hargrove, R. (1995; rev. 2003). *Masterful coaching.* San Francisco, CA: Jossey-Bass.

REFERENCES

Harris, M. M., & Schaubroeck, J. (1988). A meta-analysis of self-supervisor, self-peer, and peer-supervisor ratings. *Personnel Psychology, 41,* 43–62.

Hayton, J. C., & McEvoy, G. M. (2006, Fall). Competencies in practice: An interview with Hanneke C. Frese. *Human Resource Management, 45*(3), 495–500. doi: 10.1002/hrm.20126

Herrnstein, R. J., & Murray, C. (1994). *The bell curve.* New York, NY: Free Press.

Hewitt, M. (2007). Finding and keeping the best: Three ways to ensure that employees stay. *Workforce Management.* Retrieved from www.workforce.com/archive/article/24/62/99.php?ht=

Higgin, M. C., & Kram, K. E. (2001, April). Reconceptualizing mentoring at work: A developmental perspective. *Academy of Management Review, 26*(2), 264–288.

Hodgson, P., & White, R. (2001). *Relax, it's only uncertainty.* London: Financial Times Prentice Hall.

Hogan, R., Hogan, J., & Roberts, B. W. (1996). Personality measurement and employment decisions. *American Psychologist, 51*(5), 469–477.

Hollenbeck, G. P. (2009). Executive selection – What's right… and what's wrong. *Industrial and Organizational Psychology, 2*(2), 130–143. doi: 10.1111/j.1754-9434.2009.01122.x

Hollenbeck, G. P., & McCall, M. W. (1999). Leadership development: Contemporary practice. In A. I. Kraut & A. K. Korman (Eds.), *Evolving practices for human resources management: Responses to a changing world of work.* San Francisco, CA: Jossey-Bass.

House, R. J., Hanges, P. J., Javidan, M., Gupta, V., & Dorfman, P. W. (Eds.) (2004). *Culture, leadership, and organizations: The GLOBE study of 62 societies.* Thousand Oaks, CA: Sage.

Howard, A. (1986). College experiences and managerial performance. *Journal of Applied Psychology Monograph, 71*(3), 530–552.

R
E
F
E
R
E
N
C
E
S

Howard, A., & Bray, D. (1988). *Managerial lives in transition: Advancing age and changing times.* New York, NY: Guilford Press.

Howard, J., & Hammond, R. (1985, September 9). Rumors of inferiority. *The New Republic, 17–21.*

Howland, W., & Martineau, J. (1998, Fall). The promise and pitfalls of re-taking 360° instruments. *Perspectives.* Greensboro, NC: Center for Creative Leadership.

Hunter, J. E., Schmidt, F. L., & Judiesch, M. K. (1990). Individual differences in output variability as a function of job complexity. *Journal of Applied Psychology, 75,* 28–42.

Hurley, A. E., & Sonnenfeld, J. A. (1998). The effect of organizational experience on management career attainment in an international labor market. *Journal of Vocational Behavior, 52,* 172–190.

Hurst, D. K. (2002). *Learning from the links: Mastering management using lessons from golf.* New York, NY: Free Press.

Huselid, M. A., Beatty, R. W., & Becker, B. E. (2005, December; HBR OnPoint Enhanced Edition, March 3, 2009). "A players" or "A positions"? The strategic logic of workforce management. *Harvard Business Review.*

Jawahar, I. M., & Williams, C. R. (1997, Winter). Where all the children are above average: A meta analysis of the performance appraisal purpose affect. *Personnel Psychology, 50*(4), 905–925.

Kaiser, R. B., & Kaplan, R. E. (2000, April). *Getting at leadership versatility: The case of the forceful and enabling polarity.* Paper presented at the 15th annual conference of the Society for Industrial and Organizational Psychology, New Orleans, LA.

Kaplan, R. E., Drath, W. H., & Kofodimos, J. R. (1985). *High hurdles: The challenge of executive self-development.* Greensboro, NC: Center for Creative Leadership.

Kaplan, R. E., with Drath, W. H., & Kofodimos, J. R. (1991). *Beyond ambition.* San Francisco, CA: Jossey-Bass.

Killion, A. (2011, July/August). A giant leap. *Stanford Alumni Magazine,* pp. 52–57. stanfordmag.org

Kluger, A. N., & DeNisi, A. (1996). The effects of feedback interventions on performance: A historical review, a meta-analysis, and a preliminary feedback intervention theory. *Psychological Bulletin, 119*(2), 254–284.

Kotter, J. P. (1988). *The leadership factor.* New York, NY: Free Press.

Kotter, J. P., & Heskett, J. L. (1992). *Corporate culture and performance.* New York, NY: Free Press.

Lamoureux, K., Campbell, M., & Smith, R. (2009, April). *High impact succession management* [Executive Summary]. Oakland, CA: Bersin & Associates and Greensboro, NC: Center for Creative Leadership.

Lawler, E. E. (1996). *From the ground up.* San Francisco, CA: Jossey-Bass.

Lepsinger, R., & Lucia, A. D. (2009). *The art and science of 360 degree feedback* (2nd ed.). San Francisco, CA: Jossey-Bass.

Leslie, J. B., & Fleenor, J. W. (1998). *Feedback to managers: A review and comparison of multi-rater instruments for management development.* Greensboro, NC: Center for Creative Leadership.

Leslie, J. B., & Van Velsor, E. (1996). *A look at derailment today: North America and Europe* (Report No. 169). Greensboro, NC: Center for Creative Leadership.

Leslie, J. B., & Van Velsor, E. (1998). *A cross-national comparison of effective leadership and teamwork: Toward a global workforce.* Greensboro, NC: Center for Creative Leadership.

Levinson, D. (1978). *The seasons of a man's life.* New York, NY: Ballantine.

Levinson, D., with Levinson, J. (1996). *The seasons of a woman's life.* New York, NY: Ballantine.

Lindsey, E. H., Homes, V., & McCall, M. W. (1987). *Key events in executives' lives.* Greensboro, NC: Center for Creative Leadership.

R
E
F
E
R
E
N
C
E
S

Linkage Third Annual Assessment of 360 Degree Assessment Survey (1999, September). Linkage Annual 360 Conference.

Lockwood, N. (2007). *Leveraging employee engagement for competitive advantage: HR's strategic role.* Alexandria, VA: Society for Human Resource Development.

Lombardo, M. M. (1986, Fall). Questions about learning from experience. *Issues and Observations.* Greensboro, NC: Center for Creative Leadership.

Lombardo, M. M., & Eichinger, R. W. (1989). *Preventing derailment: What to do before it's too late.* Greensboro, NC: Center for Creative Leadership.

Lombardo, M. M., & Eichinger, R. W. (2000). High potentials as high learners. *Human Resource Management, 39*(4), 321–330.

Lombardo, M. M., & Eichinger, R. W. (2003a). *The Leadership Architect® norms and validity report.* Minneapolis, MN: Lominger International: A Korn/Ferry Company.

Lombardo, M. M., & Eichinger, R. W. (2003b). *The Choices Architect® user's manual.* Minneapolis, MN: Lominger International: A Korn/Ferry Company.

Lombardo, M. M., & Eichinger, R. W. (2009). *FYI® for your improvement* (5th ed.). Minneapolis, MN: Lominger International: A Korn/Ferry Company.

Lombardo, M. M., & Eichinger, R. W. (2010). *Career Architect® development planner* (5th ed.). Minneapolis, MN: Lominger International: A Korn/Ferry Company.

Lombardo, M. M., & McCauley, C. (1988). *The dynamics of management derailment.* Greensboro, NC: Center for Creative Leadership.

Lombardo, M. M., & McCauley, C. (1993). B*enchmarks®: A manual and trainer's guide.* Greensboro, NC: Center for Creative Leadership.

Lombardo, M. M., Ruderman, M. N., & McCauley, C. D. (1988). Explanations of success and derailment in upper-level management positions. *Journal of Business and Psychology, 2*(3), 199–216.

Lominger International: A Korn/Ferry Company. (2010). *The Leadership Architect® technical manual.* Minneapolis, MN: Author.

Lominger International: A Korn/Ferry Company. (2011). *Succession Architect®: Best practices for building and executing a succession planning program.* Minneapolis, MN: Author.

Lounsberry, C. (2008). Compensation and performance management comparison. In J. J. Phillips & L. Edwards, (Eds.), *Managing talent retention: An ROI approach.* San Francisco, CA: Pfeiffer.

Lyness, K. S., & Thompson, D. E. (1997, June). Above the glass ceiling: A comparison of matched samples of male and female executives. *Journal of Applied Psychology, 82*(3), 359–375.

Lyness, K. S., & Thompson, D. E. (2000). Climbing the corporate ladder: Do female and male executives follow the same route? *Journal of Applied Psychology, 85*(1), 86–101.

Mallon, D. (2009, July). *High impact learning practices: The guide to modernizing your corporate training strategy through social and informal learning.* Oakland, CA: Bersin & Associates.

Martin, J., & Schmidt, C. (2010, May). How to keep your top talent. *Harvard Business Review, 88*(5), 54–61.

McBassi & Company. (2006). *Human capital and organizational performance: Next generation metrics as a catalyst for change* [White paper]. Retrieved from http://www.mcbassi.com/pdfs/HC+OrganizationalPerformanceWhitePaper.pdf

McCall, M. W., Jr. (1998). *High flyers: Developing the next generation of leaders.* Boston, MA: Harvard Business School Press.

McCall, M. W., Jr. (2009). *Recasting leadership development* [White Paper]. Marshall School of Business, University of Southern California, Los Angeles, CA.

R
E
F
E
R
E
N
C
E
S

McCall, M. W., Jr., & Hollenbeck, G. (2002). *Developing global executives: The lessons of international experience.* Boston, MA: Harvard Business School Press.

McCall, M. W., Jr., & Hollenbeck, G. P. (2008). Developing the expert leader. *People & Strategy, 31*(1), 20–28.

McCall, M. W., Jr., & Lombardo, M. M. (1983). What makes a top executive? *Psychology Today, 17*(2), 26–31.

McCall, M. W., Jr., Lombardo, M. M., & Morrison, A. (1988). *The lessons of experience.* New York, NY: Free Press.

McCauley, C. D., & Brutus, S. (1998). *Management development through job experiences.* Greensboro, NC: Center for Creative Leadership.

McCauley, C. D., Eastman, L. J., & Ohlott, P. J. (1995). Linking management selection and development through stretch assignments. *Human Resource Management, 34*(1), 93–115.

McCauley, C. D., Ruderman, M. N., Ohlott, P. J., & Morrow, J. E. (1994). Assessing the developmental components of managerial jobs. *Journal of Applied Psychology, 79,* 544–560.

McWhorter, J. H. (2000, rev. 2001). *Losing the race: Self-sabotage in Black America.* New York, NY: Free Press.

Michaels, E., Handfield-Jones, H., & Axelrod, B. (2001). *The war for talent.* Boston, MA: Harvard Business School Press.

Miles, S. A. (2009, July). Succession planning: How everyone does it wrong. *Forbes.com.* Retrieved September 21, 2011, from http://www.forbes.com/2009/07/30/succession-planning-failures-leadership-governance-ceos.html

Morrison, A. (1992). *The new leaders.* San Francisco, CA: Jossey-Bass.

Morrison, A., White, R., & Van Velsor, E. (1987, rev. 1992). *Breaking the glass ceiling: Can women reach the top of America's largest corporations?* Reading, MA: Addison Wesley.

REFERENCES

Morrow, C., Jarrett, M., & Rupinski, M. (1997). An investigation of the effect and economic utility of corporate-wide training. *Personnel Psychology, 50*(1), 91–120.

Moses, J., & Lyness, K. (1990). Leadership behavior in ambiguous environments. In K. E. Clark & M. B. Clark (Eds.), *Measures of leadership* (pp. 327–337). West Orange, NJ: Leadership Library of America.

Most, R. (1990). Hypotheses about the relationship between leadership and intelligence. In K. E. Clark & M. B. Clark (Eds.), *Measures of leadership* (pp. 459–464). West Orange, NJ: Leadership Library of America.

Mount, M. K., Sytsma, M. R., Hazucha, J. F., & Holt, K. E. (1997). Rater-ratee races effects in developmental performance ratings of managers. *Personnel Psychology, 50,* 51–70.

Mount, M. K., Witt, L. A., & Barrick, M. R. (2000). Incremental validity of empirically keyed biodata scales over GMA and the five factor personality constructs. *Personnel Psychology, 53*(2), 299–324.

Mumford, M. D., Marks, M. A., Connelly, M. S., Zaccaro, S. J., & Reiter-Palmon, R. (2000). Development of leadership skills: Experience and timing. *The Leadership Quarterly, 11*(1), 87–114.

Murphy, K., & Cleveland, J. (1995). *Understanding performance appraisal.* Thousand Oaks, CA: Sage Publications.

NACE (National Association of Colleges and Employers). (2001). 2001 Graduating student and alumni survey. *Journal of Career Planning and Development.*

Neff, T. I., & Citrin, J. M. (1999, rev. 2001). *Lessons from the top: The 50 most successful business leaders in America – and what you can learn from them.* New York, NY: Doubleday.

Orr, J. E., Sneltjes, C., & Dai, G. (2010). *The art and science of competency modeling: Best practices in developing and implementing success profiles* [White Paper]. Minneapolis, MN: Korn/Ferry Institute.

R
E
F
E
R
E
N
C
E
S

Orr, J. E., Swisher, V. V., Tang, K. Y., & De Meuse, K. P. (2010). *Illuminating blind spots and hidden strengths* [White Paper]. Minneapolis, MN: Korn/Ferry Institute.

Peiperl, M. A. (2001, January). Getting 360-degree feedback right. *Harvard Business Review, 79*(1), 142–147.

Phillips, J. J., & Edwards, L. (2009). *Managing talent retention: An ROI approach.* San Francisco, CA: Pfeiffer.

Pluzdrak, N. L. (2007). *The correlation of leadership competencies and business results: A case study on the ROI of leadership competencies* (Doctoral dissertation, Pepperdine University, 2007). Published on: http://gradworks.umi.com/32/52/3252724.html

Poe, A. C. (2000, April). Face value. *HR Magazine.*

Pressley, M., Borkowski, J. G., & Schneider, W. (1987). Cognitive strategies: Good strategy users coordinate meta-cognition and knowledge. In R. Vasta & G. Whitehurst (Eds.), *Annals of child development* (Vol. 4, pp. 89–129). Greenwich, CT: JAI Press.

Ragin, B.R. (1997). Diversified mentoring relationships in organizations: A power perspective. *Academy of Management Review, 22*(2), 482–521.

Rewick, P., & Lawler, E. E. (1978). What you really want from your job. *Psychology Today, 11*(12), 53–65.

Rogers, E., Metlay, W., Kaplan, I., & Barriere, M. (2000). *Multisource feedback: A state-of-the-art and practice report.* Unpublished manuscript.

Roth, P. L., BeVier, C. A., Switzer, F. S., & Schippmann, J. S. (1996). Meta-analyzing the relationship between grades and job performance. *Journal of Applied Psychology, 81*, 548–556.

Rothwell, W. J. (2001). *Effective succession planning: Ensuring leadership continuity and building talent from within* (2nd ed.; 4th ed., 2010). New York, NY: AMACOM.

Royster, C. (1979, rev. 1996). *A revolutionary people at war: The continental army and American character, 1775–1783.* Chapel Hill, NC: University of North Carolina Press.

Ruyle, K. E., Eichinger, R. W., & De Meuse, K. P. (2009). *FYI® for talent engagement: Drivers of best practice for managers and business leaders.* Minneapolis, MN: Lominger International: A Korn/Ferry Company.

Ruyle, K. E., Hallenbeck, G. S., Jr., Orr, J. E., & Swisher, V. V. (2010). *FYI® for insight: The 21 leadership characteristics for success and the 5 that get you fired.* Minneapolis, MN: Lominger International: A Korn/Ferry Company.

Ruyle, K. E., & Orr, J. E. (2011). Fundamentals of competency modeling. In L. A. Berger & D. R. Berger (Eds.), *The talent management handbook* (2nd ed.). New York, NY: McGraw-Hill Companies, Inc.

Sala, F. (2003). Executive blind spots: Discrepancies between self- and other-ratings. *Consulting Psychology Journal: Practice & Research 55,* 222–229.

Sackett, P., DuBois, C., & Noe, A. (1991). Tokenism in performance evaluation: The effects of work group representation on male-female and White-Black differences in performance ratings. *Journal of Applied Psychology, 76*(2), 263–267.

Schippmann, J. S., Ash, R. A., Battista, M., Carr, L., Eyde, L. D., Hesketh, B., Kehoe, J., Perlman, K., Prien, E. P., & Sanchez, J. I. (2000). The practice of competency modeling. *Personnel Psychology, 53*(3), 703–740.

Schmidt, F. L., & Hunter, J. E. (1998). The validity and utility of selection methods in personnel psychology: Practical and theoretical implications of 85 years of research findings. *Psychological Bulletin, 124*(2), 262–274.

Schmidt, F. L., & Rader, M. (1999). Exploring the boundary conditions for interview validity: Meta-analytic findings for a new interview type. *Personnel Psychology, 52,* 445–464.

Sessa, V. I., & Campbell, R. (1997). *Selection at the top.* Greensboro, NC: Center for Creative Leadership.

Sessa, V. I., Kaiser, R., Taylor, J. K., & Campbell, R. J. (1998). *Executive selection: A research report on what works and what doesn't.* Greensboro, NC: Center for Creative Leadership.

R
E
F
E
R
E
N
C
E
S

Siebert, K. W. (1999). Reflection in action: Tools for cultivating on-the-job learning conditions. *Organizational Dynamics, 27*(4).

Simonton, D. K. (1987). Developmental antecedents of achieved eminence. *Annals of Child Development, 4,* 131–169.

Sirower, M. (1997). *The synergy trap.* New York, NY: Free Press.

Sirower, M. (2000). *The synergy trap, Asia-Pacific edition.* New York, NY: Free Press.

Smither, J. W., London, M., & Reilly, R. R. (2005). Does performance improve following multisource feedback? A theoretical model, meta-analysis, and review of empirical findings. *Personnel Psychology, 58*(1), 33–66.

Soares, R., Combopiano, J., Regis, A., Shur, Y., & Wong, R. (2010). *2010 Catalyst census: Fortune 500 women executive officers and top earners.* New York, NY: Catalyst, Inc.

Spencer, L. (2001). The economic value of emotional intelligence competencies and EIC-based HR programs. In D. Goleman & C. Cherniss (Eds.), *The emotionally intelligent workplace: How to select for, measure, and improve emotional intelligence in individuals, groups, and organizations.* San Francisco, CA: Jossey-Bass.

Spencer, L., & Spencer, S. (1993). *Competence at work: Models for superior performance.* New York, NY: John Wiley & Sons, Inc.

Spreitzer, G. M., McCall, M. W., & Mahoney, J. D. (1997). Early identification of international executive potential. *Journal of Applied Psychology, 82*(1), 6–29.

Steele, C., & Aronson, J. (1995). Stereotype threat and the intellectual test performance of African Americans. *Journal of Personality and Social Psychology, 69*(5), 797–811.

Sternberg, R. J., & Wagner, R. K. (1990). Street smarts. In K. E. Clark & M. B. Clark (Eds.), *Measures of leadership* (pp. 493–504). West Orange, NJ: Leadership Library of America.

Sternberg, R. J., Wagner, R. K., Williams, W. M., & Horvath, J. A. (1995). Testing common sense. *American Psychologist, 50*(11), 912–927.

Tang, K., Dai, G., & De Meuse, K. P. (in press). Assessing leadership derailment factors in 360° feedback: Differences across position levels and self-other agreement. *Leadership & Organization Development Journal.*

Thomas, D. A. (2001, April; HBR OnPoint Enhanced Edition, November 1, 2002). The truth about mentoring minorities: Race matters. *Harvard Business Review, 79*(4), 98–107.

Tornow, W. W., London, M., & Center for Creative Leadership Associates. (1998). *Maximizing the value of 360-degree feedback: A process for successful individual and organizational development.* San Francisco, CA: Jossey-Bass.

Ulrich, D., & Lake, D. (1990). *Organizational capability: Competing from the inside out.* New York, NY: John Wiley & Sons, Inc.

Ulrich, D., Zenger, J., & Smallwood, W. N. (1999). *Results-based leadership.* Boston, MA: Harvard Business School Press.

Van Velsor, E., & Hughes-James, M. W. (1990). *Gender differences in the development of managers: How women managers learn from experience* (Report No. 145). Greensboro, NC: Center for Creative Leadership.

Watson Wyatt WorkUSA®. (2002). Weathering the storm: A study of employee attitudes and opinions. Retrieved September 19, 2011, from www.watsonwyatt.com/research/printable.asp?id=w-557

White, R. P., Hodgson, P., & Crainer, S. (1996). *The future of leadership, a white water revolution.* London: Pitman.

Wilson, M. (2008). *Developing future leaders for high-growth Indian companies: New perspectives* [Research Overview]. Singapore: Center for Creative Leadership and Pune, India: Tata Management Training Center.

Wilson, M. S., & Dalton, M. A. (1998). *International success: Selecting, developing, and supporting expatriate managers* (Report No. 180). Greensboro, NC: Center for Creative Leadership.

Wusteman, L. (2000). New dimensions to competencies: An interview with Bill Byham. *Competency and Emotional Intelligence Quarterly, 8*(1).

Yip, J., & Wilson, M. (2008). *Developing public service leaders in Singapore* [Research Overview]. Singapore: Center for Creative Leadership.

Zhang, Y., Chandrasekar, N., & Wei, R. (2009). *Developing Chinese leaders in the 21st century* [Research Overview]. Singapore: Center for Creative Leadership and Shanghai, China: Europe International Business School.

REFERENCES

Index

competencies
  85 percent model of leadership
    effectiveness, 41–44
      85 Percent Solution Table, 2.7, 42–44
      Story: A Superior Performer's
      Leadership Competencies, 46
  building a case for development
    five killers, 47–49
  building a core model, 29
    Observation: The 85 Percent Solution,
    30
  common vs. unique, 6–7
  complexity, 141
  critical
    develop a level early, 45–46
    know what they are, 19
    unique to job, 40
  DDI, 70 worldwide competencies, 7, 433
  definition of, 5
    skill, interchangeable term for
      competency, 5
  five types of competencies, 30–40,
    217–218
    common to superior performers, 35–40
    few people are good at, 33–34
    job-driven, 40
    level-driven, 34–35
    price-of-admission, 30–32
      cannot be critical differentiators, 223
      predict performance, 31
  how many (*see* competencies, number of)
  important to success, 52
  international, 433–435
  item creation and scales, 264–265
  Leadership Architect®
    Library Structure, 21
  not-for-profit/government, 436
  select for 85 percent, 45
  sizing, 262
  top 22 competencies by level, 451
  what most people are good at, 23
    top 10 across levels, 24
    top 10 across regions, 25
  what most people struggle with, 26
    bottom 10 across levels, 26
    bottom 10 across regions, 27
  See also skills
  See also Appendix A
  See also Chapter 2
  See also Chapter 12

competencies, number of
  argument for more than ten
    development can't be based on ten, 261
    don't reinvent the wheel, 8, 49
    not powerful enough to drive winning
      strategy, 217
    produces a limited diagnosis, 261
    several sets are needed to cover an
      enterprise, 29
    single set not reflective of
      performance across levels, 216
    from system standpoint, 261
    too general, 222
  argument for ten or fewer by
    organizations
    can't handle more than ten, 10
    focus on the critical few, 215
    keep it simple, 261
  solution for the "how many" dilemma, 262

competencies, research-based
  85 percent are common, 7, 8
  85 Percent Solution Table 2.7, 42–44
  don't reinvent wheel, 8, 49
  model of leadership effectiveness, 41
  not invented here syndrome, 9
  starter model, 41
  See also Appendix A
  See also Chapter 2

I
N
D
E
X

I
N
D
E
X

INDEX

INDEX

|

Excerpts

Exercises

INDEX

Figures

Observations

Stories

Studies and Surveys

Tables